W9-BZB-148

Mastering Local Area Networks

Mastering™ Local Area Networks

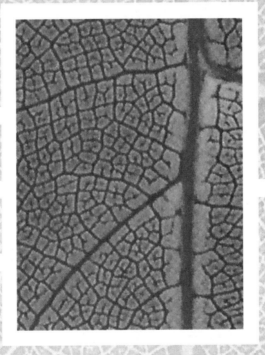

Christa Anderson
with Mark Minasi

San Francisco • Paris • Düsseldorf • Soest • London

Associate Publisher: Guy Hart-Davis
Contracts and Licensing Manager: Kristine O'Callaghan
Acquisitions & Developmental Editors: Bonnie Bills and
Brenda Frink
Editor: Valerie Haynes Perry
Project Editor: Raquel Baker
Technical Editor: Jim Cooper
Book Designer: Bill Gibson
Graphic Illustrator: Tony Jonick
Electronic Publishing Specialist: Nila Nichols
Production Coordinators: Susan Berge, Catherine Morris
Indexer: Ted Laux
Cover Designer: Archer Design
Cover Photographer: The Image Bank

Screen reproductions produced with Collage Complete.
Collage Complete is a trademark of Inner Media Inc.

SYBEX, Network Press, and the Network Press logo are registered trademarks of SYBEX Inc.

Mastering is a trademark of SYBEX Inc.

TRADEMARKS: SYBEX has attempted throughout this book
to distinguish proprietary trademarks from descriptive terms
by following the capitalization style used by the manufacturer.

The author and publisher have made their best efforts to prepare this book, and the content is based upon final release
software whenever possible. Portions of the manuscript may
be based upon pre-release versions supplied by software man-
ufacturer(s). The author and the publisher make no represen-
tation or warranties of any kind with regard to the completeness
or accuracy of the contents herein and accept no liability of
any kind including but not limited to performance, merchanta-
bility, fitness for any particular purpose, or any losses or dam-
ages of any kind caused or alleged to be caused directly or
indirectly from this book.

Photographs and illustrations used in this book have been
downloaded from publicly accessible file archives and are
used in this book for news reportage purposes only to demonstrate the variety of graphics resources available via electronic
access. Text and images available over the Internet may be
subject to copyright and other rights owned by third parties.
Online availability of text and images does not imply that they
may be reused without the permission of rights holders,
although the Copyright Act does permit certain unauthorized
reuse as fair use under 17 U.S.C. Section 107.

Library of Congress Card Number: 98-88952
ISBN: 0-7821-2258-2

Manufactured in the United States of America

10 9 8 7 6 5 4 3 2 1

To Scott, my favorite combination of user and network geek.
See—I finally wrote the book you suggested three years ago.
Told you I'd get around to it.

ACKNOWLEDGMENTS

No book is the result of only one person's hard work. My deep appreciation goes to:

- Scott Anderson, for late dinners, shoulder rubs, and periodic trips off the PC to play Settlers and rake leaves. As always, his support has been invaluable—I couldn't do it without him.

- Teresa Wagamon, for lots of remote support (the deadline's doing great; thanks for asking), as well as many suggestions and stories.

- Mark Minasi, generally for suborning me into this field in the first place lo these many years ago and specifically for asking me to work on this particular project. As with everything else I've ever done with Mark, writing this book has been both absorbing and challenging.

- Jim Cooper, for once again being the world's greatest technical editor. A technical editor can be either a hindrance or a great help. Jim's been my technical editor for several books I've written, and he's always fit in the latter category. I look forward to working with him again.

- All the Sybex editorial and production staff who contributed to this book: Raquel Baker's management of a complicated project, Valerie Perry's careful editing, Bonnie Bills's help with developing the book's structure, Brenda Frink's developmental support in Bonnie's absence, Nila Nichols's expert and speedy layout of the project, and Susan Berge's and Catherine Morris's flawless proofreading.

Most of all, thanks to all those who shared their stories and insights with me. I'm glad to be able to draw not only on my own experience but also from the experience of others in order to make this book useful to as many people as possible.

CONTENTS AT A GLANCE

TABLE OF CONTENTS

INTRODUCTION

Welcome to *Mastering Local Area Networks*! In this edition, I've both updated information to reflect current technology and expanded the book's scope to include many topics not discussed in the previous version of the book. The goal of the book remains the same as ever: to break through the jargon associated with networking. Whether you're just starting out with local area networking, have been in the field for a while, are learning about new technologies, or are simply brushing up on your knowledge of the older ones, you should benefit from this approach.

Why This Book?

The shelves of the bookstores are full of books on networking. Why pick up this one? Mostly because this book was originally developed as a teaching tool for a course designed for hundreds or thousands of people like yourself, people who wanted to learn more about networking. After a few years of teaching and getting feedback from the people who've taken the course, it's possible to refine the material and the approach. This book takes the original course material and then builds on it. The end result is a systematic approach to understanding the components of a local area network and how they fit together.

In the course of reading this book, you'll walk through the progressive steps of creating a local area network, from planning the basic structure, to configuring resource management, and setting up security that preserves the integrity and privacy of the network's data. It doesn't stop there: I'll explain documenting and troubleshooting techniques that will keep you out of trouble (or at least *help* you out of trouble), and take a peek at some technologies that aren't yet in common use but may be helpful to you in the near future. Finally, you'll learn techniques intended to help you avoid or overcome some of the hurdles of setting up and maintaining a PC-based local area network.

In short, over the course of reading this book you'll learn both the theory and practice of networking, developing both a theoretical understanding of it and preparing for hands-on experience. After reading, you should find your task of building a network that fulfills most of the expectations of your management and users a bit less daunting.

Who Should Read This Book?

I wrote this book for those either just learning about local area networking or those who are interested in a systematic approach to network development. This book doesn't delve much into esoterica (much as it fascinates me) but attempts to keep the focus on the "story" of local area networking. That is, you'll learn about how some of the various networking protocols work because this information is useful when determining which protocols to use on your LAN. However, I'm not going to discuss the specific structure of a DLC packet, for example, unless it's directly applicable to something you need to understand. The point here is *practical* networking.

What's Inside?

The basic reason to network is so you can stop worrying about maintaining a supply of floppy disks. Okay, there's a bit more to it than that, but the idea is based on information and resource sharing. Networks serve a number of different roles:

- Sharing files for greater information integrity

- Sharing peripheral devices, such as printers

- Centrally locating data for ease of security, resource management, and backup

To explain how all this works, the book is divided into four main sections, each of which describes a different part of the network itself.

In Part I, "Channels—Your Network's Nervous System," I'll talk about the theoretical and physical components of a local area network's communications system. Chapter 1 will introduce the basic elements of networking, including card types, cabling options, connectors, and, in case you were getting too comfortably rooted in components you can bite, a description of the OSI model that's crucial to understanding networking protocols. Building on these basics, Chapter 2 will describe issues associated with network architecture, namely the physical and logical topologies you're likely to encounter and the *raison d'être* for each. Chapter 3 will discuss the networking protocols from which you can choose the transport backbone of your network. In Chapter 4, I'll talk about how to install the boards and cables you've chosen based on the knowledge you've gained from the previous chapters. Got a network that's more complicated than a single segment? Join the club, and turn to Chapter 5 to read more about the devices you'll need: repeaters, switches, routers, bridges, and other enterprise hardware. To round things off, Chapter 6 will close the section with a discussion of some of the connectivity options you have for wide area networks and remote access.

The backbone of the network out of the way, Part II, "Pieces of the Puzzle," discusses the pieces of the network that those channels are charged with connecting: the servers, clients, and peripheral devices involved. Beginning with the discussion of what hardware you need to support a network server in Chapter 7, I'll then discuss the specifics of server needs in Chapter 8. You still need to get to those servers, so Chapter 9 will discuss what hardware you need to support the *client* end.

You've got channels and you've got hardware. How about something to do with that network? Part III, "Breathing Life into Your Network—Operating Systems and LAN Applications," begins with an overview of network operating systems in Chapter 10—both client/server and peer-to-peer. Networks are unexciting until you add applications to them, so Chapter 11 will discuss the types of applications you'll be using on your network, and what you need to worry about in terms of licensing those applications. I'll close this section with the basics of networking issues that are growing in popularity and you can't afford to ignore: thin client networking (Chapter 12) and creating Web sites (Chapter 13).

The network is up and running, but how will you make sure that it remains that way? Part IV, "Holistic Network Management—Resource Organization, Security, and Disaster Recovery," covers all your bases for making sure your hard work doesn't go up in smoke. Chapter 14 discusses the principles of network administration: auditing, management tools, and troubleshooting techniques. Interested in protecting data from either unauthorized access or destruction? Turn to Chapter 15 on network security. When all else fails, you'll need Chapter 16 on disaster recovery.

Feeling overwhelmed? I'll include some additional sections to help you keep up. Appendix A, "Internet Resources," is available in this book as well as on the Sybex Web site at www.sybex.com. To find the Web component of this book, click on catalog, then type **2258** in the search field, and press Enter. Appendix B, "Networking Forms," includes some forms designed to help you document your network and set up a backup schedule. Appendix C, "Sample from a Disaster Recovery Plan," shows the level of detail you're shooting for when you create your own plan. Finally,

Appendix D, "Answers," includes the responses to the exercises that appear at the end of each chapter. I've also provided a glossary of terms found in this book; those who know all the terms can skip the glossary, and those who don't have a handy place to look. (All terms will be defined the first time they appear in the book, but you can refer later to the glossary in case you've forgotten or aren't reading the book straight through.)

Features and Conventions

That's an awful lot of material for one book, so in addition to those appendices I've included some additional elements to help you absorb the information and to highlight especially important points.

First, note the exercises that occur at intervals throughout the book. I've developed these to help you solidify your knowledge of the content included here. No one's going to make you complete them, and this book is not designed to be an MCSE guide. However, if you can answer the questions in the exercises, then you'll know that you've been paying attention and that what you've been reading has sunk in.

Second, note how the text looks. The first time a new word appears and is defined, it will be in *italics*. Notes, Tips, and Warnings also draw your attention to various kinds of important or (hopefully) interesting information that doesn't quite fit into the main body of the text, as seen here:

NOTE   Notes contain interesting points about networking or about a particular component or tool.

TIP   Tips contain information about how to use tools to make your network run better or to protect it.

WARNING   Warnings call your attention to information that can help you avoid networking mistakes and possible data loss. If I think it's important enough to put into a Warning, it's pretty bad.

And Finally...

Time to quit blathering and get on with it, so I'll close here. I'd like only to say that when writing a book of this kind there's an awful lot of information to absorb and to include. (Yes, I keep saying that—keep reading and you'll see how right I am.) I've made every effort to make this as organized, coherent, and comprehensive as possible. However, as you're either aware or will be soon, this is an incredibly dynamic field and it's not always possible to cover all topics as thoroughly as you would like. If you have questions to ask or comments to make, please feel free to e-mail me at `candersn@adelphia.net`. I travel from time to time, so don't panic if I don't write back right away. I'll get back to you when I return to the office, I promise.

Now, on with the show....

Christa Anderson

Sybex Technical Support

If you have questions or comments about this book (or other Sybex books), you can also contact Sybex directly.

For the Fastest Reply

E-mail us or visit the Sybex Web site! You can contact Sybex through the Web by visiting `http://www.sybex.com` and clicking Support. You may find the answer you're looking for on this site in the FAQ (Frequently Asked Questions) file.

When you reach the support page, click `support@sybex.com` to send Sybex an e-mail. You can also e-mail Sybex directly at `support@sybex.com`.

Make sure you include the following information in your e-mail:

Name   The complete title of the book in question. For this book, it is *Mastering Local Area Networks*.

ISBN   The ISBN that appears on the bottom-right corner of the back cover of the book. This number looks like this:

0-7821-2258-2

Printing   The printing of the book. You can find this near the front of the book at the bottom of the copyright page. You should see a line of numbers, as in the following:

10 9 8 7 6 5 4 3 2 1

Tell us what the lowest number is in the line of numbers. This is the printing number of the book. The example here indicates that the book is the first printing.

> **NOTE** The ISBN and printing number are very important for Technical Suppport because they indicate the edition and reprint that you have in your hands. Many changes occur between printings. Don't forget to include this information!

For a Fast Reply

Call Sybex Technical Support and leave a message. Sybex guarantees that they will call you back within 24 hours, excluding weekends and holidays.

Technical Support can be reached at (510) 523-8233 ext. 563.

After you dial the extension, press 1 to leave a message. Sybex will call you back within 24 hours. Make sure you leave a phone number where you can be reached!

Other Ways to Reach Sybex

The slowest way to contact Sybex is through the mail. If you do not have access to the Net, e-mail, or a telephone, write Sybex a small note and send it to the following address:

SYBEX Inc.
Attention: Technical Support
1151 Marina Village Parkway
Alameda, CA 94501

Again, it's important that you include all the following information to expedite a reply:

Name The complete title of the book in question.

ISBN   The ISBN that appears on the bottom-right corner of the back cover of the book and looks like this:

0-8721-2258-2

Printing   The printing of the book. You can find this near the front of the book at the bottom of the copyright page. You should see a line of numbers, as in the following:

10 9 8 7 6 5 4 3 2 1

Tell us what the lowest number is in the line of numbers. This is the printing number of the book. The example here indicates that the book is the first printing.

> **NOTE**   The ISBN and printing number are very important for Technical Support because they indicate the edition and reprint that you have in your hands. Many changes occur between printings. Don't forget to include this information!

Page number   Include the page number where you have a problem.

No matter how you contact Sybex, Technical Support will try to answer your question quickly and accurately.

PART

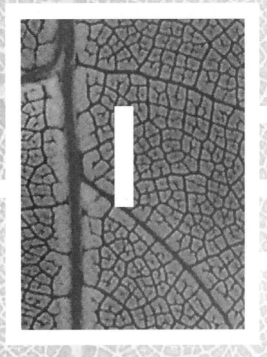

I

Channels— Your Network's Nervous System

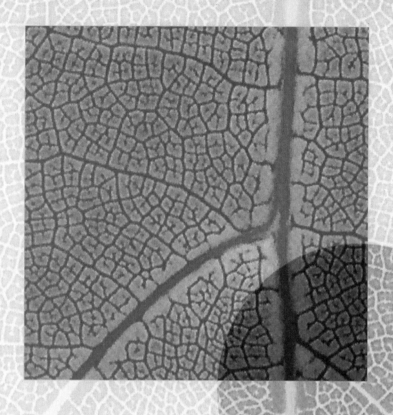

Basic Networking Concepts and Componen

In this chapter, I'll cover the basics that you'll need to understand the rest of this part of the book. Be warned: this is not a throwaway chapter full of fluff suitable for airplane reading. In the following pages, I'll discuss the elements of LAN channels, including network cards, cables, connectors, and the ever-popular OSI model. But first, some real basics.

What Is a LAN?

Strictly speaking, a local area network (LAN) is a group of computers connected together within an enclosed area, such as a building. LANs can vary greatly in size. They can consist of two Windows 98 workstations in the same room or several hundred workstations spread out over several floors in an office building. The key to the definition of a LAN is that all of the computers on the network are grouped together in some fashion and connected somehow, and in the same building. On most LANs, the medium of connection is some sort of cable. However, as I will discuss later in this chapter, some LANs use wireless communications to link together their member computers.

NOTE   If the network extends beyond the borders of a single building, it's no longer a LAN but some type of *wide-area network* (WAN). There are a couple of different kinds of WANs. If the network is big enough, it's just a WAN, but the smaller ones may be named somewhat differently. For example, a WAN that extends through a major urban area may be referred to as a MAN (metropolitan area network). A WAN that connects the buildings of a university might be identified as a CAN (campus area network). Generally speaking, LANs are contained within the confines of a single building and WANs are not.

That's the textbook definition, but in the real world LANs are generally defined more by their function than by their physical characteristics. In this more usual sense, a LAN is a means of linking computers to allow them common access to individual hardware. That is, subject to security restrictions, all computers on the LAN can access each other's shared hardware (printers, scanners, CD-ROM drives, hard disks, modems, and so on) as though that hardware were available locally. Because the members of a LAN can share hardware, they can share the data on that hardware, too.

Therefore, not only can all computers on the LAN access certain parts of each other's hardware (subject to security restrictions, which I'll discuss later), but they can also use that hardware as though it were available locally. This implies that the users of these computers can share data.

Although the first office computers—mainframes and terminals—were networked, the first personal computers (PCs) in an office setting were typically stand-alone devices. The oldest form of the LAN is commonly referred to as *SneakerNet*, an official-sounding name for an unofficial way of doing business. In this arrangement, one PC user would copy data from his computer to a floppy disk, then walk that floppy over to another computer, either to print out the data at the printer attached to that computer or to give a copy of the data to someone else. If you don't have all that much data to transfer, it's not a terrible solution (and for some situations, it still works just fine) but it's got several serious drawbacks:

- The risk of losing data to lost or accidentally formatted floppy disks is high.

- It's difficult to keep all versions of a document current if more than one person needs to work on it.

- Floppy disks only hold up to 1.44MB of data and modern files may be quite a bit larger than that.

- What if both users don't have the same applications on their machines? The second user may not be able to open the shared file.

- Security is a problem—how do you keep those floppy disks from walking out the door?

- It's quite time-consuming for users to have to copy files, walk them to another PC, and then wait for the file's recipient to copy or print the data in question.

For anything other than very simple purposes, SneakerNet is not the way to go. In modern offices, you need a solution that permits:

- Easy sharing and transferring of data, and protection of that data

- Application sharing

- Easy interaction with other users on the network

- Sharing of peripheral devices

Let's take a look at these needs in some more detail.

File Management

Sharing, transferring, and securing information between computers on a network is generally known as *file management*. One of the primary purposes of a LAN is to provide a common storage area so that a number of people can access the same files. The PC that shares the files or directories is called the *file server*.

File sharing can help ensure that there is only one version of a file going around, and that anyone who uses that file is always working with the most recent version of the information. If you don't want to share a file with the network but you need someone else to do some work on it, you can transfer it to that person—just move it from your hard disk to theirs, or else send it as an e-mail message.

The act of sharing a file with the network does not automatically give everyone on the network access to it. In modern network operating systems, you can restrict access to shared files or directories based either on a password system or on a user account. This capability may be fine-tuned to permit a variety of types of file access—at a minimum, read-only or full access. Therefore, you can keep others from seeing your work or just stop them from making changes to your work when they're not supposed to.

What about protecting that data from loss? The most valuable asset your company has is its data. This data is far more valuable than the putty-colored boxes called computers on your desk, which are already obsolete from the moment you bought them and inherently replaceable. If your data is lost or corrupted, that signifies a disaster of monstrous proportions. The good news is that networking can make backing up all that data much simpler than it is with stand-alone computers. You can either store all the data on a single server and back up that server regularly, or provide a central backup system on the network to which each PC user must copy all important files from his or her computer's hard drive. If managed properly, LANs can provide a degree of data security unheard of in stand-alone computing environments. I'll talk much more about backups and backup strategies in Chapter 14, "Network Security."

Sharing Applications

One of the great advantages of a LAN is that it can make the process of distributing applications to the users in your office much easier. Many applications—not all, but most—will permit you to install them on a central computer called an *application server* and let people access these applications from the network.

There are a couple of advantages to installing applications in this manner. First, as the bulk of network-installed applications will reside on the server rather than the client, this means that less disk space is needed on clients than if the application is installed on every PC. This is no small consideration in a world where a popular office suite requires almost 2GB of space to install fully. As common as large disks are nowadays, you won't necessarily have those large hard disks installed in every computer in your network. Second, installing and upgrading applications is much easier if you can install the program files on a single point instead of on all computers in the network. Although this doesn't work for all applications or in all situations, when application sharing is feasible, it can save a lot of time and energy.

How does this work? When a client PC connects to the copy of an application installed onto an application server, a copy of the application is loaded into the client's memory. As the client interacts with the program, it interacts with the copy stored in its own memory, not the one on the server, so more than one client can access the same application simultaneously.

NOTE   There's an advanced sort of application sharing called *thin client networking*, which requires almost no resources on the client side at all. Thin client networking is the topic of Chapter 12.

One word of caution, however: installing applications on an application server for use by the rest of the network does not mean that you only have to buy one license for that application. Typically, you must buy one license for each user of the application, whether concurrent or total. (The requirements differ depending on the application.) If you don't have proper licensing for all your applications, you are guilty of software piracy, which is a federal crime. You don't think that anyone will know or care? This is not necessarily the case. The sole purpose of the watchdog organization called the Software Publisher's Association (SPA) is to care about piracy issues, and it will prosecute violations against its member organizations. If you're unfamiliar with the subject of licensing, don't worry. It's covered in detail along with the SPA in Chapter 11, "LAN Applications."

Enhancing Office Interaction

As offices get larger, it can be hard to keep people apprised of important events and to get them together. Networks can help encourage office cohesion by use of e-mail and group scheduling software.

Group scheduling was once probably one of your office manager's favorite ways of accumulating gray hair. It can be made much easier with the use of a network and some specialized scheduling software. Without these tools, organizing departmental meetings can be a nightmare as the organizer tries to sort through everyone's schedules to find a compatible time to meet. Group scheduling software can make this task much more approachable. The idea is this: everyone enters their schedules into a calendar program. Only they or selected people can see their own schedules, but the times are stored in a central database. When you want to call a meeting, you enter the names of the people you want to be present, then pick a time. If all the people listed are free at that time, the scheduling software will notify you. If not, it will notify you that there's a conflict and with whom, and (depending on the package) may be able to suggest the first time when all the people listed will be free. Once a time has been set, you can use the scheduling program to e-mail everyone invited to the meeting, telling them of the date and time.

Speaking of e-mail, it's useful for a lot more than just scheduling office meetings. E-mail is probably the most ubiquitous networking application today. A lot of e-mail–related network traffic may entail tired jokes, but it's also invaluable as a method of asking for quick answers to quick problems, or scheduling private meetings between people. E-mail is good for communication too simple to require scheduling software between people who are sufficiently busy that they can't just drop everything for each other's convenience. Not only is it faster than dropping by someone's office to ask a question or talk, it's more private. Everyone notices if the boss stops by your cubicle, but if she sends you an e-mail asking you to stop by for your performance evaluation then no one knows about it except you and her. Essentially, think of office e-mail for any communications that require relative privacy, mass dissemination, or brevity.

Another advantage of e-mail over telephone calls or in-person meetings is that most e-mail systems permit you to attach binary files to e-mail messages. For example, you can send someone a file to review with your comments separate from the document itself. The recipient of the message can just open the file and read or edit the data. Sending binary files in this way is like sharing the file with the network, but has four main advantages for some applications:

- You can explain anything confusing about the data in the e-mail message or emphasize the importance of the information.

- You can ensure that the recipient is getting the intended file and you don't have to worry that he or she will open the wrong one by mistake.

- You don't have to worry about setting the proper permissions on the file or muck around with passwords because only the recipient of the e-mail message will get a copy of the file you send.

- You can send files to people with whom you don't share a LAN connection, such as those to whom you only have e-mail access via the Internet.

In short, the introduction of LANs is one of the best things to ever happen to office communication and information-sharing.

Sharing Peripheral Devices

When personal computers were originally introduced, they were stripped-down boxes that included little more than a motherboard, memory, and a floppy drive—as recently as ten years ago, even hard disks were extra. As the PC matured, more and more devices that were originally expensive extras became part of the typical hardware profile. As additional devices become standard parts of an off-the-shelf PC, you may get confused as to what's a peripheral device and what isn't. If a printer is a peripheral device, is a CD-ROM drive? What about a hard disk?

A *peripheral*, or *peripheral device*, is simply any piece of hardware that attaches to the motherboard of your computer, whether directly or indirectly. Not all peripheral devices are external to the computer case, and not all can be shared. However, for those that can be shared with the rest of the network, peripheral sharing can be a good way to make these devices available to everyone and make it easier for people to use them. For example, rather than having people line up at the PC with the printer attached, they can send print jobs to it as though it were attached to their machine and pick up those jobs at their leisure.

Sharing peripheral devices can save network users both time and money. It's true that even without a network you don't have to buy printers or CD-ROM drives for every computer on the network. One or two devices distributed throughout the office can work just as well if demand isn't high or people don't mind standing in line to use them. However, if people must waste time waiting for a device to be free, then the money saved by not having a printer at every desk may be spent in lost productivity.

Like shared folders, shared peripheral devices aren't necessarily available to everyone on the network or at the same level of control. Thus, you can share that color printer that uses the really expensive cartridges with the network but protect it so that only the graphics people can access it, not every Tom, Dick, and Harry with a rough draft to print out.

These are the basics of what you can do with a LAN. Now let's take a look at the pieces of the backbone that make all of this possible: cards, cables, and connectors.

Understanding Network Components

Okay, you're convinced—your office is never going to enter the twenty-first century until you get those PCs connected. You know that you need computers to make that work and you've got them. What hardware will enable you to connect those computers and make them talk to one another? For a simple network, you'll need network cards, some sort of cabling, and connectors to affix the cables to the cards inserted in each PC.

Door to the Outside World—Network Cards

The *network interface card* (NIC), known also by such aliases as the *network board* or *adapter*, is the add-in card that you'll plug into the motherboard of your computer to provide an interface to the network. A network card really isn't fundamentally different from any other daughtercard: it plugs into a slot on the motherboard, requires certain resources in order to operate, and has a jack on the side that sticks out the back of the computer into which you can plug the tool into the card controls. If this were a sound card, you'd plug in speakers to produce sound. Since it's a network card, you plug in a network cable to produce connectivity.

You can divide NICs into categories in a few different ways. First, there's the type of network they support. For practical purposes, there are currently two main LAN types: Ethernet and Token Ring. I'll go into more detail about what makes these network types different in Chapter 2, "Planning a Network Architecture." For now, just understand that these two types represent different methods of communicating. You can't make Ethernet cards and Token Ring cards talk to each other without the help of one of the internetworking devices discussed in Chapter 5, "Additional Networking Hardware."

Second, there's the type of cable that the cards support. The jack on the back of the card must be of a type into which you can plug the cable you want to use. The good news is that many modern cards support more than one type of cable. For example, Ethernet cards often support the type of Ethernet that requires coaxial cable as well as the kind that requires unshielded twisted pair (UTP) in a single card. You could use this type of card to start out your Ethernet network with coaxial cable. Then, you could switch to UTP (which uses an RJ-45 connector) as the network got larger without having to install new network cards. Figure 1.1 shows the back of a network card that includes ports for both types of interfaces, as well as an attachment unit interface (AUI) port.

FIGURE 1.1:

A dual-jack network card for both UTP and coax

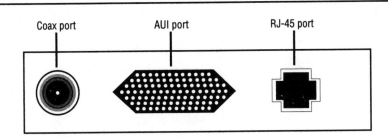

Coax port   AUI port   RJ-45 port

Third, there's the card's bus type, which governs how fast the NIC can talk to the motherboard. Most modern cards for desktop machines will be available with one of the following bus types:

- Industry Standard Architecture (ISA)

- Peripheral Component Interconnect (PCI)

NOTE   Laptop users must use network cards with the Personal Computer Memory Card International Association (PCMCIA) interface, also called *PC cards*. Can't remember the abbreviation easily? Try it as "People Can't Memorize Computer Industry Abbreviations."

The difference between the ISA and PCI buses is mainly one of speed. ISA communicates with the motherboard at 16 megabytes per second (MBps) and 8 megahertz (MHz), which is how fast PCs operated when the ISA standard was originally developed. For reasons of backward compatibility, this hasn't changed.

PCI, supported by modern computers, communicates with the motherboard at a rate of 32MBps and a clock rate of 33MHz. It's faster than ISA, although ISA is doomed because it lacks PCI's speed and other enhancements, which are discussed in Chapter 3. However, ISA is taking a good long time to die because of its enormous installed base. Die it will, though. So it's a good idea to plan ahead now and look for PCI network cards even if they do cost a bit more than their ISA counterparts.

NOTE   External data transfer rates are typically described in terms of bits per second (bps), whereas internal data transfer rates are typically described in terms of bytes per second (Bps). One byte equals eight bits. How much is that? One ASCII character can be expressed in one byte.

Fourth, there's external data transfer rate, typically measured in megabits—that is, millions of bits—per second (Mbps). The data transfer rate that the network card you choose can support isn't the only factor that determines network speed, but it's one of them. Token Ring networks run at 4Mbps, 16Mbps, or 100Mbps, and Ethernet runs at either 10Mbps or 100Mbps. Although you can plug a PC with a 10Mbps card into a 100Mbps network, the speed of the PC's connection to the LAN will be determined by the speed of the card connecting it to the LAN.

NOTE   There's a faster version of Ethernet, called Gigabit Ethernet, supporting transmission speeds of up to one billion bits per second (Gbps). The NICs designed for these high speeds are currently very expensive and designed for the high-end server market, rather than for client PCs or ordinary servers.

The Silver Link, the Silken Tie—Network Cabling

Sir Walter Scott may not have been talking about network cables when he wrote of these bonds, but the description fits: network cables are indeed the sometimes almost invisible but essential pieces for tying together a network. The types of information that will be sent between computers (text, complex graphics, video, or audio), the distance between computers, and the environment in which those cables must operate are all determining factors for the type of cable you will need to use. As each type of cable is used for a particular kind of network, the kind of network you want to create will determine which cable type you choose.

Copper wire, used within twisted pair and coaxial cable, may be either stranded or solid. *Stranded wire* is made of smaller wires combined, while *solid* is a single wire. Stranded cables are more flexible than solid and thus better for short runs that may require stress to the cable that might break a solid wire, but they are also more vulnerable to signal loss.

What are the options? There are several, divided between copper wire and fiber optic. Each of them is designed to solve, in a different way, one of the most nagging problems facing any kind of transmission: interference, *radio frequency noise,* or *RF noise.* The problem is that copper wire was originally chosen as a medium for network transmissions because it conducts signals terrifically well, but that same ability makes it susceptible to interference from other sources of electrical signals, thus endangering the integrity of the original transmission. To get around this, the various cable types use one method or another of protecting the wire from outside interference or even making it immune to such interference.

RF noise is a product of electromagnetic interference (EMI) and thus is not produced only by transmitting devices. Large electric motors produce EMI, as do power lines, radar signals, other cables if not properly protected, and, of course, high-powered radio devices.

The less susceptible cabling is to interference, the faster it is because transmission speed along analog channels, such as copper wire, is a function of frequency. Before your eyes glaze over, understand that this is important. Copper cables are sometimes described in terms of the frequencies they can support, so if you don't understand what this means then you're not going to understand those descriptions.

Frequency describes the rate at which electrical impulses travel through a certain area. It's expressed in hertz, or cycles per second, the cycles being how fast the pulses can be created. They can be illustrated as sine waves (see Figure 1.2). In other words, a signal that runs at 8MHz can run eight million cycles in one second. The higher the frequency, the faster the data is traveling because more 1s and 0s are being packed into a single second.

FIGURE 1.2:

The more bumps of a sine wave in a given time period, the higher the frequency

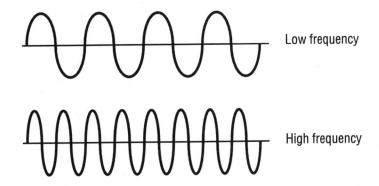

Low frequency

High frequency

Higher frequencies are more susceptible to interference than are lower frequencies because more data is compressed into a given instant. If you're unsure as to why this is so, take a look again at Figure 1.2. Suppose that something interfered with both the low-frequency signal and the high-frequency signal for a half-second (a long time, but this is to make the point, not to show precise measurements). During that half-second, the data transmitted along those channels would be corrupted and lost. In the case of the higher-frequency signal, we've lost a larger proportion of the data because more data was crammed into that half second. The lower-frequency signal lost much less data.

The maximum frequency supported by a given cable does not imply that the data transfer rate of that cable always uses that frequency, but only says what the physical medium of the cable is theoretically capable of supporting, if undamaged and installed correctly. For example, Category 5 UTP (discussed in the following section) operates at a maximum frequency of 100MHz, but to support speeds of 100Mbps a frequency of only 62.5MHz is required. That's just how fast the cable could transmit data under ideal conditions if the data were pushed through it that quickly. I'll discuss frequency and its relationship to signal strength and carrying power further under "Wireless Networking," later in this chapter.

Another variable in physical cable types is their reach. When reading the descriptions of the cable types, you'll notice that they vary in the length of the cable that they can use. That's due in part to a phenomenon called *attenuation*. Essentially, attenuation is the degree to which the signal weakens over distance. The more vulnerable the cable is to interference, the more it will be affected by attenuation. The good news is that devices, such as repeaters, can rebroadcast the signal on long cables so they can run for longer distances.

Interference versus Attenuation

Although interference and attenuation have similar effects on data transmission (they're not good for it), they're not the same thing. *Interference* is a stray electronic signal that distorts the signal being transmitted, possibly corrupting the data being carried by adding extra humps in the sine wave or otherwise interfering with the signal. *Attenuation* is the increasing weakness of a signal as it travels. Just as a sound loses power from the time it leaves its source, but may still be audible at any given distance from its source, all signals experience attenuation. The problem arises when the signal is so severely attenuated because it's traveled farther than it was meant to that the fading signal can distort the data.

Continued on next page

Both interference and attenuation work a lot like sound. Interference is the problem that you run into when a lot of people are all talking at once and it's difficult to sort out who said what, or even to distinguish the sound of one voice as it gets overrun by the sound of another. Attenuation is the problem you run into when someone's too far away for you to hear their voice properly and you may misunderstand them. Interference problems are resolved by shielding out other "conversations;" attenuation problems are resolved by boosting the signal.

Twisted Pair Cable

If you wrap one good conductor around another one, they form a field that protects the conducting wires from RF noise. That's the approach taken by twisted pair cable. There are in fact two types of twisted pair cable: unshielded twisted pair (UTP) and shielded twisted pair (STP).

There are two differences between the types of twisted pair cable. First, UTP has four pairs of wires and STP has two. Second, and the key to the difference in their names, STP has an extra conducting layer surrounding the twisted wires to give the cable an extra level of protection from interference. This does not necessarily imply that STP is always better protected from RF noise than UTP, but only that the two cable types take different approaches. The theory with UTP is that the two wires wrapped around each other individually conduct noise, but cancel out each other's noise.

The theory with STP is that the conductors are best protected with a layer of conducting wires rather than the two conductors being wrapped around each other. This extra layer of protection can make the STP cable hard to work with because it stiffens the cable and the shielding only works as long as it's both properly grounded and not torn. You can see the difference between UTP and STP in Figure 1.3.

FIGURE 1.3:

Sections of UTP and
STP

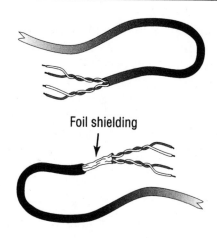

Foil shielding

NOTE   STP cable is commonly used in Token Ring networks. UTP is used in Ethernet networks (10BaseT and 100BaseT) and occasionally in Token Ring networks.

The Electronics Industry Association (EIA), Telecommunications Industry Association (TIA), and National Electrical Manufacturers Association (NEMA) established a five-grade standard for UTP. They then commissioned Underwriters Laboratories to certify and grade cable sold in the United States according to these standards. The higher the grade number, the more twists per foot and the more often the pattern of these twists must vary to throw off RFI (radio frequency interference). Thus, although no cable is entirely uninfluenced by interference, the higher the grade, the more immune that category of UTP is to RFI and EMI and the faster it can accurately transmit data. Technically speaking, Category 3 cable, rated for transmissions of up to 10Mbps and with at least three twists per foot, is LAN-capable, and may be found in existing LANs. However, any new LANs using UTP will most likely use Category 5 cable, which is rated for transmissions of up to 100Mbps and capable of extending up to about 90 meters.

Beyond Category 5

Note that Category 5 cable is the highest *certified* standard of twisted pair cable. As of this writing, there are also a couple of not-yet-certified standards: enhanced Category 5 and Category 6.

Enhanced Category 5 cable is like Category 5 (high-speed UTP) except, well, it's enhanced. It's got more variance in its twist patterns and uses a higher grade of wire than does ordinary Category 5 cable and can typically support frequencies of up to 200MHz. It's not certain how the standard will define enhanced Category 5 cable—whether this will be the frequency rate required or if it will have to be as fast as 300MHz.

Category 6 cable is a kettle of fish of a different color because it requires a foil wrapping around the twisted pair cable and is thus STP, rather than UTP. It's unclear as yet just how high its frequencies will be when and if a standard is defined. On the low end, one possibility is 350MHz, but on the high end, rates of 600MHz are bandied about. There are a lot of hang-ups attached to a Category 6 standard, such as what type of connector to use, the fact that it's STP instead of UTP, and the speed at which it's supposed to run. So Category 6 products are not likely to be widely available in the United States until some of these issues are sorted out.

Category 5 cable is able to keep up with the needs of Fast Ethernet, which supports data transfer rates of up to 100Mbps. Why are faster cables needed? Mostly because of the specter of ATM and Gigabit Ethernet networks, which require frequencies in the hundreds of megahertz (350MHz for ATM) to keep up with them. These high-speed networks make Fast Ethernet look like your father's Oldsmobile. At a top frequency of 100MHz, Category 5 cable can't keep up with those needs, so the options are either to improve UTP performance or switch to fiber optic cable.

IBM also maintains standards for a variety of types of twisted pair cables (and two types of fiber), organizing them by function rather than in order of immunity to RFI. The twisted pair types are as follows:

Type 1   Is solid-wire STP used for data transmission. It has two pairs of wires in each cable.

Type 2   Combines four unshielded solid wires and two shielded solid wires in the same sheath. The UTP is intended for voice transmission and the STP is for data.

Type 3   Contains four pairs of solid-wire UTP to be used for voice or data.

Type 6   Contains two pairs of stranded-wire cable. It's essentially like Type 1 except that it uses stranded wire instead of solid.

Type 8   Is a special type of STP designed to be flatter than ordinary cable so it can be run under carpets.

Type 9   Consists of two pairs of STP covered with plenum rather than polyvinylchloride (PVC) and is meant to be used between floors in a building. PVC emits toxic smoke when it burns, so plenum is required to meet some fire codes.

Twisted pair networks typically connect each individual NIC to a centrally located switching area, either a hub or a *punchdown block* connected to a hub, which is a place to plug in lots of cables. I'll talk about hubs in Chapter 5, "Additional Networking Hardware."

Coaxial Cable

Coaxial cable, often referred to as either BNC cable or Thinnet, is made of a single copper wire encased in insulation and then covered with a layer of aluminum or copper braid that protects the conducting wire from RF noise. As you can see in Figure 1.4, coaxial cable has four parts:

- The central wire, called the *inner conductor*

- A layer of insulation, called the *dielectric,* which surrounds the inner conductor

- A layer of foil or metal braid, called the *shield*, which covers the dielectric

- The final layer of insulation (the part you can see), called the *jacket*

FIGURE 1.4:

Coaxial cable

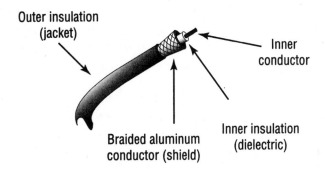

With a top data transfer rate of 10Mbps, coaxial cable is slow by modern standards, but it's got a couple of advantages over UTP for some installations. First, it can extend for longer runs. The top length for UTP cable runs is 100 meters, but coaxial cable can extend for more than 800 meters. However, after 185 meters you'll have to boost the signal with a device called a *repeater*, which will be described in Chapter 5, "Additional Networking Hardware."

The second advantage is that you can use coaxial cables to connect PCs to each other directly (rather than to a central hub) in a daisy-chain effect. This can be handy for those who have only a couple of computers in the same room to connect and don't want to go to the expense of a hub.

NOTE   There's actually a second kind of coaxial cable known as *Thicknet*, which is used in older networks but not often installed new today. This cable can stretch for longer distances than can Thinnet cable, but it's much harder to work with. One contractor I know who used to have to work with it refers to Thicknet as "frozen yellow garden hose" because of its stiffness. Thicknet doesn't actually connect to the PCs themselves, but forms a backbone to the network that the PCs connect to with short patch cables.

Fiber Optic Cable

One way of getting around the problem of how to protect your data medium from EMI is to whack that Gordian knot in two. Make that cable utterly immune to EMI by not using electronic signals for transmission at all. That solution is called *fiber optic cable*.

Fiber optic cable is indifferent to RF noise because of the difference in its conductive medium; rather than using electronic pulses to send data, it uses light. The light is conducted through a hairlike glass or plastic fiber that is covered with a thin insulating layer called *cladding*. The cladding is then surrounded with a plastic jacket to protect the delicate fiber. You can see a drawing of fiber optic cable in Figure 1.5.

FIGURE 1.5:

Fiber optic cable

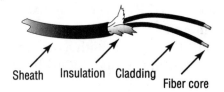

Sheath   Insulation   Cladding   Fiber core

As you'd expect, the fibers are the crucial element of data transmission. At each end of the fiber is a device called a *codec*, or coder/decoder. The codec is responsible for encoding the data into light pulses and then decoding them back into the electronic impulses that a computer can understand. To transmit data, a light-emitting diode (LED) or a laser at one end of the fiber sends signals along the cable. When those signals reach the other end, they're decoded into their original form.

It might sound as though traffic through a fiber optic cable is limited to a single path of data, but this isn't true for a couple of reasons. First, fiber optic cable may have more than one fiber in it, meaning that multiple data pathways exist. The more fibers a cable has, the more data can pass through it at once, just as a four-lane highway can carry more traffic than a single-lane road.

Second, there are two types of fiber optic cable: single mode and multimode.

NOTE   A *mode* is a ray of light entering a fiber at a particular angle.

Single-mode fiber sends transmissions along a single path, like a flashlight. This beam of light is very intense, so single-mode fiber can carry more data for longer distances and is thus suitable either for applications that are very traffic-intensive or need to travel for long distances.

Multimode fiber allows multiple modes to pass through the cable at once. There are actually two kinds of multimode fiber: step index and graded index. In *step index fiber optic cable,* the light beams bounce around inside the cable in a zigzag pattern. *Graded index cable* has a more rounded pattern to the light movement, like a sine wave (see Figure 1.6).

FIGURE 1.6:

Multimode cable sends more than one beam of light down the fiber at a time.

Step index system: Light bounces along an angular path inside the cable.

Graded index system: Light follows a more rounded path.

Both kinds of multimode fiber optic cable are prone to *modal dispersion*—spreading of the received light impulse—due to the number of light beams traveling through the cable. When the signal spreads, it moves more slowly, so single-mode cable transmits faster than multimode cable. To understand this behavior, try imagining what would happen if you threw a ball down a pipe. If you threw just one ball and it went through without hitting the walls of the pipe, it would move faster and more accurately than if it bounced off the walls of the pipe. Just as bouncing off the walls of the pipe slows down the ball's travel speed, bouncing off the walls of the cable slows down the light signal.

> **NOTE**   Single-mode cable is more expensive than multimode and can extend further without requiring the signal to be boosted. Multimode cable is more often used within buildings; single-mode is reserved for inter-building use.

Fiber has had notable success as a LAN backbone, combined with UTP taps to each workstation, for those with high-traffic networks and deep pockets. Fiber's not often run to the desktop at this point for a couple of reasons. First, it costs more per foot than does UTP and requires some specialized knowledge to install it, driving that cost up as well. Second, with the advent of Fast Ethernet, which supports speeds of up to 100Mbps over copper wire, UTP is much faster than it used to be, not quite reaching fiber's speed when used in an FDDI network (see Chapter 2) but rivaling it. However, as higher speeds are required for some applications and the costs of fiber drop, you can probably expect to see fiber run to the desktop more often.

If fiber's too expensive to run to the desktop and no longer always hugely faster than UTP, then why use it at all? First, it *is* really fast and eminently suited to demanding sorts of traffic such as video. Second, since it transmits light, not electricity, fiber optic cables are completely resistant to EMI and RFI, so signals are sometimes able to travel several miles without any degradation. Some kinds of fiber can transmit up to three miles in LAN environments and across the country via a high-powered laser device in WAN environments. Fiber optic cable is also useful in hazardous environments because it can't spark (as electric transfer cables potentially could). Furthermore, it doesn't contain any metal, so it resists corrosion. Finally, fiber optic cabling is harder to tap into than is copper-based cable, so it's more secure and therefore popular for top-secret communications.

A relatively new kind of high-end fiber network called *fibre channel* seeks to blur the distinction between individual devices and the network even more than the LAN does already. Fibre channel can operate at even higher speeds than does FDDI.

Wireless Networking

Wireless networking is less esoteric than it may sound. Essentially, it's any method of connecting two devices without having a cable running between them. It's best suited for the following situations:

- When wiring isn't possible or is prohibitively expensive because of logistical problems

- When clients (such as laptop users) join and leave the network frequently, or don't have access to a desk with a network connection

- When network clients need to move around a lot

Unless there's a specific reason to make a network or part of it wireless, it's not a good idea. Wireless networks are slower than their wired counterparts and more prone to interference. That said, there are also times when they're invaluable. For example, doing inventory is much easier with a wireless laptop that you can carry around than with a wired terminal that you must keep running to in order to enter numbers.

Wireless networks operate on the same principle as do wired networks; signal strength and speed are a function of frequency, or how often information can be passed during a given interval. The frequencies used depend on the signal, but generally speaking, wireless types may be divided into two classes: radio signals and infrared signals. *Radio signals* have a wider range and (like radio) are relatively immune to most barriers, but in exchange have a low transmission speed. *Infrared signals* have a very high frequency and high speed, but are easily disrupted.

Getting Connected—Cable-NIC Connectors

Getting NICs and cables is a large part of the business of putting together a LAN, but you still need something to make those NICs talk to those cables, and that's where connectors come in.

Coaxial Cable Connectors

Three types of connectors are associated with coaxial cable:

- T-connectors
- BNC connectors
- Terminators

T-connectors (see Figure 1.7) plug into network cards where they stick out the back of the PC and provide an interface to plug in the BNC connector.

FIGURE 1.7:

FIGURE 1.7:

A T-connector creates the interface into which you plug the BNC connector.

A BNC connector (see Figure 1.8) plugs into the T-connector attached to the NIC. This links the card and the cable, with the cable forming the crossbars of the "T" (see Figure 1.9), and may also be used to link sections of coaxial cable.

FIGURE 1.8:

The BNC connector may link coaxial cables to each other or to T-connectors.

FIGURE 1.9:

The BNC connector attaches the T-connector to the coaxial cable.

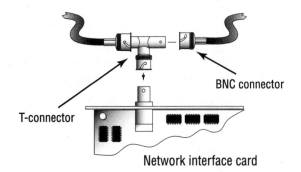

BNC connector

T-connector

Network interface card

The terminators are the final piece of the coaxial puzzle (see Figure 1.10); they are used to define the ends of the cable. If you don't have terminators at each end of a coaxial segment, then the signal will "echo" from the end of the cable and *shadow packets* will result. Shadow packets slow down network speed by increasing traffic and may corrupt data if confused with real packets. Terminating the segments ensures that packets will be destroyed when the signal reaches the end of the segment.

FIGURE 1.10:

Terminate the ends of coaxial segments to avoid shadow packets.

NOTE   Terminators are made for either 50-ohm or 75-ohm cable. The standard is usually a 50-ohm terminator. Pay attention when you're buying terminators because they won't work if you mix them up. Most coax network cable systems require 50-ohm terminators.

Twisted Pair Connectors

Most UTP cable uses RJ-45 connectors, which look like chunkier versions of the connectors used to plug your telephone into the wall (see Figure 1.11). The RJ-45 connectors are attached to both ends of the cable; one end plugs into your computer card and the other plugs into a hub or a punchdown block in the wiring closet. Essentially, it looks like a somewhat bulkier version of a telephone cord.

FIGURE 1.11:

Each end of UTP network cable has an RJ-45 connector on it.

Okay, I lied—not all UTP cables connect a hub and a network card. You can use crossover cables in some implementations to daisy-chain computers together. *Crossover cables* are wired to perform the function of a hub.

STP cable doesn't use the same connectors as UTP cable. You'll use a D-shell connector (see Figure 1.12.) with STP to connect the cable to the NIC. You'll need an IBM Data Connector (Figure 1.13) to connect it to a multistation access unit (MAU) or hub.

FIGURE 1.12:

A D-shell connector connects the cable to the machine's network card.

FIGURE 1.13:

An IBM data connector connects the cable to the MAU.

> **WARNING** You may notice that the D-shell connector used to connect to a Token Ring card is the same one that is used to connect to a video card. Be careful not to plug the network cable into your monitor.

Fiber Optic Connectors

Unlike copper-wire cables, in which the transmission medium is the biggest source of signal loss, fiber optic is most susceptible to signal dispersion at its connectors. Fiber optic cable uses two kinds of connectors: *SMA* (screw-mounted adapters) and *ST* (spring-loaded twist). The ST connector uses a spring-loaded twist to clamp to the cable while the SMA screws onto the end. ST connectors (see Figure 1.14) are more common than SMAs.

FIGURE 1.14:

An ST connector and a connector cover

Summary of Cable and Connector Types

Having trouble assimilating all of these cables and connectors? Table 1.1 lists the cable types discussed, their speeds, their maximum lengths, and the means they use to minimize electrical interference.

TABLE 1.1: Cable and Connector Types

Cable Type	Top Speed	Maximum Supported Length	Anti-Interference Measures Used	Connector Used
Coaxial	10Mbps	2500 feet	Copper braid around transmitting wires	BNC
Unshielded twisted pair (UTP)	100Mbps	300 feet	Twisted pairs	RJ-45
Shielded twisted pair (STP)	100Mbps	300 feet	Twisted pairs combined with metal shielding	D-shell
Fiber optic	155Mbps or greater	10Km	Transmission without electrical signals	ST or SMA

The OSI Model

So far, I've covered the basics of the physical elements of a network. Another important concept is the way in which data is transmitted along those physical elements. I'll talk about those methods in the following chapters when I discuss network types and transmission protocols. However, those methods are more easily understood if you have a context in which to place them so you can understand how all the various levels of networking interact. This context may be provided with a tool called the OSI model.

What Is the OSI Model?

In the early days of networking, inter-computer communication systems were developed in a vacuum. Communication between various vendors' protocol stacks was not given priority.

In the interest of promoting networking protocol stacks that *could* communicate with each other, the International Standards Organization (ISO) developed a model that could be used to develop *open systems*—networking systems that could easily communicate with other networking systems because they would all use the same communications model. That dream didn't entirely work out, but the Open Systems Interconnection (OSI) model, released in its final form in 1984, provides a convenient framework for understanding how the various parts of networks talk to each other.

NOTE   Few, if any, existing protocols fit perfectly into the OSI model. In most cases, I'll provide some examples of networking protocols, or sometimes hardware, that perform the functions the standard defines for each layer. These protocols will be discussed further in this section of the book.

Fundamentally, the point of using a system like the OSI model to develop networking standards is to gain flexibility. If you change your physical medium, you shouldn't have to change the entire networking structure.

The OSI Model—A Return to the Warlord System?

Feudal Japan was not ruled by one government, but was divided into adjacent but more or less independent provinces, each ruled by their individual warlords. You couldn't travel from one part of Japan to another and expect the rules from one province to apply to another. Not until Ieyasu Tokugawa united the country by force was there any kind of central government.

Although not introduced by force, the OSI model is like the Tokugawa regime in that it's an attempt to unify a divided world, to get all the pieces to cooperate.

Continued on next page

In an August 1998 internal memo leaked to the public (and confirmed by Microsoft as genuine), one Microsoft employee suggests the possibility of returning to this model. The reason? To stomp out competition from open-source operating systems, such as Linux, which depend on open networking. Read a copy of the memo (annotated by Eric Raymond, an open-source software advocate quoted in the memo) at `http://www.opensource.` `.org/halloween.html`.

Will it happen? Since the publication of the memo, there's been sufficient public outcry that it would now be politically difficult for Microsoft to create a proprietary stack. This is especially true given that Microsoft is already under investigation by the Department of Justice for antitrust activities. However, even if the open systems are ruled to remain open, this should be taken as a warning: open systems are dependent upon intra-community cooperation, not competition.

Layers of the OSI Model

As shown in Figure 1.15, the OSI model divides networking functions into seven layers, each describing a different part of the physical or logical network. Typically, this model displays the layers in a stack, but the relationship between the layers is clearer if you think of the layers as concentric circles, as shown in Figure 1.15. Generally speaking, each circle supports the ones further in. For example, UTP is a physical layer medium that provides a physical connection between two points of the LAN. Ethernet, described in Chapter 2, is a data link layer medium creating a virtual channel within the physical channel by specifying the source and destination physical addresses for the transmission. IP, a network layer protocol described in Chapter 3, travels within the virtual channel created by the data link layer protocol.

FIGURE 1.15:

The OSI model

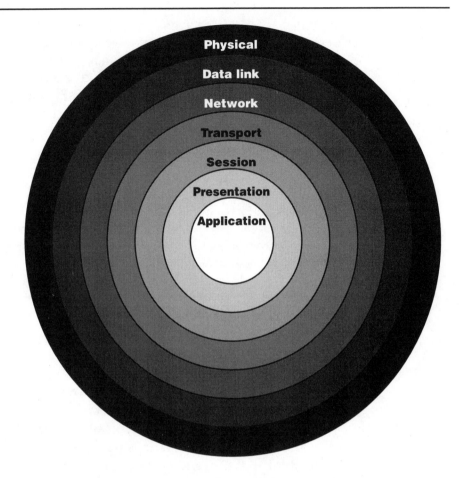

FIGURE 1.15:

The OSI model

The support relationship between the layers of the OSI model is most pronounced in the physical, data link, and network layers, but even in the inner circles all layers are supported by the layers around them. Application protocols, for example, cannot function without the client/server sessions established by the session data protocols.

> **TIP**   Having trouble remembering the names of the layers and the order they come in? From the inside out, the first letters of each layer spell "All Pizza Seems To Need Diet Pepsi."

The Physical Layer

The *physical layer* describes the physical medium by which networking takes place: copper wire, fiber, satellite, or what have you. If the network is composed of more than one medium defined at the physical layer, you'll have to set up hardware that permits the various physical media to talk to each other.

Data is passed to the physical layer as a series of bits, with no framing information or anything other than a stream of data. Depending on the type of connection, the stream may be serial or parallel and transmission may be either *duplex* (able to send and receive simultaneously) or *half-duplex* (only able to send or receive at any given time). If the signal weakens, it's amplified here with a device called a *repeater*.

At the physical level, no formal addressing exists except a virtual circuit between sender and recipient. Formal addressing of a kind comprehensible to humans is handled at higher levels.

The Data Link Layer

The purpose of protocols functioning at the *data link layer* is to make sure that the bits traveling along the physical medium get to their destination in as error-free a manner as possible. No medium is completely error-free, so data link protocols include some mechanisms for error checking and retransmittal of problem packets. For example, Ethernet, as you'll read in Chapter 2, is prepared to deal with the possibility of two packets being sent at the same time (meaning that neither packet can be delivered) and can recover from that problem.

At the data link layer, the raw stream of bits passed to the physical medium is trapped and framed for delivery. *Framing* means that data is packaged into little segments called *packets* or *frames*. Each packet not only contains data but also addressing information and (sometimes) a record of the amount of data in each packet.

This way, the network will know whether any data is lost. The contents and structure of the frames will vary with the network type. So, if your network contains two different data link protocols (such as Ethernet and Token Ring), then you'll need a device called a *bridge* to permit them to communicate.

As bits are sent via the physical layer of the network in the order in which they get to the channel, it's the job of the data link layer to make sure that all data arrives at its destination in the proper order. Essentially, the data link layer protocols provide reliable channels for communication between network layer processes.

The Network Layer

The *network layer protocols* are responsible for finding the best path for routing data between computers. At this level, logical network addresses such as those used with IP (the network layer half of TCP/IP) are defined for use by the upper-level protocols. As routing takes place at the network layer, hardware devices called *routers* determine the best way to get information from one segment of a network to another; routers operate at the network level. Protocols operating at the network layer aren't concerned with whether the data reaches its destination; they just find the best path.

At the transport layer (discussed next), it doesn't matter whether the physical network is composed of a variety of media, or whether more than one type of protocol at the data link level defines the packet size and contents. All it's concerned about is routing packets between logically defined addresses. That said, the network layer may package data into its own units for easier routing because it's using addresses unknown to the protocols defined at lower layers. The transport layer will use those addresses to make sure that the data reaches its final destination at the logical address defined in the network-layer packets.

The Transport Layer

Protocols operating at the *transport layer*, such as SPX or TCP, take care of getting data to the logical addresses supplied by the network layer protocols. These protocols subdivide the data packets sent to them and repackage them to be smaller, reassembling them when they reach their destination.

Transport layer protocols are a bit slower than their network layer counterparts because they contain more error-correcting information in case something goes wrong. This is the final layer of the OSI model that's concerned in most networking.

The Session Layer

The main purpose of the *session layer* is to provide support for the presentation and application layers. At this level, the way that two remote systems communicate with messages called *remote procedure calls* (RPCs) is defined. To do this, the session layer has two functions: dialogue control and data separation. *Dialogue control* provides an orderly means of beginning conversations, relaying messages between the remote systems, and then, when the session is over, shutting down the connection. *Data separation* refers to the points inserted into the messages to permit each workstation to tell where one message ends and another begins. Both are important to the session to make sure that both machines get the message, the whole message, and nothing but the message; the exact contents of the message is of no concern at this layer. NetBIOS provides session-layer services.

The Presentation Layer

Presentation protocols are responsible for making sure that the data being passed between systems is in a form that the recipient can understand. Compression/decompression and encryption/decryption all take place at this level. "Presentation" refers not to what the interface looks like, but to the manner in which the data are presented.

The Application Layer

Finally, the *application layer* is responsible for passing necessary information from the application interface to any network resources it needs. Protocols running at this level vary enormously in their size and complexity, with some passing enormous amounts of data between server and client and some performing only a small set of tasks. In a well-designed protocol stack, the application layer can comprise up to 90 percent of the data passing back and forth across the network, so network efficiency is more or less defined at this layer.

Summary

This chapter has given you a lot to chew on for the first chapter of a networking book. Here, you've learned the basics of how networking can enrich your office. You've also been introduced to the different kinds of copper and fiber, and the connectors that are used to join cables to the various types of network cards. In a nutshell, this chapter covered the following points.

Local area networks are networks that are confined within a single building. LANs can help you share files and peripheral devices more easily, and can form the backbone of your office by making available communication media, such as e-mail and office databases.

Network cards may be organized according to network type supported, bus type, speed, or other variables, but in all cases the network card is a peripheral device that makes your computer network-ready. Network cards are built to support the various cable media; some modern cards can support more than one kind.

Network transmissions are adversely affected by interference. There are two solutions to this problem. Copper-wire cables avoid interference by providing a protective layer of copper (either by twisting cables or in the form of a sheath) that protects against outside influences. Fiber optic cable is immune to electrical interference because its transmission medium uses light, not electricity. The only trouble with fiber optic cable is that it is much more expensive than copper-wire media.

Network cables are attached to the network cards with hardware called connectors. These connectors, which are cable-specific and meant to be used with a certain kind of port on the network card, create the interface between the network-ready PC and the network. Some network types not only require connectors but also terminators, which are devices that let the network know the locations of its ends.

Networking may be broken up into a seven-layer model called the OSI model, which describes the various protocols used in networking. Although most protocols in common use span more than one layer of the OSI model, it's a handy tool for understanding how the parts of networking fit together.

That's enough to get you started. In Chapter 2, "Planning a Network Architecture," we'll take this basic knowledge of LAN components and begin to apply it, starting with the concept of network topologies.

Exercise 1

In the chart below, fill in the missing information about each cable listed.

Cable Type	Top Speed	Maximum Supported Length	Anti-Interference Measures Used	Connector Used
Coaxial cable		2500 feet		BNC
	100Mbps	300 feet	Twisted pairs	
Shielded twisted pair	100Mbps		Twisted pairs combined with metal shielding	
	155Mbps		Transmission without electrical signals	ST or SMA

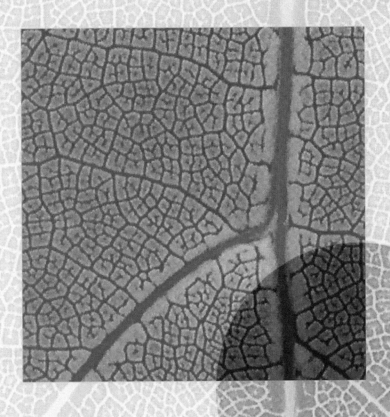

2

Planning a Network Architecture

Chapter 1, "Basic Networking Concepts and Components," covered the basics of network channels. At this point, you should have a pretty good idea of the defining characteristics of network cards, cables, and connectors. But the question remains: how do you organize those channels, and what network type will you use to have them talk to each other? In this chapter, I'll talk about the essentials of planning a network architecture and what that means in terms of physical arrangement and logical communications. Or, to use the proper jargon, the physical and logical topology of your network.

You may not be familiar with the term, "topology." In its mathematical sense, it refers to the study of the properties of geometric structures that aren't affected by stretching or twisting. In the networking sense, however, topology has two meanings. The *physical topology* refers to the physical layout of your network, or the way it would look if you drew a bird's-eye view of it. The *logical topology* of your network refers to how data packets are passed around, how only one network station is permitted to "talk" at a time (all network stations use the same wire), and how low-level error checking works to be sure that data gets where it's supposed to go.

NOTE   Although there's a little overlap in the names of the physical and logical topologies, the two have nothing to do with each other. For example, there's a bus physical topology and a bus logical topology, but a logical bus network does not have to be arranged in the bus physical topology.

Physical Topologies

The physical topology you choose for your network influences and is influenced by several factors:

- Office layout
- Troubleshooting techniques

- Cost of installation

- Type of cable used

First, there's the simple matter of looking at how your office is arranged. Those people setting up only a few computers in a single room will have more options than those with many computers distributed throughout several floors of a building.

Second, troubleshooting techniques and requirements are determined to some degree by the physical topology you use. For example, some topologies have built-in physical redundancy to prevent breaks in the cable from interrupting communications. Other topologies isolate each cable in the network so that a single break won't bring everything down.

Third, not all physical topologies are equal in terms of cost. Some of this cost is going to depend on your office layout, to be sure; it's more work to wire a network that extends over a larger area, and cost will reflect that extra effort. However, some of the cost will be affected by the complexity of the topology you choose and more important, how hard it is to make the topology fit into your space. The bus topology, for example, is simple when done in a small area but could be a major headache to cable if you attempted to run it through a multi-floor network.

Finally, to a significant degree, the physical topology you choose for your network determines what kind of cable you'll get for it and vice versa. As you may recall from Chapter 1, "Basic Networking Concepts and Components," UTP uses RJ-45 connectors to connect each computer on the network to a central hub. This particular configuration is called the *star topology* because it looks like rays radiating from a central point. You can't use coaxial cable in the star physical topology because the cables simply don't fit together that way.

That said, let's take a look at the most common physical topologies you're likely to encounter.

The Bus Physical Topology

For simple networks in a small area, the bus physical topology (known in the Mac world as daisy-chaining) may be the best solution. In the bus topology, the cable runs from computer to computer, making each computer a link of a chain. All computers on the network share a single cable and this cable is typically coaxial cable.

NOTE   A network using twisted pair cable could use the bus physical topology if you connected the individual PCs with patch cables, but this really isn't practical for connecting more than a couple of computers.

You can connect a bus topology in two different ways, depending on the type of cable you're using. If your network is using the Thicknet coaxial cable described in Chapter 1, "Basic Networking Concepts and Components," then the bus network will have a central backbone cable that's the thick coaxial cable. Smaller, thinner (and more flexible) cables called *taps* or *drops* will run from the backbone to each PC in the network. A small device called a *transceiver* actually connects the thinner cable to the Thicknet backbone. You can see an example of this topology in Figure 2.1.

FIGURE 2.1:

The bus physical topology using Thicknet coaxial cable

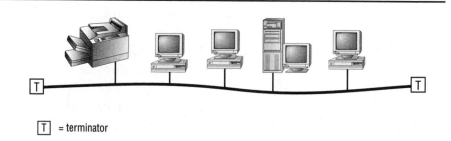

T = terminator

The thick Ethernet configuration is normally used in mainframe and minicomputer networks in a setup like the one illustrated in

Figure 2.1, but its popularity is diminishing as PCs get smarter and mainframe-based networks become less common. For new networks using the bus physical topology, you're much more likely to use thin coaxial cable.

As opposed to thick Ethernet, *Thinnet* eschews the backbone idea and connects all network devices directly. Rather than using thick cable, Thinnet uses the more flexible coaxial cable described in Chapter 1, as shown in Figure 2.2. This is a more popular version of the bus physical topology today than the thick counterpart that uses taps and transceivers. It's mostly a matter of simplicity; the thick cable that Thick Ethernet uses is a pain to work with—it's very stiff and clumsy.

FIGURE 2.2:

In the bus physical topology, PCs can also connect directly to the backbone.

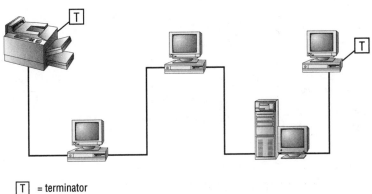

T = terminator

The biggest potential problem with a bus network is that if it's not terminated correctly (remember, I talked about terminators in Chapter 1), then your network can't transmit properly. If you are using the bus physical topology, you must do what you can to prevent breaks in continuity along the cable. Those breaks can be caused by malfunctioning nodes and cable breaks.

The network won't transmit correctly if even one node on the network is malfunctioning because the system depends on every node being in proper working order so that it can pass along the data. This doesn't mean that every machine on the network must be powered up and logged onto the network for the network to work. There is an important distinction between malfunctioning (the cable connection being not quite snapped together, for example) and the node being off. If the node is turned off, then data will pass through the T-connector plugged into the NIC to the next active node. In this case, the network is unaware that an inactive node is present. However, if the node is active and malfunctioning, then problems will occur. The active node will still attempt to process packets, but will do it inaccurately, thus slowing down the whole network or bringing it to a screeching halt.

Cable breaks will also cause problems for the bus topology because proper functioning of the network is dependent on the cable running unbroken between its terminated ends. If the cable is damaged at some point along the way, the network won't work, and it can be time-consuming trying to figure out just where that break took place so you can replace the broken segment of cable. You might need to inspect every node to make sure that the cables are securely fastened, that no one tried to reboot or log off when a signal was being passed, or that any number of other things were in order.

The bus topology does have one great advantage: it's cable-efficient and therefore can save you money on the most expensive part of your network. On the other hand, it can be difficult to implement if the machines in your network are not neatly lined up in a row. A network extending throughout a building, for example, is not a good candidate for the bus topology and would be better served by the star physical topology.

The Star Physical Topology

In the *star topology*, each server and workstation plugs into a central hub that provides connections to all other devices connected to the hub. If seen from above, a network using the star topology would look something like the schematic shown in Figure 2.3.

FIGURE 2.3:

In the star topology, all resources connect to a central device.

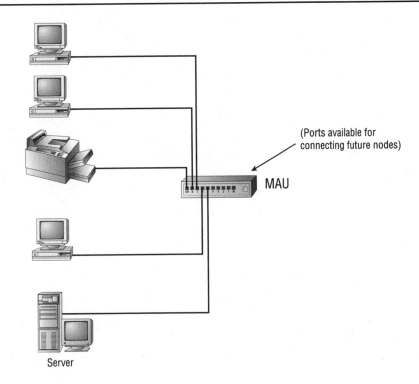

(Ports available for connecting future nodes)

MAU

Server

The first data communications networks used a star topology to connect dumb terminals to the mainframes. Why is this topology still around? Mostly because it's really easy to work with. Each workstation and server on the network has its own connection to the central switching point. This means that each connection is independent of all other connections; a break in workstation A's cable won't affect workstation B's connection. It also means that the network is relatively easy to cable because you don't have to worry as much about where the computers on the network are in relation to each other. So long as each workstation and server is no more than the maximum cable length from the hub, then that's all you need to worry about.

The centerpiece of the star topology is a hub. Hubs come in several different flavors, but the basic design is simple: they're devices that provide a central junction point for all network cables, providing a connection between each port to permit the computers plugged into it to talk to each other. I'll discuss hub design in Chapter 5, "Additional Networking Hardware."

Another big advantage to the star topology is that it's easy to troubleshoot. As described earlier in the section, "The Bus Physical Topology," if your bus network fails, it can be very difficult to pinpoint exactly where the problem lies without a node-to-node search. On a star network, it's very easy to find the source of a problem. If one node doesn't work, the problem probably lies somewhere between the port on the hub and the node that it is physically attached to. You should check to see if the problem lies with one of the following:

• The terminal itself

• The cable between the hub and the terminal

• The port on the hub that services the troubled terminal

If none of the network nodes are able to establish a connection to the server and the hub's fine (a good reason to keep a spare hub around if you can), the problem probably lies with the server. If so, it's time to hope that you planned for fault tolerance and that you did your backups.

The star topology is also nice for physically distributed networks. Imagine a network with four computers—three workstations and one server. If one workstation is upstairs and two are downstairs but in separate rooms, it's a lot easier to cable the network if you don't have to worry about connecting all the nodes to each other, and can just concentrate on connecting the individual workstations to the hub.

Of course, the star topology has one major drawback: the large amount of cable it uses. Each piece of the network requires its own cable run. Having a centralized hub just isn't the most cable-efficient arrangement, so if you're concerned about cable costs and your nodes are close together, you might want to consider the bus topology.

The Distributed Star Physical Topology

For larger networks, a single hub may not be able to support all the nodes. Perhaps it doesn't have enough ports for all the computers on the network; perhaps the computers are too far apart for the cable you're using—perhaps both. To connect everyone to the network, you're going to need more than one hub, but the idea of having three or four separate networks in the same building isn't very appealing. How do you get around this problem?

That's where a variation on the star physical topology comes in. This variation, called the *connected star* or *distributed star*, daisy-chains together the hubs on your network so that all the hubs can communicate (see Figure 2.4). This configuration does have some of the drawbacks of the bus network in that a break in the cable connecting two hubs will isolate the part of the network beyond the break. However, this drawback is compensated for by the fact that without the bus the hubs would be isolated anyway.

Use a distributed star topology to connect multiple star networks.

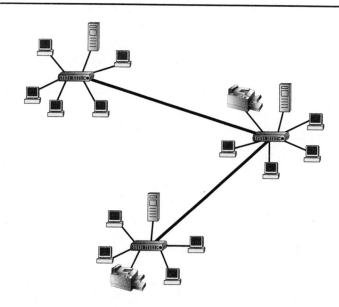

The Ring Physical Topology

Finally, there's a physical topology that you're not likely to encounter but is worth mentioning. The *ring* physical topology (see Figure 2.5) connects all PCs on the network in a loop, running double cables between each node in order to maintain network integrity. It could work, but it's a real pain in the neck to cable and puts your costs through the roof because of the double cabling costs.

FIGURE 2.5:

The ring physical topology connects all networked machines in a loop.

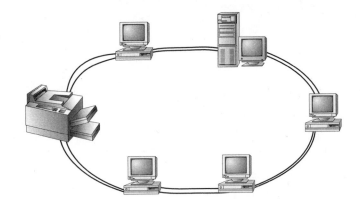

The ring physical topology has its applications. Fiber wide area networks sometimes use this physical topology because it's not a bad way to give a number of sites in a metropolitan area access to the fiber network. However, the only LAN I've ever seen use the physical ring topology was an old IBM office automation system called the 8100. You're not likely to come across one of these and even less likely to want to cable one if you're building a network from scratch, so you can note that this topology exists and then forget about it. An exception to this rule is fibre channel technology (see "Speed Demons—Fast Ethernet and Gigabit Ethernet," later in this chapter), which may use a physical ring to create a high-speed physical layer path between network nodes and other hardware. Due to the high cost of fibre channel, this isn't one you're likely to see either, but it does exist.

Maybe some of you are scratching your heads at this, saying, "I know of someone who's got a ring network!" You're probably thinking of a Token Ring network. Token Ring is an IBM wiring system that uses the ring *logical* topology of token passing, and I'll discuss that in just a minute.

Logical Topologies

Logical, or *electrical*, topologies describe the way in which a network transmits information from one node to the next node, not the way the network looks. It's not all theory, however, because the way you want your network to transmit information can directly affect your options when it comes to purchasing cable and network interface cards.

As I head into the discussion of logical topology, remember that the physical topology does not have a direct bearing on the logical topology. You can have a physical star and a logical ring; a physical star and a logical bus; and so forth.

The Bus Logical Topology

Ethernet is probably the best-known example of a logical bus network; it's the most popular LAN type. Ethernet is an example of a *logical* bus topology; as you'll see in a minute, it is not always a *physical* bus topology. (I know that I keep hammering that home, but the concept isn't always easy to grasp.)

How does the logical bus topology work? Simply put, each time a node on the network has data for another node, the sending node broadcasts the data to the entire network. The various nodes hear it and look to see if the data is for them. If so, they keep the data. If not, they ignore the data. Every Ethernet card has a 48-bit address peculiar to itself, and each piece of data that travels the network is directed to the address of the card in the node that should receive the data.

NOTE What if a packet is intended for more than one workstation? Network software can set an Ethernet card to listen for specific multicast addresses. If a packet is intended for the entire network, then the destination address will be entirely 1s, thus signifying that every card should collect that packet.

Whatever anyone on the bus says, everyone hears. It's something like the old telephone party lines, where a number of neighbors would share a telephone number. Each person sharing the telephone was assigned a distinctive ring to determine who was receiving a call. If your code was, say, three quick rings, and you heard the telephone ring three quick rings, you could pick it up and know it was for you. On the other hand, if you heard two long and one short, you'd know that the call was for your neighbor Burt and you'd ignore it. In all cases, everyone heard the rings, but only one person responded—the person who was supposed to receive the call. The bus topology works in a similar fashion, although the bus networks work better than the old party lines in that your neighbor's machine won't gossip with the other PCs on the network about data not sent to it.

If that's how data finds its destination on the network, how do networked computers send it in the first place? On a bus network, every workstation can send out information in a package called a *packet*. Data transmitted on a network of *any* type must conform to the strict format, called the *Data Link Layer Frame* format, which that network type uses for arranging data. This format is defined at the data link layer of the OSI model described in Chapter 1, "Basic Networking Concepts and Components."

NOTE   As described later in this chapter under "The 802.3 Standard," Ethernet packets can be of varying lengths, but each packet can be no longer than 1518 bytes, just to make sure that one workstation doesn't hog the network for too long.

Before a workstation broadcasts to the network, it listens to see if anyone else is using the network. If the coast is clear, then the workstation broadcasts.

What if the coast isn't clear? The biggest problem with the broadcast method of network transmittal is distance. If the distance between two computers on the same network (let's call them Node A and Node B) is too great, they may not hear each other on the line. If they can't "hear" each other, then Node A can't tell whether Node B is transmitting or not. Thinking that all is quiet, Node A may therefore begin its transmittal when Node B is already transmitting data. If this happens, and two nodes transmit at the same time, an event called a packet collision occurs, causing a frequency "ripple" on the cable. The first node to detect this increased frequency ripple will send out a high-frequency signal that will cancel out all other signals. This signal tells all nodes that a collision has occurred and that all nodes on the network should stop sending packets. At this point, each node waits a random amount of time, then tries broadcasting again. They will do this up to 16 times before giving up. Take a look at the sidebar, "How Nodes Recover from Collisions," later in this chapter, for more details of how this works. Figure 2.6 illustrates this process for Ethernet networks.

FIGURE 2.6:

How packets are sent on a network using the bus logical topology

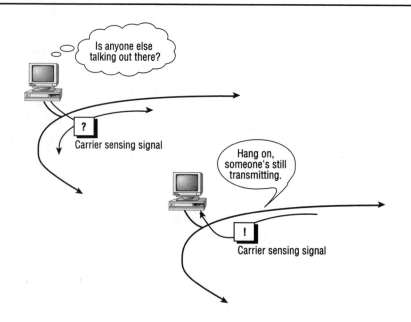

How Nodes Recover from Collisions

The system that nodes use to decide when to resend their data is known by the unfortunate name *truncated binary exponential backoff*. (No, unlike almost everything else in the LAN world, it doesn't have a convenient and commonly used acronym or abbreviation.) In plain language, this means that after two nodes collide, each node on the network randomly generates a whole number between one and two, multiplies that number by one half, and then waits that number of milliseconds before retransmitting. Of course, the first time out the chances are 50/50 that A and B will pick the same number, so they might have to retry again. The next time, A and B will each randomly pick a number between one and four and do the same thing. If they pick the same number again, they'll each pick a number between one and eight. This goes on, doubling each time, either until A and B choose different numbers and send their information, or the 16 attempts are up and they stop trying. The chances are pretty good that both A and B will get to send their data, but by the time they get to the sixteenth try, this could be up to half a second delay. Realize that for a network transmitting data at 100 million bits per second, half a second is an eternity. It's very rare for a bus network to need that many retries.

How likely are collisions? Having cable no longer than it's supposed to be decreases your chance of a collision because the nodes can hear other nodes broadcasting. (For example, on Ethernet networks, that means a cable can be no longer than 185 meters before the signal must be boosted.) In fact, the way the bus logical topology works *increases* the likelihood of packet collisions. If a node can't broadcast until the network is clear and more than one node has information to send, what's going to happen as soon as the line's free? Both nodes will leap to get their information out first and the result is a collision.

Keep in mind that all of this processing takes place at the Ethernet NIC. Therefore, if you are going to use the Ethernet topology, all of your nodes must have Ethernet cards. Ethernet can run on top of a physical bus, physical star, or physical ring.

NOTE   Ethernet isn't the only example of a bus logical topology, but it is the most common one. Other networks using the bus logical topology include ArtiSoft's LANtastic and the LocalTalk/AppleTalk network built into Macintosh computers. LocalTalk only transmits at one quarter of a million bits per second, but employs many of the basic design principles of Ethernet.

The Ring Logical Topology

The bus logical topology is a broadcast system—what one station says, all stations hear—but the ring topology doesn't work that way. In the ring topology, used by Token Ring and Fiber Distributed Data Interface (FDDI) networks, every station must repeat what it hears from the previous station, making a kind of "bucket brigade" of data. When a piece of data gets back to the originator, it stops. An entire file can't be transmitted in one packet, so its pieces will be transmitted in succession as illustrated in Figure 2.7.

FIGURE 2.7:

Sending data with the ring logical topology

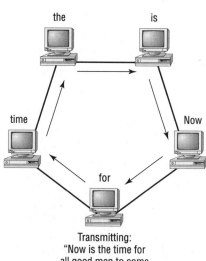

Transmitting:
"Now is the time for
all good men to come
to the aid of their party."

The heart of the ring logical topology is the *token packet*. To avoid packet collisions, the ring topologies ensure that only one workstation can send information across the network at any given time. The method used to ensure that this occurs is the token packet, which works like the "talking stick" that you might have to resort to to maintain order at a noisy meeting. Only the node that has control of the token packet can send information across the network.

How does the token packet move around the network? When a workstation is done with the token packet, it releases it to whatever station is next in line. If nobody grabs it, the workstation releases it a second time. If nobody responds to the token packet for a second time, then the workstation sends out a general query, known as a *solicit successor frame*. This frame goes out over the network, asking, "Who's supposed to get the token next?" If a workstation responds, the sending workstation addresses the token to that workstation and passes the token. Because no single node can transmit for longer than it takes for a piece of data to make a complete circuit of the network, no PC ever waits more than one circuit's worth of information before getting a chance to transmit.

In the ring logical topology, data is not broadcast on the network but passed from node to node. Thus, timing is important to make sure that frames passed on the network are received properly, and the token is responsible for maintaining this timing. Given the token's importance in keeping order on a network using the ring logical topology, one computer is dedicated to token management. This computer, called the *token master* or *active monitor*, detects lost tokens, monitors frame transmissions, and creates a new token when necessary. The active monitor also maintains a regular clock tick on the network that keeps all other nodes synchronized.

IEEE Standards

Some network types have become standardized by the Institute of Electrical and Electronics Engineers (IEEE). They're defined at the physical and data link layers of the OSI model described in Chapter 1, "Basic Networking Concepts and Components." These layers overlap, as the standards describe both physical media and methods of packet transmittal. In other words, you can know how a network that conforms to one of these standards will behave and how that network is designed to work. Below, I'll review some of the IEEE standards for which you're likely to see references when dealing with networking.

NOTE   All of these standards begin with "802" because the 802 committee of IEEE is in charge of LAN standards.

The 802.2 Standard

The 802.2 standard defines the rules for data link communications for networking topologies 802.3-802.5. Working for both Token Ring and Ethernet, it provides the interface between networking protocols such as TCP/IP and the network types. The 802.2 standard can function either in connectionless mode (for protocols that don't require an explicit connection to be established before they start transmitting data) or in connection-oriented mode for protocols that do require such an explicit connection to be made.

The IEEE divides the data link layer into two sections: the *logical link connection* (or *data link connection*; both terms are used) and *media access control* (MAC). The LLC handles the interface between all networking topologies and their network-layer communication protocols. To do this, the LLC relies on the MAC layer to provide it with certain addressing information. The method of addressing information it uses defines the network type.

The Ethernet (802.3*n*) Standard

Ethernet was originally designed in the 1970s by Dr. Robert Metcalfe as part of an "office of the future" project. At that point, it was a 3Mpbs network. In 1980, Ethernet was standardized as a 10Mbps network by the DEC-Intel-Xerox (DIX) consortium, and then in 1985 standardized by the 802 committee of IEEE. Since then, new Ethernet technologies have followed the basic pattern of that original Ethernet design, which called for a logical bus topology and a method of error detection and recovery called carrier sense multiple access with collision detection (CSMA/CD). The various forms of Ethernet use different physical topologies (bus and star, for example) and cabling types (such as UTP, coax, and fiber).

NOTE   All Ethernet-type networks—10Base2, 10Base5, 10BaseT, or 10BaseF— use variations of the 802.3 standard.

Ethernet Basics

Information travels an Ethernet network in packets consisting of six parts:

Preamble   Consists of eight bytes of information used to coordinate the rest of the information in the packet.

Destination address   Consists of the hardware address (burned into the Ethernet card) of the workstation or workstations that are to receive this information.

Source's address   Allows the receiving workstation or workstations to recognize the workstation that sent the information.

Type   Designates the type of information that is held within the data part of this packet, whether it is graphic information, ASCII text information, or whatever.

Actual data   Can be anywhere from 46 to 1,500 bytes long.

Frame checked sequence   Resembles a packing slip; it's used to verify that the rest of the packet reached its destination intact.

You can see the parts of an 802.3 Ethernet frame in Figure 2.8.

FIGURE 2.8:

The structure of an 802.3 Ethernet frame

Preamble 7 bytes	Start delimiter 1 byte	Destination address 2-6 bytes	Source address 2-6 bytes	Length 2 bytes	Data 46-1500 bytes	Frame check sequence 4 bytes

There are several different kinds of Ethernet, each with its own number and its own name by which it's more commonly known. These types are described in Table 2.1.

Interpreting Ethernet Names

The various Ethernet types have common names by which they're more often known than by their IEEE committee numbers. These names take the form of numbers and letters and may not appear much more descriptive than the IEEE numbers. They're not perfectly descriptive, but the basic idea is that the first number represents the top speed of the network in megabits per second. The word "base" means that the transmission is baseband, or transmitted serially, as opposed to broadband networks such as those sometimes used for WAN connections, in which data may be transmitted along a parallel path. Finally, the last letter indicates something about how long (in meters) a segment of the network may be.

This final part isn't really very helpful as it's not always accurate. For example, 10Base2 networks have an actual run length of 185 meters. Also, it isn't always a number but instead refers to cable type, as in 100BaseT (twisted pair) or 100BaseF (fiber) networks. However, if you've ever wondered why a 10Base2 network was called that, this is why.

TABLE 2.1: Some Ethernet Types and Descriptions

IEEE Number	Common Name	Physical Topology and Media	Bandwidth
802.3	10Base2	Thin coaxial cable in a bus topology	10Mbps
802.3	10Base5	Thick coaxial cable for the backbone; taps to the backbone from each PC	10Mbps
802.3u	100BaseT or Fast Ethernet	Unshielded twisted pair in a star topology	100Mbps (10Mbps version is 802.3)
802.3z	Gigabit Ethernet	Fiber optic for the backbone, coax for the taps to the hub, all in the star topology	1000Mbps

NOTE No matter what the physical topology of the network, an Ethernet network always uses the bus logical topology, which means that all cables in the LAN are part of the same path and are available to all networked PCs.

Whichever type of network it's running on, the 802.3*n* standard's most salient feature is the *carrier-sensing multiple access with collision detection* (CSMA/CD) designation. Carrier-sensing multiple access with collision detection; quite a mouthful, eh? It gets to the heart of the basic Ethernet problem I've discussed before: how can you send vast amounts of information simultaneously across the network without causing collisions?

The short answer is that you can't. However, that's not bad news; Ethernet is *supposed* to experience collisions from time to time. To understand CSMA/CD, let's break it apart. "Carrier sensing" means that all nodes on the network listen to the network to see whether it's clear before attempting to transmit.

"Multiple access" means that all nodes on the network have access to the same cable—that signals are broadcast across the entire LAN. Finally, "Collision detection" means that each node can tell if another node starts transmitting data at the same time the first node is already sending data. In short, CSMA/CD provides a means for reducing packet collision by having each PC broadcast a signal known as the *carrier-sensing signal* before transmitting in order to see if any other workstations are broadcasting. If not, the signal gives the workstation the "all-clear" and the workstation transmits its packet. However, if the carrier-sensing signal detects another workstation's transmittal, the workstation waits before broadcasting.

This process avoids collisions so long as network traffic isn't heavy and the LAN's cables aren't any longer than their rating. If either of those conditions exist, then collisions are likely to happen regardless of CSMA/CD. CSMA/CD isn't in charge of making sure that only one workstation transmits at a time: it's in charge of making sure that all workstations are quiet before one transmits. If two workstations happen to begin transmitting at the same time, there's nothing that CSMA/CD can do to avoid the collision.

If two packets collide, CSMA/CD tries to avoid a repeat collision. As I discussed earlier in this chapter, the first time a collision happens each workstation chooses a random number between one and two before transmitting again. If the workstations choose the same number, causing another collision by beginning their broadcasts at the same time, they each choose a number between one and four and try again. This process goes on until either the workstations have both successfully completed their transmissions or they've tried 16 times without success. If they flunk out by the sixteenth try, both workstations have to pause and give the other workstations a chance to transmit.

TIP If 16 tries doesn't produce a successful transmittal, then something is wrong. Check for broken cables or a heavily overloaded network.

The list below shows the range of numbers possible at each repeated attempt to transmit:

Retry Number	Range of Numbers
1	1-2
2	1-4
3	1-8
4	1-16
5	1-32
6	1-64
7	1-128
8	1-256
9	1-512
10-16	1-1024

In short, CSMA/CD isn't designed to prevent every collision, but it tries to minimize the time that collisions tie up the network. You can see the entire process in Figure 2.9.

FIGURE 2.9:

How CSMA/CD
recovers from collisions

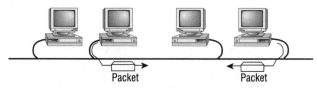

Two packets, not having heard each other, both start down the network.

The packets collide!

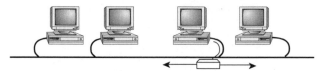

The node closest to the collision detects it and sends out a jamming signal,
notifying all nodes that a collision has taken place.

Each node on the network waits a random number of milliseconds before
transmitting, in hopes that they won't coincidentally wait the same
amount of time and send the packets at the same time again.

Speed Demons—Fast Ethernet and Gigabit Ethernet

As noted, Ethernet originally ran at 3Mbps and was upgraded to
10Mbps. This 10Mbps speed lasted for quite a while, until Fast
Ethernet, running at 100Mbps over Category 5 UTP, was released
as an official standard in 1995. This trend has been continued
with the development of Gigabit Ethernet, a backbone technology
designed to allow Ethernet networks to operate at line speed over
fiber optic cable. As its name implies, Gigabit Ethernet runs at
1000Mbps, or 1Gbps.

NOTE Gigabit Ethernet as a LAN technology currently requires multimode fiber optic cable, but the IEEE is investigating methods of running it over Category 5 UTP. Most LANs using this high-speed form of Ethernet will use 100BaseSX, which is Gigabit Ethernet over backbones that can be up to 260 meters long. CAN or MAN channels using single-mode fiber can be up to 3 kilometers long.

Generally speaking, the main differences between the various types of Ethernet lie in the physical media used and the speeds derived from using the faster media. All types of Ethernet use CSMA/CD, and all use the same frame type illustrated in Figure 2.8. The greater transmittal speeds of Fast Ethernet and Gigabit Ethernet come about largely because of the media used, not from significant changes to the framing standards or transmission methods. This means that Ethernet networks of varying speeds can be connected without requiring changes to the packet structure. In fact, it's fairly common for an Ethernet network to combine a couple of different speeds, perhaps supporting both 10Mbps and 100Mbps connections, or supporting 100Mbps to the desktop with a 1Gbps backbone. That's why you can have one network card that supports both 10Mbps Ethernet and Fast Ethernet with a single connection. Each type of Ethernet works a little differently on the physical layer, but all use the same data link layer standards, so they can interoperate.

Gigabit Ethernet supports half-duplex transmission for shared areas of the network (those on which nodes are contending for bandwidth) and full duplex for unshared switch-to-switch areas. The shared areas, which use CSMA/CD to manage packet collisions, operate slightly differently than shared areas under slower types of Ethernet. The problem is the high line speeds. As the network speeds are so fast, the timing had to change; otherwise, nodes wouldn't be able to "hear" each other before their transmission was over. Thus, in Gigabit Ethernet, for devices operating in half-duplex mode (network nodes), the minimum time slot available for each packet has been increased from 64 bytes to 512 bytes—that is, each node will be given windows sufficient to transmit 512 bytes instead of 64 bytes. Packets smaller than 512 bytes will be padded to accommodate this increased time slot. As this larger time slot slows down packet transmission by reducing the "clock tick," Gigabit Ethernet supports packet bursts so that groups of smaller packets can be sent during a single time slot. However, this change to timing doesn't affect interoperability with slower types of Ethernet, particularly because the full-duplex areas of the Gigabit Ethernet network use the same 64-byte time slots as slower versions of the 802.3n standard.

This change in network timing led to another innovation especially for Gigabit Ethernet networks to be used on the backbones—a device called a *buffered distributor*. The buffered distributor is a hub-like device connecting two or more Gigabit Ethernet segments, like a repeater (described in Chapter 5). The main difference between a buffered distributor and a repeater is that a repeater forwards packets to the outgoing segments as it gets them, while the buffered distributor can buffer frames to get better use out of existing bandwidth.

You're not likely to see Gigabit Ethernet to the desktop any time soon; it's too expensive. More likely, the technology will be initially deployed as a means of creating a high-speed connection between routers or switches (described in Chapter 5) on an Ethernet network. Deployment to the desktop will come when prices fall, as they did with Fast Ethernet.

Using Fiber for High-Speed Networks

Gigabit Ethernet wasn't created in a vacuum. Its methods of getting line-speed network transmission out of a channel are related to those originally developed for fibre channel networks.

Continued on next page

Fibre channel was originally conceived as a method of blurring the distinction between network hardware and the network, but not in the way that this kind of blurring is usually done. Rather than logically making all parts of the network accessible from a single location (as networking attempts to do), fibre channel physically makes all parts of the network a single unit by replacing network cables and high-speed data channels, such as SCSI connectors (described in Chapter 8), with high-speed fiber channels that run at gigabit speeds. Thus, a server can be connected to a hard disk across the room from it, but still treat that hard disk as though it were a locally attached piece of hardware.

Fibre channel conceives of connections as possibly being one of three types. First, a connection can be point-to-point, connecting two devices. Second, it can be arranged in a physical ring, with all devices looped together. Third, it can be arranged in what's called a *fabric*, in which devices are part of a physical and logical mesh.

As fibre channel is a high-end and high-cost technology, it's not one you're likely to encounter often. However, it's worth noting now both as a contributor to Gigabit Ethernet and as a rival to SCSI because it allows all parts of the network to be physically distributed in the manner most convenient to the people using it, not by the limitations of the data channels.

The Token Bus (802.4) Standard

In an effort to design a standard less prone to collisions than the 802.3, the IEEE 802.4 subcommittee designed a combination bus/ring topology that transmitted information via a token but would use the bus physical topology. The 802.4 standard is designed around the observation that computers are prone to the same fallibility as humans: give 'em half a chance, and they'll talk right on top of each other. To get around this problem, the 802.4 committee described a token packet that the network could use to decide which machine got to "talk." So it is with the 802.4 standard.

Only the workstation that has the token can send information, and once that workstation has received acknowledgment of the receipt of that information, it must then pass the token to the next workstation in line. How does the network determine who's next in line? In the 802.4 standard, the network keeps track of who gets the token next. Just as the business manager could get the talking stick more often than the person in charge of office decorations, it's possible for some workstations to have higher priority to get the token than others.

The method of controlling collisions isn't the only way in which the 802.4 standard differs from the 802.3 standard. First, the medium is different to some degree; a Token Bus network runs on either 70-ohm coaxial cable (unlike the 50-ohm used by 10Base2) or fiber. Second, as you can see in Figure 2.10, an 802.4 Ethernet frame looks different than an 802.3 frame in that it contains the following: a preamble, a start frame delimiter, a frame control, a destination address, a source address, information, a frame check sequence, and a frame delimiter.

FIGURE 2.10:

An 802.4 Ethernet frame

Preamble	Start frame delimiter	Frame control	Destination address	Source address	Information	Frame check sequence	Frame delimiter

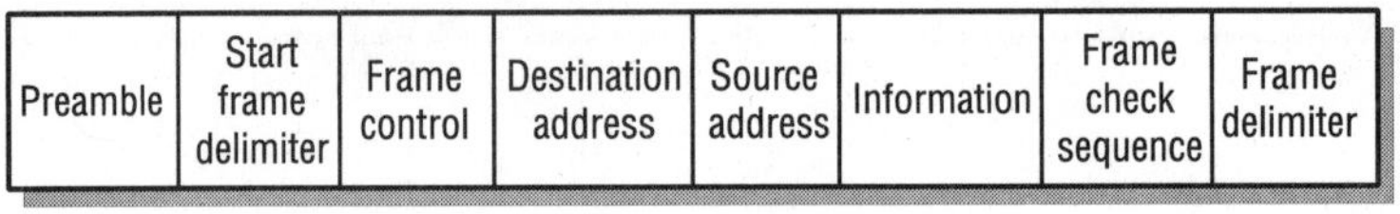

Although the token/bus combination avoids collisions, the 802.4 standard still has some disadvantages that have kept it from common usage. Most shortfalls of the token/bus format come from malfunctioning hardware, which can result in the token being lost or shadowed tokens that make it look as though there are multiple tokens on the network. Imagine a board meeting with more than one talking stick!

The Token Ring (802.5) Standard

The IEEE 802.5 committee developed the 802.5 standard in conjunction with IBM. This standard is specifically designed for Token Ring networks that use the token specification to pass information from one workstation to another.

As in the 802.4 standard, the workstations on a Token Ring network use a token to determine which workstation gets to transmit data at any given time. If a workstation doesn't need to transmit anything, it passes the free token to the next workstation and so on until it gets to a workstation that needs to transmit something.

Data travels from the originating workstation to every node on the network in succession. Each workstation examines the address on the data packet. If the data is for that station, it keeps a copy of the data and sends the original on. If the data isn't for that station, it merely sends it to the next workstation on the network. When the sending workstation gets back the copy of its first data packet, it knows that it's time to stop transmitting and passes the free token to the next workstation. This process is illustrated in Figures 2.11, 2.12, and 2.13.

FIGURE 2.11:

How Token passing
works (stage 1)

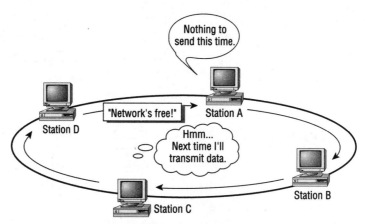

A free token is passed from node to node until one node has data to transmit.

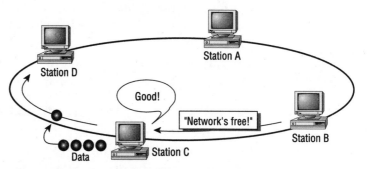

Station C has data to transmit to station B. Upon receiving the free token, station C
begins to transmit data instead of passing the free token to the next station.

FIGURE 2.12:

How Token passing
works (stage 2)

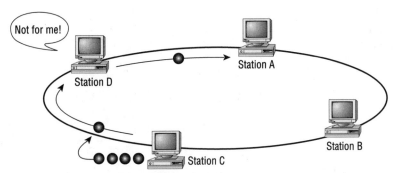

Station D receives the data and recognizes that it isn't for it, so it passes the
data along and forgets about it.

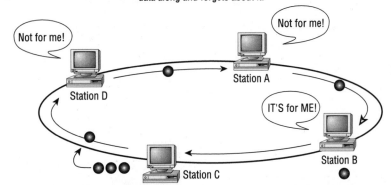

Station A likewise receives the data, notes that it isn't for it either, and passes it
along. Station B, however, recognizes that it is the destination address and makes
a copy of the data for itself. Then, instead of halting the transmission, it continues to
send the data around the ring.

FIGURE 2.13:

How Token passing
works (stage 3)

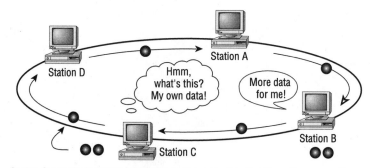

Station C sees the incoming frame of data and recognizes that it was the source. Once
it notices its own data, it quits sending data (regardless of whether it's finished) and
releases a free token instead.

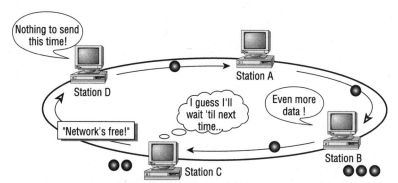

The free token gives someone else on the ring a chance to transmit. Once station C
receives the free token ring, it can finish sending its data to station B.

The 802.5 standard has some qualities to recommend it. With a
smart hub, the Token Ring standard can help the network recover
from problems due to malfunctioning hardware—a nice feature
that the Token Bus standard doesn't have. If a workstation mal-
functions, either not releasing the token when its turn is up or
jabbering over the network, the smart hub can tell that there's
trouble and cut that workstation from the LAN, allowing the rest
of the network to function normally. An 802.5 network can also
extend for longer distances than either the 802.3 or the 802.4
because the packet travels from one workstation to another,

retransmitted at every step, and so it never has very far to go before being retransmitted.

A Token Ring board attaches to the MAU with a D-shell type connector on one side and an odd-looking IBM connector on the other. The Token Ring connector just pops into the MAU. Eight PCs can attach to an MAU; from there, those MAUs attach to other MAUs. There are no terminators on Token Ring networks; one end of the cable plugs into the board, the other plugs into the MAU.

As with the hubs for 10BaseT, you can most easily arrange your Token Ring network so that cables extend from a central wiring closet on each floor to workstations on that floor, and put the MAUs in the wiring closet. The cables between the MAU and the network device can be up to 45 meters long, providing enough space for most floor plans to be cabled with a wiring closet.

Although the Token Ring network has a ring logical topology, it uses a star physical topology. Instead of hubs, Token Ring uses either concentrators or, more commonly, MAUs. Don't confuse this MAU with the media attachment unit, which is a transceiver connecting to the AUI port on an Ethernet adapter.

Summary

That's a flying view of the network types you'll see, both from a logical and a physical perspective. Most often, you'll use one of two logical topologies. The bus topology, used by the various incarnations of Ethernet networks, broadcasts its data all along the network to be picked up by the network node to which it's addressed. Only one network node can transmit at a time, so before transmitting each station must listen to see whether the coast is clear. If not, then the node waits and tries again. If the coast is clear, then the node transmits, and if by coincidence another station chooses to transmit at exactly the same time, then both will have to stop transmitting and wait for the coast to be clear. The ring logical topology avoids two stations using the channel at the same time in a somewhat different manner. A packet called the *token packet* is passed around the network, with each station only allowed to transmit so long as it has control of the packet.

Somewhat confusingly, there's also a bus and ring physical topology to consider. In the bus physical topology, all computers connect to the same backbone, either with taps or directly, and run in a line. The ring physical topology, not often used, is similar except that it runs in a physical loop and may be double-cabled to avoid network failures due to breakages. The physical topology most likely to be found in small offices that need some degree of flexibility but don't use a backbone is the star configuration, in which each PC is connected to a central hub.

Of all the logical and physical topologies discussed here, the most common today is probably 100BaseT. It is the Ethernet network that combines the bus logical topology with Category 5 cable in the star physical topology to achieve speeds of up to 100Mbps. It's certainly the most likely to be used in new LANs. The popularity is due to this network type's speed and flexibility. As I've said, Token Ring networks are found mostly in IBM installations or those requiring mainframe connectivity, and 10Base2 is best suited for very small organizations with all their computers packed into one space. Take your physical environment into account when choosing a topology and find the one that's best for you.

Choosing a physical topology may be the easy part. In Chapter 3, "Networking Protocols and Programming Interfaces," I'll discuss low-level networking software, including redirectors, network card drivers, and network transport protocols. If you don't remember how the OSI model works, this would be a good time to review it in Chapter 1, "Basic Networking Concepts and Components," because I'll be delving into it heavily next.

EXERCISE 2

1. In case of network failure, which of the following physical topologies would be easiest to troubleshoot, and why? What is the name of each topology shown here?

   Topology 1:

   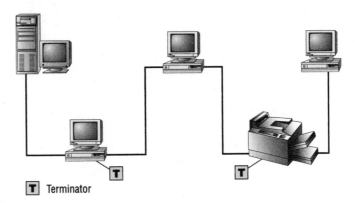

   T Terminator

   Topology 2:

   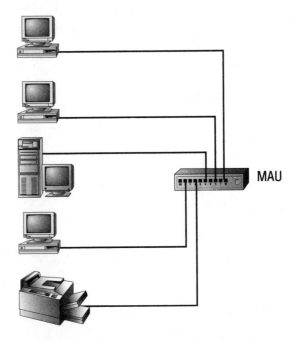

   MAU

EXERCISE 2 CONTINUED

Topology 3:

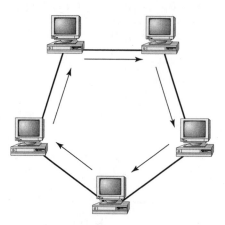

2. Describe two network types mentioned in this chapter that combine one physical topology and one logical topology.

3. What device do you need to translate 10Base2-compatible Ethernet frames to Gigabit-compatible frames?

4. The token bus network architecture is described in which IEEE standard?

5. Which Ethernet technology supports packet bursting?

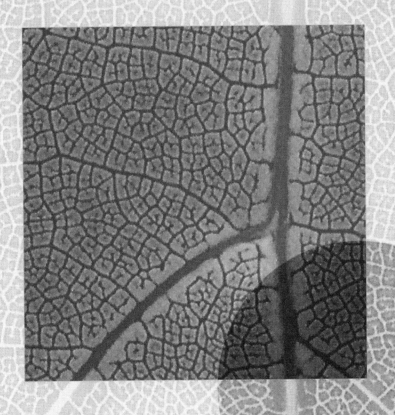

3

Networking Protocols and Application Programming Interfaces

For data to get from point A to point B on the LAN, you need not only the hardware discussed in Chapter 1, arranged in one of the configurations described in Chapter 2, but also networking software to package that data for transmittal. That networking software consists of three main parts:

- A redirector to send requests to the network instead of the local hard disk

- Network card drivers to provide communications between the operating system and the network card

- Networking protocols to send the data on its merry way and pick it up at the end of its journey

The flow of information described here is illustrated in Figure 3.1.

FIGURE 3.1:

LANs allow applications to utilize centralized data.

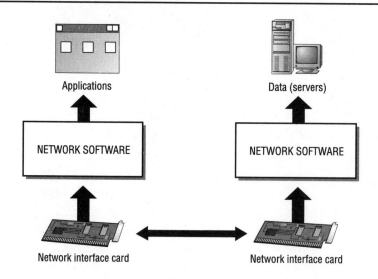

So, for example, if Fred tries to save a WordCruncher file from his computer to a shared drive on the network file server, the following happens:

1. Fred clicks Save and chooses to save the document to his drive G:, which is in fact a network connection to drive D: shared from the file server.

2. The redirector examines the request to save, notes that drive G: is not locally available, and redirects the request to a part of the operating system called the *network file system driver.*

3. The file system driver passes the request to the network card driver.

4. The network card driver passes the request—and the data—to the network card.

5. The network card packages the data for transmission across the network and sends it.

6. The file server's network card notes that a package has arrived for it, and receives it.

At this point, the process is reversed: the server's network card driver passes the request to the file system driver in the operating system, and writes the file to the local drive.

If you're building a network, chances are excellent that sooner or later the network you create will be connected to another one in some manner or other. After all, that's how the Internet itself got started; local networks were given the means to connect to each other in a larger whole. Most networks grow in stages, rather than emerging full-blown in their final form, so they often include a hodgepodge not only of hardware but of network operating systems and communications needs as well. This, in turn, means that the network needs more than one type of redirector, must use more than one type of network protocol, and that not all the cards use the same driver. In short, sometimes even with careful planning it can be a bit of a mess as networks grow and merge. In the course of this chapter, I'll discuss the various parts of the networking process so you can better understand what you're dealing with when it comes to managing networking software in all its varied parts.

First, I'll discuss the role of the redirector in arranging communications between applications and the operating system to reach network-accessible data. Second, I'll look at the role of the network card driver. Finally, I'll examine the three transport protocols used most often in PC-based networks.

The Role of Redirectors

As illustrated in Figure 3.2, from the perspective of the PC initiating a network request, the first actor in the networking process is the redirector. Its role is to fool an application on the local machine into thinking that it is getting data from a local drive, rather than from a network drive. The point is that it shouldn't matter where the file being requested is stored; it should be accessible in the same way, no matter what.

For example, what happens if you are running WordCruncher and open a file stored on a network drive? From WordCruncher's point of view, there *is* no network. It knows only that there are one or more disk drives available with names consisting of a letter and a colon, as in A:, B:, C:, and so on. Like other application software, WordCruncher was not built to accommodate storage devices that aren't on the local machine. Thus, there must be a layer of software (placed just below WordCruncher) whose job it is to present a common drive-letter interface to WordCruncher when supplying data stored on the network. WordCruncher thinks that it is addressing local drives, but its requests for information from network drives must be *redirected* to network requests. So, if you tell WordCruncher to get the data from directory DOCS on the server named BIGDOG, the redirector software initiates the request as described in the introduction to this chapter.

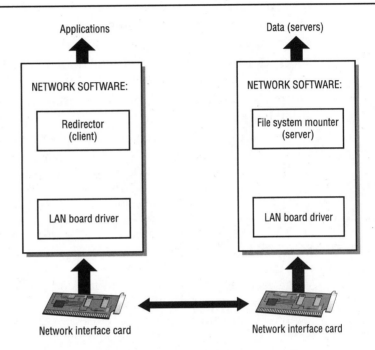

FIGURE 3.2:

The redirector's place in networking

Applications

Data (servers)

NETWORK SOFTWARE:

Redirector
(client)

LAN board driver

NETWORK SOFTWARE:

File system mounter
(server)

LAN board driver

Network interface card

Network interface card

NOTE   Redirectors are often referred to as *clients* (as in, the Windows 98 Client for NetWare Networks) because they're a required part of a client machine.

Therefore, before you can join a network, you must install a redirector that's compatible with the network type. Not all network operating systems use the same redirectors, so you must install the one that corresponds to the operating system on the network to which you're connecting. The difference lies at the presentation layer of the OSI model, which was described in Chapter 1, "Basic Networking Concepts and Components." For example, Microsoft networks use Server Message Blocks (SMBs) to pass data back and forth, so they need a redirector that can phrase things in terms of SMBs. Novell networks use NetWare Control Protocols (NCPs) for the same job. So, to make requests of a NetWare server, you must use a redirector that can phrase requests in terms of NCPs. Note that having a transport protocol such as TCP/IP in common is not enough—you must have a redirector that works with the operating system to which you're connecting. The good news is that redirector support can overlap if the presentation layer protocol is the same for more than one operating system. Thus, if you're using Windows 98, you can use the SMB-supporting Client for Microsoft Networks to connect to any operating system that supports SMBs.

Redirectors and APIs

As you've already read in the introduction to this chapter, most user applications are unaware of the network or networks that they use. But some, such as e-mail or groupware programs, must be cognizant of the network, and exist only *because* of the network. They need to be able to "plug in" and communicate with other programs running on other machines in the network.

Programmers build network-aware programs to be tailored to sets of commands that a network offers to applications programs. Those sets of commands are called APIs, or *application program interfaces*. Think of an API as being somewhat like the dashboard of a car. Your car's dashboard is the interface that you see, and you must learn to use it in order to operate the car. You actually have no idea while you're driving about what's under your car's hood—you just push down on the accelerator and the car goes faster.

Thus, you don't have to know precisely how a car works to drive it. Not only that, but once you know how to drive one car, you can drive just about any car because the controls—the API—are the same.

Continued on next page

(I discovered while driving a friend's Volkswagen one night that Volkswagens do not use the same API for "reverse" that other manual shift cars do, but this analogy generally works.)

A dashboard consists of just a few primitive commands: brake the car, accelerate the car, shift the car's transmission, and so on. There is no command "back the car out of the driveway," and yet you can still back a car out of a driveway by just assembling a number of the primitive commands into the actual action of backing a car out of a driveway. You have, in a sense, built a program with your car's dashboard controls arranged in a certain order.

Your computer's API functions in pretty much the same way. Your network services, like the redirector, can sit on top of different transport protocols. Without an API, the programmers of your network software would have to develop one redirector program to connect Microsoft NT (a network operating system) to IPX/SPX and a different redirector program to connect Microsoft NT to TCP/IP. It is the same redirector; it is just talking to different transport protocols. The way to avoid this is to provide a common "dashboard" for all of the network services. Thus, the redirector service is not written to a protocol, but rather is written to an API (in our example, NetBIOS). NetBIOS can sit on top of IPX/SPX, NetBEUI, and TCP/IP. This means that the transport protocol can change, but you do not have to rewrite your network service because it is written to the API (NetBIOS).

Sockets are a well-known type of API. They are temporary communication channels set up for passing information between a client program and a server program. These programs can be running either on the same machine or across the network. There are three network APIs that you'll probably come across in the networking world:

- Novell Sockets

- NetBIOS

- TCP/IP Sockets

The API will take your network request and perform the task through the proper transport protocol.

File System Drivers

The redirector is the piece on the end of the connection that's making the request. Its counterpart on the end of the connection that's complying with that request is the file system driver.

File system drivers aren't used just for networking, but are part of any request for access to storage media. In Windows NT, for example, the network file system driver is one of the supported file systems: FAT, NTFS, CDFS, and the network.

> **NOTE** FAT is the file allocation table, originally developed for use with floppy disks and ported to use with hard disks up to 4GB in size. NTFS (New Technology File System) is Windows NT's native file system. It incorporates support for large disks and security features that FAT does not cover. PC-based CD-ROM devices use CDFS, the Compact Disc File System.

In general, the role of *any* file system driver is to organize data on the storage media with which it's used. To take a commonly used disk drive file system, FAT numbers each cluster and notes which files are stored in which cluster. If a file's data requires more than one cluster to hold it all, then each cluster will also include a pointer to the next cluster on the disk that's used to store that data; the final cluster has an End of File marker so the FAT file system knows when to stop looking. How does the file system know where the clusters are? When you format a disk, you're cataloging the space on it with the file system you use.

When you ask to retrieve a file, the FAT file system is in charge of finding the data you want and making sure that all of it is retrieved (as chances are excellent that not all data will be in the same cluster). Similarly, when you attempt to save a file to disk, the FAT file system finds the first free space on the disk and stores the data associated with that file in those clusters, marking the clusters to point to the next one used as required.

NOTE   Depending on where disk space is available, those clusters may not be contiguous. The file system doesn't look for the first group of unused clusters that's large enough to store the file; it looks for the first unused cluster, period. If all the file's data won't fit into that space, then the file system will store the remaining data in the next free cluster, wherever that cluster happens to be on the disk.

Disk Geometry

Confused about all this talk concerning clusters and storing data in them? The principle is simple: for Microsoft-based file systems, the cluster is the smallest logical unit of storage. A disk's surface is divided into concentric circles called *tracks*, and pie-shaped wedges called *sectors*. At 512 bytes, the sectors are the smallest physical unit on a disk.

Clusters are logical groups of sectors, with the exact number of sectors in a cluster depending on the file system being used and the size of the disk. Generally speaking, the larger the disk, the more clusters are in the file system, although modern file systems are tending toward smaller clusters. Larger clusters may reduce disk access times as more data may be stored in a single cluster and thus is more likely to be found in a single location on disk. The trade-off is that large clusters on a disk used to store small files can lead to wasted space because a file may not be stored in a unit smaller than one cluster. Thus, if you store a 4KB file on disk, but the cluster size for that disk is 8KB, then 4KB is wasted and cannot be used to store other data.

The network file system is just one more interface for reading disk space. The only difference is that it's used for network access instead of local access as are the other file systems. Thus, on the server end, when the server receives a request for disk access from some network client, the request goes to the network file system, which does what must be done—retrieve data, store a file, or whatever. The important aspect to this is that the network file system makes the local format of the server's hard disk immaterial to the client. Even if the file system with which the disk is formatted is not supported by the client, it doesn't matter because the local file system isn't the one used to satisfy network requests. So long as the client can talk to the server, the server will interpret the file system for the client.

The Role of Network Card Drivers

Now you know how a request gets from the application to the operating system, or is satisfied on the operating system side. How does that request get to the network? That's the role of a piece of software called a *network card driver*.

Generally speaking, any device driver is a piece of software that lets an operating system and a piece of hardware talk to each other. Some device drivers are included with an operating system's files. Others must be loaded from floppy disks or may be downloaded from the Internet, but they're always required to act as an interface between the network card and the operating system.

Why not just build functionality for network cards right into the operating system, particularly considering that modern operating systems are built with networking in mind? Mostly because it's impractical to do so. There are tens or hundreds of manufacturers making hundreds or thousands of different models of networking cards, and each model requires its own driver. It's simply not practical to build support for every network card out there into the operating system. Even if such a scheme were practical, it wouldn't be desirable. It would make the operating system take up more room than is really necessary; if you've only got one network card installed, you really don't need drivers for dozens more installed as well. Not only that, but updating drivers for better support of the hardware would mean replacing the operating system. Do you really want to have to reinstall the operating system each time there's an improvement made to your network card's drivers? Didn't think so.

That said, some operating systems use a modular design to incorporate certain functions of a driver into the operating system, meaning that the hardware manufacturers only have to write a stub portion. As illustrated in Figure 3.3, the idea is this: although each individual network card may handle data transfer between the operating system and network in a slightly different way, the main function of network cards is the same in all cases. So, those functions can, in fact, be built into the operating system. At that point, all the creator of a network card driver has to do is write the card-specific instructions required to let the card access the functionality built into the operating system.

FIGURE 3.3:

How microdrivers cooperate with the operating system

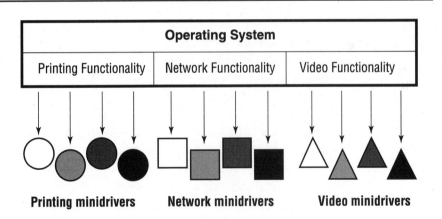

Enough with the discussion of network card driver design. Let's go on to the meat of the matter—what these drivers do.

What Network Card Drivers Do

Network drivers are responsible for managing any extra-computer communications, including those required to access the Internet. You'll have one network driver installed for each model of card used. Thus, for example, if you have a PC with a cable modem connection to the Internet and a network connection, you'll need two drivers installed. If you have more than one network card installed (perhaps if your PC is acting as a router) and they're of different kinds, you'll have one driver installed for each. However, if you have two network cards of the same type installed, you'll only have to install the one driver. Basically, these drivers install data link network support for the PC, allowing it to access an Ethernet network, for example.

Network Binding Interfaces

It is possible to build a network driver that can both send data to the card and arrange to have that data sent across the network—essentially, a driver that incorporates a driver and network protocol in one. Such drivers are called *monolithic device drivers*.

Note that I said this was *possible.* It's no longer a recommended practice for much the same reason that device drivers aren't built into operating systems. Modularity engenders flexibility. Assuming that your network card's driver includes the transport protocol you'll be using to access the network, if you need to change that transport protocol or add a new one, you'll need to change the driver as well. Bad idea, particularly as that means you can load support for only one transport protocol at once.

Rather than using monolithic device drivers, modern drivers use another tool to bind the network cards to the transport protocols. In general terms, this tool is called the *network binding interface.* As shown in Figure 3.4, it serves as the interface between a NIC driver and a transport stack.

FIGURE 3.4:

The network binding interface makes it possible for several protocols to communicate with a single driver.

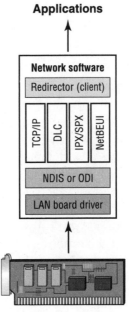

Network interface card

> **NOTE**   If you're familiar with the concept of binding a protocol to a network card, then the network binding interface is where the binding takes place. It's essentially a means of "marrying" a NIC driver and a network transport protocol.

What's going on here is fairly straightforward. The network binding interface clumps each installed driver with each installed transport protocol. The name of the clump depends on the network type—for example, NetWare networks call them "modules." Communication between modules is handled by a program called LSL under NetWare and PROTMAN.SYS under Microsoft networks. Any configuration information required for the binding interface is contained in a text file, such as PROTOCOL.INI for Microsoft networks, or NET.CFG for NetWare networks. However, if the default values for the drivers are used, there won't be much information in these configuration files.

The Ties That Bind

I've said that one of the handy things about network binding interfaces is that they permit you to use more than one transport protocol with each network card driver. By default, all network transport protocols are bound with all installed network card drivers. When you attempt to send data across the network and more than one transport protocol is installed, which protocol gets used? The answer depends on the order in which the transport protocols were bound. You can edit the binding order to place the protocol that will be used most often first, so as to reduce the number of retries required to find the protocol needed to access a particular server.

If you want to cut off communication to a server that's using a particular protocol, you don't have to uninstall it—just remove it from the list of protocols bound to the network card. Confused? Good. If you're confused now, you'll still be interested when I talk more about this in Chapter 15, "Network Security."

There are two competitors for the title of world standard network binding interface: Novell's Open Datalink Interface (ODI) and Microsoft's Network Driver Interface Specification (NDIS). These two binding interfaces have a lot in common in terms of what they do and how they do it. The main difference between them is that ODI-compliant drivers operate in real mode. This means that they must use memory in the first 640KB of the memory installed in your machine, and that they can't cooperate with other drivers that may be installed in the system. NDIS-compliant drivers, in contrast, run in protected mode so they can multitask with other drivers and don't use scarce conventional memory.

Why use ODI-compliant drivers if they can't run in protected mode? Mostly because your redirector sometimes requires them. Not all redirectors will work with the NDIS-compliant drivers. If you're not sure, check with the documentation for your particular operating system to find out the requirements of your particular redirector. Generally speaking, both NDIS and ODI work with all transport protocols; any limitation is on the driver side.

Network Transport Protocols

Sneakily, throughout this chapter I've been referring to transport protocols without ever really explaining what they were. First, what *is* a protocol? One of the best ways to understand a protocol is to know that it is simply a standard or set of rules.

You are confronted with protocols in various aspects of your daily life. For example, if your phone in your house rings, you pick it up and say, "Hello?" Why do you say "hello" first? Why doesn't the caller identify himself first? The answer is that it's a tradition. It is the custom in the United States that the person answering the phone should respond first. In other words, this is the American *protocol* for answering the phone. If you were in mainland China, you'd pick up the telephone and wait for the other person to say, "Wei," to signal that they were there. When you meet someone, do you hug, kiss, or shake hands? Once again, the answer is determined by protocol.

How does this apply to networks? Network transport protocols determine how data is transmitted across the network, and how that data is packaged and addressed. For two computers on the same network to communicate, they must be using the same network transport protocols because the protocols used determine how the data is packaged and delivered.

NOTE   Technically speaking, *any* convention that determines how a network transmits data is a protocol, whether that convention operates at the data link layer or the application layer. However, you'll often hear the conventions that govern how data is packaged and delivered on the network as protocols, and that's what I'll be referring to below. NetBEUI, IPX/SPX, and TCP/IP all operate at the network and transport layers of the OSI model. Because they operate at more than one layer, they're often referred to as *protocol stacks*, not just protocols.

The good news is that modern operating systems can simultaneously support more than one protocol, so you can use one for each type of connectivity you need. The bad news is that not all operating systems support all transport protocols; in fact, they tend to specialize, and even some like-named protocols are not useable across all platforms. However, today there's enough overlap that some degree of communication and interoperability is possible across all major operating systems.

TIP   Loading more than one network transport protocol uses up RAM, so even though it's possible to load more than one transport protocol with modern operating systems, it's a good idea to install support only for the ones you need.

Please be aware that the following sections are *introductions* to the three main protocols used in PC networking, and are not complete. TCP/IP, for one, is an enormously complex protocol with sufficient configuration options to write a book about them, or a lot of books. What's here is simply intended to help you understand the basics of how each of these protocols work and what's involved in it.

The NetBEUI Protocol

Back when IBM first started marketing their PC network, they needed a basic network protocol. They had no intention of building large networks, just small workgroups of a few dozen computers or less.

Out of that need grew the Network Basic Input/Output System, or NetBIOS. NetBIOS is just 18 commands that can create, maintain, and use connections between PCs on a network. IBM soon extended NetBIOS with the NetBIOS Extended User Interface, or NetBEUI, which is basically a refined set of NetBIOS commands. Over time, however, the names NetBEUI and NetBIOS have taken on a different meaning. NetBEUI is the transport protocol, while NetBIOS is the set of programming commands that the system can use to manipulate the network; it is actually an API. To return to that pesky OSI model, NetBIOS operates at the session layer, whereas NetBEUI operates at the network and transport layers.

NetBEUI is one of the fastest protocols that you can use in terms of its speed when slapping data into packets for transmittal and unwrapping said data on the receiving end. It's also beautifully simple to set up: you install it and bind it to a network driver, and it works. No configuration is required, and the address of the computer is an easy-to-remember name that you assign.

NOTE   Computer names on a network using NetBEUI are actually NetBIOS names. They can be up to 16 characters long and are not case-sensitive.

However, there is one problem with NetBEUI, and this problem really limits its usefulness: you can't route it. In other words, if your needs are larger than those of a single segment, you can't use it to transport data beyond your local segment. It's also only supported by Microsoft operating systems and OS/2, so if you planned to communicate with the UNIX file server or NetWare print server, well, you're out of luck.

Today, NetBEUI's usefulness is somewhat limited. TCP/IP is faster than it used to be, so NetBEUI doesn't have the performance advantage it did at one time. As Internet access becomes ever more ubiquitous, you need TCP/IP anyway, as it is the protocol required to use that network. Even though some NetBIOS applications require support that NetBEUI can give, you can now use NetBIOS over IP to get the same effect.

In short, NetBEUI's not useless, but its usefulness is limited to small, single-site networks that don't need Internet connectivity, and not a lot of those are around.

The IPX/SPX Protocol

IPX/SPX, Novell's proprietary transport protocol, is actually two protocols—IPX and SPX. IPX, or Internet Package Exchange, is a network-layer connectionless protocol. It's responsible for finding the best path for packets to take to reach their destination, or for picking them up when they arrive. Packet addressing and routing are handled by the IPX protocol. So, logical network addresses (as opposed to the hardware ones used at the data link layer that are burned into the network card at production) are assigned at the IPX level. An IPX address consists of a four-byte (32-bit) network number and a six-byte (48-bit) node number.

What do these numbers mean? The *network number,* also called the *external network address,* identifies the physical segment to which the computer is attached. If two or more servers are on the same network segment, then they'll all use the same external address.

NOTE   External network addresses are assigned only to NetWare servers. Client machines on a NetWare network inherit their external network addresses from the server they log into.

The *node number,* or *internal network address,* is usually the hardware address of the network card inside the PC. This is handy, as it means that no translation has to take place from software-assigned names to hardware-assigned names. When installing a Novell NetWare server, you are asked to accept or change the internal IPX number. It then becomes that server's ID number. If you type **slist** from a workstation, you'll see this ID for each server listed.

Figure 3.5 shows the format of a complete NetWare IPX address.

FIGURE 3.5:

A NetWare logical address

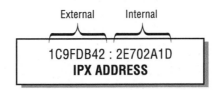

TIP   For those occasions when NetBIOS support is required, you can enable support for NetBIOS over IPX/SPX.

Note that *routing* is handled by the IPX protocol. In other words, IPX/SPX is a routable protocol, unlike NetBEUI, and can therefore be used to connect network segments separated by a router. To find the most efficient paths, every 60 seconds, IPX issues a broadcast with the Routing Information Protocol (RIP) or the NetWare Link Services Protocol (NLSP) and sends it to an expected location along all available paths. A sort of echo returns from this broadcast, and IPX determines the shortest path to the known location by how long it takes for the packet to get back. The only trouble with this method is that it makes IPX/SPX a rather "noisy" protocol prone to generating a lot of network traffic as it attempts to keep up to date with current routes. I'll talk more about routing in Chapter 5, "Additional Networking Hardware."

As IPX includes no support for error handling, for some purposes it's supplemented by the services of SPX, the Sequenced Package Exchange. This transport-layer protocol is connection oriented, so it makes sure that a solid connection has been established before it attempts to send data across the network. Because it's reliant on a valid connection, the SPX protocol is responsible for handling lost packets and other errors. Its main function lies with client/server computing, which is dependent on error-free communications.

Even though IPX and SPX are proprietary to Novell, their usefulness is not limited to Novell networks because of IPX/SPX-compatible protocols that aren't the original protocol but can communicate with it. These compatible protocols have been instrumental for permitting Microsoft networks to communicate with Novell ones, as the two network types have no other transport protocols in common. NetWare IP and Microsoft's TCP/IP are not mutually intelligible.

The TCP/IP Protocol

The Department of Defense developed the Transmission Control Protocol/Internet Protocol (TCP/IP) in conjunction with ARPANET (Advanced Research Projects Agency Net) to handle the problem of connecting networks with dissimilar hardware, for example, Sun systems talking to mainframes and mainframes talking to PCs. Each of the two halves of the name, "TCP/IP," describes a different task.

NOTE   Strictly speaking, there are more than two parts to TCP/IP—it's actually a suite of protocols. However, the best known are IP and TCP, so I'll concentrate on them here.

Working at the network level, the *Internet Protocol* (IP) provides a standard set of rules and specifications for the different networks to follow if they want IP to route their packets from one network to another. IP is designed for communications between both LANs and individual machines. The Transmission Control Protocol (TCP), on the other hand, operates at the transport layer of the OSI model. It takes network information and translates it into a form that your network can understand. In this way, it supports process-to-process communication between two machines or clients. You could think of IP as the part of the protocol that sets the rules of communication and TCP as the part that does the interpreting.

You can tell how good TCP/IP is at its job by its current task. It's the transport protocol for the Internet, the system that connects thousands of individual computers and networks over the world. Although originally designed for use by universities and the military, TCP/IP is becoming more popular for business applications. It can be used to connect LANs, UNIX hosts, DEC VAX minicomputers, and many other kinds of computers.

What happens when a Mac in a remote office wants to send data to a PC in headquarters? First, TCP establishes a connection that provides full duplex error-checking (error-checking of data in both directions) between the two platforms. Second, IP lays down the rules of communication and connects the ports of the PC and the Mac. At this point, TCP has prepared the data, so IP takes it, breaks it into smaller pieces if the original was too big, and puts a new header (a "forwarding address") on the packet to make sure it gets where it's going. The TCP packet is also labeled with the kind of data it's carrying and how long it is. Next, IP converts the packet into a standard encoded format and passes it to the PC at headquarters. Finally, the PC's TCP translates the encoded packet back into "PC-ese," that is, its own networking protocol. You can see the process in Figure 3.6.

FIGURE 3.6:

Sending data from a Mac to a PC through a TCP/IP network

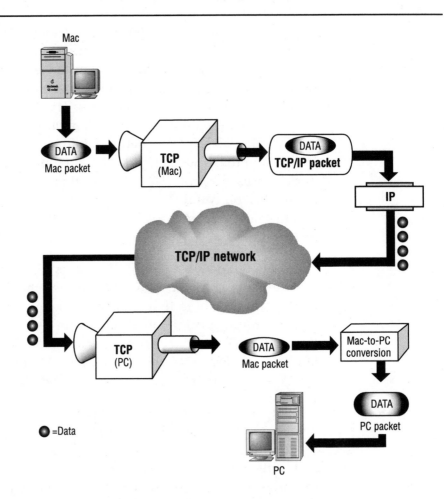

TCP/IP has become the default protocol for many of the world's networks. It's the only universal communicator that permits computers of all types—PCs, Macintoshes, and UNIX workstations—to communicate, and it's required for communication on the Internet. It is a little slower than NetBEUI, but its wide support more than makes up for any performance hit. It's better to be a little slow and able to talk to the whole world than really fast and able to talk to only small groups.

Configuration Requirements for TCP/IP

One catch to TCP/IP is that it can be difficult for novices to set up, as there are so many addresses and servers to assign. As we've discussed already in this chapter, NetBEUI and IPX/SPX are pretty simple to set up addresses for. In the case of NetBEUI, you assign a computer name, and in the case of IPX/SPX you assign a network identifier and let the system assign its own node identifier based on the hardware address of the PC's network card. However, TCP/IP can require a whole slew of addresses, including:

- A local IP address

- The IP address of the Domain Name Service (DNS) server, which translates the easy-to-remember names, such as computer.company.com, into IP addresses

- On NT networks using NetBIOS names to identify computers, the IP address of the WINS (Windows Internet Name Service) server, which translates NetBIOS names into IP addresses

- The default gateway (that is, the portal to the next network segment), which is even required for Internet access

- The number (called the *subnet mask*) that identifies the network segment to which your computer is attached

- If dynamic IP addressing is enabled, the IP address of the server assigning IP addresses

If you've spent any time on the Internet at all, you're probably familiar with the concept of IP addresses. Simply put, they're a

32-bit (four-byte) number that identifies a computer on the network. This is the software address of the PC, as opposed to the hardware address burned into the network card. In its binary form, an IP address might look something like this:

11000000 01101010 01111110 11000001

It's not wildly easy to read by anyone but a programmer or a computer, so for the convenience of humans, IP addresses are normally written in what's called "dotted quad" format, converting each byte of the 32 bits into a number using the base-10 system, as shown below:

192.106.126.193

Each network card attached to a TCP/IP network has a unique IP address that identifies it on the network—not just the physical segment to which it's attached, but the entire network.

Where does this IP address come from? How do you know what numbers to include in it? The answer depends on the scope of your network. If you're creating IP addresses for a local TCP/IP network that will never have any contact with the Internet whatsoever, then you can more or less make them up if you want to, just so long as no two network cards have the same IP address. However, if you want to connect to the Internet, you'll need to get unique IP addresses, and that's where an organization called the InterNIC comes in.

The InterNIC, simply put, is an organization in charge of assigning Internet addresses to companies and organizations that request them. In broad terms, it assigns groups of IP addresses to organizations based on their sizes, by assigning specific numbers for the first byte (or first two, or first three) and then letting the organization use any numbers they like for the other addresses. So, for example, if you requested a set of Internet addresses from the InterNIC, they might give you the set 192.106.X.X. This would mean that all of your IP addresses would have to start with the

192.106. prefix, but that you could assign numbers (up to 255) as you chose for the final two quads of the address. The parts assigned by the InterNIC are called the *network* portion of the address, and the parts assigned internally are called the *host* portion.

> **TIP**
>
> If your eyes aren't boggling at the idea of having to assign an IP address for each computer in your organization, they should be. Not only must you assign the numbers but you must also create a file mapping computer names to the IP addresses. The file with the name mappings must be kept up to date on every computer on the network. To reduce the complexity of this problem, you can run a Dynamic Host Configuration Protocol (DHCP) server to assign IP addresses from a pool, and then use a WINS or DNS server to resolve name-address mappings. WINS servers take care of NetBIOS names, and DNS servers take care of domain names.

A key part of Internet addressing lies in identifying not just a specific computer, but identifying the *subnet,* or part of a network, to which it belongs. That's done not with an external network number, as with IPX/SPX addresses, but with a *subnet mask.* The subnet mask is a number that can be overlaid onto the IP address. If the network portions of the IP address match the subnet mask, then the IP address is on the same subnet. If the network portions don't match, then the two IP addresses are on different subnets.

It's easy for two computers on the same subnet to communicate with each other; TCP/IP broadcasts the data, and the computer with the destination address that matches the one in the IP packet picks up the data. If a computer on one subnet wishes to communicate with a computer on another subnet, then the request must go to the router that connects the two subnets. The router looks at the network address of the destination address, decides whether that address is on the local subnet, and if it isn't, forwards the packet to the next subnet. Then that router examines the destination IP address, decides whether the address is on *that* subnet, and either broadcasts the message for pickup or forwards the packet again to the next subnet. This procedure continues until the correct subnet is found. The subject of routing can be a bit complicated, so I'll return to it in Chapter 5, "Additional Networking Hardware."

When a packet arrives at its destination, a protocol called the *Address Resolution Protocol* (ARP) resolves the IP address to the network card's hardware address. ARP is also responsible for translating the addresses for outgoing data.

Where Do We Go from Here? Part I—IP Version 6

The Internet has become the global network forecast in science fiction. Because TCP/IP is the protocol that makes that network function, TCP/IP's changes reflect the needs of this global network.

NOTE   The current version of IP is IP version 4. There is no version 5.

As of late 1998, the Internet protocol—the part of the TCP/IP suite responsible for routing packets across a network—is being adapted to better manage the increasing traffic levels on the Internet, as well as changes in the types of data transmitted. The changes to the protocol fall into five main categories:

- Increased addressing capabilities supporting longer (128-bit) addresses, as well as *cluster addresses* or *anycast addresses* that identify a group of nodes on the TCP/IP network

- Simplified header formats in order to reduce the impact that the larger IP packets will have on the network

- Increased support for extensions and options, including space for blank extensions so that the packet format can be easily changed in the future as needed

- Flow labeling to identify a stream of packets as coming from a particular node

- Additional extensions to increase error-checking capability and user authentication, and (optionally) data confidentiality

The complete gory details of IP version 6 (IPv6) are outlined in Request for Comment (RFC) 1883, but I'll review here the parts that matter to someone not planning on designing routers for a living.

More Flexible Addressing The logic behind making IP addresses isn't difficult to figure out: there are only so many addresses that you can squeeze out of 32 bits (it's 4,294,967,296, or approximately 4 billion, if you're interested), and every device on the Internet needs its own IP address. The number becomes even more limited when you consider that you don't even have all of these addresses available for the following reasons:

- The decimal value of each quadrant of the 32-bit address can be no greater than 255.

- Many of the addresses are reserved for purposes other than ordinary IP addresses—for example, addresses with "10" in the first quadrant are for local use only.

- Groups of addresses were assigned to companies and organizations, and those organizations get all the addresses within that group whether they need them or not. For example, all the addresses that begin with 192.233.x.x belong to Novell. Even if address 192.233.54.5 is unused, no one outside of Novell can use it.

Several steps were made to reduce the number of IP addresses needed (DHCP servers for address leasing, CIDR, and the like). But the population of the Internet keeps growing, thus, the 128-bit addresses. I'm not exactly looking forward to this any more than I enjoy using 10-digit telephone numbers when I go to a part of the country that uses them, but the 128-bit IP addresses are necessary to the Internet in the same way that the 10-digit numbers are necessary to the switching network—we ran out of the shorter identifiers.

The use of anycast addresses is intended to make it easier to address packets to a group that isn't necessarily a subnet or network. Rather than having to send packets to each member individually, you'll be able to send them to the cluster, which is a logical grouping instead of a physical one.

NOTE   Anycast addresses will replace the broadcast addresses used in IPv4.

Flow Labeling Longer addresses will be a bit of a pain for the humans who have to type them, but they'll make the problem of unique identification on the Internet a bit simpler. Another problem that plagues the Internet today is traffic.

When the Internet was first implemented, it supported little traffic; most of the internetwork data transfer consisted of file transfers and e-mail. As time went on, the traffic diversified to include support for newsgroups and bulletin board services where people could post messages to each other in a public forum; chat rooms; the Web; and now, services, such as telephone over the Internet, are available. The data load keeps increasing, as not only are these services new and used by a lot of people, they're traffic intensive in a way that file transfers are not.

I'll be covering routers in Chapter 5, "Additional Networking Hardware," but understand for the moment that the Internet is a collection of networks connected by routers. Each router is responsible for identifying the best possible path for data to reach its destination. To do this, a router must identify the destination of each packet it receives. That's a lot of packets to open and examine. Thus, IPv6 packets have a field that can be filled in to indicate that a packet is part of a particular flow. The idea is, if a router can tell that a packet is part of a stream of packets all going to the same place, it doesn't actually have to know where that place is after it's examined the first packet in the flow group.

NOTE   By default, a router will only be able to "remember" a flow's label for six seconds, but this value can be increased manually.

Packet Priority Sometimes, Internet traffic gets too heavy to handle and packets can be lost. As it stands, packets are dropped without respect to their function. However, with IPv6, IP packets will be able to be prioritized according to their purpose.

Priority values are divided into two ranges: 0-7 and 8-15. Low-valued packets within a particular range are dumped first when congestion gets too great, although each of the ranges is considered exclusively. That is, a packet with priority 6 will not necessarily get dropped before a packet with priority 8 because 6 is a high-ranking packet for its range.

Values 0-7 are used to specify the priority of traffic for which the source is providing congestion control. That is, traffic using an upper-level protocol such as TCP to monitor whether the system can handle the data stream backs off accordingly when congestion gets too bad. The values suggested in the IPv6 specification to prioritize congestion-control traffic are as follows:

0   Uncharacterized traffic (traffic not assigned a priority)

1   "Filler" traffic (netnews)

2   Unattended data transfer (e-mail)

4   Attended bulk transfer (FTP, NFS)

6   Interactive traffic (telnet, display protocols)

7   Internet control traffic (routing protocols, SNMP)

> **NOTE**   Priorities 4 and 5 are reserved for future categories.

Values 8-15 are used to specify the priority of traffic that does not back off in response to congestion, such as voice or video packets being sent at a constant rate. They're not labeled in the specification, but as a general rule, more essential information (such as low-resolution voice) will have a higher priority than information that it would be nice to transmit but is nonessential (such as high-resolution video).

Support for Bigger Packets Among the other extensions available to make IPv6 more responsive to conditions on the Internet is one that allows IP packets to be bigger than possible with IPv4—that is, to carry a larger payload of data. This is a nice capability because bigger packets means fewer packets for the same amount of data, which means in turn less latency when it comes to routing those packets.

Where Do We Go from Here? Part II—Migrating to IPv6

You'll notice that there are a number of differences between the current IP implementation and the one looming large on the horizon. Addressing will be the big headache because the other options, such as priority and flow control, aren't required; if no settings exist for them in a packet, then the capabilities are ignored. Migrating to the new protocol isn't going to happen automatically; you're not going to wake up one morning and discover that all your network nodes have been upgraded to use IPv6.

The subject of migrating from IPv4 to IPv6 is not a simple one. Classes are already being offered on how to deal with the problem and some online resources are available. An excellent one is at http://www.ewos.be/coexist/etg071/gintrod.htm#INICIO.

To be very brief, though, there are four ways to attack the problem of how to make your network support IPv6:

- Support both protocols.

- Include addresses for both protocols within a single packet.

- Tunnel IPv6 through IPv4.

- Translate headers so that IPv6-only nodes can communicate with IPv4-only nodes.

NOTE   Not sure what these options mean? Tunneling is described in Chapter 6, "Wide Area Network Considerations." Header translation is described in the context of bridging in Chapter 5, "Additional Networking Hardware."

If or when you decide to go the full migration route, you'll need to upgrade the pieces of your network in the following order:

1. Upgrade the DNS server to support the new addresses.

2. Upgrade the nodes to support both IPv4 and IPv6.

3. Deploy the upgraded nodes.

4. Upgrade the area (segment of a network) to IPv6 only with routers on the area borders supporting both protocols.

5. Upgrade the routers to support IPv6 only.

6. Deploy the new routers.

You are upgrading the name resolution system, then working from the inside out to spread IPv6 throughout the network while maintaining compatibility all the way through the process.

Multiple Transport Stacks

Two things should be obvious by now. First of all, there is no single best network protocol. Second, you may conceivably want to run all three of the protocols (NetBEUI, IPX/SPX, and TCP/IP), each for a different reason, and the good news is that you can. One of the values of the current networking model is that it supports multiple transport protocols. This is shown in Figure 3.7.

FIGURE 3.7:

A network using multiple transport protocols

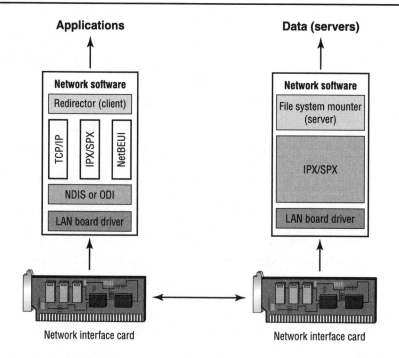

In this example, you see that the client machine has four transport protocols loaded and the server has one protocol loaded. This could happen if the client machine connected to more than one server. The IPX stack might talk to a Novell server, the TCP/IP stack might talk to an Internet server, and even NetBEUI might be used for local access with Microsoft machines. Each transport protocol binds to the drivers and redirector installed on each machine. As discussed earlier in this chapter in the section, "Network Binding Interfaces," you can change the binding order for the various protocols so that IPX/SPX (or a compatible protocol) may be used first when connecting to a NetWare server, or TCP/IP for connecting to the Internet.

Summary

In order for PCs to transmit data across the network, you need not only hardware but also a suite of programs collectively called *networking software.* This networking software includes the following:

- A redirector, which makes sure that requests are sent to the proper file system driver for network access

- A network file system to map the disk area for the operating system

- A network driver to let the operating system and network card communicate

- A network transport protocol to package the information and send it across the network to its destination

Each of these parts is separate so as to make the system more flexible and easy to change as needed, but all are vital to inter-computer communications.

In the previous chapters, I've talked a lot about the parts of network communications and introduced you to the pieces you'll need. In the following chapter, I'll talk about what you must do to put these pieces together into a local area network.

EXERCISE 3

1. Review the following diagram. Which of the transport protocols discussed in this chapter could be used to send data from PC A to PC D? If any limitations exist, what are they?

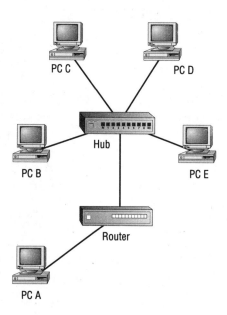

2. You're running Windows 98 on one PC and DOS on another. Will the network drivers you use for each be ODI-compliant or NDIS-compliant, or does it matter?

3. Which of the transport protocols mentioned in this chapter uses a default gateway?

4. IPv4 addresses are _____ bits long; IPv6 addresses will be _____ bits long.

5. Which part of networking software is responsible for handling application requests for data found on a network-accessible drive?

Exercise 3 Continued

6. An API used to facilitate communication between a client program and a server program is called a _____.

7. What is a monolithic device driver?

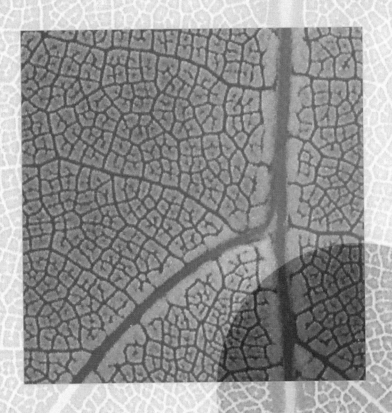

4

Installing Cards and Cables

I've spent three chapters talking about theory and you're probably anxious to get your hands dirty. Therefore, in this chapter I'll be talking about installing cards and cables to build the network that will connect your PCs.

Cable Installation Considerations

Most of what I'm going to talk about here concerns how to prepare for a contractor's help and what you need to know about your physical installation before the cabling process begins. This is not a complete tutorial in cable installation. First, I don't have room. Second, it's difficult to tailor such instructions when you can't see the environment in which the cable will be installed. Third, complex cabling is often a specialist's job. Therefore, I'll talk about the basics, so far as you need to know them for simple cabling jobs or for overseeing someone else doing a more complex one. After reading this, you'll be better prepared to instruct the cable installer in what you need done. Outsourcing this kind of work isn't cheap, and the meter's always ticking, so it's best to be prepared.

Plan Ahead

This is one of those really obvious but easily overlooked hints: don't just think about what your needs are now, think about what they'll be five or 10 years down the line. Cabling a building is not so much fun that you're going to want to do it twice, so plan ahead.

First, know your situation. Get the blueprints for the building you're in and study them. Where is the ductwork? Where's the electrical wiring and how is it shielded? Are there any surprises waiting to happen? What are the fire codes for your area? What do they say about where you can use polyvinylchloride (PVC) coated cable and where you must use plenum?

Get the fastest cable you can afford. Even if you don't need it now, the chances are excellent that sooner or later you'll use it, when your company starts implementing databases, or video to the desktop, or some such thing. Buy that 100Mbps Cat 5 now, or even fiber if you can justify it, and you'll save yourself money later in not having to pay for two cabling installations.

Give Yourself Some Slack

Don't plan out your cabling needs to the last foot, but anticipate quite a bit of extra cable. First, you'll need this because you can't just plug PCs into the network on top of each other; if you're using the bus physical topology, you'll need about 10 feet between taps or connections to the PC.

TIP   Conveniently, some coaxial cable comes with marking every 10 feet, so you can tell how far apart to make the connections.

In addition, the extra room will give you flexibility. If you have just enough cable for your needs, then sooner or later Joe User is going to want to move his PC five feet to the left and that's going to completely throw off your entire network if your plan has no flexibility built into it. When running the cable along the ceiling or floor, leave a few loops (six to eight feet for backbone cable) at each corner, or each doorway, or anywhere that's a permanent physical feature in the building so you can find it again. Secure the loops with electrical tape to keep them neat and out of the way. When you need a little more length in your cable, you'll have it. Otherwise, you'll have two options: splicing the cable yourself, or paying someone else to do it. Contractors typically charge not only for the length of the cable they run but also for the number of terminations they must do. Splicing the cable means paying for two useless terminations that don't do anything but give you more length that you could have had from the beginning with a little planning. Similarly, when running taps from a backbone or hub, give yourself a spare 10-15 feet so that you can move the PC at a later time if you need to do so.

WARNING   If you haven't planned for flexibility and need to extend your cable, splice it rather than attempting to stretch it. Stretching can damage cable—especially stranded cable—and damaged cable is far more prone to interference.

Giving yourself elbow room applies to conduit, too. In big installations with high security needs, you'll often have a central backbone run in a large duct, with smaller conduits branching off from it. This is an expensive configuration and larger conduits will make it more expensive yet. Regardless, you should seriously consider getting conduit a little larger than you need now. For example, if the 1/2-inch variety will let you run two taps from the backbone, get the 3/4-inch variety so that you can run three or four taps if you need to do so. Once again, even if it's more expensive up front, giving yourself room to grow will save you money down the road when you don't have to buy new conduit, pay to have it installed, and scrap the stuff you already paid for.

Neatness Counts

Keep in mind that you're going to have to deal with this cable at some point after it's installed, so make it as easy to get at as possible. When it comes to ceiling installations, you may be tempted to just throw the cables across the floor because it's less work. It's true, this is less work initially, but when you have to work up in that ceiling later you're not going to like it if you have to trip over cable snaking across the floor. To avoid this, tie the cables to something such as the supports of the drop ceiling; clamps are made for the purpose, or you can use the plastic snap ties. You may also want to consider attaching the cables to air conditioning or heating ductwork.

As a last resort, leave all the cables on the "floor" of the ceiling, but bundle and tie them so that they're out of the way. That way, if you have to move them you only have to move one lump, not six individual cables all tangled up together.

NOTE   Not all drop ceilings can support cable, so you may have to tie the cables to the supports or ductwork to make this work at all.

Running cables under the floor requires similar planning. Again, lay the cables neatly so that they're easy to get to. If you've got the money, consider getting ductwork to run the cables in so that they stay in one place. Also, put the cables somewhere where you can get to them *after* the furniture has been put into the room. It might look neater to have the cables running along the wall, but the chances are excellent that cubicles or an extremely heavy table will be along the wall. The middle of the room, where there's less likely to be furniture, is a better bet.

If you're running cable *on* the floor, then the rules are a little different. In that case, you'll do well to keep the cables against the wall and out of harm's way. That way, people will be less likely to trip over them (injuring themselves and/or the network in the process). Also, janitorial staff are less likely to damage them with enthusiastic cleaning. Tape down cables as best you can to avoid the chances of them being tripped on or wandering away.

Finally, label *everything*. At troubleshooting time, you're going to want to know which cables go where without doing this routine: "Okay, Karen, when I say 'Go,' shake the cable so I can tell which one it is." That exchange is normally followed by this routine: "Okay, it wasn't that cable. When I say so, shake the one next to it."

To avoid this, you can use different colors of electrical tape wrapped around the ends of the cables, or little adhesive numbers, or (if you've got deep pockets) color-coded cables themselves. These make it easier to tell which cable you've got at the end and also make it possible to tell which cable you're holding when you're crouched in the ceiling. I don't recommend hand-printed labels, as they can be hard to read. Unless you've got a really complicated cabling system that requires extensive description, symbols are probably the way to go. You can identify them at a glance and don't have to decipher someone else's handwriting or turn the cable over to read the whole thing. A little more than 10 percent of the male population can't tell red from green, so consider using symbols or avoiding green and red cables.

> **TIP**   Keep a legend of cable codes around so people can tell what they're looking at even if you're out of the office.

Play Well with Others

Finally, think about what's going to be running in the same place as your network cable. Got lots of interference-producing devices around? Consider cable with extra shielding, such as coaxial or STP, or, better yet, RFI-immune fiber.

> **TIP**   Fluorescent lights emit a lot of EMI, so don't run cables over the top of them.

Are electrical cables already in place? Don't run your network cables parallel to them, particularly if you're looking at big bundles, such as those leading up to a fuse box. If new electrical cables are going in after the network has installed, avoid introducing new interference problems by asking for armored cable (run in a metal sheath) rather than the ones enclosed in the plastic sheath. Once again, it will cost more up front, but these extra precautions may save you money later.

Things to Know Ahead of Time

I've talked about some of the specifics you need to be aware of before the cabling process begins. Here are some questions for your contractor. Figuring out these details early in the process can save you time, money, and lots of headaches.

Do you have wiring conduits? Many buildings provide you with built-in places in the walls and ceilings where you can run your cable. Often, these wiring conduits are themselves plenum-rated. This means that you *may* be able to use a cheaper PVC cable.

How are you testing your cables? You will want to know the precise method that is being used to test the cables after they are installed. Common sense reigns supreme on this issue. (Keep in mind that common sense really isn't that common.) Make sure that you get a written description of the testing method and follow the testing logic from start to finish to ensure that it makes sense for installation.

How are you documenting your cables? Make sure that the cables are being documented and labeled according to your company's set standard. If your company has not set one, then it should do so. You want to be sure that the labeling system makes sense to you, so I recommend that your company set the labeling standard, not the contractor.

What is the repair policy for the cable installation? You will want at least a 24-hour on-site response from your contractor. Many contractors say they have a 24-hour response to cable problems, when what they mean is, "We will call you back within 24 hours and it may take us up to a week to actually get there." You don't want that; you want the contractor at your site in 24 hours or less. Cable problems are mission-critical problems.

Can you get at least three local references from the contractor? You will want three local references from your contractor so that you can personally see the quality of his or her work and documentation of it. Most companies will not mind taking you on a tour of their cable systems if they are happy with the work the contractor has done. Don't forget to reciprocate when prospective clients call you to come see your expertly designed and installed cable system.

Are you following building and fire code requirements? To ensure the safety of all your employees, follow all local building and fire codes. You want to select a contractor who can demonstrate by experience and references that she or he is well versed in the local regulations. When in doubt, call the city or county offices yourself and ask questions.

Do you need to notify anyone else in your building or locale of your plans? You may need to check with other tenants in your building to make sure that the cable installation will not conflict with their workflow. This is usually more of a courtesy than a requirement. Often, if you notify building management, they will notify all of the other tenants in your building.

How long is the guarantee on the cable installation valid? Verify the length of time the contractor will guarantee his or her labor and the cables themselves. A service contract at least one year long is advisable. Reasonable costs for an annual service contract should not exceed 12 percent of the overall cable installation cost.

Wireless Networking

Preparing for a wireless network—or, more likely, a wireless portion of a wired network—isn't significantly different from preparing for a wired one. You still have to think about environmental factors and how the data is going to get from point A to point B.

Two kinds of wireless networking are used in LANs. Most common are the radio-frequency (RF) wireless networks, which can be used to connect PCs and servers over a fairly wide area, but have low transmission speeds (around 1Mbps). More specialized applications, such as wireless printers and keyboards, use infrared (IR) technology to create a high-speed short-range link.

Interference is the biggest problem you're likely to encounter with wireless networks. Infrared communications have an extremely high frequency, so in order to use them, the sender and receiver must be close and in the line of sight. If you can't stretch a piece of string between the sending device and the receiving one, they can't communicate. Therefore, if you've got an IR printer, it's a good idea to place it somewhere that IR notebook users can access it without people walking between the two devices.

NOTE   As discussed in Chapter 1, "Basic Networking Concepts and Components," frequency determines the amount of data that can be sent during a specified interval. Because of this, high-frequency communications are more easily interfered with than low-frequency ones.

RF devices are less prone to interference because their lower frequencies mean that the signal can more or less go around obstacles instead of being blocked by them. For this reason, although IR devices are confined to the room in which they operate, RF wireless devices can roam up to about 300-500 feet away from their source if indoors, or 800-1000 feet away if outdoors. Thick walls or metal barriers will interfere with the signal, but otherwise they're pretty flexible.

Installing and Configuring Network Cards

The cables are in. Now, you're ready to attach them to something. If you're not familiar with cable installation and configuration, read on. You'll learn how to get the card in the box in the first place and how to make it work with the other cards in the box once it's in there.

Installing Network Cards

If you have any experience at all in installing cards in a PC, the mechanics of installing a network card are pretty straightforward. Power down the PC, don your antistatic strap, open the computer case, and find a slot in the PC that's free and fits the kind of card you have.

TIP   If you can, choose a slot that's not next to another card in order to keep the airflow inside the PC's box as open as possible.

If you're removing another card to insert the new one, follow these steps:

1. Make sure that the card is disconnected from any outside cables.

2. Unscrew the small screws attaching the card to the PC case and lay them aside.

TIP   I keep an egg carton around to hold screws. They're perfect for the task—cheap, accessible, they have lots of little slots where you can put the different kinds of screws, and you can close the tops to keep screws from flying everywhere if you knock the carton off the table. The only disadvantage lies with well-meaning people who don't understand why you have egg cartons lying around and throw them out.

3. Pull gently on the card, using both hands to wiggle it back and forth slightly to disengage it from the connectors. This may take a little tugging, but if the card doesn't come fairly easily, stop and make sure that the card is indeed fully disconnected from the PC.

4. When you've got the card out, set it aside. Wrap it back up in its original sheath, if you kept it and plan to use the card again. Don't touch the gold connectors on the card; the oils in your skin can corrode the gold and thus reduce the card's connectivity.

Installing a card is much the same process, in reverse:

1. Unwrap the card, being careful not to touch the gold connectors, and set it aside.

2. Power down the PC and open it up.

3. Find an open slot on the motherboard that matches the bus required by the card. An ISA card needs an ISA slot; a PCI card needs a PCI slot.

NOTE   ISA and PCI are the two card types you're most likely to be dealing with. MCA and EISA cards are very rare, and I'd be surprised if you found a network card that required that you use either bus type. It's possible to find EISA network cards, but they're fairly uncommon.

4. Unscrew the plate that covered the open slot's opening to the rear of the computer and set the plate and screws aside. You may need the plate later, and you'll need the screws in just a minute.

5. Align the network card with the slot in the PC, and push gently but firmly to seat the card in its slot. You may need to push fairly hard for this to work, which can be somewhat intimidating if you're not used to inserting cards. If you've got the right slot and push straight in, then the card should snap into place.

6. Using those screws that you set aside in step 4, screw the card into the little holes in the case to hold it in place. If the card is in all the way, this extra step won't affect the card's positioning all that much, but will keep it from sagging or working loose.

7. Replace the case and, if the cables are already in place, connect them to the card.

Installing Network Card Drivers

The process for installing the drivers for the card depends on your operating system. Like other add-in cards, network cards come with a floppy disk containing drivers. To install these drivers, follow the instructions that come with the network card. The setup process is usually initiated with really complex operations, such as running INSTALL from the A: drive. This type of installation program will have an interface like the one shown in Figure 4.1.

TIP The operating system may include drivers for the card, but if the operating system is more than a year old, the drivers that come with the card itself are likely to be newer.

FIGURE 4.1:

Installing network
cards from a
floppy disk

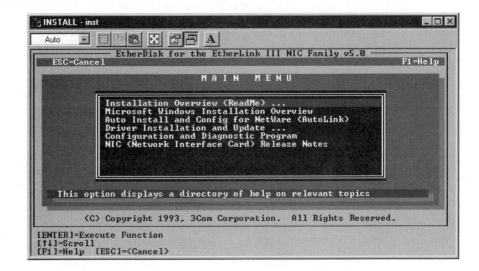

More recent versions of operating systems may include drivers
for the cards that you can load using an interface within the operating system. For example, Windows 95/98 includes the Add
New Hardware wizard, which you can use to detect the card and
automatically load the required driver. That said, you may end up
using the disk anyway, as the drivers on the floppy disk may be
more recent, or may be better optimized for the card than are the
drivers included with the operating system. Consider the 3Com
EtherLink III NIC used for the previous example (see Figure 4.1).
When installing the card for use with NT, you're not supposed to
use the drivers that come with the operating system. Instead, you
should manually select the card to be installed and install the drivers from the floppy. Not sure what you should do? Read the documentation for the card included in the package or often on the
manufacturer's Web site.

Speaking of Web sites, if you've got Internet access, you may
not want to use the drivers provided on the floppy disk *or* in the

operating system because they're both extremely likely to be out-dated. Instead, turn to the Web site for the network card's manu-facturer and find the section for software downloads. Select the type and model of card you're using. There will often be a page like the one shown in Figure 4.2 from which you can connect to download sites for that particular model of card.

FIGURE 4.2:

Downloading newer network card drivers from the Web (Copyright NeoPlanet. Copyright Bigfoot)

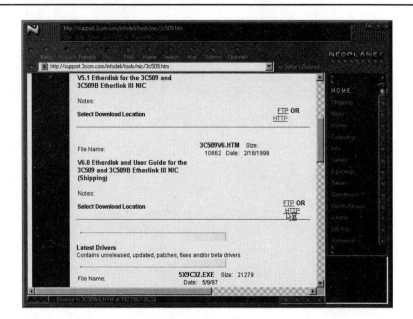

By the time you read this book, drivers updated in February 1998 may not seem all that recent. However, when you compare them with the drivers on the floppy disk that were saved in 1993, you can see the advantage of checking out Web and FTP sites for the most recent versions of card drivers. (Note that I bought this particular card in 1996, so the drivers were old then.)

> **TIP**
>
> This tip about downloading drivers from the Internet applies not only to network cards but also to any device you're installing. Not all device drivers are frequently updated, but it's always worth looking.

Configuring Card Resources

In a lot of ways, installing the card physically is the easy part: you plug it in and you're ready to go. Configuring it is another matter entirely. In Chapter 3, "Networking Protocols and Application Programming Interfaces," I talked about the logical addresses that the cards use. I also discussed how those addresses must be unique on the network, but that's not the hard part. The hard part lies in making sure that the network card has access to the CPU and a place to store its data while it's waiting for the CPU to process that data. In other words, it needs its own interrupt, I/O address space, and (rarely) DMA channels.

> **TIP**
>
> On modern cards, interrupts, IO buffers, and DMA settings are software configured, either with a SETUP program or by automatic detection in the operating system. On older cards, some of these settings may be set with hardware jumpers or switches on the card itself. So, before installing a card in the machine, note whether the card is software configurable or hardware configurable.

If you're familiar with all these terms, you can skip the next few pages. Here, I'm going to review what these configuration settings are and why you'll need them.

TIP

If you're using only PCI cards and have installed an operating system that supports Plug and Play, you don't have to worry about any of the configuration issues mentioned in the remainder of this chapter. PCI cards support Plug and Play, in which the cards are self configuring. The cards still use the same resources described here—you just don't have to hand-configure them.

Getting the CPU's Attention—Interrupt Requests

The network card is in charge of sending and receiving information across the network. However, it can't *do* anything with that information. All number-crunching, moving to main memory, or data manipulation must be handled by the CPU.

This is fine, but every other device in the PC or attached to it— the keyboard, hard disk, video card, sound card, and what have you—is also contending for access to the CPU. Those peripheral devices could get access in one of two ways. First, every few milliseconds (thousandths of a second), the CPU could periodically go over to the NIC and ask, "Excuse me, NIC, but have you any information that needs to be processed?" This method of "nagging" the cards in your system periodically is known as *polling*, and you can see how it would work in Figure 4.3.

This works, and some older network cards really do require the CPU to poll them to find out their status. The trouble is, this process is terribly inefficient. If the CPU were to do this, it would constantly have to stop doing what it loves to do best (processing), just to nag the NIC for information that may or may not be there. That's a whole lot of wasted CPU time, especially as there are many other devices in the PC that would also be polled. In a polling-only computer, the CPU could conceivably spend all of its time virtually rushing from device to device, asking, "Have you got anything for me?" This doesn't leave a lot of time for number-crunching, which is what the CPU is best at and designed for.

FIGURE 4.3:

The CPU polling the NIC for data

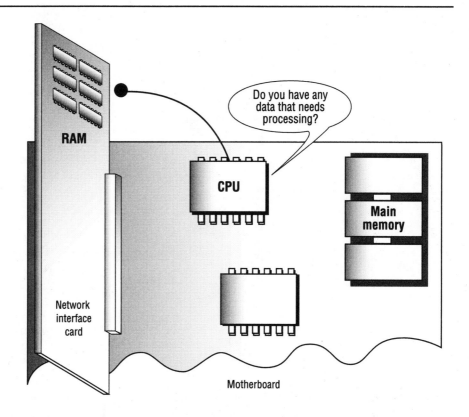

Polling: The CPU periodically asks the networking card if it has any information to transfer.

The alternative is the method preferred in modern systems: interrupts. When the network card has packets waiting to be processed, as shown in Figure 4.4, they're stored in the NIC's memory. When a packet arrives in the "waiting room" or memory on the NIC, the NIC goes over to the CPU, taps it on the shoulder, and says, "Excuse me, CPU, but there is some information sitting in the memory of the NIC. When you get a chance, will you please interrupt what you are doing and process this information or move it over to main memory?" When the NIC does this, it is making an *interrupt request*.

FIGURE 4.4:

The NIC asking the
CPU to move data

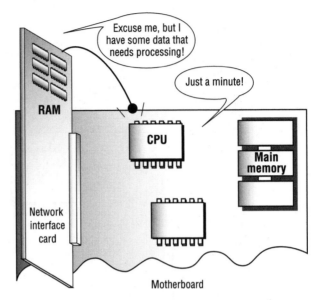

A more efficient process is to have the network card
notify the CPU when it has data that needs to be
transferred to main memory.

Once the CPU receives this request, it goes ahead and continues working. However, when it gets a free moment, the CPU will then go over to the NIC and start processing the information or move the information from the NIC to main memory.

Having trouble imagining this? Think of the CPU as the CEO of your PC, and each peripheral device as a department head. The CPU keeps its door locked, but has an array of telephones on its desk, each a different color so it can tell them apart. Each telephone is a hotline from one department or another. So, if the pink telephone rings, it's the hard disk requesting that data be pulled from cluster 492 into main memory. If the green telephone rings, it's the keyboard insisting that the keystrokes in its buffer be registered before they're lost, and if it's the black telephone... well, you get the idea. Each device gets its own hotline to the CPU so that it can ask the CPU to do something for it. When a particular telephone rings, then the CPU can immediately identify who needs help and if it's already dealing with someone else's request, the CPU can prioritize based on the urgency of requests associated with that particular telephone.

The only trouble is that the number of telephones is limited. Also, in most cases, each peripheral device needs its own telephone line—they can't share. Some devices can only use one of a few telephones at all; for example, your network card may only work with a blue or orange telephone, not with a purple or black one. Thus, you must assign one telephone to each device you want to use, and that line must be one of the ones that work with that particular device. If you ever wondered why so many network people are either prematurely gray or losing their hair, this is part of the reason.

How does this work? The telephone analogy isn't too far off. There are metal traces or wires embedded in the motherboard, and those wires act as pathways to connect various cards sitting in their bus slots to the CPU. Some of these pathways are known as *interrupt request* (IRQ) *lines*. There are 16 IRQ lines going to each slot on the motherboard, numbered from 0 to 15.

Generally speaking, each device on your network that needs an interrupt must have a different IRQ line assigned to it. To return to the telephones, if the CPU had two red telephones on its desk and both were ringing, it wouldn't know which device needed its attention. In that case, one device or the other—maybe both—simply wouldn't work. When the red telephone rang, the CPU wouldn't know who was calling, so it might ignore both lines, or it might sometimes answer one and not the other. Similarly, if you assign the same IRQ to both the network card and the LPT2 port, sometimes one won't work, sometimes the other, and sometimes neither will work.

How do you find out which interrupts your network card can use and which of those are free? The first question can be answered by reading your network card's documentation. Somewhere, it should list supported interrupts. Most network cards support two or three interrupts, one of which is likely to be IRQ 5.

TIP If no supported interrupts are available for your network card but some interrupts are available, look to see whether a device in your system could switch to the one that's free. For example, suppose that your network card supports only IRQs 5 and 10, but IRQ 7 is the only one available. If your sound card is using 5 but will support 7, switch the sound card's interrupt to 7.

You can answer the second question in a couple of different ways. One method is to meticulously document each interrupt, I/O buffer area, and used DMA channel and write them down on a sheet of paper that's kept in an envelope taped to the computer case. There are a couple of advantages to this method. First, you can always get a good idea of your system's configuration, even when the computer is turned off. Second, it's easy to see the configuration at a glance—something not always true when dealing with software diagnostics. The only catch to this method is that you *must* keep it updated, or you're lost.

Well, not entirely lost. Although software diagnostics have historically not been all that great at correctly identifying which devices were using which resources (including IRQs), with Windows 95 the situation got a lot better. The Device Manager tab in the System applet available in the Windows 95/98 Control Panel can tell you what resources some devices are using. As shown in Figure 4.5, select the device for which you want information, then click the Properties button. You'll move to the Properties sheet for the device. Turn to the Resources tab, as shown in Figure 4.6, and you'll be able to see the system resources that a particular network card is using.

FIGURE 4.5:

The Windows 95 Device Manager

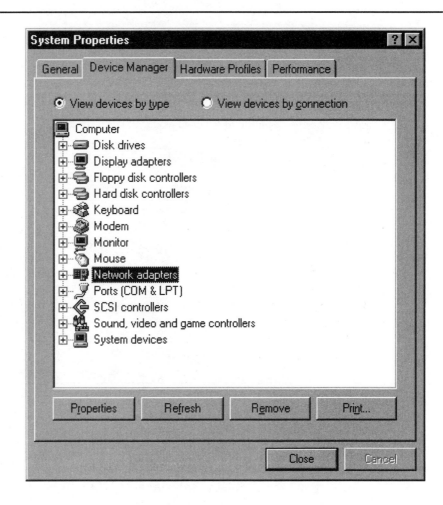

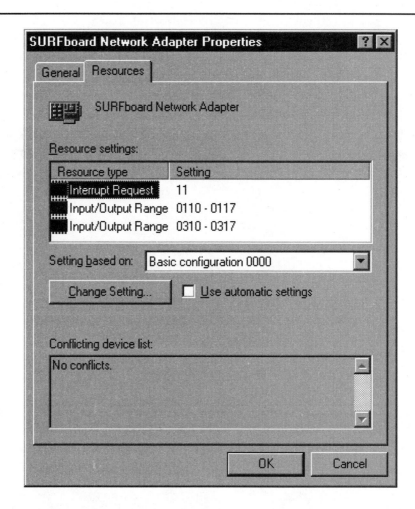

You can use the Device Manager not only to determine current system configuration but also to change it. To change the interrupt a device is using, click the Change Setting button on the Resources tab and enter a new IRQ number in the space provided. If you choose an interrupt not supported by that device, Windows 95 will tell you and offer you another option. If you choose an interrupt that *is* supported but is already in use by another device, the Device Manager will alert you to the problem, as shown in Figure 4.7. If you insist on making the devices conflict, the Device Manager will show the problem device in the list with an exclamation point next to it (see Figure 4.8).

FIGURE 4.7:

The Device Manager will warn you if you assign an interrupt already in use by another device.

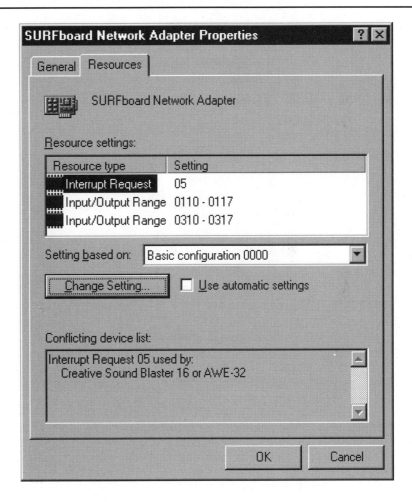

FIGURE 4.8:

Devices currently not working will have an exclamation point next to their entries in the list of installed devices.

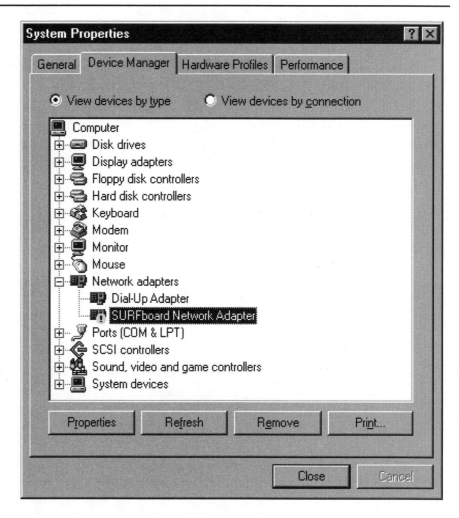

An exclamation point next to a device in the list of installed devices doesn't necessarily indicate a resource conflict, but could herald some other problem with the device that keeps it from working.

WARNING Another option for Microsoft Windows users is MSD, the DOS-based system information tool. You can use it to get configuration information about your system, but unless you run it from DOS (not from a DOS window in Windows), then it's likely to be inaccurate. For example, note that the network adapter shown in the previous example is using IRQ 11. When I run MSD on the same computer, it reports that IRQ 11 is free and open for use; that is a troubleshooting nightmare waiting to happen.

Where Does This Data Go? Choosing a Base I/O Address

Now you know how the network card gets the CPU's attention when it has information to pass along. Where is this information stored? For that matter, when the CPU passes instructions to the peripheral device, where are those instructions stored?

The answer to both questions lies in the I/O addresses. Essentially, they're a mailbox that the CPU can use both to pick up data waiting for it and drop off instructions for the device to which that I/O area belongs. Each device must have its own I/O area so that the CPU will drop off the appropriate instructions to each device; it's going to cause no end of confusion if the CPU asks the network card to play a sound. Therefore, you'll either need to tell the device which I/O addresses to use or let the system configure itself to avoid conflicts. The *base* I/O address is the one defining the bottom of the range.

NOTE Normally, you'll configure the base I/O address and the rest is taken care of for you. However, some cards will require you to define a range, letting you pick from one of the ranges supported by that card.

Why Do Memory Addresses Have Letters in Them?

I/O addresses and memory addresses are written in hexadecimal, a base-16 numbering system like the familiar base-10 numbering system. The reason for this is complex, but basically it's because computers think in a base-2 numbering system called *binary*, and binary numbers tend to be long and unwieldy for the human brain. If you're like an old roommate of mine who could read a binary number on a license plate and at a glance get the joke, then you can feel superior to me. If she hadn't explained after she started laughing, I probably would have caused an accident doing the "Okay, carry the one," conversions to decimal while driving along.

In an effort to make these numbers easier to absorb, programmers began using first a base-8 system and now hexadecimal, so as to express the numbers in a more efficient form. Why not use decimals? Mostly because of bytes, which are eight bits. The 10-based decimal system didn't accommodate the 8-based bytes all that well; a system more easily divisible by four made the conversions easier.

As the base-10 numbering system we're used to doesn't have 16 distinct characters used to express numbers, the hexadecimal system must be supplemented with letters in the alphabet. A-F make up the missing six digits. Therefore, up to the number nine, hex and decimal numbers look just alike. At 10, things start looking a bit off. Ten is A in hexadecimal; 11 is B; 12 is C; and so forth until we get up to 16 and run out of letters. Sixteen decimal is 10 hexadecimal; 17 is 11 hexadecimal; and so on. Hexadecimal numbers are often written with a lowercase "h" at the end so that you can tell that the number is written in hex, not decimal, like so: 330h. The "h" is not part of the number.

Continued on next page

You can do conversions if you want to, but for most of us, the simplest way to convert hexadecimal to decimal is to break out the Windows calculator and run it in Scientific mode. Make sure that the calculator is set to display in the number system you're starting out in (say, hexadecimal), type in the number, and then change the display to the numbering system to which you're converting. This doesn't impress people the same way that converting in your head does, but you don't have to *tell* anyone you used the Windows calculator.

Getting Information to the CPU—Direct Memory Access

I have already talked about getting the CPU's attention to let it know that there is a packet of information sitting on the NIC. However, once the CPU is aware of this, how does the information actually get from the NIC to main memory?

On the first PCs in the early 1980s, the CPU was in charge of moving data from the NIC to main memory, and the CPU was not happy about this. More to the point, the users were not happy about this. Why? Because when information was moved from a card in your computer to main memory, it had to go through the CPU one bit at a time (see Figure 4.9). This method of transferring information is referred to as *Programmable Input/Output (PIO)*. PIO is very processor-intensive, which means that your processor has less time to get any real work done.

FIGURE 4.9:

The CPU moving data from the network card

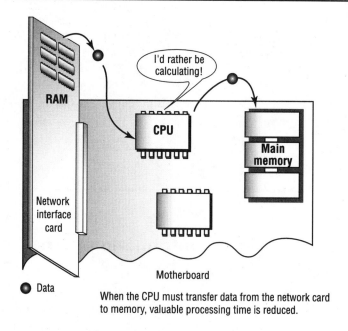

When the CPU must transfer data from the network card to memory, valuable processing time is reduced.

In the mid 1980s, a new chip known as a *direct memory access* (DMA) chip was developed, delivering a whole new way to move data around in your computer. We already know that when a packet arrives at your workstation, it goes to the memory of the network card. At that point, the network card issues an interrupt to the CPU to ask it to do something with this data that it's just received. With the advent of DMA chips on the motherboard, the CPU no longer had to stop what it was doing and move the data itself. Instead, it could pause for a moment in its calculating of that really engrossing spreadsheet and tell the DMA chips on the motherboard, "Please move this information for me and let me know when you're finished." The real power of direct memory access is that the DMA chips now can move information back and forth while the CPU is still calculating.

When the DMA chip is finished moving the information, it lets the CPU know that it is done. With DMA chips on board, we can now process and move information faster and more efficiently on each computer system, as demonstrated in Figure 4.10.

FIGURE 4.10:

Moving data from memory using a DMA chip

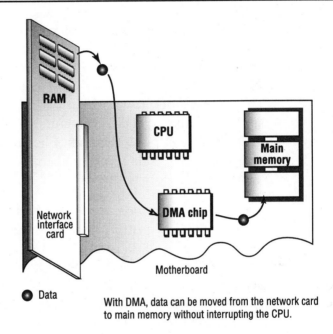

RAM

CPU

Main memory

DMA chip

Network interface card

Motherboard

● Data

With DMA, data can be moved from the network card to main memory without interrupting the CPU.

On modern motherboards, there are two DMA chips. Each DMA chip supports four *DMA channels* (dedicated pathways across which information is moved), so there is a total of eight DMA channels on the motherboard, numbered 0 through 7.

As with IRQ lines, every device on your network that needs to use DMA must use a unique DMA channel to avoid traffic jams and system crashes. There are really no software utilities that document this information well. The best way to keep track of your DMA channels is to document the settings of your cards as you install them. As most cards—especially newer ones—don't use DMA channels, this isn't too hard to do.

DMA isn't just for motherboards. A special type of network card known as a *bus-mastered network interface* card (actually, this could be any kind of card) has a DMA chip on the card itself. Why do they call it bus-mastered? The slots where you place your video card, sound card, SCSI card, and so on are known as expansion slots or *bus* slots. The card sitting in the bus slot will control—that is, *master*—its own DMA transfer, hence the title, bus-mastered. As soon as you put a DMA chip on any card, you now have a bus-mastered card. Today, you can purchase bus-mastered NICs, hard disk controller cards, and SCSI cards.

In 1989, IBM introduced some of the first bus-mastered cards, asserting that by putting the DMA chip on the card itself, the card could process and do direct memory access transfers faster than the two DMA chips on the motherboard. As it turned out, they were right. With its own DMA chip, a bus-mastered network card can communicate with main system RAM without additional processing intervention by the CPU. You can see this in Figure 4.11.

FIGURE 4.11:

Bus-mastered network cards can transfer information without the help of the CPU.

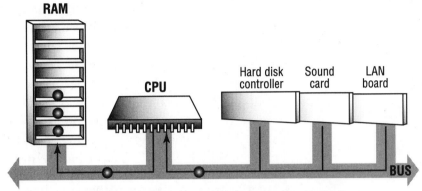

Without bus mastering, all data transfers from the system's interface cards to memory must be processed through the CPU.

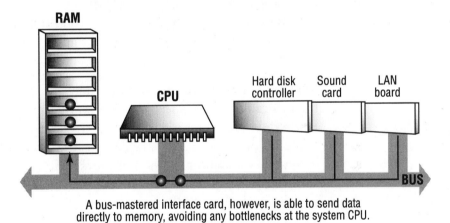

A bus-mastered interface card, however, is able to send data directly to memory, avoiding any bottlenecks at the system CPU.

Summary

In the previous pages, I covered the basics of installing your cabling system and network cards. Neither are difficult tasks, but both are made much harder if you don't prepare ahead of time.

When installing cables, the most important thing to keep in mind is planning ahead. Know what you're dealing with before you start. Build flexibility into your design. If need be, spend a little more money on cables or wider conduit now so that you can expand later. The most expensive part of your network is not going to be the machines that are part of it, but the cable. It's hard to install and harder to upgrade; plan ahead so that you only have to do the installation once. Finally, document everything so that when troubleshooting time comes around you're prepared and can tell which cable is the problem child.

Network cards are like any other add-in card for your computer. When installing them, you must configure them to have their own interrupts, I/O buffers, and perhaps DMA channels for quick transfer of data between network card and motherboard. Once again, proper documentation—whether by hand or with the help of diagnostic programs—is key to trouble-free card installation.

In the course of these first four chapters, you've learned about the basics of a LAN and how to put one together. Before I conclude the discussion of channels, I'll expand our LAN with an explanation of the hardware devices required to connect and extend those channels: hubs, routers, bridges, and so forth.

EXERCISE 4

1. IRQs 5 and 7 on your computer are unused. You have a network card to install that supports IRQs 10 and 11. Can you install the network card? Why or why not? If not, then what can you do to make it installable?

2. Which of the following is/are rarely used by modern network cards? Choose all that apply.

   A. Base I/O addresses

   B. DMA channels

   C. IRQs

   D. None of the above

3. If running cable under the floor, where's the best place to put it? Why?

4. True or false. You can have I/O address ranges that overlap between two adapter cards, so long as the base I/O addresses are not the same.

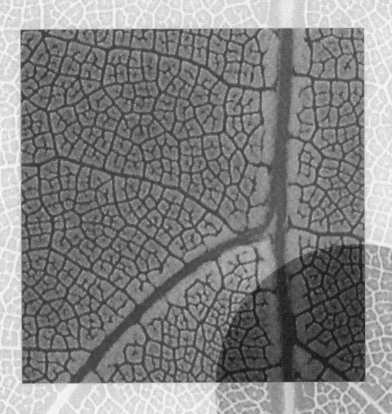

5

Additional
Networking
Hardware

It's not enough to create a single LAN. These days, the chances are excellent that your LAN will either start out connected to another network or it will be connected at some point. That's when you've got to move on from the simple network topologies I discussed in Chapter 2, "Planning a Network Architecture," and start dealing with internetworking and intranetworking devices.

Intranetworking *and* internetworking devices? Yup. The basic difference between the two is that *intra*networking devices extend your LAN, and *inter*networking devices connect two different LANs or networks of any size or breadth. This isn't a perfect division, by any means. Why? Because it's sometimes hard to tell where one network ends and another begins. Some devices include both extending and linking capabilities, but the internet/intranet division is a start for organizing networking hardware.

NOTE   The higher up the OSI model a piece of network hardware operates, the more likely it is to connect or merge separate networks, not extending a single one. For example, a hub connects the parts of a single Ethernet network, but a router is required to connect an Ethernet LAN to the Internet.

When I started writing this chapter, I thought I'd make a nice neat model to map networking hardware to a particular layer of the OSI model (described in Chapter 1). A lovely idea, but it didn't work well for one simple reason. Although you could perhaps separate the functions of networking hardware into those layers (physical layer functionality, data link layer functionality, and so forth), the devices themselves resist such a mapping because their functions overlap. Bridges have some purposes that you could describe as operating at the data link layer, for example, but most modern bridges also creep into the network layer of the OSI model. While the OSI model is a convenient organizer for describing what's going on in a network, it doesn't always map well to the real world, and in this case it doesn't map well at all.

Thus, I'm not going to dwell much on the OSI model as it applies to networking hardware. On a theoretical level, you can divide the hardware as follows and elaborated upon in the sidebar that follows this list:

- Repeaters—physical layer
- Bridges/hubs/switches—data link layer
- Routers—network layer

Models of Network Functionality

You can fit some aspects of networking hardware into a simple model, so long as you don't strain the model overmuch.

Physical layer devices, such as repeaters, operate like an extension of network cable, allowing the network to transmit its signal farther than would otherwise be possible.

A **data link layer device** has some functions specific to a particular kind of network, such as Ethernet or Token Ring. The degree of complexity of these functions varies with the device. For example, hubs are mostly concerned with connecting the members of a network indiscriminately; switches may forward information to only the particular segment where a frame's destination address may be found; and bridges may actually permit two disparate network types to be connected. However, the basic idea remains the same; they're concerned with hardware only. A data link layer device doesn't know or care what networking protocol is in place on the network, what network operating system is in place, or what applications are running on the network.

Continued on next page

The data link layer of the OSI model is not itself monolithic, but it is divided into two sublayers: the media access control (MAC) and the logical link control (LLC). The MAC layer is concerned with hardware addresses and connectionless data transfer, whereas the LLC layer actually makes connections before passing along data. Most data link devices are more concerned with MAC functions than with the LLC functions, but, as you'll see, bridges may use some capabilities defined at the LLC level.

Network layer devices, such as routers, are concerned with networking protocols, such as IPX/SPX or TCP/IP, not with network type.

Don't get too hung up on these distinctions, though, as they won't necessarily hold true. That is, most modern bridges and routers overlap in their bridging and routing capabilities, some switches have bridging characteristics, and *every* powered device on an Ethernet network is a repeater. You can trust these divisions to some degree. That is, if you need to connect your network to the Internet, then you're not likely to find the functionality you need in a hub. However, they're not perfect. Instead of focusing on the OSI model, think about what capabilities you need to add to your network and choose a device based on those needs. This means that you'll spend a lot of time reading spec sheets and comparing functionality between products, but you'd be doing that anyway.

Repeaters Extend the Network's Reach

Repeaters are devices that regenerate an electronic or photonic signal so as to increase the distance that that signal can travel, basically, to boost it at some point after its original transmission. All repeaters do is strengthen the signal by repackaging and rebroadcasting; they do not connect disparate networks, filter packets, or route data to other subnets.

The sole purpose of a repeater is to reduce the effects of attenuation. I discussed attenuation briefly in Chapter 3, "Networking Protocols and Application Programming Interfaces." As you may recall, that's the Techese for "signals get weaker as they travel." As signals get weaker, they're more easily corrupted by other signals. This shouldn't be news to anyone who's ever used a radio while on the road. Say you're driving along, listening to Bela Fleck. As your drive approaches the end of the broadcast area, Bela doesn't immediately disappear, but has a disturbing habit of suddenly breaking off and sounding like the Bee Gees, because the radio station in the new broadcast area is having a "Best of Disco" show. Bela fades out and the Bee Gees fade in. What happens with radio also happens to networks; no matter what type of signal it is, how well it's shielded, or how immune to interference, sooner or later it will fade to the point at which it's no longer "intelligible" at its destination.

You can take two approaches when it comes to solving the problem of attenuation. First, you can boost the signal with increased voltage, which is what your radio station is doing when they start boasting about getting a new transmitter. The new transmitter will have no effect on the signal's quality for the original broadcast area. However, it will improve it on the outer edges of the broadcast area and extend it to new areas. Sooner or later, the signal will still fade, but with the stronger original signal, it will travel further before doing so.

The second approach, and the one taken by networks and inherent in repeater design, is to repeat the signal, so as to start it out fresh again.

What Can Repeaters Do for You?

In repeating the signal, repeaters can have a couple of beneficial effects. First, in Ethernet networks they can help you avoid collisions, or allow you to have a bigger network and spare you from worrying as much about collisions. Second, they can allow you to isolate parts of your network.

> **NOTE**   All segments of a network connected with repeaters must be using the same data link and network protocols. That is, you cannot use a repeater to connect a Token Ring network to an Ethernet one, or to connect an Ethernet network running IPX/SPX to one running TCPI/IP. Both networks must be of the same type (Ethernet) and both running the same transport protocol.

Avoiding Collisions

Like other baseband networks, Ethernet networks have only a single "path" on which data can travel at a time. As you may recall from Chapter 3, "Networking Protocols and Application Programming Interfaces," collisions occur on Ethernet networks when two or more PCs' network cards begin transmitting data on the network at the same time. Therefore, before a PC on an Ethernet network begins transmitting, it listens to the network to make sure that all's quiet on the western front before it begins. However, a PC can only hear so far, and if a node too far away to hear—but on the same segment—is already transmitting, then they'll collide. Admittedly, collisions are inherent in the Ethernet design and to be expected on a properly functioning network, but they can slow down the network by requiring retries. You don't want to have collisions more often than is strictly necessary. Repeaters can help you avoid excessive collisions by boosting the signal so that all PCs on the network can "hear" each other.

Isolating Segments

Ethernet segments, specifically those using the bus physical topology and thus sharing a single backbone among all PCs on the segment, are vulnerable to downtime caused by breaks in the cable connection. If you've got some parts of the network that are more prone than others to network downtime, then a repeater could isolate those segments, letting them go down in flames without affecting the rest of the network. For example, say that you're running a PC training firm and want your instructors to get lots of hands-on experience. Therefore, you set aside part of the network to let them mess with it and with testbed servers. After all, the last person you want within reach of the mail server is someone playing, "What happens if I do *this*?" However, if that segment is connected to the rest of the network, then removed cables, forgotten terminations, and other network problems could have a bad effect on network functionality elsewhere. That is where the repeater can help you; even if the cable segments are shorter than the 185m maximum, you can still use a repeater to keep the dead bits of the network from affecting the living ones.

How Do Repeaters Work?

So now you know that the function of a repeater is to regenerate a signal so that it can travel further. Strictly speaking, this isn't quite true; rather than just boosting the signal, repeaters repackage a signal and rebroadcast it. Essentially, what happens is this: when data packets arrive at the repeater, the device takes them apart and repackages them in the same form in which they started out. The repeater isn't actually affecting the data, or touching the addressing information. However, it is revitalizing the signal from scratch, not just resending the original signal. That said, there's no error control built into this process. If a packet is corrupted when it gets to the repeater, it will be corrupted when it leaves the repeater.

NOTE   On Ethernet networks, every device is a repeater.

Repeaters versus Extenders

You'll have gathered that repeaters don't just repeat, but actually repackage. There *is* a device that just repeats; it's called a LAN *extender* and this device fulfills the function that you'd expect from something called a repeater. Extenders function similarly to repeaters in that they permit you to have longer networks without increasing the chances of collisions, but they don't add to your repeater count. What's repeater count? You can only have up to four repeaters in a single network and the number you have is called your *repeater count.*

There's no reason to *not* use a repeater in place of an extender, except that you can only use so many repeaters in a network and you're not limited in the number of extenders that you can use.

The sidebar contrasting repeaters and extenders refers to repeater count. You can only have up to four repeaters in a single network, or else Bad Things (such as network failures or delays) can happen. There are two reasons for this.

First, overuse of repeaters can actually increase the number of collisions on the network. Every time a package is disassembled and reassembled, there's a tiny delay. This delay isn't long enough to matter when a package is only being reassembled once, but, the more repeaters on the network, the more tiny delays you'll have. Eventually, the delays will accumulate until a point at which a sending node is waiting too long to hear back any acknowledgment of its transmission, and resends its data. The trouble is that when the sending node does this, its original packet is still in transit. If the sending node resends the data while the original transmission is still limping on toward its final destination, then the two packets will collide. Once again, collisions are to be expected in an Ethernet network, but you don't have to go looking for them.

The second potential problem with too many repeaters is data corruption. Each time a repeater breaks down and reassembles a packet, there's the chance that it's putting the data back together incorrectly, perhaps substituting a 0 for a 1 at some point along the line. (If that doesn't sound like a big deal, then consider this: 11001100 binary is 204 decimal, but 11101100 is 236 decimal. Someone just got an informal raise.) It's like the old game of Gossip that perhaps you played in grade school. Person A would whisper something in the ear of person B, and person B would whisper what they heard in the ear of person C, and so forth around the circle. Finally, person O would say what he or she heard and it turned out to be an extremely garbled version of what person A said in the first place. Funny then (at least fourth graders get a big kick out of it), but not good when what's getting garbled is not tongue twisters but your network's data.

The four-repeater rule is not carved in stone; your network will not work perfectly with four repeaters then crash in flames as soon as you add the fifth. However, it will become more unreliable as you increase repeater count, and four hops is the recommended upper limit.

Hubs Connect the Dots

"Hub" is a catch-all term for a device that connects networked devices to each other. They can range in complexity from unpowered patch panels to complicated devices that can connect disparate LAN types, or even plug those LANs into a WAN.

The term "hub" is used most often to apply to devices used in Ethernet networks. Token Ring networks use multistation access units (MAUs), which, like the network itself, function differently from the Ethernet hubs. However, both hubs and MAUs serve the same basic function of joining together the PCs on the LAN.

The Types of Hub Models

Most hubs come in one of three forms:

- Stand-alone
- Stacked
- Modular

Stand-alone hubs are what they sound like—powered or (more rarely) unpowered devices that may or may not include the capability to connect to other hubs with a short run of cable, perhaps fiber or twisted pair, in which case they're stacked. Stand-alone hubs, both in stand-alone and in stacked form, are shown in Figure 5.1.

FIGURE 5.1:

Stand-alone hubs may be used alone or linked to other hubs.

Unmanaged stand-alone hubs are generally pretty inexpensive (I picked up one LinkSys hub with five PC ports for $59), but hubs get more expensive as more ports are added. If you don't need management capabilities, buying two stand-alone hubs and linking them may be cheaper than buying one big one.

Modular hubs are built with a backplane that hub cards can plug into, as shown in Figure 5.2.

FIGURE 5.2:

Modular hubs look like add-in cards plugging into a motherboard.

Add-in card for additional ports

If built to be "intelligent" (I'll discuss this in the following section), the hubs in a modular or stacked design may be managed by one hub that's the master, while the rest are slave hubs. Why choose a modular or stacked hub? Mostly, it will depend on how your network will grow. You can add modules to a hub chassis, or you can get stackable hubs to distribute them throughout your building wherever they happen to be needed.

Some Hubs Are More Equal Than Others

Hubs come in a variety of forms ranging from extremely simple designs that act as a cable interface to those that offer some advanced management techniques. You can theoretically divide hubs into three categories:

- Passive

- Active

- Intelligent/managed (two terms for the same thing)

Passive hubs are unpowered devices, such as patch panels, that provide an interface for cables to transfer data back and forth. They're appropriate for some applications, such as wiring a house for a network, but you're more likely to find an active and/or managed hub in most LANs.

NOTE　　All completely passive devices are unpowered, as a powered hub regenerates the signal and is therefore active.

An *active hub*—that is, any powered hub—has repeating qualities, repackaging and regenerating the signal as described in the earlier section of this chapter on repeaters. Otherwise, active hubs serve the same functions as passive hubs, blindly making sure that data put on the network is broadcast to each connected segment so that whomever the data is for can pick it up. One advantage that most powered hubs seem to have is *status lights.* If a PC's connection to the network is working, then the light for the port it's plugged into comes on. If the PC isn't connected to the network, then the light is out. Another status light on one hub I have shows a scary-looking red light whenever collisions take place, but recall that some collisions are a normal and expected part of Ethernet operations.

Intelligent, or managed, hubs have a module that allows them to do a bit more than just shove data along the network; they can be used to help you troubleshoot or keep tabs on your star network. If you see a hub sold with a managed device interface (MDI), it's an intelligent hub.

I'll be discussing management protocols in Chapter 14, "Principles of Network Management." However, the basic idea is this: management protocols, such as the Simple Network Management Protocol (SNMP), have two parts. A monitor runs on a management server, and an agent runs on the devices to be managed. The monitor and the agent can communicate. In the case of SNMP, the most common generic management protocol, the monitor queries the agent and collects information from it, perhaps including the following:

- Hub and/or port-level status and activity information
- Performance statistics on a per-port basis
- Network mapping of all SNMP-capable hardware on the network
- Event logging of network errors and activity

You can also use management software to do things to managed devices, such as:

- Change network security by denying unauthorized people access to the hub.

- Set tolerances for activity, error levels, and performance so that if those tolerances are exceeded you know about it.

NOTE   This is a sample of the kinds of information that may be available with managed hubs, not a complete list or one that will apply to all managed hubs. The precise information that the management software delivers depends on the agent installed, and may vary with the model.

Managed hubs aren't always necessary. If your network has only a single 5+1 hub and this hub is easy to get at, you can probably check it out in person as easily as you can call up diagnostic software. The more PCs that are on the network, and the harder the hub is to get at, the more complicated troubleshooting gets. What's simple with one hub becomes a nightmare when you've got 10 hubs with 16 PC ports each. In that case, some kind of management software can help you keep your sanity when it comes time for troubleshooting.

TIP   When choosing managed hubs, look for management modules that can be upgraded with flash ROM. That way, when improvements become available, you can upgrade the module rather than replace it.

Hub Architecture

At its most basic level, a hub is a device that offers an electrical connection for cables that can't be hooked into each other directly. The logical topology of the network and the type of cable it's strung with are irrelevant to the definition, as is the specific chassis type. However, hubs are part of the star *physical* topology, as shown in Figure 5.3.

FIGURE 5.3:

The hub is the center of the star physical topology.

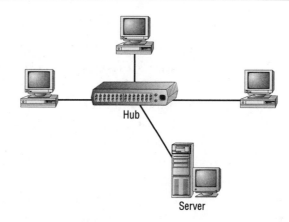

Hub

Server

Ports, or the little holes you stick the cables in to connect them, are relevant to the definition of any hub, as shown in Figure 5.4.

FIGURE 5.4:

Inserting STP cables into a hub

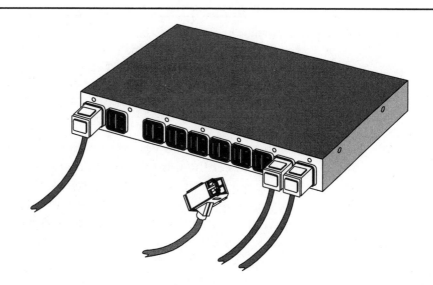

Ports are important; the ports in a hub determine:

- The cable type that the hub supports
- How many PCs may be connected with a single hub

- Whether the hub is expandable and may be remotely managed when the network is down

Like network cards, hub ports are designed to accommodate only particular kinds of cable connectors like the ones discussed in Chapter 1, "Basic Networking Concepts and Components." For example, thin coaxial cable and UTP require different ports, and STP requires ports different from those used by fiber. Like other network devices, hubs can only be used with the type of cable with which they're compatible. Also like other devices, they're logically compatible once the cables fit. That is, if you buy a hub that supports connections to RJ-45 connectors like those used with UTP, then you should be able to use that hub for your 10BaseT network whether the hub came from Ye Olde Hub Shoppe or 3Com—the physical interface remains the same. To make a live network connection, you provide power to the hub and plug in the cables.

NOTE Some hubs have ports for various sorts of cables. This allows them to connect to more than one type of network so that you can physically connect, say, an AS400 to your PC-based 10BaseT LAN. Or, you can connect hubs in the distributed star logical topology with backbone cables made of thick coaxial cable or fiber optic cable.

Those ports won't do you any good unless there's some mechanism to connect them internally so that packets from one cable may be passed to the rest of the network. To let ports—and thus the nodes plugged into those ports—communicate, there's an internal bus system inside the hub providing each port with a receiving connection and a sending connection. The way that data are sent to each port depends on the type of network involved. For example, Ethernet networks broadcast data to all parts of the network, leaving it to the nodes to sort out whether a packet is intended for them or should be ignored. Thus, data coming into a hub from a PC on a 10BaseT Ethernet network is broadcast to all segments plugged into the hub, as illustrated in Figure 5.5.

FIGURE 5.5:

Data sent on a 10BaseT network is broadcast to each PC plugged into the hub via the ports.

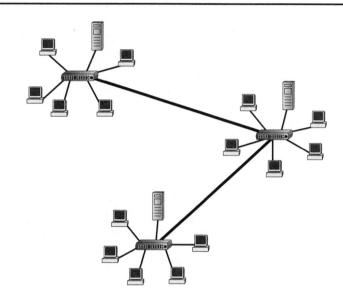

Some intelligent hubs note the physical address of the network card associated with a particular port. These hubs may either be preprogrammed with a static list of address-hub mappings or they may create mappings through discovery. Static address mappings can be used to keep unauthorized people off the network. As shown in Figure 5.6, if a hub is given a static list of port-address mappings, and a PC with a physical address not found in that list attempts to connect to the network, a smart hub can isolate that port. Once isolated, the unauthorized PC can't actually connect to any of the other PCs plugged into the hub.

FIGURE 5.6:

Intelligent hubs can use static lists of authorized physical addresses to keep unauthorized PCs off the network.

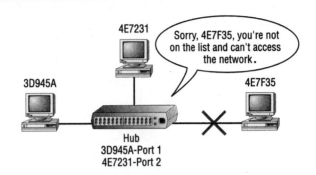

The internal bus of the hub operates at the same speed as the network, or, more precisely, the speed of the network using the star topology is determined in part by the speed of the hub. Therefore, if you want to run a 100Mbps network, you'll need a hub with an internal bus that supports that speed.

Not all the ports in a hub are for plugging in computers. One, called the *attachment unit interface* (AUI), may be present to let you connect the hub to another hub or to another device such as a bridge or router, as shown in Figure 5.7.

FIGURE 5.7:

Use the extra port to link hubs to each other or to internetworking devices.

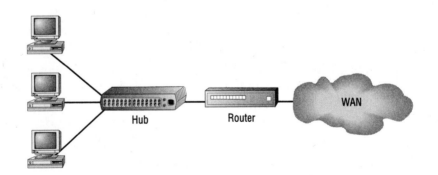

Models with AUI ports typically list the number of ports like this: 5+1, meaning that the hub has five ports for PCs to plug into and one AUI. The type of cable that plugs into the AUI port depends on the hub; some models may use fiber or thick coaxial, while others may use RJ-45 and look like one of the PC ports. More expensive hubs may have fiber AUI connections. However, even the cheap $59 hub that my network supports can connect to other hubs at 100Mbps because its AUI supports Category 5 cable.

TIP   The more ports a hub has, the more expensive it's likely to be, and the expense may be greater than the cost of another hub with the same number of ports. Check costs—it may be cheaper to attach two hubs with their AUIs rather than to buy a single hub with the number of ports that you need.

In addition to their AUI ports, some hubs will have a serial port interface. This interface allows you to connect the hub to a PC or modem and thus get remote management capability that isn't affected by network crashes not related to the hub itself. Such management is referred to as *out of band* management, as it takes place independent of ordinary network transmissions.

Switching Hubs

You'll notice that some smart hubs don't just blindly shove data onto all the segments of the network that are plugged into them. Instead, they notice the MAC addresses of the network cards associated with each port and can discriminate based on those addresses. Switches carry this capability somewhat further to identify the destination's MAC address and only forward the packet to the segment on which that address is located.

The distinction between an ordinary hub and a switching hub is the difference between the office switchboard operator getting an incoming call and paging the intended recipient to pick up the call and calling a specific office and patching through the call directly. Figure 5.8 illustrates this concept.

FIGURE 5.8:

Switching the signal versus broadcasting the signal

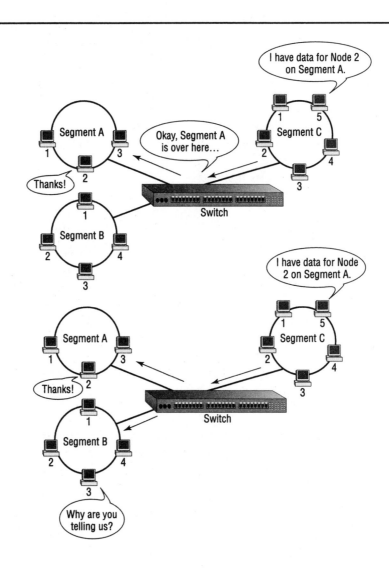

Why bother with switching the signal instead of broadcasting it? One major reason is traffic control. If every time there's a telephone call into the office, the switchboard operator makes everyone listen to the page and then decide whether to pick up, that's more of an interruption to the office than it is to directly notify the call's target. Similarly, when a hub broadcasts all frames to all segments attached to it, then every PC on the network has to stop and "listen" and can't talk themselves lest they cause a collision. If the signal is switched only to the part of the network where it needs to go, then the rest of the network isn't bothered. It can in fact transmit data on the other segments without interfering with the first transmission.

Switching also makes it possible to reserve more bandwidth for high-traffic applications. With ordinary hubs or repeaters on a 10Mbps network, all ports share the same 10Mbps pipe. With switching, each port can have its own 10Mbps pipe, unencumbered by traffic from other ports. Switching makes it possible to connect multiple LANs to get all the advantages of being linked without the disadvantages of sharing bandwidth.

The role of a switch is a bit more complex than simply that of a hub with a little more on the ball than average. As illustrated in Figure 5.9, you typically don't plug individual PCs into a switch but plug hubs into the switch's ports so that each segment of the network has its own port. Depending on where you put the switches in the LAN, you can use the switch to isolate portions of the network at the workgroup, departmental, or backbone level.

FIGURE 5.9:

Use switches to isolate parts of the network, not to isolate individual PCs.

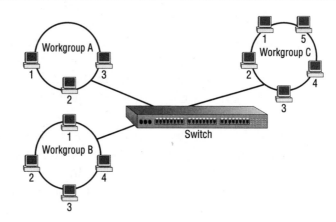

> **NOTE** Although switches are often used to connect LAN segments, you can connect an individual PC to one if you want to devote a large amount of bandwidth to a single power user or server.

Switching Methods

Most switches use one of two methods to accomplish their mission: cut-through or store-and-forward. In *cut-through switching*, the switch only reads the MAC address in the frame to be switched. It starts forwarding the frame to the appropriate port on which that MAC address is to be found as soon as the switch knows where to send it—usually after only 20-30 bytes of information have entered the switch. (Recall that an Ethernet frame has about 1500 bytes of information in it, so this pause to inspect 30 bytes of the frame represents very little latency.) Thus, cut-through switching operates essentially at line speed.

Store-and-forward, a function also found in bridges, receives the entire frame and then inspects it to determine its destination

MAC address and checks the frame for errors. Only frames that are in good shape get forwarded.

Figure 5.10 illustrates the difference between the two methods.

FIGURE 5.10:

The switching method you choose depends on whether it's more important for your network to be error free or very fast.

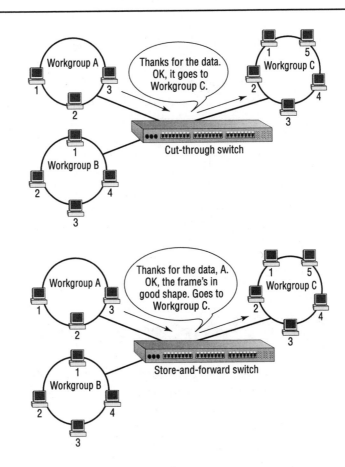

Which method is better? Cut-through switching is generally faster, as the frames can be shoved onto the appropriate segment as quickly as they arrive at the switch. However, this method carries the hazard of forwarding damaged frames and thus increasing network traffic with useless bits. Store-and-forward switching is slightly slower, as each frame must be inspected for errors before it's forwarded, but is less likely to propagate errors on the network. It's not slow, exactly, but there's a degree of latency found with store-and-forward switching not found with cut-through switching, and the larger the frame, the greater the delay. This is an issue that affects bridged networks as well.

Therefore, cut-through switches are best for networks that need high throughput more than they need to reduce the chance of error propagation; smaller, simpler networks can benefit from them. Store-and-forward switches may be necessary for more complex networks that can't take the chance of wasting time on garbage frames.

NOTE   Some switches support both methods. Ordinarily, they use cut-through switching and monitor error rates without storing the frames. If error rates exceed a predetermined tolerance, the switches change to store-and-forward switching.

Bridges Extend the Network

I mentioned earlier in "Switching Methods" that, like some switches, bridges do store-and-forward frame routing. The truth is that the line between bridging and switching can at times be annoyingly fuzzy. I distinguish them based on function. If the idea of *switching* is to separate one network into separate (but still connected) segments, the idea of *bridging* is to combine separate networks into one. More precisely, bridging permits communication between two (or more) distinct networks while still keeping their traffic separate (see Figure 5.11).

FIGURE 5.11:

Bridges permit commu-
nication between like
networks.

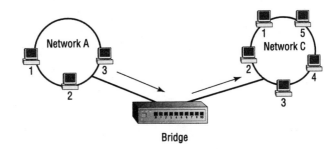

Bridge

Bridges are protocol independent. Typically, they don't care whether the transport protocol is IPX or TCP/IP. As long as the bridge can read the source address and the destination address of the packet, it can determine whether to filter or forward the packet.

NOTE   Just to drive home the point about the blurring boundaries between types of networking hardware, some bridges can discriminate between packets using a particular transport protocol (such as IPX versus IP). Generally speaking, however, bridging is a data link layer operation.

The examples here will discuss Ethernet bridging for the most part unless otherwise stated, but most principles apply as well to Token Ring networks.

How Do Bridges Work?

Every time a frame is broadcast on a bridged network, the bridge, like every other device on the network, "hears" the broadcast and can read the MAC address of the frame's destination. Based on this information, the bridge determines whether the packet can be picked up by one of the machines on the local segment or if it is on another segment. In the first case, the bridge doesn't have to do anything; the PC for which the frame was intended has already picked it up. If the packet's destination is on another segment, it's forwarded to that segment. The only exceptions to this are broadcast and multicast frames; that is, frames that are either sent to the entire network or to more than one recipient. Those frames are sent to all ports of the bridge.

> **NOTE** Sending packets to all connected segments is called *bridge flooding*. Some flooding is intentional; some is accidental and should be avoided.

How does this work in practice? There are a couple of different bridging methods, so let's start with the simplest—one used on Ethernet networks. This method is called *transparent bridging*.

Let's assume you have two Ethernet networks with a bridge between them. If you want to send information from Node A on Segment 1 to Node B on Segment 2, the process looks like this:

1. Node A broadcasts a packet across the network.

2. When that packet gets to the bridge, the bridge looks at the source address and the destination address of the packet.

3. If this packet is destined for another workstation on the same segment of the network upon which it originated (the same side of the bridge), then the bridge will not broadcast the packet to Segment 2. This process, known as *filtering*, is illustrated in Figure 5.12.

FIGURE 5.12:

Frames are filtered (dropped) if their destination is on the local segment.

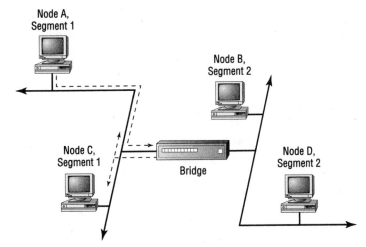

Filtering: If the bridge determines that the packet's destination is in the same segment where it originated, then it broadcasts only to that segment.

4. However, if the packet is destined for the other segment of the network (as in this example), the bridge will then forward it to that segment of the network, across the bridge, as illustrated in Figure 5.13.

FIGURE 5.13:

Frames are forwarded if their destination addresses are not on the local segment.

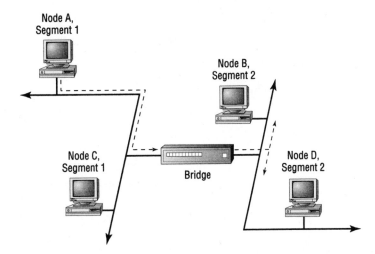

Forwarding: If a packet's destination is not on the same segment from which it originated, the bridge forwards it to the other network segment.

How does the bridge know whether a physical address is located on the local segment? The answer lies in the way that network cards resolve hardware addresses to software ones. Recall that there are a couple of different layers of network addresses: the physical ones that apply to network cards and which the network understands, and the logical ones needed by upper-layer networking operations that wouldn't know a 48-bit Ethernet address if they tripped over it. For example, a PC running the TCP/IP protocol to send data to a particular node on the network will need some method of mapping the logical addresses to the hardware addresses.

This mapping is done with a method of discovery that may use one of several protocols depending on the network-layer transport protocol in use. For example, TCP/IP uses the Address Resolution Protocol (ARP), but all perform pretty much the same function. The first time that a networked PC running TCP/IP tries to send data over the network after being rebooted, it has to map the IP address the networking software understands to the MAC address that the network will understand. So, in anticipation of sending out the data, the node broadcasts an ARP REQUEST packet over the network with an IP address. The node with that address (each node must know its own IP address) will respond with a REPLY ARP packet of its own containing its physical address. Once the requesting node gets the reply, it adds the mapping to its ARP table and discards the packet.

The clever bit to this lies in what happens when the bridge forwards the ARP request to all other segments; as it's a broadcast, it's automatically forwarded. Before sending the packet on its merry way, the bridge inserts its own MAC address in the sender's space of the packet so that it gets the replies back. When it does, the bridge adds the mapping to its own MAC table. If another ARP request changes the first mapping, the bridge will update the table.

Bridging Standards

If your network grows, you may need to start adding bridges, and simple transparent bridging won't work anymore. Multiple bridges can expose you to *bridge looping* in which two copies of a packet get to a bridge and confuse it. The difficulty is that the bridge doesn't know which segment the original packet came from and therefore cannot accurately update its MAC tables. The problem arises when more than one path lies between two segments. For example, say that PC Aries is located on Segment Andromeda, which has two bridges on it: Bridge Gamma and Bridge Beta. Bridge Gamma connects to Segment Cassiopeia, and Beta to Segments Bonham and Cassiopeia. See Figure 5.14; this is going to get complicated.

FIGURE 5.14:

Multiple bridges and segments can lead to bridge looping.

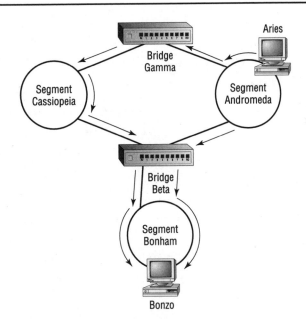

Now, the first time after booting when PC Aries sends a packet to PC Bonzo on Segment Bonham, things are going to get tricky.

Segment Andromeda has two bridges, neither of which has heard of Aries since boot-up. So, they're going to get involved in the ARP discovery broadcast and both flood their segments with Aries' packet to Bonzo. This is bad for two reasons:

- Bonzo gets two copies of Aries' ARP packet (and any future packets), which wastes bandwidth.

- More seriously, Bridge Beta "hears" Aries' ARP packet from two directions: Segment Andromeda and Segment Cassiopeia. Therefore, it can't tell which segment Aries is on so that it can have a correct entry in its MAC tables.

To prevent Beta from going into an electronic nervous breakdown, some kind of logical ordering of the bridges is necessary, and that's where bridging algorithms come in. These algorithms organize network traffic so each packet sent on the network has only one path available to reach its destination.

Spanning Tree Algorithm

The *spanning tree algorithm* (STA) permits bridges to establish a best route to reach a given segment and then blocks off any other possible routes that are less desirable. If only one path is available to each segment, then a bridge can't loop.

Under STA, each bridge is identified on the network according to its MAC address. In addition, each port has a three-part identifier created by the network administrator: its priority, cost, and identifying number. This information allows flexibility in the network, as one path will be preferred. If the preferred path is interrupted, other less efficient paths will still be available.

NOTE *Cost* is a function of the number of hops a packet would have to make to reach its destination. Fewer hops mean a lower cost.

When the network powers up, all the bridges broadcast Bridge Protocol Data Units (BPDUs) containing information about their addresses and relative priority until one bridge is recognized as having the lowest priority and becomes the *root bridge*. (If two bridges have the same low priority, then the bridge with the lowest MAC address becomes the root bridge.) All other bridges define themselves in relation to the root bridge; this algorithm uses a tree logical topology (see Figure 5.15).

FIGURE 5.15:

The spanning tree algorithm prioritizes paths according to their efficiency.

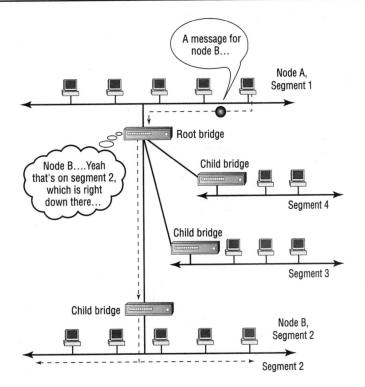

In addition to one bridge becoming the root bridge, one port of each bridge becomes the root port, chosen based on the cost of its connection to the root bridge. Once again, if two ports have the same path cost to the root bridge, then the port with the lowest priority is made the root port, or *forwarding port,* for that bridge. Thus, every segment of the network has identified a lowest-cost path to the root bridge, and this is the path used unless it's unavailable. Other possible paths are blocked (that is, the ports don't transmit packets) until such time as the path using the forwarding port is unavailable. Then, the bridge may set a blocked port (chosen for its low cost or high priority) to the forwarding state.

As most of the parameters of the spanning tree algorithm are hand set (the port number, port priority, and path cost), it's very important that you choose your paths carefully when configuring the bridges. Be sure to figure out the most efficient paths. If you're not careful, you can end up sending packets to their destination by way of segments they never needed to traverse, which won't exactly hurt anything but will cause unnecessary traffic on those segments.

Source-Route Bridging

The spanning tree algorithm is semi-static; it is only updated when paths are found to be dysfunctional. Source routing (SR), originally developed by IBM for use on bridged Token Ring networks, is more like routing than bridging in that it dynamically does path discovery based on packets broadcast to the network. Based on the information garnered during route discovery, nodes identify the best path to a given destination and store a record of that path for their own use.

Network nodes learn the path to their destinations in one of two ways:

- All-paths broadcast routing
- Spanning tree broadcast routing

Both of these methods operate to collect data about the logical structure of the network.

All-Paths Discovery A node configured for all-paths broadcast routing starts the process of route discovery by broadcasting multiple all-routes explorer (ARE) or all-paths explorer (APE) frames. They're the same thing; the distinction lies mostly in whether you'd rather talk about "APE frames" or "ARE frames" when discussing source routing methods. Each of these ARE frames takes a different path to get to its destination.

As each frame traverses a bridge, the bridge appends the packet with the following:

- The *incoming ring* from which the packet arrived (recall that source routing is for Token Ring networks)
- The segment and bridge identifiers
- The *outgoing ring* to which the packet will go on the way to its final destination

As shown in Figure 5.16, after the bridge adds this information to the packet, the bridge sends the ARE packet again on its merry way. It intentionally floods all ports with AREs so that multiple packets may appear on the network.

FIGURE 5.16:

All-routes exploration floods the network with discovery packets.

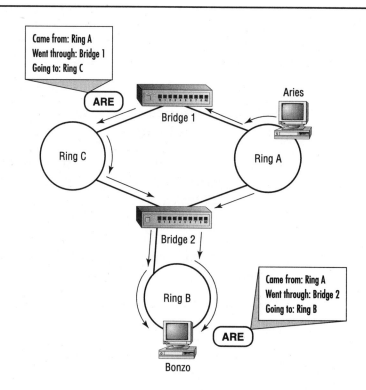

This process is continued until the ARE packet arrives at its final destination. Thus, each ARE packet includes a unique path from the source to the destination.

Spanning Tree Broadcast Routing Spanning tree broadcast routing (STBR) takes a tack for route discovery similar to that of the STA. The node seeking the route generates a spanning tree explorer (STE) frame, but in this case the frame is only forwarded on active ports—those that are blocked do not forward the packet. Thus, only a single STE frame is on the network, following a single predetermined path, as illustrated in Figure 5.17. Essentially, it's STA for Token Ring networks.

FIGURE 5.17:

Spanning tree
broadcast routing
packets follow a
single path to
their destination.

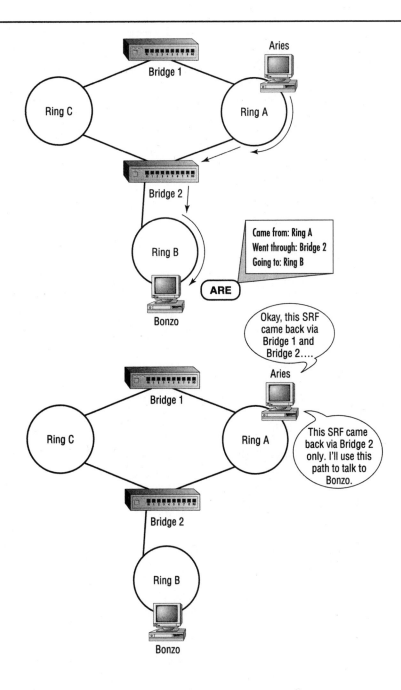

> **NOTE** If the bridged network is looped, then the bridge that sent the packet along in the first place will also receive a copy of the ARE packet. In this case, the bridge will discard the packet, rather than forwarding it again.

The main differences between STBR and STA lie in the network type (STA runs on Ethernet and STBR on Token Ring) and in the recipient of the information. With STA, the nodes are not responsible for routing packets; it's done automatically depending on how the network administrator sets port cost and priority.

Specifically Routed Frames In either case, what's happening here is that when a particular network node needs to communicate with another for the first time since reboot, the node sends out the data to be sent with discovery extensions. However, when a node receives its ARE or STE packets, the job is not yet done—the sending node still has no idea of how the packets got there, or what is the best route.

Thus, when a node gets an ARE or STE frame, it responds with a specifically routed frame (SRF). This means that STEs generate a single response and AREs generate as many responses as there are AREs. Each SRF contains the routing information of the explorer packet that it's responding to. The SRF is returned to the original sender of the explorer frame, which evaluates the paths in each SRF it receives and caches the preferred path for all future communication with that particular node. This process is shown in Figure 5.18.

FIGURE 5.18:

Source-route (SR)
bridging controls
traffic at the node
level, not the
bridge level.

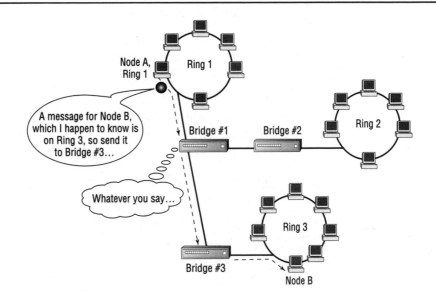

NOTE   As packets sent on an SR network carry a "road map" with them, they
may vary in size depending on the size of the road map, which may be
up to 18 bytes long. It takes two bytes of information to name a
bridge and port, and the original port must be in the road map. The
road map may be no more than seven hops long.

SR bridging isn't used as often as transparent bridging (discussed next) or STA bridging for a couple of reasons. First, as you
can see, it generates a lot of traffic. Perhaps more importantly,
Token Ring simply doesn't have the installed user base that Ethernet does. Because source routing is done on Token Ring and FDDI
LANs, more demand for Ethernet creates less demand for source
routing. That said, source routing does have the advantage of
flexibility, allowing route choosing in a manner more like that
used by routers than that of STA.

Transparent Bridging

Ethernet LANs use STA. Token Ring LANs use SR. STA depends on bridges to know which port to send a packet with a given destination address to. SR bridges have to know nothing about routing instructions—they just forward the packet based on the mapping that the sending node included in the packet. Can Ethernet and Token Ring LANs communicate, or are they doomed to mutual incomprehensibility?

The two bridging types can communicate, with a combination of a variant of the spanning tree algorithm and protocol conversion. The spanning tree determines which ports are set up for this cross-cultural communication, and the packets sent over those ports are converted to a format comprehensible on the new network type.

Earlier in this chapter under "Spanning Tree Algorithm," I discussed how the spanning tree operates. This instance of it works alongside the spanning tree already in place for Ethernet-only communications, not replacing it. Each bridge's ports may be configured to be in the blocking state, the forwarding state, or the forwarding-and-converting state.

Converting packets from the 802.2 Ethernet to 802.2 Token Ring isn't difficult. As shown in Figure 5.19, the two frame types are nearly identical, except that where the Token Ring frame has a variable-length routing information field (RIF), the Ethernet frame has a fixed-length Length field. This is because it contains no routing information. When a packet is passed to a port in the forwarding-and-converting state, the field is converted to match the requirements of the destination domain.

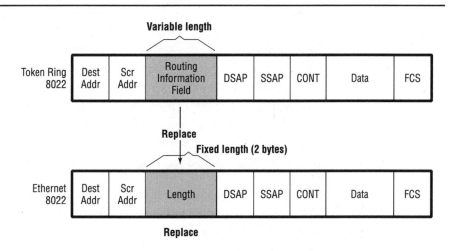

FIGURE 5.19:

Translating Ethernet
and Token Ring packets

If the Ethernet network uses 802.3 packets instead of 802.2, the process is a bit more complicated and slightly different. Regardless, the idea remains generally the same—the packet's routing information (or lack thereof) is edited as needed to be passed along the new network type.

Where do the translation bridges get the information they need to convert the packets? Two databases store the addresses needed. A *forwarding database* contains the list of addresses that require packet forwarding to be accessed. For example, an entry might mean "To reach address 12345, send the packet to Port A." A routing information field (RIF) database contains routing information for all workstations on the network, no matter which side of the translation bridge they're on. To continue the previous example, an entry might mean "To reach address 67890, send the packet to Port A, then Port D, then Port C." The two bridges are updated when the translation bridge learns an address on the SR side, adding the routing information to the RIF database, and the address and port information to the forwarding database.

The information stored in the two databases doesn't remain static; the exact interval at which old information is discarded to be replaced with new depends on how the bridge is configured. If a timer is set, say, for 15 minutes, then every time an address is confirmed (when the translation bridge receives a packet from a specific address, for example), then the timer for that address is restarted. That is, entries are not automatically deleted when they expire. Only those addresses that have not been confirmed for a while will be discarded.

Thus, the two bridge types still work as expected. The STA side still pushes packets in the direction of the port that will get them to their final destination. The SR side still keeps a roadmap that it can affix to packets to help them find their final destination. When an SR frame is moved to the STA side, its routing field is removed, and when an STA frame is moved to the SR side, it's given its routing roadmap.

Routers to Link Networks

Routers are network layer devices that can link networks with a common routable networking protocol. If you've got a dial-up connection to the Internet, you've got one view of how packets are transferred on a routed network. Using some variant of Windows? When configuring the dial-up connection, you had to specify the default gateway. This default gateway is, in fact, a router. You don't send packets directly to an address, but broadcast them on your local network. As will be described shortly in "Gateway to Your Mainframe," the default gateway decides whether the packet is addressed to a node on the local network or not. If it is, then the router ignores it. If it isn't, then the router forwards it to the next network, where the same thing happens until the packet locates and reaches the network that is its final destination.

> **NOTE**   As routers connect multiple networks, the nomenclature can get a little tricky. All the networks connected by routers are collectively called an *internetwork*, with the Internet being the best-known example of one.

Before I begin, there are a couple of points that need clarifying. First, in this section, I'll focus mainly on TCP/IP routing as that's the most commonly used protocol. Second, the term "router" refers to a machine that performs the tasks described in the following pages. This machine may be a black box with blinking lights (a hardware router) or it may be a computer with multiple network cards installed and running an operating system such as Windows NT that supports routing (a software router). In either case, the basic functions remain the same.

How Does Routing Work?

As shown in Figure 5.20, all communication on an internetwork is based on routers, not on individual nodes, as opposed to a bridged network in which communication is based on individual addresses and the bridges provide the information needed to help the packet get to its final destination. Each area of a network subdivided with routers is called a *segment* on the entire network.

FIGURE 5.20:

Routers connect two separate networks, or segments of a single network, while bridges extend a single network.

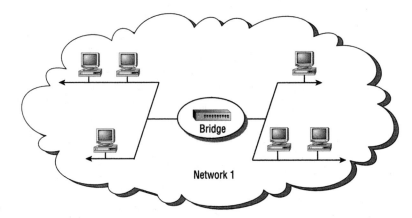

A bridge connects two segments of one network.

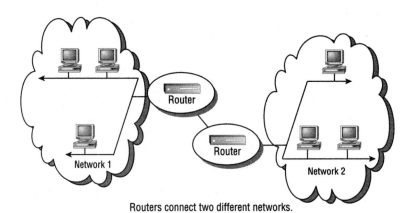

Routers connect two different networks.

To take a simple example, when Node Argus on Segment 1 wants to send data to Node Cameron on Segment 3, the process goes something like this:

1. Argus broadcasts his data on his local segment, where it is heard by all other nodes on the segment. It is also heard by Router 1, the segment's default gateway.

> **NOTE** A network may have more than one router connection to other networks, but one router will be defined as the default gateway and that router will handle data transmittal. The only exception to this rule is if the default gateway isn't working properly, in which case the alternate (if an alternate is defined) will kick in.

2. Router 1 examines the destination address in the packet and compares it to its *routing table*, a list of addresses located on the local segment. It asks itself, "Is this packet for someone here?" As the answer is "no," Router 1 puts the packet back together and routes it to Segment 2, the next segment, making the packet an SEP (Somebody Else's Problem).

3. When the packet is broadcast on Segment 2, Router 2 hears the broadcast and examines the destination address of the packet. Again, the destination address is not located on Segment 2, so Router 2 repackages the packet and sends it on to Segment 3.

4. On Segment 3, the same thing happens, but this time, Router 3, Segment 3's default gateway, finds the destination address in its routing table. At this point, the packet is no longer Router 3's responsibility. The packet was broadcast on the segment. Node Cameron heard it and collected it, and everybody's happy.

In the previous example, the routing decisions were pretty simple. Each segment had one router that was connected to one other segment, so the data were able to travel in a straight line to their destination. Many routed networks aren't that simple, however. The Internet is a perfect example of an enormously complicated routed network.

Therefore, routing on a complex network needs to solve a couple of problems:

- If more than one path from the source to the final destination is available, which one is chosen?

- How is routing information obtained, and who's responsible for storing it?

Read on to find out how routers resolve these problems.

Finding the Best Path

One of the crucial points of routing networks is providing traffic control. Certainly, packets will be broadcast on some segments other than the one with the final destination in the interests of minimizing network traffic. After all, more than one node on a network is transmitting data at any given time. It's best to find a short path or a fast one, so as to clear the network as quickly as possible. In order to find the path with the least number of hops, a packet's path may change in midstream to compensate for changes in network traffic or availability. It's not like bridging, in which a path is predetermined at the beginning of data transmittal and, by golly, that path is going to be used for the entire transmission no matter how tied up it is. Routing is flexible.

For example, say that Node Argus is attempting to communicate with Node Diana, located on Network 5 (see Figure 5.21). To get from Network 1 to Network 5, the packets must hop through Routers 1-4.

FIGURE 5.21:

The original path between Argus and Diana

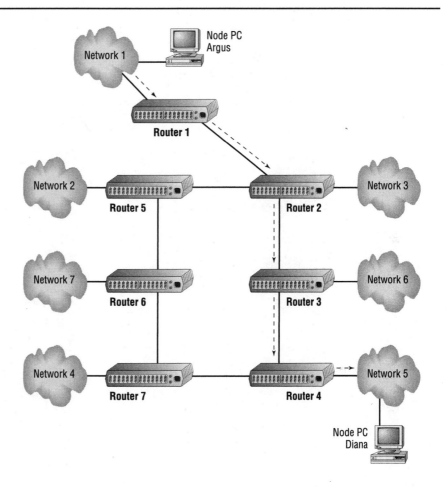

However, when the packet gets to Router 2, Router 2 might take a look at the situation and observe, "Well, I could pass this packet along to Router 3, but 3's looking pretty harried right now. Why don't I pass it along to Router 5 instead and hope that that path works out?" This alternate path (shown in Figure 5.22) actually requires more hops, but is more efficient than the original path would have been because it doesn't send packets to a router that's already busy.

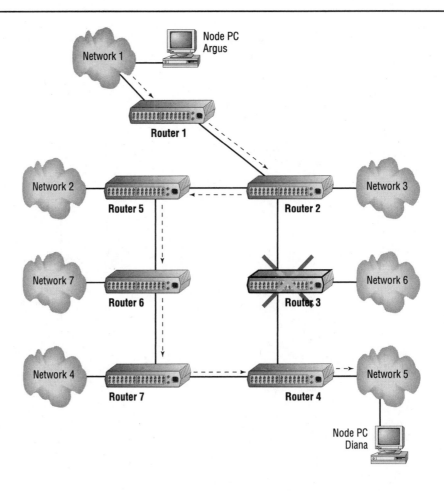

FIGURE 5.22:

An alternate path between Argus and Diana

All this said, routing can potentially take a little bit longer than bridging because of its flexibility. The reason is simple: if the state of the network must be evaluated each time a packet hits a router, then the time it takes to make that evaluation must be added to the packet's travel time. This is a worthy trade-off; if a router can evaluate network conditions to reduce unnecessary network traffic, or to find the least busy path between source and destination, then it's all to the good of overall network performance. However, that latency means that it's generally a good idea to keep the number of hops to a minimum.

Who's Minding the Store?

What information goes into determining the path a packet takes to reach its destination, and who's responsible for choosing that path? The answers depend on how the network's set up and what is supported by the network type and hardware.

Routing information can be either node based, with the initial path determined by information stored on the sending node, or router based, with the path determined by information stored on the network routers.

NOTE   TCP/IP networks support node-based routing; IPX/SPX networks do not.

Node-Based Routing To send a packet on a network using node-based routing, first the node must reconcile the recipient node's name (for example, Argus) with its internetwork address (for example, 12.45.2.15), using a table obtained from a server holding a list of name/address mappings. In a TCP/IP network, this table would be a Domain Name Service (DNS) server. The internetwork address identifies the network on which the destination node is located, as well as an individual locator for the node itself once the network is found.

Once the internetwork address has been determined, or *resolved*, the host compares the network portions of its own address and that of the destination. In the case of a TCP/IP network, it would run the destination address through its own subnet mask as described in Chapter 3, "Networking Protocols and Application Programming Interfaces." If the source and destination are on the same network, then the source can send the packet directly to the destination.

If they're not on the same network, the node has two options:

- Send the packet to a router on the network and let the router take things from there

- Supply a complete path to the network destination

In the first case, the host will send the packet to an intermediate router, choosing this router (if more than one is available) by one of several means, described in Table 5.1.

TABLE 5.1: How Hosts Can Find Routers

Method	Description	More Information
Static routing table	Each host maintains a list of all routers and the ones that should be chosen to reach certain networks.	This method is fast, but large internetworks require a large table. It's also not easily updated in the case of changes to the network.
Dynamically updated routing table	The TCP/IP suite includes a protocol that allows routers to periodically update the host routing tables with the information in their own tables.	When routers discover a better path to a particular destination, they send a message to the nodes on their network, allowing the hosts to update their tables.
Eavesdropping	Some networks support a routing information protocol that allows nodes to collect data without broadcasting any.	Windows NT networks use Silent RIP for this functionality.
Default gateway	A node may have a certain router designated as the default gateway to be used for all internetwork communications.	If more than one default gateway is assigned for reasons of fault tolerance, the second one takes over only if the first is not functioning.
Network query	When a node is ready to send a packet, it broadcasts a message to the network, asking the best route to the given destination.	All routers on the network will respond to the query, and based on the responses, the node will choose one router to use.

Although not often done, it can be technically possible for a node to supply not only the router to send a packet to, but an entire path from source to destination. This is known as *source routing*. In IP source routing, for example, the sending node specifies the entire route to take by providing the internetwork addresses of the routers that should be used. At each router, the destination address of the IP datagram is updated to that of the next router to which it will be sent.

Supplying a complete path to each destination on the network is much more difficult than supplying a path to a router that should be able to route the packet on its way. The source node must either already know the path to take or perform path discovery, as in SR bridging. The router's only role in such a situation is bridge-like; it's responsible for storing and forwarding packets, but has no input into their path.

NOTE   Source routing (SR) bridging and node-based source routing are not identical, as source routing relies on data link layer MAC addresses and the routing described in this section relies on network-layer IP or IPX addresses.

As source routing of this kind is traffic intensive and slow, it's not often done except as a troubleshooting measure when the network administrator is attempting to find a downed router or other part of the network.

Router-Based Routing Even node-based routing generally has to get the routers involved in some way. Once a packet has left the sending node, the router is in charge of making sure that the packet gets where it's supposed to go. If the destination node is on the network to which the router is attached, the job is easy— the router addresses the packet to the destination node and all is well. If not, then the router must consult its routing table to choose the router to which it's connected that looks like the best bet for getting that packet where it's going. Routers build their tables through a process of discovery.

Using Routing Tables

A routing table may contain either path information for getting to a specific network on the internetwork, or a specific node on the internetwork. A routing table may also potentially contain default routes, to be used when no other path is available. This saves routers and hosts from having to maintain explicit instructions for getting to every possible destination on the network—if a path is not specified, then the default is used.

Table 5.2 lists the information normally found in a routing table. The field names may not match those in your routing table, but the information remains the same.

TABLE 5.2: Routing-Table Information

Entry	Description
Network ID	If the entry is for a network, contains the network address. If for a specific node, contains the internetwork address for that node.
Subnet mask	In an IP network, contains a 32-bit number used to identify the network and distinguish it from other networks.
Forwarding address	Contains either the address to which packets sent to that node or network are to be forwarded, or is blank if the node or network is connected to the router. The address may be either a physical or network layer address.
Interface	Identifies the port that will be used to forward those packets, either by hardware number or network layer address.
Metric	Indicates the preference for a specific route so that if more than one route exists, the lowest-cost route may be used. As the metric is a function of the cost of a route, the lower the metric, the more likely the route will be used. Metrics may be calculated in one of several ways: hop count, delay (a function of the speed of the path or the degree of congestion), the effective throughput for a path, or the path's reliability.
Lifetime	Used with routes that dynamically update each other's information. Indicates how long the listed path is considered valid before expiring so that the routers may reconfigure themselves to match the network. This column won't be visible in the routing table.

If you're running a Windows machine on a TCP/IP network, you can examine the routing table for your computer by typing **route print** at the command prompt, as shown in Figure 5.23.

FIGURE 5.23:

Output of the route print command showing local routing tables

Network Address	Netmask	Gateway Address	Interface	Metric
0.0.0.0	0.0.0.0	24.48.12.136	24.48.12.136	1
24.0.0.0	255.0.0.0	24.48.12.136	24.48.12.136	1
24.48.12.136	255.255.255.255	127.0.0.1	127.0.0.1	1
24.255.255.255	255.255.255.255	24.48.12.136	24.48.12.136	1
127.0.0.0	255.0.0.0	127.0.0.1	127.0.0.1	1
224.0.0.0	224.0.0.0	24.48.12.136	24.48.12.136	1
255.255.255.255	255.255.255.255	24.48.12.136	0.0.0.0	1

Building Routing Tables

I've discussed how hosts build their routing tables, but the routing demands placed on a host are fairly simple. Generally, all a host must do is know where to find the router connecting it to the internetwork. For routing to work properly, the routers must know about each other. Individual routers make themselves known to the rest of the WAN by a process known as *advertising*.

Every time a router enters the network environment, it advertises to the other routers its address and the networks to which it is attached. In doing so, it is essentially telling all the other routers, "Hello! I'm Router A. If you are trying to get to networks 1, 2, or 3, I can get you there." Once the router broadcasts this information to the other routers, the other routers add this information to their routing tables. As you can see in Figure 5.24, as more routers enter the picture, each router's routing table gets larger.

FIGURE 5.24:

Router advertising helps other routers figure out how to direct traffic.

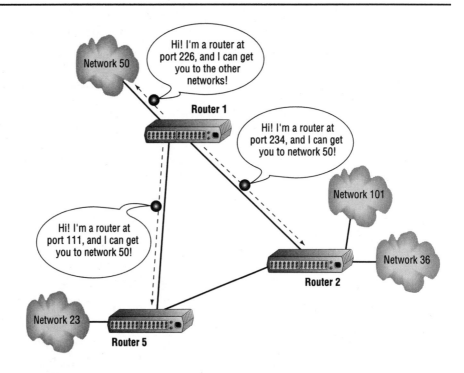

Routers will continue to announce their presence at intervals after their first appearance on the networking scene. If any changes (such as downed ports) take place, then the other routers will edit their routing tables to reflect the change in the internetwork's logical structure. Otherwise, any repeats of earlier announcements such as, "I'm still Router A and I can *still* get you to networks 1, 2, or 3," are ignored.

The format and content of routing tables is determined by any of various routing protocols that regulate how routing tables are generated. The protocols also keep track of particulars such as how the table is constructed, what type of information is kept in it, and how each router interacts with other routers. There are several routing algorithms out there, but I'll stick with a couple of the ones you're most likely to encounter in a LAN: RIP and OSPF.

The Routing Information Protocol (RIP) The oldest routing protocol still in use is called the Routing Information Protocol (RIP). Although described in some documents as being obsolete, it's still in wide use on small networks; Windows NT machines configured for IP routing support RIP.

By default, routers supporting RIP announce their current status to the rest of the network every 30 seconds. Routes to a given network (identified by network number and subnet mask) not otherwise updated are assumed to be valid for up to 180 seconds, the timeout period. If a route times out, it's not immediately removed from the routing table. Instead, six updates—nine minutes—must occur before the route is finally removed from the routing table. Similarly, when new routes are announced, they don't immediately supersede similar routes already defined in the routing table. If the route isn't already defined, it's immediately added. If the route already existed in the routing table, then the replacement with the new route is delayed a certain interval (to confirm it). The length of this interval depends on whether the route was already timed out or still valid. Routes with the same metric but defining a different path won't ordinarily replace an existing route unless that route was in the process of timing out anyway.

Therefore, routers aren't always operating with the most up-to-date information. Although this isn't necessarily the end of the world, sometimes it's less than ideal. Delay in confirmed information can be especially critical when a route is lost or very congested.

Thus, two kinds of changes to the routing structure must be announced as soon as they happen: route deletions and increases in a route's metric—an increase in a route's cost. When either of these events occur, the router in question makes a *triggered update*. Triggered updates will include all information that's changed since the last regular update, but, to save bandwidth, won't include any information that hasn't changed. In this, they differ from regularly scheduled updates, which are a complete broadcast of all routing information, changed or not.

All this broadcasting, updating, and triggering sounds like a traffic nightmare waiting to happen, and it is. Therefore, as illustrated in Figure 5.25, the current implementation of RIP prevents routers from broadcasting information more than one router away. After that, the update packets expire. This doesn't keep routers several hops away from one another from updating each other's routing tables, as the routers still share their complete routing tables. However, it takes a while for Router 5 to get updated with the contents of Router 10 as the updates trickle down from Router 10's network in a bucket brigade of data.

FIGURE 5.25:

RIP routing only allows routers to update the routers next to them in the internetwork.

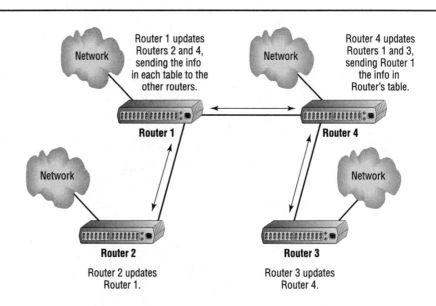

Open Shortest Path First (OSPF) OSPF announces itself with a Hello packet as each router on an internetwork starts up, and at regular intervals afterwards. The routers one hop away "hear" this Hello and collect the data. Similarly, the router announces its state at intervals to all the routers in the internetwork, which allows all the routers in the internetwork to determine which routers are functioning and how busy they are.

The other routers take this router status and route table information and run algorithms on it to determine *their* shortest path—or, more precisely, lowest-cost path—to a particular network, identified by both network number and subnet mask. Identifying the shortest path doesn't necessarily include detailing the entire path, but instead points to the router that should provide the lowest-cost path. If more than one valid path with the same metric is available, then the router will use all those paths, distributing traffic among them to even out network usage. This is in contrast to RIP, which maintains only one path from each source to each destination.

Notice that although routers only share their routing tables with the routers adjacent to them, they share their state with the entire internetwork. To keep traffic down, routers using OSPF can be divided into groups called *areas*. Network flooding is intra-area only, with backbone routers designated to forward route tables between areas, as shown in Figure 5.26. Secondary area routers connect each area to the backbone, which maintains a logical tree shape.

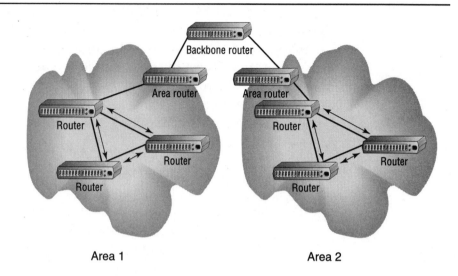

As each router is only supposed to identify the shortest path to
its destination, the backbone router must maintain more than one
version of the routing algorithm. Obviously, the shortest path in
one case will not be the shortest path in another. The results of
processing the information through the algorithm are then passed
to the appropriate area.

Gateway to Your Mainframe

Most people reading this book won't have to worry about mainframe connections, but if you do then you'll need a device called
a *gateway*. Gateways have a more complex job than either bridges
or routers. Bridges simply take your packet information, look at
the source and destination addresses, and then pass the information to the proper location. Routers look at the packet information
and pass the packet from router to router, changing the source and
destination data-link addresses along the way, but not changing

any of the other information inside the packet. Gateways can effectively transform the information from one protocol standard to another one. Gateways handle data transfer between networks using disparate protocols in one of two ways: *tunneling* and *terminal emulation*.

Connecting with Protocol Tunneling

The most common method and the least processor-intensive is *tunneling*. It is the means by which the gateway transfers packets by taking the information from the first network in one format, wrapping it in a mutually intelligible format, and transferring it to the other network using the other format. Conceptually, tunneling looks like interoffice mail. If you've got a memo circulating in your main office that Tom in the branch office needs to see, you can't just drop the memo in the mail by itself. The addressing system used on the memo (To: and From:) works fine within the office, but the post office won't know what to do with it. Thus, you've got to package the memo in an envelope—a mutually intelligible format, one that you, the post office, and the branch office can all understand. Once the envelope gets to the branch office, it gets routed to Tom, he strips off the outer envelope, and there's your memo.

For example, let's say I want to send a Novell IPX packet from my PC network to a Macintosh machine on an AppleTalk network. Both NetWare and AppleTalk understand TCP/IP, so I can use it to transport the information. To get the IPX packet to the Mac network, the PC network encapsulates the packet within a TCP/IP "envelope," and sends the packet over to the Mac. Once it's there, the Mac can strip off the TCP/IP envelope and get to the actual packet. Note that the Mac must still do some kind of data conversion to put the PC data in a form that it can understand. Conversion is not the gateway's problem; once the data is transferred from the PC network to the Mac network, the gateway's job is done. You can see how tunneling works in Figure 5.27.

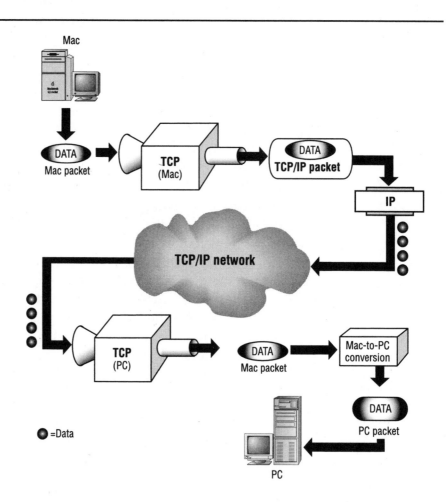

Connecting with Terminal Emulation

Another gateway method of data transfer is called *terminal emulation*. Mainframes were not originally designed to talk to PCs; they're used to communicating with dumb terminals. Thus, when a PC needs to communicate with a mainframe, it must pretend to be a dumb terminal for the duration of the conversation. There are two methods of terminal emulation: terminal emulation cards and emulation software, such as Reflection or Attachmate.

There are two ways to implement terminal emulation successfully in a network environment: PC emulation cards and gateway servers. In the first case, you can insert a terminal emulation card into every PC that needs access to the mainframe. This can be hard to configure correctly. As you can see in Figure 5.28, you are now putting two communication cards in a system that may need to access the mainframe and network simultaneously, which can lead to hardware conflicts and hanging problems. This is also an expensive option.

FIGURE 5.28:

Using individual terminal emulation cards to access a mainframe

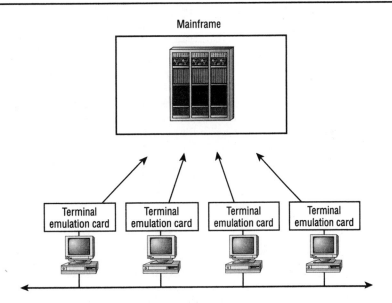

Putting a terminal emulation card in each computer on the network is an expensive and problem-prone option.

Alternatively, you can assign a PC to handle all the emulation for the network so that this PC becomes the gateway server. The terminal emulation card(s) will reside in this machine, as illustrated in Figure 5.29. Users will access the gateway server and the mainframe by using terminal emulation software located on each workstation.

FIGURE 5.29:

Using terminal emulation software and a gateway machine to access a mainframe

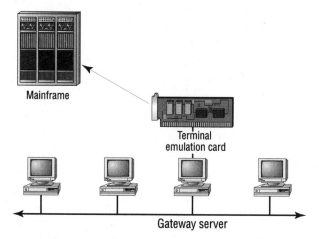

Mainframe

Terminal emulation card

Gateway server

A terminal emulation card can be placed in one computer on the network, which will then serve as the network's gateway to the mainframe. Other computers can then access the mainframe via terminal emulation software.

Terminal emulation has three main drawbacks:

It's expensive.   You must purchase additional hardware or software to let your PCs communicate with the mainframes.

It's slow.   Any time that you've got one operating system pretending to be another one, it takes time.

The additional hardware or software exposes you to more equipment conflicts.   Not that terminal emulation cards are any more prone to conflicting than other cards, but your computer has only so many interrupts and DMA addresses available to it.

To get around these problems a little, you may want to consider using a gateway server—dedicating a machine to handle all the mainframe/PC communication. Even with a gateway server, you'll still run into these problems, but they'll be confined to one machine rather than to every PC that needs to access the mainframe. The machines connecting to the gateway server will still need emulation software, but they won't need their own emulation card.

Summary

As you can see, networking hardware is a complex subject. Unfortunately, it's also unavoidable. Even in the simplest networks, you'll often need a hub to provide connectivity between network nodes. As the networks become larger and more complicated, you'll need repeaters to extend the network's reach; switches for traffic control; bridges for traffic control and connectivity between Ethernet and Token Ring networks; and routers for traffic control, connectivity, and packet filtering. For this reason, you'll find many devices that combine the functionality of more than one device, such as combination hub/switches and bridge/routers.

The final aspect of your network's nervous system entails using some of the internetworking devices discussed in this chapter. Chapter 6 will take you on a tour of wide area networks, the networks most likely to use the router.

EXERCISE 5

1. You're attempting to link two LANs: one Ethernet and one Token Ring. What device do you need to accomplish this?

   A. A transparent bridge

   B. A router

   C. A source-routing bridge

   D. A switch

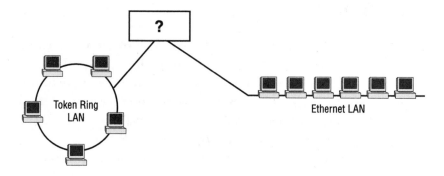

2. What capability do some switches share with bridges and what is its purpose?

EXERCISE 5 CONTINUED

3. The following diagram illustrates one method of router advertising. What is its full name?

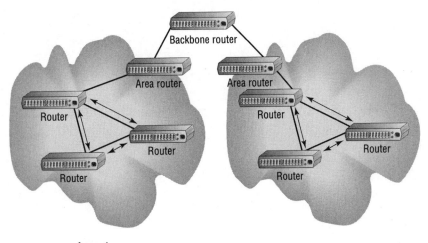

Area 1

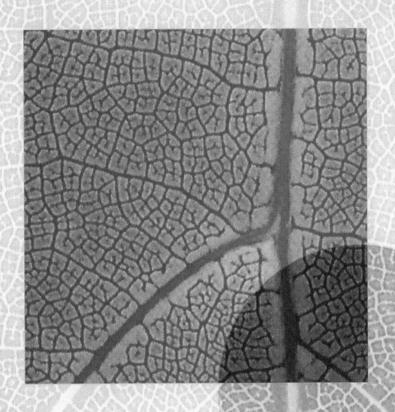

6

A Tour of Wide
Area Networks

Just as local area networking extends the reach of individual PCs, wide area networking extends the reach of local area networks. Not all networks will require wide-area connections, but if a permanent wide-area connection isn't necessary, even an intermittent connection can offer advantages, such as:

• Information sharing

• Improved communications via e-mail and online scheduling software

• Centralized backups and file protection

There's more. Almost every advantage a LAN offers can also be offered through a WAN—it's just extending the scope of your network. The advantages are limited mostly by speed, as, for reasons of expense, WAN communications typically run at a fraction of the speed offered by local area networks.

In Chapter 8, "Server Types and Additional Hardware," I'll be talking about some of the hardware that you can use to create a communications server, or provide any computer a direct connection to the outside world. For the moment, however, let's take a look at the technologies available to provide your network with wide-area capabilities, whether those capabilities offer point-to-point communications or worldwide private networking.

WAN Terminology

Although the terminology used to describe local area networking and wide area networking overlaps, there's some additional jargon to know. Also, some of the emphases are a little different once you're talking about a network extending across state lines instead of one ending in the next room.

Units of Data

Most current WAN technologies are described in terms of transmitting data in the form of *packets* that contain both data and addressing information. It helps to think of packets in the form of regular postal mail, in that:

- An envelope identifies the packet as a unit in the flow of correspondence, and marks it as a discrete chunk of data distinct from the other data being passed through the network

- The addressing information identifies the packet's recipient and (usually) the sender

- The addressing information comes first in the packet, with the data stored in the middle of the packet

The envelope, or the structure of the packet, puts the data into a format that the connection can understand. Just as a mail system meant to send FedEx packages won't know what to do with a UPS Ground letter, most connections require the data to come in some sort of standard format. The size of a given packet depends on the type of packet involved. *Frame relay networks*, for example, transmit packets called *frames* that may vary in size. *Cell relay networks*, such as the Switched Multimegabit Data Services (SMDS), transmit 53-byte *cells*.

NOTE   Not all packets are identical. As you'll see, different types of packet-switched networks include different information in their packets. For example, X.25 packets include error-checking information, but frame relay packets do not.

Just as with a LAN packet, for a WAN packet to get to its destination it needs some kind of addressing information—even if you broadcast the packet on every channel of the WAN, without a destination address the proposed recipient wouldn't be able to tell that the packet was for it. If some kind of acknowledgment is required, then the packet must also include the sender's address. Otherwise, the recipient just takes the packet and that's the end of it. An unacknowledged packet is called a *datagram*.

NOTE   Modern WAN connections use datagrams, as they're faster and in wide-area connections speed is critical. Older methods, to be used when communications are less reliable, will still use connection-oriented transmissions.

To the network doing the transmitting, the envelope type is crucial and so is the addressing information. However, no one cares about the format of the data being transmitted except the node that finally receives the packet and strips off the envelope and addressing information.

Packet Switching versus Circuit Switching

Packets are important because they're the basis of one WAN type: *packet-switched networks*. The method of switching used indicates how data finds its path from its source to its destination, like routing (described in Chapter 5).

Circuit-switched networks define a static path from one point to another. In a circuit-switched network, at the beginning of each transmission a connection between sender and recipient is established. This virtual path will be used for the duration of the session; all data traveling between sender and recipient will follow this path. Because only a single path is available, it's not necessary to include as much addressing information with the data, as the packets cannot get lost. Thus, the packets can be smaller, as less data is in them. The other result, however, is that once this virtual circuit is established it will be used for the duration, even if a more efficient path becomes available.

Packet switching, in contrast, is more like the routing described in Chapter 5, "Additional Networking Hardware," in that it does not establish a virtual circuit between sender and recipient. Rather than creating a single path, a packet-switched network is a mesh of switching points that can be used to send the data on its way. This means that there's a slight delay at each switching point as the most efficient path must be determined. This delay is not long by human standards, but it means that packet-switched networks don't deliver the same quality of transmission for real-time transmissions as do circuit-switched networks. If you've used voice over IP technology, you know that it doesn't sound as good as voice over the circuit-switched voice lines. Table 6.1 offers a comparison between the two routing methods.

TABLE 6.1: Packet Switching versus Circuit Switching

Network Feature	Packet Switching	Circuit Switching
Type of connection.	Connectionless.	Connection-oriented.
Static path or dynamic routing?	Does not use a predefined path for an entire session, but routes according to traffic levels.	Defines a static path between points for the duration of a session.
Contents of packets?	Includes routing information in data packets.	Includes addressing information in data packets.

Network Speed and Reliability

Nowhere is it written that WANs must be slower than LANs, but they almost always are because of the cost of high-speed links. A good WAN connection has a practical throughput of about 2Mbps—a far cry from the 100Mbps possible with a modern Ethernet network. This isn't necessarily a problem, so long as you don't ask your WAN to do more than it can handle, but it's something to be aware of.

Line speed is not necessarily an accurate measure of a WAN link's effectiveness. True network speed—*throughput*—is calculated from a combination of factors: available bandwidth and network speed. *Bandwidth* describes the size of the pipe, or the number of pipes available, and is the amount of data that can be squeezed into the pipe at one time. More contention for bandwidth leads to slower connections as packets must wait their turn, just as driving down a road will take more or less time depending on how much traffic is using the road at any given time.

Network speed is a function of how fast data travels through the pipe. As discussed in Chapter 1, "Basic Networking Concepts and Components," not all transmission media send data at the same speeds. The better a channel is protected from interference, the faster data can travel through it. This combination of bandwidth and speed determines throughput.

NOTE   Throughput is not always unidirectional. WAN technologies may be either *half duplex* or *full duplex*. These terms describe the flow of packets through the pipe. Half-duplex communications permit data to travel in one direction on the pipe at a time, whereas full-duplex communications permit data to travel upstream and down at the same time. Half-duplex communications have greater bandwidth (as channels can be combined), but full-duplex communications have greater flexibility.

Another function of the network is its reliability. If the channels through which the data passes are prone to interference, or if more data is squished into the pipe than the pipe can handle, then some packets may be lost.

Corruption due to interference is also a possible issue. Some sort of error control is needed to make sure that the data that arrives at point B is the same data that left point A, and that no data are missing. Recall that most modern WAN technologies transmit with datagrams, so that no receipts are sent to the original sender. How does the sender know when to resend packets, or how are errors corrected? Not all wide-area technologies use error control, but those designed for unreliable transmissions do.

Most error control involves methods collectively known as *cyclic redundancy checking* (CRC). Before a packet is transmitted, the sender runs a particular algorithm on the packet, using the packet's data and addressing information as variables in the equation. This algorithm and the expected result are included in the packet along with the rest of the packet's contents. When the destination node gets the packet, it runs the algorithm. If the answer it gets doesn't match the one included in the packet, then the packet's recipient sends a message to this effect back to the original sender. It then asks for a resending of the original packet. Notice that the recipient can't correct the packet—that's beyond the scope of CRC technologies. The check just allows the recipient to be sure that the data came through without corruption and to ask for a resend if necessary.

NOTE   CRCs make for highly reliable transmissions but reduce throughput by making bigger packets. Therefore, reliable communications such as these are reserved for networks that are not designed to be reliable on their own, such as the Internet or X.25 networks.

Frame Transmission versus Cell Transmission

I mentioned earlier under "Units of Data" that a packet—the "envelope" used in WAN transmittal—can take the form of either a cell or a frame. It's not news to you that different network types will use different packet organizations. Recall that Token Ring and Ethernet are mutually incompatible because their packets don't include quite the same information and what information *is* the same is organized differently. However, in the case of WANs, the differences are somewhat more profound. The differences in Token Ring and Ethernet are largely related to traffic control—of how to keep more than one node from talking at a time. WAN technologies, on the other hand, are concerned with the problem of how to make best use out of limited traffic space. The method they use influences the kinds of data that are best suited to a particular environment.

Framing Technologies Framing technologies are designed to squeeze as much throughput from available bandwidth as is possible. The idea is that most network transmissions are intermittent—bursty, to use the appropriate jargon. This is true of LAN transmissions as well as WAN transmissions. When working at your computer, most of the time you don't need the network all that much. Most network-accessible data can be stored or cached locally, so most of the time the wire lies idle. When you do use the network, you're apt to use it for only a brief period, and not use anything like all the available bandwidth in the network.

When you're talking about local area networks, the high network speeds make it acceptable for one person to hog the entire network for the duration of his or her transmission. This is possible because the duration simply isn't that long, and, if traffic problems crop up, the network can be subdivided to keep traffic down. However, the case is a little different with wide area networks. Generally speaking, they're both slower and more crowded than local area networks. Furthermore, having one LAN's node take over the entire WAN just to send e-mail is not acceptable behavior. Therefore, framing technologies mix the transmissions of everyone who's using the network into a jumble and send everything all at once. Once the data gets to the other end of the network, the data are sorted out and routed to their final destinations. The entire pipe is used at once and by more than one device. Thus, a network using framing technologies has an effective bandwidth significantly greater than that of the actual pipe itself, were the pipe to be in use on a local area network.

This method of transmission has a couple of implications. First, if at any given time more bandwidth is needed than is available, then some frames are crowded off the highway—dropped. Using a mechanism I'll discuss more in the upcoming section on frame relay, dropped frames are discovered and re-sent. Second, not all frames will arrive at their destination in the order in which they left. Because of these two issues, there's a third: data does not arrive at its destination in a nice smooth stream, but rather as it's ready and has been sorted out at the end of its ride across the framing network.

For most communications, this doesn't matter; a server can interpret a request for a file to be opened just as easily in scrambled order as in the original form. It *does* matter for real-time communications, however, and that's where cell relay technologies come in.

Cell Relay Technologies Rather than being designed to squeeze the most use out of available bandwidth, cell relay technologies are designed to transmit a variety of data as smoothly as possible. All data (textual, video, voice, and so on) transmitted over a cell relay network is split into 53-byte chunks called cells. Those cells are pushed over the network in a steady stream, with real-time data types, such as voice having first priority. When the data arrive at their destination, they arrive all at once and in the order in which they left.

Dial-Up Network Access

When you hear the term, "wide area networking," your first image may be one of those maps showing the main office in Chicago and branch offices around the country. However, not all wide area networking is a matter of connecting offices to each other. Sometimes, the connection is a bit more limited—a telecommuter who needs to pick up her office e-mail, or a salesman on the road who needs access to his customer database. If you need it while in the office, you can probably think of a reason to need it outside the office.

For those who can't afford a complex wide-area solution or who need something that provides more flexibility than a permanently wired wide area network can provide, some form of dial-up access can be useful. Today, there are three main options:

- Dial-up presence on the network (remote access)

- Remote control of a host computer

- Remote access to a computer running a multiuser operating system

All three options have three elements in common. First, the computer on the network end must have software installed that allows it to accept a telephone connection. This software is referred to as the *server element*. Second, the client computer, the one doing the dialing in, must have software installed on it that allows it to dial out and connect to another computer. This software is referred to as the *client element*. Third, the client must have installed not only a network protocol for communicating with the network once it's established the dial-up connection, but also an additional protocol called a *line protocol*. This is needed to connect to the dial-up server. This line protocol is either the Simple Line Internet Protocol (SLIP) or the Point-to-Point Protocol (PPP). In most cases, the server will support PPP, as it's the more efficient of the two and requires less user setup than does SLIP.

Dial-Up Security

I'll be discussing LAN and WAN security in Chapter 15, "Network Security." For the moment, understand that remote control and remote access open a couple of security cans of worms that are not an issue with LANs. This is because these capabilities make a private LAN part of an international and insecure network. If the problem isn't clear, think of this: hacking into a LAN not connected to the outside world requires physical access to the LAN. With remote control (or remote access, for that matter), physical access isn't required. Rather, physical access is easier to achieve because the entire telephone network is connected to the LAN. Considering how ubiquitous Internet access is nowadays, this isn't anything new, but it is something to think about. Remote access and remote control systems have some built-in capabilities that you can use to increase dial-up security, and you should use them.

Remote control systems have an additional security liability. They're giving a remote user access to a host computer and running applications on that host without knowing who's standing watching those applications run and those files displayed on the screen. The problem of people who don't mean to look but just happen to be wandering by can be avoided by turning off the monitor. To foil potential intruders on the host end, you'll need remote control software that doesn't display anything on the host end's monitor, just on the client. This isn't an issue for remote access systems as they're not using a computer on the network, but logging into the network separately. Similarly, it's not an issue for thin clients because the sessions on the terminal server aren't displayed on the server screen.

Remote Control Systems

Remote control software allows you to remotely "possess" a computer (stand-alone or networked), controlling it with input from your keyboard and mouse. As shown in Figure 6.1, all the processing takes place on the host computer. All the client computer does is provide an input area and display what's happening on the screen of the host computer in the office. Remote control software is also often used for file transfer and file synchronization.

FIGURE 6.1:

Remote control link to a computer

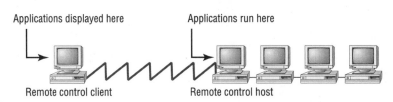

As noted in the previous sidebar, "Dial-Up Security," remote control software permits you to run a computer from a distance by dialing into it. During the remote control session, your mouse clicks and keyboard strokes are uploaded to the computer on the network (the *host*). The images on the screen are downloaded to the computer at the remote location (the *guest*).

Remote control does not necessarily require any kind of separate authentication on the network, but does require a dedicated machine to act as the host. You can't remotely control a computer that someone else is using. Well, you can, but it's a troubleshooting measure, when you need to fix a problem on that person's computer. For example, a friend of mine has installed remote control software on her computer as well as her parents' computer so that she can troubleshoot e-mail problems more easily. Two people cannot work on a remotely controlled machine at the same time.

Remote control software comes in two parts: a host side (to be loaded on the office computer that's being controlled) and a client side (to be loaded on the computer that's doing the controlling from afar). These parts aren't always separate from each other.

Even if you load the same software onto both computers, there's still a host and client component.

TIP   Some packages allow you to separate the host and client components, loading each explicitly so that you can hard-wire the computer roles. If you want one computer to be able to control another, but not the other way around, this is useful.

Once you're plugged into the host computer, you can use it as though you were sitting in front of it. Remote control packages typically support file transfer, or even file synchronization so that you can automatically update the files on your client computer. The applications you're using don't have to be loaded on the client machine, or even supported on it—you can even run 32-bit software from a client running a 16-bit operating system such as Windows 3.x. The client machine just has to be able to display the images on the host end.

The type of connection used for remote control of a network computer means that the connection isn't exactly the same as the one you'd get if using the computer directly. A modem connection will typically support about 40Kbps; 56Kbps modems don't actually transmit at 56Kbps. That's a far cry from the 100Mbps possible on the local network, even if all you're asking the line to transmit is images and sometimes files. Therefore, remote control software typically supports some kind of bitmap caching on the client end so that previously downloaded parts of the host desktop don't have to be downloaded every time the mouse moves. Similarly, to avoid demanding file transfers, remote control software supports file updating. File updating, as opposed to file replacement, downloads only changes to the file, not an entire replacement copy. This may not seem terribly important when you're talking about text files, but a salesperson attempting to update his or her client database via remote control will appreciate that only changes to the database will be sent across the wire, not the whole thing.

Remote Access Systems

In contrast to remote control software allowing a remote computer to take control of a computer on the network, remote access software permits dial-up authenticated direct access to a network. The client computer itself becomes a part of the network that is connected with telephone line instead of the 100Mbps twisted pair everyone else in the network gets to use (see Figure 6.2). Just as if you were sitting at a desk in the office instead of miles away, data are downloaded from the file server and loaded into the remote computer's memory for manipulation. Any applications being run use the computing power of the client computer.

FIGURE 6.2:

Remote access link to a network

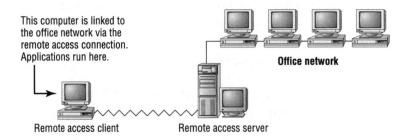

This computer is linked to the office network via the remote access connection. Applications run here.

Office network

Remote access client   Remote access server

To connect to a LAN with remote access, you need three things:

- Remote access server software running on the host end

- A remote access client installed on the client

- A preexisting account on the network

Once you have those three things, you dial up to the server, log into the remote access server, and you're in. Once connected, you can do anything on the network for which you have permission: edit files, check e-mail, or copy files between computers. The set of rights may be identical to those that you'd have if logging in normally. You may have a more restricted set of rights for dial-up access, even perhaps being limited to the remote access server and not permitted to reach the rest of the network.

Remote control gives you a one-to-one ratio of hosts to clients. Not so with remote access in which one server can support one or hundreds of remote connections. The exact number depends on the capabilities of the software. For example, Windows 98's dial-up server product supports a single connection but Windows NT's supports 256 connections.

As remote access makes the client computer part of the network, the client must support any processing it wants to do. This means that the client must be a bit more robust than is required with a remote control client, in which it can rely on the capabilities of the host computer.

Multiuser Connections

The third kind of direct dial-up access, and one gaining in popularity, allows you to connect to a multiuser server and run applications on it using a thin client protocol (see Figure 6.3). Remember, in thin client networking the applications run on the server and are displayed on the screen of the client computer. As with remote control, mouse clicks and keystrokes are uploaded to the server and interpreted there.

FIGURE 6.3:

Dialing up to a multiuser Windows server

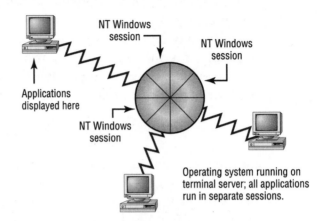

It works like this. On the network side, a server runs a multi-user version of some operating system, such as Windows NT. Each thin client on the WAN dials up to the server and logs in. At that point, the server creates a Windows NT session in a virtual machine for that client's exclusive use. Multiple clients can dial up in this way, with the upper number being limited only by the licenses available and the demands placed on memory availability and CPU cycles.

The setup is like remote control of a machine in that it allows you to run applications remotely. It is also like remote access in that the client computer, the one dialing in to make the connection, is in its own way a separate machine on the network. It is connected just as it would be locally except that the connection is via a telephone line instead of the network cable.

Frankly, of the three types of dial-up access available, this is the one I've found easiest to use. Remote access can be difficult to set up and get working properly, and remote control requires that spare machine. However, a thin client dialing into a multiuser version of Windows worked the first time and didn't require a machine waiting for someone to dial into it.

There is a catch, of course. First, it's too expensive for casual or occasional use. You need a multiuser version of Windows on the server end to make this work, and that's not cheap. A machine that can support multiple users needs to be fairly heavily loaded up in terms of CPU power and even more important, memory, and that also adds up. Finally, for each session run on the multiuser Windows machine, you need a separate client license, and that *really* gets expensive quickly, depending on how many licenses you need.

Second, not all display protocols are created equal. For example, Microsoft's Windows Terminal Server (WTS) comes with the Remote Display Protocol (RDP) for downloading images of the session to the client and uploading user input. However, RDP works better for local thin client networking than for remote dial-up; it works, but screen redraws are slow enough to make the client experience uncomfortable. A faster protocol, such as Internet Computing Architecture (ICA) provided with the Metaframe add-on available from Citrix, can make quite a bit of difference.

Virtual Private Networks

One disadvantage common to every dial-up network I've described so far is that they all use the telephone network for connectivity. This means that:

- The packets are traveling on an unsecured network; more on what this means in Chapter 14, "Principles of Network Management."

- If the server and client are a long-distance call from each other, you have to pay long-distance charges for the connection.

- One line is needed for each connection.

One way to get around both of these problems is to create a virtual private network (VPN) within another network, such as the Internet. To the user, it looks like a direct connection to the host network (see Figure 6.4). Instead, the connection is tunneling through the public network—within it but separate from it. (See "Tunneling Mechanics" later in this chapter for details.)

FIGURE 6.4:

A client accessing the company LAN via a VPN

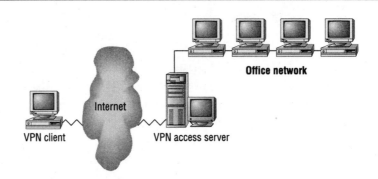

VPNs can be used in a number of different ways. Individual users can dial into the company network and use remote access or remote control; you can connect entire networks; or you can even use a VPN to connect a stand-alone machine to network resources without having to connect it to the LAN.

> **NOTE** Most people associate VPNs with the Internet. This is the usual option because the Internet is the most commonly accessible public network in the world and the one I'll be referring to in examples. However, the Internet is not the *only* option for virtual private networking. Any public network can be the backbone of a VPN.

As virtual private networks are intended to extend the security of the private LAN across a public network, they have some stringent requirements, including:

- Support for user authentication so that user identity can be verified against an account database. Additionally, logins and file access should be capable of being logged for security reasons.

- Clients must have an address for use on the private network and this address should be restricted to the private network.

- Data encryption should be supported so that private information remains private. Additionally, the VPN software should generate and refresh the encryption keys.

- The VPN must support transport protocols used on the public network.

In short, VPNs are a secure, inexpensive, and fairly simple way to allow multiple routes into a network, whether for a single user or an entire LAN at another location. The only catch is the other traffic contending for space on the public network.

Tunneling Mechanics

How does all this work? Recall that remote access and remote control clients use a line protocol to dial in, and that PPP is the most widely supported line protocol. In addition to PPP, the computers on a VPN will use another protocol to carry their private network data over the public network. This involves a technique called *tunneling*. Tunneling encases the packets of one network within those of another network, like concealing an envelope within a plain brown wrapper. This wrapper isn't for purposes of concealment, but rather to add the routing information needed to send the original packet on a network that couldn't ordinarily support it. When the packet reaches its destination—the corporate LAN, for example—it's stripped of the extra header information and reverted to its original state.

Why is this encapsulating necessary? As I discussed in Chapter 3, "Networking Protocols and Application Programming Interfaces," in order to convey information on a network, you need to transmit packets with the protocol in use on that network. Tunneling acts as a means of providing packets with an alternate identity.

For example, IPX packets can assume the identity of IP packets (more precisely, of PPP packets) for their trip across a network that uses IP. Once the packets get to the end of the IP network and are back in IPX Land, they strip off their IP disguise and regain their original identities. The tunneling protocol is responsible for encapsulating the packets and then removing the encapsulation once the packets reach their destination.

A Bestiary of Current and Forthcoming Tunneling Protocols

Tunneling isn't a new technology. It's been around in the form of NetBIOS over TCP/IP and SNA (Systems Network Architecture—it's a protocol for connecting PCs to IBM mainframes.) tunneling over IP networks for quite some time. Some newer tunneling protocols include:

- The Point-to-Point Tunneling Protocol (PPTP)
- Layer 2 Tunneling Protocol (L2TP)
- IP Security (IPSec) tunneling mode

Tunneling works slightly differently depending on whether a data link or network tunneling protocol is in play. Data link layer protocols are connection oriented. This means that before tunneling can occur, the endpoints must agree to the tunnel and arrange compatible encryption, compression, and other factors. They also depend heavily on the capabilities of PPP or another network layer protocol to provide security. Network layer tunneling protocols don't have to explicitly establish a tunneling session before beginning, but instead assume that all those arrangements have been made without their help. Their focus is on encrypting and encapsulating packets in more packet headers. As with networking protocols, whichever tunneling protocol is used, all members of the VPN must be using the same one.

The Point-to-Point Tunneling Protocol (PPTP) PPTP is a draft standard of a data link layer protocol used to tunnel packets across IP networks, such as the Internet. It can be used with any network that supports NetBEUI, IPX/SPX-compatible protocol, or TCP/IP, but is designed for IP internetworks. The tunneling protocol uses a two-channel system to pass data and session control information. Data runs through one stream and control information through TCP, a connection-oriented protocol that's part of the TCP/IP suite.

PPTP has wide support. Although it's mostly pushed by Microsoft, the original work for the draft standard was largely done by Ascend Communications. In fact, the Microsoft implementation of the draft is slightly different from the one proposed to the Internet Engineering Task Force (IETF). This is because Microsoft included support for stronger encryption than was planned for with the original standard.

The Layer 2 Tunneling Protocol (LT2P) Widespread as its support is now, PPTP may be set aside for LT2P, a faster tunneling protocol that's derived from it. L2TP is another data link layer protocol designed to support NetBEUI, IPX/SPX-compatible protocol, and TCP/IP. It's intended for use on any network that supports UDP datagrams (connectionless sessions), such as frame relay, ATM, X.25, or IP.

As I just mentioned, LT2P looks likely to supplant PPTP as the premiere tunneling protocol. Why? First, Microsoft is supporting it. Although current Windows operating systems don't support the protocol, the next generation of NT-based Windows will. Even apart from this support, however, LT2P has the potential to be a faster protocol than PPTP, as it relies on a single channel of UDP datagrams rather than the dual-channel design that PPTP uses. Its connectionless design makes it less reliable, but reliability is less of an issue than it once was as channel quality, at least in the

United States, is high so less error checking is needed. Use of UDP over GRE is also important as more firewalls support UDP than GRE. Additionally, LT2P will be more flexible than PPTP, supporting not only the Internet but also almost any WAN architecture.

NOTE   As of fall 1998, L2TP is not yet a standard. However, a draft standard has been submitted to the IETF, and a proposed standard is in the works. PPTP isn't a full standard either, so not being a standard won't stand in the way of LT2P.

Although LT2P can use the security functions built into PPP, it's designed instead to cooperate with IPSec, only using PPP if this network layer protocol isn't available.

The IP Security (IPSec) Protocol   Whereas LT2P and PPTP are Microsoft standards, IPSec is in the "everybody else" category. IPSec is a network layer protocol that encrypts IP packets and gives them a new header with which to be sent across an IP network. The whole process of authentication is done with certificates—attachments to data transfers that authenticate the sender's identity. The computer initiating the session sends a certificate to the target across the public network. The target accepts the certificate, then confirms its identity with a certificate of its own. The two computers then use their public or private keys to establish settings for the session, including what encryption and compression should be used for the duration of the connection.

As noted, LT2P uses IPSec by default to supply it with security. Why not just use IPSec and be done with it? Mostly because of the need to support dial-up access from multiple locations. IPSec in its native form provides only for machine-level security, not user-level security. Notice that the machines on each end of the connection use certificates to identify themselves and certificates are machine specific. IPSec implementations typically have extensions that allow them to authenticate on a per-user basis, but these are not part of the standard.

For user-level security, you need one of the data link layer tunneling protocols that can authenticate on a per-user basis and then use the network layer encryption algorithms. If the user base of the computers in your VPN is static and your network operating system (NOS) supports IPSec, then IPSec can be a good choice.

NOTE   Not sure what user-level security is and how it might be different from other forms of security? Turn to Chapter 15, "Network Security."

A Sample PPTP Session

You can start a VPN session with a remote access client. A tunneling session between members of a VPN will begin as follows:

1. PPP uses the Link Control Protocol (LCP) to initiate a session between two nodes on the VPN. LCP is responsible for selecting the communication mode and compression factors to be used, but does not actually implement them during this step.

2. The client (the node initiating the connection) presents its credentials to the server for authentication. It uses one of several authentication protocols that prevents a third party from impersonating the client or capturing the password. The server authenticates the client's access or terminates the connection if the client can't be authenticated. Optionally, the server will sever the connection and call back the client at a prearranged number to make doubly sure that the client is who it claims to be.

NOTE Password authentication protocols will be discussed in Chapter 14, "Principles of Network Administration."

3. The client machine is assigned an address and the compression and data encryption methods chosen by LCP are implemented.

At this point, the connection has been made; the client's identity is established and authenticated; all session settings have been chosen and implemented; and secure data transfer can begin.

Are VPNs always superior to other forms of dial-up access? Not necessarily. They save money by reducing long-distance charges, but they have one drawback: as VPNs use the same public Internet as a lot of other people, their performance may be slow. If the Internet's slow, then your VPN will be slow. Your traffic may be private, but even in its brown paper wrapper it's still contending for bandwidth like everyone else.

Packet-Switched Networks

As mentioned earlier in this chapter under "Packet Switching versus Circuit Switching," not all WANs operate in the same way. I'll take a look at a couple of packet-switched WAN technologies:

X25 An older one used for unreliable networks (it's still in use anywhere that lines are not at their best).

Frame relay A more modern one that's frankly the most likely contender for new WAN users in the United States because it offers the most efficient use of bandwidth.

Both WAN technologies work in much the same way. The major difference between the two is the additional error-control information that is included in every X.25 packet, which is not part of frame relay packets.

Esperanto for WANs—X.25

X.25 is an access protocol for packet-switching networks, establishing a virtual circuit between the two ends of the network. It works like this: an X.25 card has one or several physical ports, each of which can support a number of virtual connections. When you send a packet to the X.25 network, the packet travels on one of the virtual connections to its destination.

X.25 is not very fast by modern standards, typically limited to a 64-256Kbps connection. Outside the United States, it's a very popular WAN type for two good reasons: in areas with wiring at all, it's pretty universally available and it's very reliable even if the connection isn't. As it's both slow and designed for use with packet-switched networks, it's not really meant for any kind of streaming data, such as video; but it's admirably suited for bursty transmissions, such as those used by file transfers, e-mail, and database entries.

X.25 is not precisely a network type, but a way of defining how data gets onto a packet switched WAN and what information needs to accompany that data. This protocol operates on the lowest three layers of the OSI model:

- At the physical layer, X.25 is defined as using an RS-232 serial connection, so any router meant to be used with an X.25 network must support that connection type.

- At the data link layer, data to be sent on the WAN is packaged into a frame, and a connection is established.

- At the network layer, the data is transmitted and error checked to be sure that it reaches its destination in one piece. If there are errors, the original sender resends the data.

The error control aspects of X.25 are dependent on the CRC information in the frame. When the frame arrives at the other end of the X.25 network, the CRC is checked. If the answer to the test algorithm doesn't match the answer provided in the frame, the recipient asks the sender to resend the data. If the answer is correct, then the recipient confirms that the data got through in one piece. Either way, the sender waits to discard data until it's heard one way or another from the recipient.

Another aspect of X.25's reliability comes from its ability to keep tabs on a session. First, if a virtual circuit is shut down unexpectedly and the session ends, X.25 can note the status of the session when it ended. When the virtual circuit is reestablished, it can continue where it left off in sending any packets remaining from the interrupted transmission. Second, X.25 has mechanisms for *flow control*, so that the recipient never gets more frames than it can handle at once. If a recipient doesn't acknowledge the successful receipt of a frame, the sender stops sending frames until it does get some kind of acknowledgment. In some cases, the recipient can actually send an explicit message to the sender to tell it to stop sending until further notice.

That's X.25, a slow but reliable on ramp to a packet-switched network. When line quality is a bit better, you can use frame relay. This is a technology that was originally supposed to be a temporary stand-in for leased lines until something better came along. Ultimately, it proved to be the most popular access technology for new wide area networks.

Making Better Use of Bandwidth with Frame Relay

The most likely choice for a company needing wide-area connections between offices is frame relay. Why frame relay? Consider these reasons:

- It's a known quantity—it's been around for a number of years.

- It's good for bursty communications of the type that most networks still use, such as file transfer.

- It uses bandwidth efficiently.

- It's become much faster than it was originally designed to be, so it can keep up with even fairly demanding data streams.

Frame relay was originally designed to be a stopgap measure while a viable alternative to leased lines was finished. *Leased lines* are dedicated private lines for point-to-point communications between members of a WAN, as shown in Figure 6.5. Each of the branch offices (B-E) needs a connection to the corporate server located in office A.

FIGURE 6.5:

Lease lines connecting offices

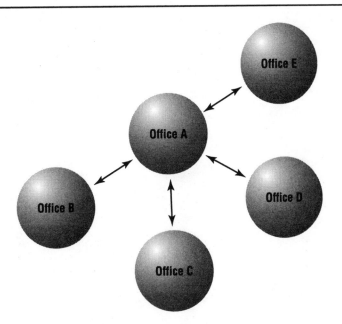

Leased lines work very well for providing connectivity, but they have one major problem: they're expensive, and the more there are and the faster they get, the more expensive they are. Additionally, no one needs those expensive links all the time, so you're paying for a lot of unused bandwidth. Slower lines are cheaper lines, but then you've got a performance hit.

There's a high-speed network across the United States now. Why not let people use parts of that, sharing it with other subscribers so that less bandwidth is wasted? That's the idea of frame relay—to give people access to the same high-speed lines that they might have used with a leased line. However, they must share it, sending data through virtual circuits so that no two subscribers interfere with each other. There is no physical point-to-point connection as with leased lines, but, as shown in Figure 6.6, the connectivity is the same. In fact, for the same size line, it's actually improved because of the more efficient way in which frame relay uses bandwidth.

FIGURE 6.6:

Frame relay connecting offices

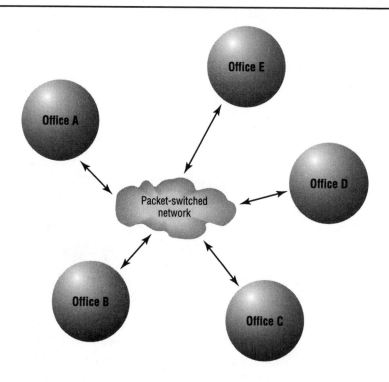

By allocating bandwidth in this more efficient manner, frame relay networks can get about twice the effective speed from a channel as would be possible with a leased line. The exact speed depends on the real bandwidth of the channel. Frame relay most often runs on T1 (1.55 Mbps) lines or 56Kbps lines, but ways of running it over T3 (45Mbps) lines have been tested. Whether you can buy the service at T3 speeds is another matter entirely, but the technology exists.

Coulda Been a Contender

I've referred to frame relay originally being considered a low-end technology to replace leased lines. The alternative was the Switched Multimegabit Data Services (SMDS). SMDS had a lot going for it. It was fast, with the ability to send data at 45Mbps; connectionless to allow greater flexibility in the network; and good for streaming data. Frame relay, on the other hand, was quite a bit slower, connection oriented, and best for bursty transmissions—even voice over frame relay is still a work in progress.

Frame relay won the battle of the WAN types not because it was a better architecture, but because of cost. Although SMDS was no more expensive than frame relay when it came to the amount of bandwidth you could get, it was a lot more expensive than frame relay in absolute terms. Most people didn't need high-speed WAN links enough to make the increase in cost worthwhile, so frame relay won by default.

Inside the Cloud

Frame relay allocates network bandwidth using *statistical multiplexing* (stat mux), in which bandwidth is not allocated on a user-by-user basis but by packets. The difference is this: If you divide a pipe into virtual channels, then each virtual channel gets its bit of bandwidth whether it's using it or not. Given that most network communications take place in short bursts, that means that a lot of bandwidth goes to waste (see Figure 6.7).

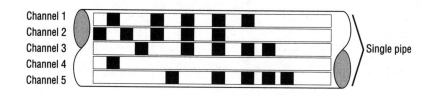

If you don't subdivide the channel and instead allocate bandwidth by network traffic, then the senders that need lots of bandwidth get it. Additionally, the ones that don't need much bandwidth won't hog space they're not using, as shown in Figure 6.8.

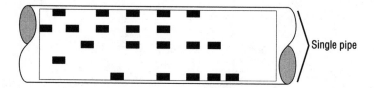

If all the subscriber's frames are jumbled up within a single packet-switched network, then how do they get sorted out for delivery? Each frame is identified by a data link connection identifier (DLCI). DLCIs work like loading docks, as frames are routed not to a destination address but to a location specified in the DLCI. When a frame reaches its destination, the telco box connecting the subscriber to the network examines the DLCI and determines whether it corresponds to an address accessible from that destination. If so, then the packet is sent on to its final destination. If the frame was routed there in error, the frame is dropped.

Congestion Handling

Frame relay, therefore, is a more efficient use of bandwidth than is dividing a physical circuit into multiple logical channels. However, cramming bandwidth full of data has its own share of difficulties. This is because more subscribers using the network at one time means slower transmissions for everyone. Frame relay providers offer a committed information rate (CIR) that's the measure of the average rate of throughput. You might get a CIR of, say, 50Kbps and have actual throughput of 100Kbps, but the provider promises that you'll always get at least 50Kbps. Frames in excess of that amount are marked and shown to be above and beyond the circuit's call of duty. If the link gets congested, the marked frames will be the first to be dropped.

The actual CIR offered depends on the service. Technically, it's possible for a provider to offer a CIR of 0, meaning it guarantees none of your data, but this isn't likely. A lower CIR is generally cheaper, but may get you a lower rate of effective throughput.

Summary

Current WAN architectures rely most not on point-to-point communications, but on access to a public packet-switched network that routes data to its destination via a collection of virtual circuits. The most popular WAN technology for new WANs is frame relay. VPNs are a likely second for networks that can support a slower connection and extend over a broader area. This isn't an exhaustive look at all WAN types available, but it does examine some of the more common ones, and the ones you're most likely to be using.

That's about it for the channels in your LAN (and beyond). In Part II, "Pieces of the Puzzle," I'll get to the software (server operating systems and applications) that breathe life into your LAN. I'll also introduce you to the "bodies" (server and client computers) that give that life a staging area.

EXERCISE 6

1. Under what circumstances would you use the X.25 protocol over frame relay?

2. In the office, you've got a Pentium 200 with 64MB of RAM. At home, you've got a 386 with 8MB of RAM. Assuming you had the necessary hardware and software in place, what kind of dial-up connection could you establish with your office to let you run the same applications at home that you can run in the office? Choose all that apply.

   A. Remote access

   B. Remote control

   C. Thin client

   D. Virtual private network

3. What protocol is needed to support virtual private networking over a frame relay network?

4. What is the committed information rate (CIR) for a 56Kbps frame relay connection?

PART

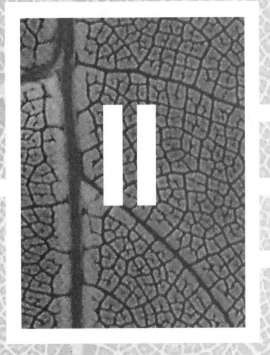

II

Pieces of the Puzzle

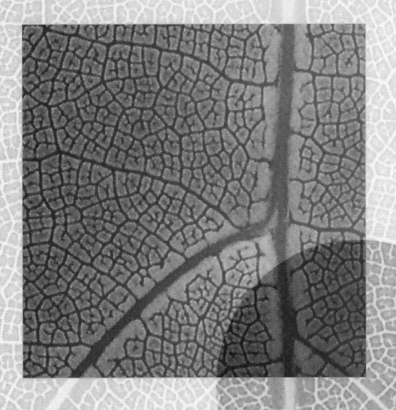

7

Building the Better Server

In the previous chapters, I spent a lot of time talking about the various methods you can use to connect the PCs in a network to each other. I've also discussed the materials—cables, protocols, networking hardware, and the like—that you must have to accomplish this. But what about the PCs themselves? What configurations are likely to make your PCs good members of a network? For that matter, what devices other than PCs are involved in a network? In this and the other chapters in Part II, "Pieces of the Puzzle," I'll talk about the kinds of client and server machines and the peripheral devices you'll also be using.

What Is a Server?

A *server* is any networked computer that provides some service to the other computers on the network. This service may include one or more tasks, such as file storage, print services, or application sharing. However, the type of service provided is less important to the definition than placing emphasis on the server's role.

> **NOTE** As will be discussed in Chapter 10, "Network Operating Systems," a server doesn't even necessarily have to be dedicated to its task. However, in peer-to-peer networks, it will play the dual role of network client *and* server.

The type of server depends on what it's doing for the network, but the basic components of all servers remain the same—disk space, memory, CD-ROM, and so forth.

A server, by definition, has to do processing not only for itself but also for other computers on the network. Because of this, it behooves you to get the fastest and best components possible for your servers. What's acceptable when only one person is using it can be miserably slow when 60 folks are making demands. What's fast, though? You can't tell what's fast and powerful until you know a bit more about it. Let's take a look at these components in more detail.

Can You Keep Up with the Joneses?

If you pay any attention to hardware developments, you know that new hardware, which outclasses the old, has been coming out fast and furious lately. It's not worth holding out for the absolute fastest, top-of-the-line components because in six months they won't be the fastest anymore. If you wait for the fastest chips/disks/memory/CD-ROMs, then you'll never buy *anything*. The best reason to wait for faster components to come out is that they'll make the prices on the next-most-recent drop through the floor as soon as they're released.

Rather than waiting for the Ultimate Server, look for solid PC components that will serve your needs now, and make sure that they're on a good upgrade path. If/when the time comes that the components you bought in 1999 aren't able to keep up with your network's demands, you can replace them then. In the meantime, don't drive yourself crazy trying to keep up with every new hardware development out there. It's an impossible task.

By the way, this isn't a complete guide to every possible component on the market. Given the rate of CPU development alone these days, by the time this book gets to print, Intel will likely have released six new varieties of CPU. (Okay, I'm exaggerating, but you get the point.) However, based on what's written here, you should be able to evaluate new products even if they are released after this book has gone to print.

Central Processing Units

Since you know enough about computers to be at least considering a LAN, I'll assume that you know that a *central processing unit* (CPU) is the brain of the PC. The CPU handles everything the PC does, from processing read requests for the hard disk, to pulling data from main memory into a temporary storage buffer, to calculating the spreadsheet you're working on. Without a functioning CPU, the PC is "brain dead;" like a human body without a brain, you could technically run power to it, but it wouldn't be able to do anything.

CISC versus RISC

One of the basic differences in CPU types lies in a really low-level matter: the way in which those CPUs process instructions. In this light, there are two categories of processors, the Combined Instruction Set Chip (CISC) and the Reduced Instruction Set Chip (RISC). Their names hold the key to their differences.

How Do the Algorithms Differ?

CISC chips combine a number of lower-level instructions to create one task built into the chip's logic, whereas the RISC chips keep the logic functioning at the low level of the individual instructions. Due to the differences in their design, a CISC chip will generally have a larger instruction set (a set of commands built into the chip's logic) than a RISC chip. This is because the CISC chip has to make each command work on its own and the RISC chip can mix and match commands to accomplish the desired result. It's much like the difference between the Roman alphabet (in which 26 letters can spell any word in the language but an individual letter means little unless combined with others) and the thousands of Chinese ideograms, each of which is a word on its own.

Reducing Complexity—What's an Instruction Set?

An *instruction set* is an array of instructions built into a chip. When computers were first developed, the instruction sets were hard-coded into the CPU. These CPUs were extremely fast, as there was no delay while the CPU interpreted software. However, they were inflexible—a change in software required a change in CPU design and vice versa. To make the systems a bit more flexible, computer engineers designed a software language to build into the CPU's logic that could accomplish the same thing as the hard-wired instructions. This language was called *microcode*.

Microcode had a number of advantages over the hard-wired instructions even apart from flexibility. First, the programs running on microcode could be shorter than the previous programs as they could call on the combined functions built into the CPU. Second, shorter programs meant lower memory requirements, which was a very good thing considering that memory was expensive.

As the instruction sets became increasingly complex over time, problems surfaced. Not all instructions required the same amount of time to execute; the more complicated the instruction, the longer it took. After the situation became extremely complicated, some chip manufacturers tried a different approach, one in which every instruction was a set size and could be executed in a single clock tick. Essentially, this represented a more modular approach to computing. When this new paradigm surfaced, it was called RISC, and that's when microcode changed its name to CISC. CISC is still alive and well, however. The new paradigm did not kill off the old one.

How much do instruction sets change over time? Not necessarily all that much. Today's Pentiums use much the same instruction set as did the 386 chips (that's why they're all part of the *x86* "family") with some additional video-enhancing instructions added with the MMX iteration of the chip. However, MMX functions are now part of the basic Intel instruction set.

To oversimplify a bit to make the point, where a CISC chip performs one complex task, the RISC chip performs five very simple tasks, but each chip could be accomplishing the same thing in the end. Confused? Try an example. If you had a CISC chip and a RISC chip, and you wanted each to set the table for dinner, you'd have to address the order differently for each. When it came to the CISC chip, you could tell it, "Set the table," and it would do so. This is because the subset for Set Table includes all the parts of setting the table—the chip has been preprogrammed that way. However, give the RISC chip the same instructions and you'll confuse it—an order to set the table means nothing to that chip. Instead, you'd have to tell it, "Put the plates on the table. Put the silverware on the table. Put the napkins on the table," and so on. Ultimately, the two CPUs are performing the same function and the end result is the same, but they go about it differently.

Why these two approaches? It's a difference in design tactics. Until the mid-80s, new CPUs used the CISC design (at the time, it was called microcode). As the chips became more powerful, their design became increasingly complex. This was because more and more instructions had to be built into the CPU logic, so the chips had to include more and more transistors. The designers of the RISC system figured that simpler instructions would be faster to carry out *and* wouldn't require the complexity of the CISC chips. This is because fewer individual instructions would have to be added in order to make the RISC chips smarter, so the chips could be cheaper.

The Perennial Question—Which Is Better?

Which approach is better? It depends on the application. RISC technology isn't always suited to applications where the set of instructions likely to be used is limited. For example, networking hardware is not suited for RISC intelligence because you've got a good idea of the situations you're likely to encounter. Most of them can be anticipated, so lots of tiny little instructions slows things down. On the more server-oriented end of things, CISC technology has generally been considered superior for tasks such as file and print sharing, as the requirements can be easily anticipated. On the other hand, RISC technology has been favored for more unpredictable applications, such as database and application serving.

NOTE   Many pieces of networking hardware, including the Windows terminals discussed in Chapter 12, "Thin Client Networking," use RISC chips.

The question of the best approach isn't always as important as knowing which technology is supported. Both approaches work when it comes time for number-crunching. However, software is designed to work with one type of logic or the other, not both, so it's more likely that you'll have to pick a chip type based on the software you had in mind. Some types of software are available in a RISC and a CISC version. For example, you can buy Windows NT and install it to run either on a server based on a DEC Alpha (a RISC chip), or an Intel Pentium Pro (a CISC chip). However, the pieces installed will be different on each machine. You couldn't just copy the installation from one to the other even if the server hardware were otherwise identical.

NOTE   Software emulation to run RISC applications on CISC machines and vice versa is available, but the applications take a serious performance hit.

Generally speaking, UNIX and Macintosh systems run on RISC chips. PC operating systems, particularly personal system, such as Windows 9*x*, run on CISC chips. Windows NT used to support an array of RISC chips in addition to the *x*86 CISC design. But because of the very limited demand for non-CISC chips, NT has dropped support for the Power PC and the MIPS. The only RISC chips currently supported are the Alpha chips designed by Digital

Equipment Corp (now part of Compaq). In other words, if you want to use Macintosh machines you'll have RISC chips in your machines. If you want to use Windows of some flavor, you'll likely have CISC chips in your machines.

Determining Chip Speed

As you've seen so far in this chapter, you don't get a lot of say in whether your computer will use CISC chips or RISC chips. I'd advise letting your application choices drive your CPU design requirements instead of allowing your CPU design choices to drive your application requirements. However, you do have a say in the speed at which those CPUs will execute the instructions they get. That speed is influenced by several factors:

- The number of cycles per minute

- The number of instructions that can be processed at once

- The number of instructions that can enter the CPU for processing at once

- The size of the buffer area in which recently used instructions can be kept for quick retrieval

In Techese, these are the megahertz per second (MHz), the word size, the data path, and the cache size, respectively.

NOTE   Up through the 486 processors, the existence or absence of a math coprocessor also affected chip speed, but math coprocessors are now a standard part of all modern CPUs. This is the part of the CPU that allows it to do complex mathematical functions, such as multiplication, instead of treating those operations as long addition problems. You can do the functions without a coprocessor, but it takes longer. It's the difference between 5×6 and 6+6+6+6+6.

MHz Considerations

The first thing you're likely to notice when looking at CPUs is the MHz, which represents a rough approximation of the chip's speed. I say "rough" because this number describes one aspect of what makes the chip fast: the number of clock cycles it runs per second. This number says nothing about how many instructions will be carried out during those clock cycles. (Well, let me qualify that. It says nothing unless you're talking about a RISC chip, in which case the ratio is 1:1. But you still don't know how many of those instructions will be necessary to carry out a single operation). However, all other things being equal, a greater clock speed will translate to a faster chip. As of this writing, the fastest CISC chips available operate internally at 400MHz.

Clock Doubling

That's *internally* at 400MHz. Note: Motherboard bus speed still has a top speed of 60-66MHz. What this means in real terms is that hardware operations—including getting data in and out of main memory—have a top speed of 66MHz (100MHz on the newest boards), while internal operations, such as calculations, have a top speed of 400MHz. The difference is made possible with a technology called *clock doubling*, which became widespread in the middle 1990s and is still common today; it's just gone underground.

Clock doubling is based on a problem of motherboard design that makes it difficult to develop a motherboard that runs faster than 66MHz—the hardware can't handle higher frequencies. However, this limitation does not apply to the internal workings of the CPU, so the CPUs can be faster and faster, operating in some multiple of the 60 or 66MHz limit.

Thus, the 486 33MHz that I still have (look, it works, and for what I ask it to do, the slow CPU speed is no limitation) has a motherboard and a CPU that operate at the same speed. A 200MHz Pentium Pro's motherboard and CPU run at drastically different speeds—it's got a motherboard running at 66MHz and an internal clock cycle three times that. (No, 66x3 does not equal 200, but rounding up makes the marketing people happy.)

Continued on next page

Is the disparity between internal clock speed and external bus speed a problem? Not necessarily. Although main memory can't talk to the CPU at the same speed that the CPU can talk to itself. All this means, however, is that you get better performance from the machine when it's doing internal calculations than when it's communicating with its peripherals. Clock doubling is no longer an option, but an expectancy, so it's not as though there's a price trade-off anymore.

How Much Is a Mouthful? Word Size

Another factor in determining CPU speed is its *word size*, or the amount of data that the CPU can process at one time. The greater the word size, the more data that can be operated on at once and, therefore, the faster the machine. People have various word sizes, too. For example, if I'm getting complex directions to go somewhere and have nothing to write with, I can remember about two turns and a stop light. Then I have to stop and ask someone else to give me directions for the rest of the way. My word size isn't large enough to handle a complete set of directions.

Data Path into the CPU

The word size determines how much data the CPU can process at one time, but how quickly can all that data get into the CPU for processing? That question is answered by the size of the *data path*. Essentially, the data path represents the gateway into the CPU. The wider the data path, the more data can go in at one time.

The data path is not necessarily capable of keeping up with the word size. To use an old example, the 386SX has a 16-bit data path and a 32-bit word size. Therefore, even though the CPU is capable of processing 32 bits of data at one time, only 16 bits can enter at a time. Additionally, there will be a microscopic delay while the second set of 16 bits enters the CPU for processing. A chip like the 386DX, with its 32-bit data path, can be much faster because the entire word can enter the CPU at once.

Cache as Cache Can

So far, I've talked about how fast the CPU can think, how much it can think about at once, and how fast it can start thinking about something new. The remaining piece of the puzzle lies in how much it can remember, which is determined by the size of its cache.

You're probably familiar with the concept of cache in a general sense. Many parts of the PC store information that's likely to be reused in the near future in a buffer called the *cache*. The CPU has a cache as well. In fact, it has two. Older CPUs only had an internal cache called the L1 cache. Modern CPUs have both the L1 cache and a larger external cache made of static RAM (SRAM) called the L2 cache. In these caches are stored information (both code and data) that the processor has recently used, the idea being that the processor is likely to need that information again soon. This concept is illustrated in Figure 7.1.

FIGURE 7.1:

L1 and L2 caching

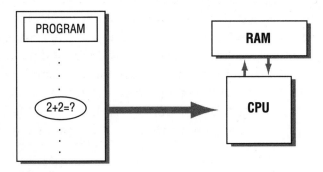

When a program calls for a function, in this case 2+2, the CPU must go to the operating system (in RAM) to get the summation instruction for each instance of the call.

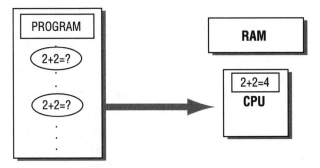

A CPU with a cache can store the first instance of the function within the cache. For every subsequent function call, it can get the information directly from the cache, resulting in speedier processing.

NOTE   *SRAM* is a kind of memory that remembers everything from the time the data goes into memory until the time the data is either removed or the machine is turned off. Unlike dynamic RAM (DRAM), which is what main system memory is made of, SRAM does not need to be refreshed every four milliseconds, so it's much faster than DRAM. It's also a lot more expensive.

As the L1 is internal to the CPU and thus runs at the same rate as the CPU clock, it's faster than the L2 cache. So, recently used data is stored in the L1 cache first. (SRAM is far from slow, but it's slower than internal clock speeds.) However, the L1 cache isn't very big (8KB to 64KB, depending on the processor), so when it's used up, the additional data goes into the L2 cache, which is quite a bit larger—up to 1MB in some cases.

NOTE   The Pentium Pro's L2 cache is semi-internal to the CPU. It is housed within the same package but in an additional module on the CPU instead of being part of the main piece.

A higher-speed chip does not necessarily mean a larger cache. For example, the Pentium Pro runs at 200MHz internally but has only an 8KB L1 cache. The lower-end Celeron processors (266MHz and 300MHz) have no L2 cache whatsoever. As caching power may be more important to performance than the number of cycles per second, this is worth your attention. When buying a server with a particular CPU, look for one with plenty of internal cache and a good-sized secondary cache as well.

Combining Processor Power

In recent years, multiple-processor systems have become a viable alternative, not just for Fortune 500 companies, but for smaller organizations as well. A multiple-processor system is useful because it allows you to harness the power of multiple processors within a single machine.

NOTE   Not all operating systems support multiprocessor systems, but the modern network operating systems do. So, you should be able to have them on your servers if you like. Check with your operating system's documentation to see the number of processors it will support. For example, Windows NT Server supports four.

There are two paradigms of multiple-processor support: symmetric multiprocessing (SMP) and asymmetric multiprocessor support (AMP). The difference between the two is what it sounds like. In SMP systems, all processing is distributed more or less evenly among all available processors, with the least busy processor usually getting handed new jobs as they come in. In AMP systems, one set of software, such as the operating system, is assigned one CPU for its exclusive use. Additional software contends for the other CPUs even if the operating system's CPU isn't busy.

Once again, the one you choose is less dependent on which you think is a good idea than on the needs of your software. Support for SMP is more common, so look for machines that use that algorithm.

How Important Is CPU Speed to Server Performance?

Good question. CPU speed is important, but it's not the factor that's going to make or break a server's performance on the network. Consider this: when running a server, you're making the entire machine available to the clients, not just the CPU. A fast CPU combined with slow peripheral devices make for a slow server.

Thus, if you're pricing servers and picking out desirable components, don't look just at CPU speed and ignore the rest of the package. As you'll see in the coming pages, there's a lot more to a server than its CPU.

Bus Types

I talked about some of the basics of bus design in Chapter 1, "Basic Networking Concepts and Components," when discussing network cards as base network components. For all practical purposes, when it comes to modern servers, there are two options: ISA and PCI.

You may recall that Industry Standard Architecture (ISA) is an 8-bit or 16-bit bus that runs at 8MHz because that's the top speed of the original AT bus it was designed for. It's changed little since 1984, when it was widened to 16 bits from its original 8-bit path, largely for compatibility reasons. You can see an ISA slot in Figure 7.2.

FIGURE 7.2:

ISA slots are still found on most motherboards.

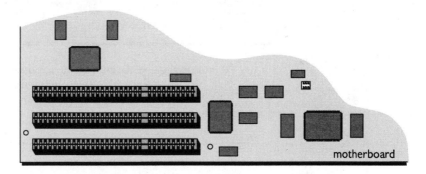

ISA slots (typically black) are still found on most motherboards.

The Peripheral Component Interconnect (PCI) is a local-bus architecture. It took some of the good ideas introduced with the VESA (Video Electronics Standard Association) local bus standard and extended them. This architecture abandoned the problems inherent in the VESA design—lack of Plug and Play support, trouble running with the Pentium, and problems with having more than two VESA slots on a motherboard while maintaining a high-speed connection to the motherboard. Local bus technology runs at the speed of the motherboard, which means that if the motherboard is running at 33MHz, the board can too, instead of poking along at 8MHz. A PCI slot is shown in Figure 7.3.

FIGURE 7.3:

PCI slots are used for high-speed cards that can operate at mother-board speeds.

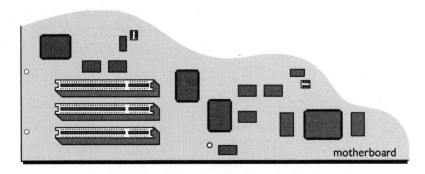

PCI slots (typically white) are used for high-speed cards that
can operate at motherboard speeds.

NOTE   Local bus technology was originally developed to improve video per-formance, but people quickly saw that what was good for video could be good for other peripherals as well.

If PCI is so much faster than ISA is, why is ISA still around? The first factor relates to the same reasons that it's remained unchanged for more than 10 years: compatibility. No one's quite ready to say,

"This is unbearably slow. Let's trash it and make all those ISA cards unusable," and become the bad guy. Second, although it's a little slow for server applications, ISA functions quite nicely for clients, and ISA cards are cheaper than PCI cards. Third, PCI can't support everything; for example, serial and parallel ports must use the ISA bus, not PCI.

A Need for Speed

As of late 1998, PCI is the fastest bus available, but it's not the end of the road. The year 1999 is expected to see shipment of a 64-bit/66MHz PCI bus from Intel. If that's not enough, an extension to PCI, called PCI-X, has been developed by Hewlett-Packard, IBM, and Compaq. This new bus is designed to run at 133MHz, transferring data between the CPU and peripherals at 1Gbps.

PCI-X is only a stopgap measure to improve PCI while something else comes along. The Next Big Thing (expected some time in 2000) is anticipated to be fabric-based connections between peripherals and the motherboard. Rather than connecting to a bus, peripherals will have a high-speed connection to a subsytem, chip, or even another server. This connection method has been in use on mainframes and supercomputers for some time, but is only now being applied to the PC market.

PCI is a better choice for those server peripherals that support it. By now, it's been around long enough that you shouldn't have any problems finding PCI cards for most things. Clients can often use ISA cards without problems. On the other hand, servers, with additional demands on them, require more speed than ISA can provide. Most PCs these days offer a mixture of PCI and ISA slots.

Mostly Gone, but Not Forgotten—MCA and EISA

As I've explained, ISA was soon outpaced by motherboards in terms of speed. Why did it take 10 years from the time ISA was expanded to support 16-bit data paths to introduce something better—PCI? It didn't. Actually, the alternatives just didn't do very well.

With the introduction of the 386 machine, IBM came out with a faster bus standard, one called MicroChannel Architecture (MCA). MCA had several advantages over ISA: it had a 32-bit bus, ran at 10MHz, supported bus mastering, and—get this—supported Plug-and-Play technology. There were two problems with MCA, however. First, IBM made it proprietary, so it wouldn't work with ISA cards. This incompatibility was a by-product of the faster speeds. It probably wouldn't have represented a real problem any more than does PCI's incompatibility with ISA. But IBM compounded the error and told card manufacturers that if they wanted to make MCA cards, they'd have to license the right to develop the technology (IBM wasn't even giving that away), and also pay royalties on MCA products that they sold.

"Heck with *that*," was the general response. So, a group of nine motherboard developers began work on another bus that would have the advantages MCA had brought to the table but skip some of the liabilities. Thus was born the Extended Industry Standard Architecture (EISA) bus. It had a 32-bit data path and supported bus mastering and Plug-and-Play technology, but ran at 8MHz in order to be compatible with ISA.

Neither one did very well, though. MCA suffered from a lack of cards built for it, and EISA never caught on with the general public, although it did get some market share in server machines. It was simply easier to find ISA cards—and they worked—so people mostly stuck with what they knew until something much better came along.

Main Memory

If Dorothy Parker were a network administrator, she'd say that you can never be too rich, too thin, or have too much RAM installed.

RAM (Random Access Memory) is the mainstay of many computer operations. All code and data being used at a given moment is stored in RAM, also called *main memory*. When the amount of information you need more-or-less instant access to is greater than the amount of memory you have installed, the less-used information goes to a cache on the hard disk. From there, it can be recalled when a program you're using requests it again, at which time the data is reloaded into main memory. This process of moving data to the on-disk buffer and back again as necessary is called *paging* the data, either out to disk or in to memory.

Dragging information back from that cache on the hard disk takes time, however, so it's to your advantage to limit the frequency with which you must make your computer resort to this measure. To do that, you need more memory.

> **NOTE**   Realistically, you'll always have some data paged to disk. Modern operating systems are designed to work this way so as to permit more data to be loaded into memory than would fit if RAM were the only possible storage space. You just want to limit its use, as reading data from the buffer on the hard disk takes more time than reading it from RAM.

The main memory found on your motherboard is called *dynamic RAM* (DRAM). Calling it "dynamic" sounds good, but what it really means is that DRAM can only hold its data for up to four milliseconds before that data must be refreshed—it's as though the memory must be reminded of what it knew. DRAM isn't quite as fast as the static RAM (SRAM) used in L2 caches, but it's significantly cheaper.

> **TIP**
>
> All RAM isn't created equal when it comes to speed. Check the access times on the chip packages and get the fastest RAM you can—the lower the access time, the better.

Basic DRAM Types

Until pretty recently, most DRAM came in one format: Fast Page Mode (FPM) RAM. FPM RAM has access times of either 70 nanoseconds (ns) or 60ns, with 60ns required if you want to keep up with the 66MHz Pentium motherboard speeds. FPM DRAM accesses one block of memory at a time.

> **NOTE**
>
> The "Fast Page Mode" part of the name refers to the way that FPM RAM accesses its structure. It's designed to operate most quickly and efficiently when the next bit of data it's retrieving is in the same page as the previous bit. On x86-based machines, a page of memory is 4KB in size.

On pre-Pentium systems, FPM RAM could keep up with the rest of the computer. But even the 60ns variety operates at a maximum speed of less than 30MHz, which means that the RAM was slower than the 33MHz CPU in my old 486 machine. Now that the CPU is apt to be operating somewhere in the 400MHz range, FPM RAM can't even come close to meeting those speeds. Additionally, as motherboard speeds have leapt from 66MHz to 100MHz, the situation has deteriorated. RAM is crucial to good computer performance and needs to be at least as fast as the components around it. The need for more responsive RAM, therefore, has led to a couple of recent innovations in RAM type:

- Extended Data Output (EDO) RAM

- Synchronous Dynamic RAM (SDRAM)

These two types of RAM are discussed in the following sections.

Walking and Chewing Gum at the Same Time—EDO RAM

EDO RAM represents an improvement on the FPM RAM design, but not a radical departure from it. The FPM RAM design works on a sort of "bucket brigade" idea in which one chunk of data can be retrieved from RAM at a time. The EDO design improves on this by giving the bucket brigade a helper; while the RAM is slinging data into the CPU, the helper is running around behind the scenes locating the next bit of data to be processed and lining it up to be picked up.

The increased efficiency produced by finding the next bit of data while the first is being shoved at the CPU makes EDO RAM faster than FPM RAM. But it's still running only at 40MHz, not as fast as the CPU—or even the motherboard. Thus, as systems get faster, more drastic solutions are called for in order to keep the CPU from sitting around drumming its fingers, waiting for the RAM to catch up.

Bursting DRAM Types

To understand the next advance in RAM speed, I'm going to have to back up a bit and talk about how RAM works.

One of the biggest hurdles to making RAM fast is the "random" part of main memory's title. When we say that this memory is "random," it's supposed to mean that all of the memory is equally easy to get at.

It's equally easy to get at, but not equally *fast* to get at. If a CPU can ask for something to be done and it's accomplished in one clock tick, then you have a zero wait state machine. If the operation can't be done in that time, then it starts using wait states. A *wait state* is essentially a clock tick during which the CPU isn't doing anything. As such, it's a good idea to avoid them.

NOTE   Clock ticks are the reciprocal of the CPU speed. On a 300MHz system, there are 300,000,000 clock ticks per second. The faster the CPU, the shorter the interval that a single clock tick represents.

The memory controller accesses DRAM in four-bit bursts, with the first bit taking the longest time to access because the first step is finding the right page in memory. So, when the memory controller is reading FPM DRAM, it first takes five clock ticks to find the page the first requested bit of data is on, and then three clock ticks to read each additional bit of memory on that page. The situation is improved slightly with EDO, as although it still takes five clock ticks to find the first page, reading the successive bits only takes two clock ticks for each bit. Of course, if the next bit of memory must be read from a different page, all bets are off and the next bit will take five clock ticks to read again. The L1 and L2 caches that are part of your system's CPU help with this problem as they'll store recently used data so that the memory controller doesn't have to keep dragging it all the way over from RAM, but caches have limited capacity.

To get around this problem, *bursting technology* is used to read not just the current four bits but an entire page (4KB on an *x86*-based system) at once. With this bursting technology, once the entire page is read into memory, *no additional wait states are required to read the latter three bits in each four-bit set*. The bits are already located and no time is wasted in finding them. To find a new page, you've still got the five-tick clock cycle to contend with, but once that page is found, then only one clock cycle is required to read each bit—no wait states are required. The DRAM itself tells the memory controller how to find those next bits.

This can be confusing, so try thinking of it like this. Imagine the DRAM as a series of dark rooms, each room representing a page of memory. Data is stored in boxes (representing addresses) in these rooms. These boxes are laid out in a logical fashion so that box 6 is next to box 7, which is next to box 8, and so forth. The only catch is that the boxes aren't touching, although they are arranged sequentially.

When the memory controller wants to retrieve data from a page of DRAM, it must find the page in which that data is stored and then go get the data that it wants. So, when the memory controller starts off, it goes to the hallway from which all the rooms of DRAM are available.

With ordinary DRAM, the memory controller must find the room it's looking for, then open the door and *while still in the dark*, feel around and find the data. It takes a little while to find the first box, but once the memory controller has found that one, it can feel ahead and find the next, and the next. At that point, the memory controller can deliver the data to the CPU.

How much simpler would this process be if the rooms were lit? That's more or less what bursting technology does. When the memory controller enters a "room," if the rooms are lit, the controller must still look around to find the first address it's supposed to pull data from. But once it's done that, then it can see the next box and the next, without having to feel along to find them.

Thus, the random access part of RAM is no longer quite so random—bits are assumed to be all from the same page, or a performance hit occurs.

Now that these points are clear, let's take a look at the bursting technologies currently available: burst EDO and synchronous dynamic RAM.

Chewing Faster—Burst EDO

Burst EDO (BEDO) represents an improvement in EDO technology, just combined with the faster read-ahead time. It can keep up with the CPU at speeds of up to 66MHz.

Improved Base Rate—SDRAM

A longer-term solution is represented in modern SDRAM, which synchs itself with the CPU at speeds of up to 100MHz. This represents access speeds of 10ns.

Full to Bursting

You'll notice that the theoretical limit is now up to 100MHz, which is better than the 28MHz possible with FPM DRAM but can't keep up with current CPU speeds of 400MHz. How do you handle that?

For the moment, you don't—no chips are currently manufactured that can keep up with this speed. A couple of possible contenders are lined up, but at this point, their designs are only theoretical; you can't buy chips based on these technologies. As of this writing, you're buying EDO or SDRAM, for the most part, and sometimes BEDO although it's less common. On top-of-the-line systems, this translates to wait states.

To make memory faster, you can increase the clock speed, widen the data path, or both. The trouble with making really high-speed memory (or anything else really fast) is that the faster it is, the more important precision becomes. Without additional controls, SDRAM is about as fast as it can get. The problem of how to provide that precision is the issue driving the efforts to make faster types of memory.

The two main technologies that plan to offer higher memory speeds are called Synchronous Link Dynamic Random Access Memory (SLDRAM) and Rambus DRAM (RDRAM). SLDRAM is supported by the Synchronous Link Consortium, which consists of about 15 companies, including Hyundai, IBM, and Apple, among others. RDRAM was developed by Rambus and is supported by Intel. SLDRAM's current design calls for 64MB memory modules running at 400MHz through two pipelines, giving it data transfer rates of 800Mbps—eight times the speed of currently available SDRAM. RDRAM operates at 800MHz through two pipelines for a total data transfer rate of 1.6Gbps.

Which design will win market share? It's hard to say at this point. RDRAM is already in use on some video boards, but is not yet available in main memory. SLDRAM's design is complete and some prototypes have been tested, but as of this writing, memory based on this design is not commercially available. Intel's support for RDRAM will help that technology, but the members of the Synchronous Link Consortium aren't an insignificant bunch either.

Disk Drives and Controllers

Another key element of a fast and reliable server is a fast and reliable disk drive. Whether you're running a file server, a print server, a communication server, or an application server, all your data and programs are stored on disk. For best performance, you want those disks to be as fast as possible.

Extended/Enhanced Integrated Drive Electronics (EIDE)

There are two important parts to a hard disk: the disk itself and its controller card. In the early days of PC hard disks, a standard called the Enhanced Small Disk Interface (ESDI) made a hard disk and its controller in two pieces connected with two ribbon cables (see Figure 7.4).

FIGURE 7.4:

An ESDI hard drive and a controller card

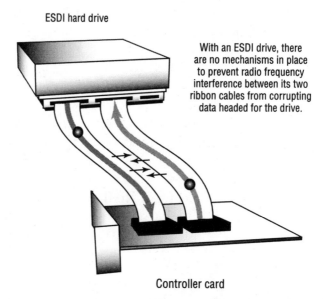

ESDI hard drive

With an ESDI drive, there are no mechanisms in place to prevent radio frequency interference between its two ribbon cables from corrupting data headed for the drive.

Controller card

This method worked, but those cables were a problem as they were prone to the same RF interference as are network cables, and inside a computer, there's a lot of RF interference—some of it is from the other hard-drive cable.

What Is the Integrated Drive Interface?

Accordingly, in 1988, Western Digital and others developed a standard called the Integrated Drive Interface (IDE), incorporating the drive controller and the hard disk into the same component. If you turn an IDE drive upside down, you can see the drive controlling mechanism on its underside. There's still a host adapter involved, but it's only for handling communication between the motherboard and the drive controller, not for doing any kind of data manipulation. The host adapter identifies each device linked to it according to whether it's a "master" or "slave" (or sometimes "secondary slave" device).

IDE technology had a couple of limitations. First, you could only plug up to two devices into the controller card. This meant that multiple drives (or other IDE devices, such as tape drives) required multiple controller cards in multiple slots using multiple IRQs. Second, they weren't very big. The maximum size of an IDE drive is 528MB, which these days is barely enough to load both an operating system and a full office suite, let alone have room for a swap file or any data.

An enhancement of IDE called EIDE (Extended/Enhanced Integrated Drive Electronics) helped alleviate these problems. EIDE controllers could accommodate up to four devices, which made things a bit more flexible and, as of this writing, can be up to 16GB in size.

Small Computer System Interface (SCSI)

Apple Computer developed another drive controller interface that eventually spread from the Mac world to encompass PCs. This technology, called SCSI, is like IDE/EIDE in that the hard drive and the drive controller are a single unit connected to the motherboard with a host adapter. It's different in the way that those devices are connected. SCSI host adapters can accommodate any kind of SCSI-compatible device in a daisy-chain that may extend outside the body of the computer and may include up to seven devices in addition to the host adapter. Although each device is connected to another device—not to the host adapter—all can communicate with the host adapter.

How does the host adapter tell which hard drive is speaking to it, or send data to the proper device? Each device on the SCSI chain, including the host adapter itself, is assigned a number called a *SCSI ID*. ID 7 is reserved for the host adapter, IDs 0 and 1 are for hard drives (with 0 reserved for the boot drive), and IDs 2–6 may be used by any other devices in the SCSI chain. The IDs don't have to go in order of where the devices are in the SCSI chain, nor do they all have to be used (that is, you don't necessarily need seven devices in the chain). The only vital points are that the reserved IDs must be used for their purpose, and you must terminate the SCSI chain on both ends. The termination is accomplished with a jumper setting; SCSI IDs may be set with hardware or software, depending on the device.

TIP   Just as I recommend that you keep records of IRQ and I/O address settings, keep track of SCSI IDs and which device is terminating the chain. It's much simpler to get this information from a list you have handy than by turning over each device to find out what its settings are, especially for internal devices.

If you want to add a new SCSI device to your system, power down the computer, plug it into the end of the chain, and terminate the chain. It's delightfully simple to work with.

Of course, it couldn't be as simple as just having a single SCSI standard, and the types of SCSI devices and host adapters are not always compatible. Table 7.1 shows the various types of SCSI currently available.

TABLE 7.1: SCSI Types

SCSI Type	Description
SCSI-2	Uses a 50-pin connector and an 8-bit bus and supports data rates of 4Mbps.
Wide SCSI	Uses a 68-pin connector and has a 16-bit bus.
Fast SCSI	Like ordinary SCSI, but doubles the clock rate to support data transfer rates of 10Mbps.
Fast and Wide SCSI	Combines the 16-bit bus of Wide SCSI and the doubled clock speed of Fast SCSI for data transfer rates of 20Mbps.
Ultra SCSI	Has an 8-bit bus but supports data transfer rates of 20Mbps.
Ultra Wide SCSI/SCSI-3	Has a 16-bit bus and supports data transfer speeds of 40Mbps.
Ultra2 SCSI	Has an 8-bit bus and supports data transfer rates of 40Mbps.
Ultra2 SCSI Wide	Has a 16-bit bus and supports data transfer rates of 80Mbps.

NOTE   SCSI-1, the predecessor to SCSI, used a 25-pin connector and did not support SCSI chains. Generally, when people refer to "SCSI" without elaborating, they're not referring to SCSI-1 but to SCSI-2.

One of the best things about SCSI is that it not only permits you to daisy-chain multiple devices from a single host adapter, but it also handles data transfers along that chain. The buses mentioned in Table 7.1 aren't just for a single hard drive, but also for all SCSI devices in the chain. A SCSI host adapter can "talk" to more than one device at a time, multitasking between them. This is important for a couple of reasons. First, it takes time for the read and write heads within the hard disk to find the right spot on the disk and then read or write the data. Also, the host adapter can think faster than its devices. Second, a single device on the SCSI chain doesn't need all the bandwidth available, so allowing the host adapter to divide the data transfer between multiple devices is more efficient.

Distinguishing SCSI from EIDE

Although it's more expensive than EIDE, SCSI is the better server technology (not technology, just *server* technology) for a few reasons.

First, SCSI host adapters support multitasking, and EIDE host adapters do not. When read or write operations for more than one device are pending, the EIDE host adapter must complete the operation for one drive before it can begin work on the second request. There are two ramifications to this. First, reads from slow hard disks or a CD-ROM (CD-ROMs are *much* slower than hard disks) must be completed before read or write operations for another device on the controller can begin. Second, the bandwidth between host adapter and drive is reserved for a single device that may not need all of it. So, as the host adapter can only communicate with a single device at one time, any remainder is wasted. The more devices that are installed in an EIDE machine, the more time and bandwidth are wasted.

Second, SCSI is more flexible than EIDE. Adding SCSI devices to a machine is as simple as powering down the machine, configuring the device's ID to make sure that it's not conflicting with any other, and making sure that the chain is terminated. Adding EIDE devices is more complicated. This flexibility will definitely pay for itself in terms of saved downtime.

Furthermore, many kinds of devices support SCSI interfaces—scanners, hard disks, CD-ROMs, removable drives, tape drives—but EIDE is supported only by hard drives and CD-ROMs.

NOTE   One SCSI device that you'll definitely want is a tape drive for doing backups. Non-SCSI tape drives run off the floppy controller and are far too slow for the kinds of data you'll be backing up from a server.

Third, SCSI drives are larger than EIDE drives. Although EIDE drives now support the unheard of sizes of 16GB, data storage needs keep growing. Application and operating system software are more, er, feature rich (I'm being diplomatic here) than ever, and show little sign of slowing down in their race to add girth. It's not just fat programs: data's also getting fatter, as multimedia files and extensive formatting are more common. On the server end, you need as much disk space as you can get.

The story on the client side is different. First, in a client/server environment, most client PCs are apt to be more static in their hardware needs than servers. After all, the point of having a network is to let you centralize your hardware in the server and share it with the clients. Second, the SCSI multitasking ability incurs some overhead that's negligible when balanced against the improved performance over five or six devices. This overhead matters when it's only a single drive. Third, most PCs come with EIDE support; adding SCSI support is an additional cost not justified for most users. Therefore, on the client side, where you're more apt to have a single hard drive so there's less contention for bandwidth and host adapter time, EIDE is a significantly cheaper and equally viable option to SCSI.

Server Display Support

The discussion of monitors on the server end should be quite brief. Simply put, there's no reason to spend a lot of money on a fancy monitor for your server because no one's going to be spending a long time looking at it. If you can get something with a decent refresh rate (75Hz or better), then a plain monitor and low-end video support should work just fine. You're spending quite enough on the SCSI recommendations and all that extra memory—no need to spend it on a 21-inch monitor that few will ever look at. As you'll see in Chapter 8, "Server Types and Additional Hardware," the story's very different on the client end.

Power Protection

Something that's *not* an option on the server end is power protection. First, power isn't getting any more reliable—quite the opposite. Electrical storms are one source of power problems. I live in Virginia, and during an ordinary summer, I can expect to lose power perhaps once a week for a short time. During a bad summer a couple of years ago, I was losing power several times a week, sometimes for short periods and sometimes for hours. Most of the power outages aren't long enough to seriously inconvenience me in terms of working, but without power protection, I would lose data every time the power went out. If they're right about the way global warming works, then this situation isn't going to improve. One side effect of global warming is expected to be more powerful and frequent storms as the ice caps melt and saturate the air with moisture.

The problem isn't simply natural, but a function of the draws on power. When the power grid was built, it was designed for fewer people and a *lot* less in the way of electrical appliances for all those people. Over time, it's become seriously overloaded with demand. One side effect of that demand is that the strength of the power sometimes sags as there are too many demands made on the available current. On a smaller scale, the same thing is true of building wiring. Modern buildings have wiring built for today's power loads and (hopefully) separated to shelter electronics from heavy motors that do Bad Things to the general power supply. However, older buildings are often still limping along with the same wiring that was designed for lights and electric typewriters.

In a perfect world, you'd power-protect all PCs on the network, not just the server. If you're at all serious about data protection, at the very least, the server must be protected from sudden power outages or sags and spikes that can damage its components.

Surge protectors are not power protection; they're a handy way of plugging a bunch of devices into a single outlet. Why don't they count as power protection? First, they don't protect you when the power goes out completely, and second, they're too forgiving of power surges. A surge that doesn't hurt the surge protector can hurt the more delicate electronics within your computer. If you have a surge protector, power-protect it.

For real power protection, you need an uninterruptable power supply (UPS). In general terms, a UPS is any device that provides battery backup for line power; when the line power fails, the battery kicks in. The battery won't last long enough to let you keep working, but it will let you close files and shut down the machine in an orderly fashion—something that makes operating systems happy.

NOTE   The amount of time that the PC will run from the UPS depends on the size of the UPS's battery, the battery's charge, and how many devices you have plugged into it. When shopping for a UPS, tell the vendor what you plan to have plugged into the device (for example, the server and the monitor) and how long you want the device to run after the outage. Then the vendor will be able to tell you how big a battery you'll need.

The devices sold as UPSes come in two flavors: switched power supplies (SPSes) and on-line power supplies, which are the true UPSes.

Switched Power Supplies

As illustrated in Figure 7.5, when the line power is working, the switched power supply (SPS) passes current from the wall straight to the PC, siphoning off a little bit of power to charge the battery. When the power fails, the line switches from the power in the wall to the power in the battery.

FIGURE 7.5:

How switched UPSes work

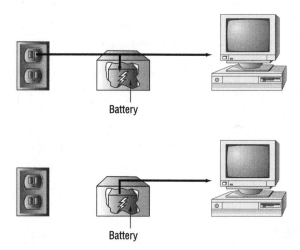

Battery

Battery

Notice a couple of things here. First, SPS devices don't necessarily offer line conditioning—that is, the power is going as is from the wall socket to the power supply, complete with any surges and sags that might be present. When shopping for an SPS, look for one with surge protection built in to offer some protection from these problems. Second, there's a point at which the power stops coming from the line. This is when the SPS says, "Augh! No power! Switch to the battery!" and turns the power feed over to the battery. In other words, there's a brief period during which the PC is getting no power whatsoever.

How long a period? These days, not long. The SPS can pass control from the line to the battery in about 4ms, which is a sufficiently short period of time that the PC won't notice. Just as you can live without breathing for a short period of time, the PC can live without power for a little while. It's just inadvisable to stop breathing *or* drawing power for very long.

Most of the devices you see sold as UPSes are in fact SPSes, and they're much cheaper than online UPSes (discussed next). They'll work just fine for most applications provided that your power is of reasonably consistent quality so your components aren't hurt by surges or spikes.

Online UPSes

If you need more protection than a switched UPS can provide, consider an online UPS. As you can see in Figure 7.6, the online UPS runs power from the wall through the battery, conditions it within the battery, and then sends the clean power from the battery to the device. Power surges hurt the battery, not the server's power supply. As the power goes through the battery, the battery gets charged.

FIGURE 7.6:

How online UPSes work

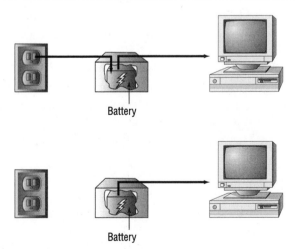

Battery

Battery

The fact that the power always comes from the battery means that there's not even a 4ms switching time when the power goes out, as the battery was providing power before the power went out anyway. As you can see in Figure 7.6, the battery continues supplying power as it always did. All that's changed is that the battery is getting no new power, so the power will only last as long as the charge does.

Choosing a UPS

Should you get an SPS or an online UPS? This depends on what you need. Both kinds of devices have become much cheaper in recent years, so buying an online UPS is still expensive but not entirely out of the question for devices that need the extra features of a true UPS. Prices range with the size of the device's battery, but generally speaking, you can expect to pay in the hundreds for an SPS and in the low thousands for an online UPS.

What do you power-protect? On the server, it's a good idea to protect not only the computer but also the monitor, as if you want to make a graceful shutdown, you'll need to see what you're doing. Don't power-protect nonessential devices, as they'll run down your battery. *Never* power-protect a laser printer as its power needs are huge and it will drain your battery almost immediately.

What about client machines? At one time, it wasn't practical to power-protect client machines, but power protection, like most other things, has become really cheap. You can pick up a switched power supply for under $100, so that might be a good $100 to spend in order not to lose data during sudden power outages.

Summary

I've spent this chapter talking about the basic bits of hardware that you'll need in just about any server. Along the way I've made some suggestions of technology that might work best in a server situation.

In the final analysis, for most purposes I'd recommend:

- High-speed CPU with plenty of on-board cache

- PCI bus so far as possible

- Modern SDRAM memory (as much as you can afford but at least 64MB; the more clients on the network, the more you'll need)

- SCSI host adapter

- A cheap monitor

- An uninterruptable power supply for the server

Armed with these components, you should have a server that can stand up to the demands of your network clients. Of course, some servers will have special needs rooted in their special purposes. In Chapter 8, I'll talk about the various types of servers you're likely to encounter and how their requirements change based on their roles.

EXERCISE 7

1. What is the location and function of the L1 cache?

2. In modern computers, which is faster: the CPU or main memory? Why?

3. ISA cards run at _____MHz, while PCI cards run at _____MHz.

4. The fastest main memory currently commercially available is called?

    A. EDO

    B. SDRAM

    C. FPM RAM

    D. RDRAM

5. Fill in all of the blanks in the following table, which is taken from this chapter:

SCSI Type	Description
SCSI-2	Uses a 50-pin connector and an ___-bit bus and supports data rates of 4Mbps.
Wide SCSI	Uses a _-pin connector and has a 16-bit bus.
	Like ordinary SCSI, but doubles the clock rate to support data transfer rates of 10Mbps.
Fast and Wide SCSI	Combines the 16-bit bus of Wide SCSI and the doubled clock speed of _____ for data transfer rates of __Mbps.
	Has an 8-bit bus but supports data transfer rates of 20Mbps.
Ultra Wide SCSI/SCSI-3	Has a 16-bit bus and supports data transfer speeds of __Mbps.
Ultra2 SCSI	Has an _-bit bus and supports data transfer rates of 40Mbps.
	Has a 16-bit bus and supports data transfer rates of __Mbps.

6. Explain the difference between an online UPS and a switched UPS.

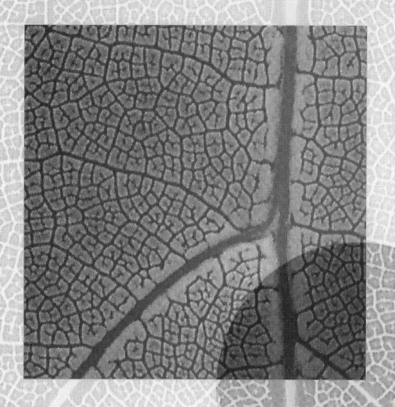

8

Server Types and
Additional Hardware

In Chapter 7, "Building the Better Server," I discussed the basic needs of your network servers: CPU types, host adapters, memory, and so forth. Those are just the bare bones of a server, however—there's a lot more to networking than storing files centrally. In this chapter, I'll examine the various types of servers that you're likely to find and take a look at the specialized hardware that these servers will require.

Of course, all the hardware mentioned here needs to be supported by the basic system components described in Chapter 7; it does you little good to have the world's fastest printer on a machine with no memory. So, I'll talk about how the basic server components support the bells and whistles that you're adding here. In addition, some servers will combine two or more server types; it's not unusual to find a single server providing file storage and print serving to the network, for example.

Data Storage

File serving is the granddaddy of all network server functions. You may not need communications serving; you may not need application serving; some networks might even be able to get along without print serving. Just about everyone running a client/server network wants an easy place to store and back up files, though.

Disk Storage Basics

Before I get deeply into disk and file servers, I should quickly review how file organization works.

Continued on next page

Computer disks are divided physically into circles called *tracks* and in pie-shaped wedges radiating from their centers. The pieces created by the intersection of the concentric circles and the pie-shaped wedges are called *sectors*. In the FAT-based and NTFS file systems, sectors are, in turn, grouped logically into *clusters*. The number of sectors in a cluster will depend on the file system in use on the disk and the size of the disk. Not all file systems organize sectors into clusters. For example, HPFS, the file system designed for OS/2, does not. In those cases, the sector is the logical unit of storage.

Every disk is formatted with a file system that numbers each logical storage unit on the disk, for example, each cluster. Once the disk is formatted, the operating system has a map of the hard disk space, what clusters are used for storing what data, and what clusters are free and where they are. Every time that data is written to or deleted from the disk, this map is updated.

Although I'll refer to the FAT file system in my examples just to keep things simple, this applies to other file systems as well. The format of the map and the way it's structured varies from file system to file system; the function of the file system remains the same.

Disk Servers

File serving originally started with disk serving. A *disk server* is a central repository for files and data, attached to the network like any other node. Its hard disk is shared, so any client on the network can map a drive letter to the shared disk as though it were local. When reading from or writing to the disk, the operating system refers to the FAT, which locates the data on the disk by its cluster number in the map.

Ah, but who has that copy of the FAT? In the case of a disk server, the client does, not the server. The first time that a client accesses a disk server after rebooting, the disk server takes a snapshot of its FAT and passes it to the client to store in its own memory. Thereafter, when the client attempts to access the server's hard disk, it uses its own copy of the FAT, as shown in Figure 8.1.

FIGURE 8.1:

A client opening a file stored on a disk server

You can probably see the potential problem. The whole point of having a server is to give all the clients on the network access to its hard disk, right? But as files are created and deleted on the hard disk, the map, as shown in the FAT, will change. Deleted files open up new clusters on the disk in which newly created files can be stored; the first open cluster is always used in the FAT file system. Thus, after a few hours of several clients working on the disk, each "map" of the hard disk might well be quite different. The map that's valid at 8:00 A.M. may be completely inaccurate by 4:00 P.M. and this could slow or halt data retrieval.

To avoid this problem, disk servers are generally divided into several volumes (one for each user) or use removable disks only accessible to one user at a time. They're still in use in some applications. For example, you might use a disk server to provide floppy disk access to users working at diskless workstations. But even though they haven't completely died out, disk servers are not nearly as common as file servers.

File Servers

Rather than sharing its physical disk with the network, a file server shares the storage area. Up to a point, file serving works like disk serving:

- The file server shares a volume with the network.
- The client maps a drive letter (or Unicode path) to the shared volume.
- The client can then read and write to the shared volume.

From the client's perspective, accessing the shared volume is just like accessing a locally available hard disk except for one difference: if the server sharing that volume is not on the network or stops sharing that volume, then the client won't be able to access the shared volume.

How Does File Serving Work?

Although file serving and disk serving may look the same to the client, they're not the same thing at all. The difference lies mainly in the matter of who's doing the work. The contrast between a disk server and a file server could perhaps be expressed like this. When a network client asks a disk server for a file for the first time after a reboot, the disk server rummages in its drawer and finds a map of the storeroom where it keeps the files. The disk server then tells the client, "Go ahead and get the file, kid, but keep the map; I've got better things to do than keep you supplied with maps." Every time a client gets something from the storeroom or returns something, the storeroom gets a little reorganized. Since it's got an automatic update, the maps that the disk server hands out are accurate. When client machines come back to look for files using their old maps, however, it's quite possible that the storeroom will now be differently arranged and that the client won't be able to find anything.

The file server, on the other hand, would rather find things itself than have a bunch of network clients rummaging through its hard disk. When a workstation requests a file, the file server says, "I'll send it right out—no, really, I'd rather do it." It then passes the request to the file system driver, which finds the file and sends the location information to the client application so it can open the file. The client never gets a copy of the server's FAT, but has to rely on the server to fulfill the request. This means that only one copy of the FAT exists, so it's always up to date.

File serving is one of the most common network server functions around for a couple of very good reasons. First, it offers a centralized location for backup purposes. Second, it permits more than one person to easily access the file. Certainly, it would be possible in many cases for a client machine to share its hard disk with the network so that locally stored files are available to others (this is common on peer-to-peer networks). The trouble is, if 40 people on a network all must share parts of their hard disks with the rest of the network, finding a particular file can be quite difficult.

The only catch with a file server is that the server *must* remain online and *must* be backed up regularly, or else it's worse than useless. If files are stored on client machines, then if one client machine breaks, the rest of the people on the network can still do their jobs. But if the file server goes down, then the network is paralyzed. Backups and fault tolerance are crucial to a good file server.

Hardware Needs

What do you need to make a good file server? File servers need large and flexible storage disks, memory sufficient to serve the requests to open and save files, and a reliable backup system. These topics are discussed in the following sections.

Hard Disk Requirements

First, you need fast and flexible disks. Returning to the discussion of disk types in Chapter 7, "Building the Better Server," the best disk type for a file server is almost certainly SCSI. SCSI disks are more expensive than EIDE disks, but they are faster when it comes to processing multiple requests on multiple disks and more flexible because of the ease of adding an extra disk to the SCSI chain.

TIP   A good network operating system includes some capability to extend volumes—that is, to logically add new disk space to a previously made partition so that two or more physical disks can appear as a single volume.

How Much Memory Is Enough?

Second, you need enough memory to support all of the file read and write requests that will be coming in. How much memory will be needed? It's not always easy to say. When running an application server (which I'll discuss toward the end of this chapter), a good rule of thumb is about 4-8MB of RAM for each user. But file serving is much less of a strain on the server than is application serving, as the file server's job is done once the read or write request is fulfilled. The file server's memory is not taxed while the file is open, and during application serving, the server maintains the application files in its own memory.

File Protection

Third, you'll need some kind of backup system. The point of having a file server in the first place is to preserve your company's data (or your personal data, if the server is part of a home network). If the data weren't important, you wouldn't be storing them in the first place. The backup method doesn't always have to be fancy so long as you're consistent about using it and know how to restore those backups when the hard disk dies.

Backups are really important to most server types, but for file servers, they're vital. Thus, let's take a more in-depth look at some of the possible backup media.

NOTE   The backup media that you can use depend on both your operating system and the backup utility you choose. Before buying, find out what hardware is supported. To record to a CD, for example, you'll need a backup program that isn't tape only.

Tape Drives

When you say "backup media" one of the first things that most people will think of are tape drives. There are a number of reasons for this: tapes can hold a lot of data, they're cheap, and in general, they're widely supported. However, not all types of tape drives are supported by all backup software; I'll get to the various types later in this section. They're not a perfect solution to the backup problem, as tapes are relatively slow both for writes and reads. Tapes are also fairly vulnerable to environmental hazards, such as heat. But their benefits outweigh their detriments for many and they're an extremely popular solution to the backup problem.

If you've ever used backup software, you've probably noticed that backups are a two-step process: first the data is catalogued and then the catalog is copied to the tape. Why not just save time and do it all in one step? The catch to some tape backup technologies (namely DAT—Digital Audio Tape) is that they aren't very efficient when it comes to small files, as each unit on the tape requires header information. Thus, it's important to copy data to the tape as large units, not as a whole collection of files.

Otherwise, much of the space on the tape will be wasted. This is why backup utilities create catalogs of data and record the catalogs rather than just blasting the data directly onto the tape.

Why Are Tapes Slower Than Disks?

One reason that you're never going to see hard disks replaced by tape drives is speed. Data that takes microseconds to read from disk takes much longer to read from tape. The difference has a lot to do with the way in which tapes and disks are designed to read and write data, as shown here.

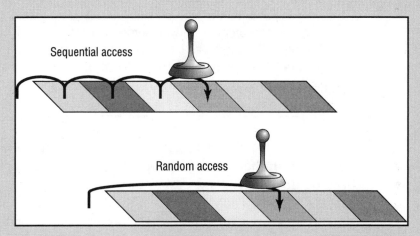

Disks are *random access* devices. This means that data can be pulled from any location as easily as another and does not have to be accessed in any particular order. The disk head can move to points A, D, Z, and L on the disk—it doesn't have to access those points in order or hit B and C on the way to point D. The closer the points are to each other, the faster the disk can access them, but the order in which the points are arranged doesn't affect retrieval time.

Tape drives, on the other hand, are *sequential access* devices. Not only must they access data in the order in which they're stored on the disk, but also on their way to reaching one location on the disk, they must pass through all locations leading up to it.

Tapes come in a variety of different formats, each of which is mutually unintelligible from the others and requires a tape drive designed for it. Generally speaking, the idea of a tape drive is to copy the data from the hard disk to the other media. Most tape backup utilities can employ some kind of compression that both increases the amount of data that can be written to tape and speeds up the write time. The only catch to this is that you may not know what you're getting.

WARNING Many manufacturers label a tape's size according to a 2:1 compression ratio so that a tape with a 1GB capacity for uncompressed data is labeled a 2GB tape. As you probably know, the degree of compression possible depends on the type of data you're dealing with, so that you may get better compression with some kinds of data and none at all with others. Choose tapes based on your needs for storing uncompressed data. That way, you'll be pleasantly surprised at your possible capacity instead of irritated that you can't store as much as you'd expected.

Of course, as hard disks get bigger, the backup media have to keep up with them. Just as floppies could be an acceptable way of backing up a 20MB hard drive but fail miserably when the hard drive is 500MB, a 40MB tape cartridge becomes useless when it's time to back up a 10GB hard disk. Tape capacity can be increased in three ways:

- Lengthen the tape
- Widen the tape
- Increase data density on the tape

Let's take a look at some common tape formats to see how they accomplish their needs for increased density and how that affects their performance otherwise.

Quarter-Inch Cartridge (QIC) "QIC" is a misnomer as modern QIC cartridges may have either .25-inch or .315-inch wide tapes. Most of what makes a QIC cartridge a QIC cartridge (shown in Figure 8.2) is the way the data's laid out on the tape and the fact that the heads are built into the tape cartridge instead of being part of the drive. The moving part of the drive is a roller that manipulates these heads, not the heads themselves.

FIGURE 8.2:

QIC cartridges are distinguished by the way that the cartridges house the heads, not just the tape.

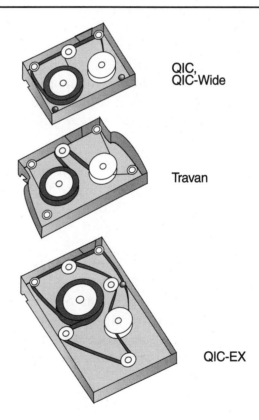

QIC, QIC-Wide

Travan

QIC-EX

There are three main types of QIC tapes today:

- Travan
- QIC-Wide
- QIC-Ex

Travan technology, developed by Imation Enterprises, uses the basic QIC format with improved media and .315-inch wide tape to make large-capacity cartridges ranging in capacity from 400MB to 10GB. QIC-Wide tapes use the basic QIC cartridge structure, but with a wider tape so as to write more tracks on the tape and therefore increase capacity. QIC-Ex also uses the QIC format, except that the tapes are longer and thus the cartridge is somewhat longer to accommodate the change. The QIC-Ex tapes may be either .25 inch or .315 inch wide.

QIC is probably the most widespread tape variety available. It supports tapes ranging from the very small (40MB) to the very large (theoretically, up to 20GB, although the cartridges sold today generally hold no more than 4GB without compression). QIC is popular for a few reasons. First, it's fast for a tape drive and supported by most backup utilities. Second, it is also backward compatible with itself, so that a drive built to accommodate more recent varieties of the standard can often read and sometimes write tapes in an older format. Travan drives, for example, can work with .315-inch tapes of any variety. Third, QIC drives and their cartridges are the most inexpensive types of tapes available; and, particularly for young LANs, this is a major selling point.

Digital Linear Tape (DLT) DLT, shown in Figure 8.3, was originally developed by Digital Corporation for VAX machines, but has since become available for PC-based LANs. Its capacity is quite high (up to 35GB) as its tapes are .5 inch wide, and it sports high data transfer rates. DLT isn't as popular as other technologies such as QIC and DAT, but it's good for large LANs.

FIGURE 8.3:

A DLT cartridge

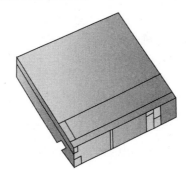

Digital Audio Tape (DAT) Digital Audio Tapes are small for backup tapes. They are actually cartridges with a 4mm-wide tape that use some form of the Digital Data Storage (DDS) standard to write data. The capacity of the tape depends on the level of DDS used: DDS has an uncompressed capacity of 2GB; DDS-2 of 4GB; and DDS-3 of 12GB. A DAT 4mm tape is shown in Figure 8.4.

FIGURE 8.4:

A DAT looks a bit like an audio cassette.

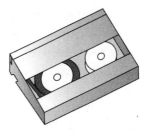

DAT recording technology operates something like video recording in order to maximize the storage space on each tape. Rather than having a fixed head like a QIC-compatible drive, DAT drives use what's called a *helical scan mechanism* that pulls the tape out of the cartridge and wraps it around the write head at an angle.

Why do this? In every backup method, when data is written to a tape, it's recorded in a series of stripes. In QIC and DLT tapes, these stripes are parallel lines running the length of the tape, like the stripes on a garter snake. You may recall that one limitation on cable speed—information density—is that an unshielded cable next to another one leads to crosstalk between the two cables, and that can lead to data corruption. The same is true of having parallel streams of data next to each other; they can corrupt each other if their density is too great.

To avoid corruption, you can either make the tracks less dense so that they don't affect each other as much, or you can arrange them so that they don't affect each other as much. DAT takes the second tack, getting around this problem in an approach similar to that taken by twisted pair cable. Tracks on a DAT tape are written not in parallel lines running the length of the cable, but as a series of diagonal stripes across the tape. The angle of each stripe is slightly different so that they're less likely to interfere with each other. For extra data security, there are two sets of heads at play during the write operation. One set writes the data, and another, set at a 90-degree angle to the write heads, reads the data directly after it's written to check it for accuracy. If what's read isn't what was written, then the data can be immediately rewritten and rechecked, with the procedure repeated until the data are read correctly. What this means in practical terms is that DAT recordings can be very densely packed with data without data corruption. They're a high-capacity storage method.

DAT's method of writing data isn't free of consequences. First, it's slower than other methods because of the additional write time taken for verification. Second, the heads on DAT drives can wear out more quickly than other drive types because the heads move instead of being fixed in place. Third, DAT technology requires expensive motors that fixed-head drives don't need, thus pushing up the cost.

Exabyte (8mm) Tape Technology Exabyte took an approach similar to DAT's to making high-capacity tapes. Like DAT, it writes data in diagonal stripes instead of in parallel lines down the tape. The main differences between the two media are the size of the tape (as you'd guess, these tapes are 8mm wide instead of 4mm wide, meaning that the tapes can hold more) and the angle of the verification heads being 221 degrees instead of 90 degrees. This means that Exabyte tapes (shown in Figure 8.5) have a higher capacity than DAT tapes.

FIGURE 8.5:

Exabyte tapes look like bigger versions of DATs.

Choosing a Tape Type As they have limited storage capacity, QIC drives are excellent for small-to-medium LANs or even for backing up individual PCs as they're so inexpensive. Although slower than QIC, DAT drives are a good and reliable method of backing up medium-sized networks. For large networks, I'd recommend either DLT or Exabyte technology. Note that theoretical tape capacities may not match what's sold, so bear that in mind when choosing a tape backup solution.

What about hardware type? Tape drives come with three types of connections:

- Parallel
- IDE
- SCSI

For backing up a server, I'd have to recommend SCSI. Parallel ports are far too slow to back up any serious amount of data. SCSI is a superior technology to EIDE for servers because of the way that media reads and writes are handled.

Optical Drives

For those with deeper pockets, the need to circulate backed-up material, or both, recordable CDs can offer another solution to the backup problem. The recorder looks much like any other CD player and so do the discs—the only difference is what you can do with this CD player.

Like CD-ROMs, your computer sees recordable CDs as ordinary drives like hard or floppy disks. You don't have to catalog data to record it to the CD, just copy the desired files or directories.

NOTE The optical drives discussed here are not necessarily CD-ROM drives. In fact, they often won't be—the CDs are too small and too slow to make good backup media for most situations.

The two catches to these recordable CDs is that they're expensive—the drives are; the CDs themselves don't cost much—and their capacity isn't great. The largest-capacity drives I've seen offered are less than 5GB in size—not small, but given the size of hard disks these days, perhaps not as big as you'll need, either.

Removable Drives

Removable drives are another backup media that can be used both for saving files and distributing them. They're not quite as flexible as optical drives; these days, almost every modern computer has a CD-ROM player, but not every one has a Zip or Jaz drive, or the equivalent. However, they're inexpensive and easy to use.

Two main types of removable drives dominate the market: Iomega's Zip and Jaz drives. The first has a capacity of up to 250MB, which isn't really enough to do server backups. The second has a capacity of 1-2GB, depending on the cartridge. This is a bit more reasonable, particularly for daily backups. It's not a solution for those managing enormous LANs who would be looking for Exabyte or DLT tape drives and optical storage, but it's viable for smaller LANs or for backing up client machines.

Print Servers

The other kind of server you'll find on just about every LAN is one offering print services. The concept of print serving is pretty easy: you connect the printer to the server, install its drivers, and share the printer with the network. All those who want to use that printer will need to install support for the printer at their own workstations. The nature of this support varies with the operating system. For example, Windows 3.*x* machines connecting to a print server need to load all drivers locally. However, Windows NT machines connecting to a print server don't have to—all drivers are automatically downloaded to them.

If the print server is just a print server and nothing else, most of what it's going to need is a good printer. Disk space isn't important as all the disk will hold is the operating system, the appropriate drivers, and spool files. A single 500MB IDE drive should be able to handle those needs for most LANs. Some memory is important as a print server may use its own memory to supplement that of the printer, but the server won't need as much memory as an application server will, for example. Even CPU speed isn't vital to a good print server—that 486 that's been gathering dust but no one can bear to give away will make a good dedicated print server.

How Does the Printer Connect to the Network?

So, you've got a printer and you've got a network. How do you hook up one to the other? There are three main ways in which you can do this:

- Connect it to an existing computer.
- Attach it to a print server device.
- Get a network-ready printer that you can connect directly to the network.

These methods are discussed in the following sections.

Printing from the Computer

This is a common configuration, particularly in smaller or new LANs. Inexpensive PCs are fairly easily come by, and remember, a print server doesn't require a lot of horsepower to do a good job. The biggest bottleneck in printing is the parallel cable (more on that in a moment when I talk about network-direct printers), so even a 386 would do a credible job if you happened to have one lying around (see Figure 8.6). So long as the PC is functioning and can talk to the rest of the network, it should work for a print server.

FIGURE 8.6:

Get that 486 out of retirement and turn it into a print server.

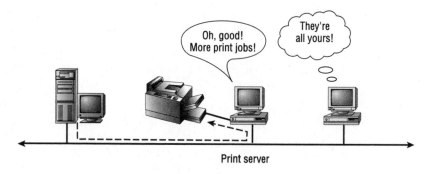

Print server

An old 486 computer can be pressed into service as a print server.

If you can avoid it, you *don't* want to keep the printer on a network client machine. Certainly, individual print jobs may not take up many CPU cycles or much memory, but an entire network's print jobs could. Think carefully about how much printing you expect to do and how much work would be done on such a PC before making a network client the print server for the network.

Printing from a Print Server

Not all print servers are decommissioned PCs. There are actual network-ready print server devices that you can plug into your network and use to create network access to several printers from a single device (see Figure 8.7). Such a device is controlled from another computer.

FIGURE 8.7:

Print server devices can make a convenient way to connect more than one printer to a single device.

Why use a print server device instead of a computer with a printer attached? Flexibility is one reason. Such a device can connect two, three, or even five printers to the network at a single location, instead of the one or two possible from an ordinary PC. Cost is another. Even taking into account dropping PC prices, print server devices are typically much cheaper than a new PC if you don't already have a spare PC available.

Network Printers

Remember, the bottleneck in print jobs is not the network, spooling print jobs from disk, or anything to do with the printer or the computer it's attached to—it's that parallel cable. (Or, worse yet, a serial cable. Hopefully, you're not trying to run a network with a serial printer.) The networked printer gets around that problem by cutting it out of the equation altogether. A network printer is connected directly to the network with the same 100Mbps or so connection that everyone else has (see Figure 8.8).

FIGURE 8.8:

Connect a printer directly to the network to avoid latency brought about by slow parallel cables.

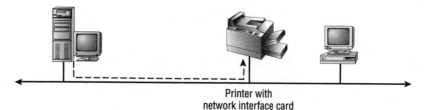

Printer with
network interface card

By installing a network interface card, a printer can become an independent
node on the network.

This solution has a couple of issues of which you should be aware. First, not all printers support direct connections to the network. You'll need one that has a place to attach a network card. Second, printing to a network printer generally requires installing a special transport protocol (such as DLC) to communicate with the printer. An alternative to installing the special printing protocol is install a service so that you can send print jobs to the printer with TCP/IP or some such protocol. Finally, as network printers have no PC or print server device to fall back on, print jobs can't be spooled from a hard disk and eked out to the printer as it can handle them. A network printer must have enough memory installed to completely handle any print job that comes its way. I'd suggest a minimum configuration of 16MB of printer memory in any network printer.

Requirements for a LAN Printer

Whether you're using a PC-based print server or a black box, much of your printer's performance will be linked to the printer attached to it. In that case, what makes a good printer? For a LAN, a good printer must be:

- Fast
- Flexible
- Reliable

Let's take a look at what this means in practical terms.

You Have a Need for Speed

Speed for printers is generally expressed in terms of pages per minute (ppm). It's not dependent on how much memory is in the printer, but how the printer itself is put together—how fast it can put the image onto the paper and crank the paper through. These days, a decent printer can produce at least 10ppm of black-and-white copy and perhaps as much as 24ppm.

Unless you're talking about really high-end printers running in the thousands of dollars, color takes longer; black-and-white copy can be produced with a single pass while color takes three passes. You should still be able to find an inexpensive printer that can produce color output at a rate of 3-4ppm, however.

NOTE Printer speeds change while you look at them, so don't be surprised if by the time you read this book even higher ppm rates are possible. Shop around a bit before buying.

Being Everything to Everyone

It's likely that you'll have a variety of printing needs to meet on a network. The graphics department needs color output on transparencies; the administrative types need black and white only; the marketing people sometimes want color on paper and sometimes only black and white—there's little point in printing a slow and expensive color copy of a draft memo.

What can you do about this? First, you could get a single printer that's capable of handling both color and black and white. If you don't mind doing periodic cartridge switching, this can work. For those who have more complex networks, more than one printer is probably in order.

If you're doing all the same colors of printing, but your paper needs change depending on the print job, consider getting a printer that supports multiple paper trays. Depending on the configuration, you can use separate trays to hold cheap paper for drafts, more expensive paper for official documents, and transparencies or labels. It's certainly possible to switch the contents of the paper tray to conform to the needs of a particular print job. However, for large networks in which the client may not be able to easily reach the printer to change the paper, multiple paper trays can save you a lot of time.

Being There When You Need It

The most commonly available printers these days are laser printers, which is a good thing from a reliability standpoint. Laser printers have few moving parts, so long as you take some elementary precautions, you should be okay.

First, keep your paper under wraps until it's time to put it in the printer. Keep the paper boxes closed and dry so the paper doesn't ripple. Crinkled paper leads to paper jams, which are an annoyingly simple problem that can be a bit of a bear to resolve as you go chasing that last scrap of paper that got caught in the roller assembly.

Think about where you're plugging in the printer. For the PC's sake, don't plug a printer into the same circuit as the PC if you can possibly avoid it, as laser printers produce the kind of EMI that leads to dirty power. For the printer's sake—and the sake of the sanity of the person sending a print job to the printer from a remote area of the building—don't plug the printer into a switched circuit that will be dead if someone turns off the lights.

Avoid printer cables more than six feet long as longer cables will be prone to interference. So long as you're buying printer cables off the shelf, this shouldn't be hard to avoid.

Finally, get bidirectional printer cable so that when there's a problem with the printer you can get more reliable notification. Simple printer cables only report an error message that there's a paper jam—whether the printer is offline, out of paper, or has some other problem.

Why Does It Matter How Much Printer Memory Is Installed?

Memory installation is not directly related to speed or reliability. However, having sufficient printer memory installed will save you a lot of time that might be spent reprinting documents and fiddling with spooling settings. Sufficient printer memory is a must and becomes more important as your documents get more complex. It's true that if you're running print jobs through a PC then you can use some of that PC's memory to hold information needed for print jobs. But sooner or later, the printer's memory has got to take on the job of storing a page or two in memory. (If you're running printers directly connected to the network or attached to a print server device, then you must have enough memory installed in the printer to handle any job.)

When that print job, or part of it, is stored in the printer's memory, then all the data required to make that print job as you requested must be stored there, too. This means that each font (typeface and type size), each graphic, each line, and so forth all must be stored in memory—and they're not wiped out when that page is done, so they're cumulative. The more complex the publishing requirements are for a particular print job, the more memory you'll need. Otherwise, you'll spend a lot of time and paper redoing desktop-published documents that came out in 12-point Courier and big X's where the graphics were supposed to be. There are ways to get around this, but the best method of avoiding this kind of problem is to have sufficient memory installed in the first place.

Stupid Printer Tricks

When sharing a printer, keep in mind that you're not necessarily limited to one printer, one share name, or one set of permissions. Depending on your operating system, or in some cases the capabilities of the printer, you may be able to make one printer look like twins; hide some printers entirely while still sharing them with select members of the network; or even combine several printers together to make one logical printer.

Creating Multiple Personalities

It's possible to share a printer more than once, assigning different access permissions to each instance. For example, for security reasons, you might have a printer configured to be available only during certain hours of the day—if someone wants to print a document after 6 P.M., that's just too bad. If someone trusted needs access to the printer at odd hours of the day, you don't have to compromise security for other people. Just re-share the printer with a different name (and security settings that prevent unauthorized people from getting access to it) and set the less restrictive times for that share.

Hiding Shared Printers

Any operating system worth its salt has some kind of security settings in place to let you set passwords or user permissions to restrict user access to shared devices or files. Printers are no exception to this rule. Printers can be protected with passwords, per-user access rights, limiting the times of day that they're accessible, and so forth.

However, the best security is realized not with extensive restrictive settings but by concealing the fact that there's anything to protect. Share the printer with a hidden name (in Microsoft networks, for example, you'd do this by ending the printer's share name with a dollar sign) and it won't show up on anyone's browse list.

Combining Printer Assets

If there's a lot of demand for one particular printer, you can avoid backlogs by getting another printer of the same kind. Just acquiring the second printer won't necessarily solve anything, however. Those accustomed to connecting to the old printer will likely continue to do so unless forcibly prevented, and the change may confuse some people.

One way of resolving this problem is to do *printer pooling* in which two identically configured printers are combined under a single name. When a network client sends a print job to the logical printer, LaserJet, the job may actually be printed out on one of two (or more) printers, depending on which one was least busy when the job request came in. The process is transparent to the user except when it comes to picking up the completed print job. If you keep the pooled printers close to each other and let people know that a job might show up in one of two places, you should avoid most confusion.

Communications Servers

The need for out-of-office communications is nothing new. Faxing's been a necessary evil for about the past 10 years. It existed prior to this, but it was about 10 years ago that people quit asking whether you had a fax and started asking, "What's your fax number?" E-mail has similarly evolved from an occasional convenience to a staple of corporate communications. In fact, in some arenas it's more popular than faxing—I give out my e-mail address easily 10 times as often as I give out my fax number.

Individual users can get online access with dial-up networking of some kind. However, that solution isn't practical for large groups of people in a single location who all need to be able to fax or send e-mail on demand for several reasons:

- It's expensive to buy a modem for every desktop and possibly to provide a line for each user.

- It's wasteful to supply dedicated connectivity to everyone equally. Some people may need e-mail 20 times a day while others need e-mail access twice a week.

- It compromises office network security to have an open line to the Internet without protection. Also, the more client connections are open, the more loopholes exist to be shut or exploited.

How can you get around this problem? You could set up a pool of shared modems to which users on the network could connect. Alternatively, you could set up a proxy server to provide Net access for the LAN via a single connection.

Modem Pooling

One solution to the problem of how to provide everyone on the network with dial-up access is to share the server's modem. That way, whenever a network user wants to check e-mail or search the Web, she could connect to the shared modem and dial out, just like using a shared printing device or a shared hard disk. For small networks with light online usage, this might be feasible, but for larger networks or those with several serious Internet users contending for modem time, it's a squabble waiting to happen. Most people will need to explore some other option, perhaps connecting more than one modem to the server.

Wouldn't connecting more than one modem to the server cause the same problems? No, because modems aren't like shared printers. Shared printers can queue one client's memo while printing another's draft of the annual report. In contrast, if a modem's busy, it's busy. Therefore, you need some method of making several modems available but always sending the connection request to the one that isn't busy. That method is known as *modem pooling*.

Modem pooling is the idea of sharing several modems with the network so that they appear to be a single device. When a network client makes a connection to a modem in the pool, any modem may be chosen. The modem chosen may be different from connection to connection, depending on which modems are busy at any given time. However this works out, it's invisible to the user—all she knows is that she established a dial-up connection. This is fine—that's all that she *needs* to know.

Most computers have one or two communications ports and a mouse is likely to be using one of those ports. So, connecting these modems in the way common to single-user machines isn't really practical. For communications servers with modem pools, a multiport add-in card with multiple comm ports is a more practical solution. Such a connection is illustrated in Figure 8.9.

FIGURE 8.9:

Connect multiple modems to a single machine.

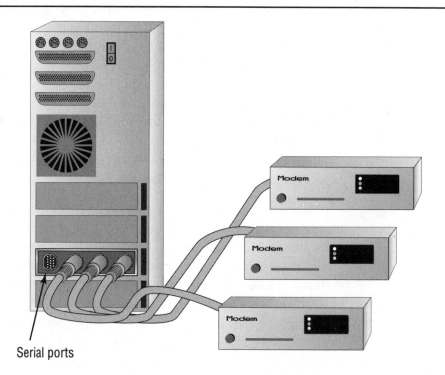

Serial ports

As network speed is far faster than any modem ever thought of being (56Kbps versus 100Mbps), clients connecting via the network won't notice any latency relative to what they'd notice if running the connection from the comm server.

The only catch to modem pooling is that each of the modems in the pool must be identical to the rest—same model, same speed, same drivers, and so forth. Otherwise, you'll run into problems as the client computers won't know how to communicate with the modem. If you have more than one kind of modem attached to the multiport board, put each kind of modem into a separate pool.

What hardware is necessary to a modem server? Memory, to be sure. Sufficient lines would also be a good thing. You don't necessarily need one line for each modem, but you'll need enough outside lines that everyone who can find a free modem can dial out as needed. As each modem has its own line, modem speed will depend on the connection, not the number of people connecting at once; they won't be sharing bandwidth.

As for software, the server will need some modem-sharing software (Windows systems, for example, do not include this capability out of the box.) and each client will need a modem client permitting them to access the shared modems. The protocols used on the clients will depend on the protocols in use on the network to which they're dialing up. Assuming that the modems are for permitting Internet access, the clients will need to have TCP/IP installed and set up for use on the Internet, just as they would for a direct connection.

Proxy Servers

A *proxy server* is a computer running software that allows it to act as a portal between network clients and another network, such as the Internet. The various proxy server software available offer an array of options such as security settings and balancing caches across servers. However, the basic idea, shown in Figure 8.10, remains the same regardless of the options.

FIGURE 8.10:

Use a proxy server to provide access to other networks via a central point.

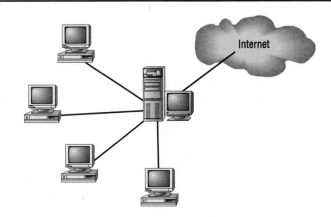

Proxy server needs are different from those of a modem server. First, as all network clients are sharing a single connection, the connection needs to support enough throughput to handle network users. Second, Internet caching takes place on the proxy server, so it needs to have a disk and use a file system that's meant for a lot of small files. As always for any server, plenty of memory is also a given.

The protocols that need to be running on a network with a proxy server depend on the proxy server software. Sometimes, all that's necessary is that the client and the proxy server have a protocol in common, and the proxy server and the other network have a protocol in common. The protocol used between the client and server doesn't have to be the same one used between server and network. In other words, a client could run an IPX/SPX-compatible protocol; the Internet could run TCP/IP; but the proxy server would need to run TCP/IP and an IPX/SPX-compatible protocol.

Connection Hardware

Several options are open to you when it comes to choosing the hardware and network type to use for your network, but the three you're most likely to choose from are modems, ISDN, and frame relay. Frame relay is describe in Chapter 6, "A Tour of Wide Area Networks," so in this section I'll concentrate on the other two options.

56Kbps Modems

Modem stands for MODulator/DEModulator; this word describes any device used to convert the digital signals used in computing to the analog ones that telephone lines can support. Just as a network card is the device that makes a computer network ready, a modem is the device that makes a computer dial-up network ready.

Due to improved compression algorithms and better quality of telephone lines, modem speeds have increased dramatically in recent years, going from 2400bps 10 years ago to today's 56000bps (56Kbps).

Like other new modem speeds, 56Kbps modems have had a tough time while the standards were hammered out. A final version of the V.90 standard for this transmission speed was not agreed on until February 1998 and not ratified until September 1998. Although plenty of 56Kbps modems were sold prior to the ratification, and some ISPs offered connections at that speed, two rival and mutually unintelligible technologies existed: K56flex (Rockwell/Lucent Technologies) and X2 (US Robotics, now part of 3Com). To get a 56Kbps connection to the Internet, you needed not only a 56Kbps modem on the server end, but you also needed a 56Kbps modem that was compatible with yours.

What happens to these technologies now that the V.90 standard has been ratified? You don't need to scrap your modem as most manufacturers are making firmware upgrades available from their Web sites. Before upgrading to V.90, make sure that your ISP has upgraded.

Although 56Kbps modems are the fastest true modems around today, their name is a bit of a misnomer. First, data speeds aren't the same for both directions; the X2 standard defines methods of supporting data transfers of up to 31.2Kbps for uploading and up to 56Kbps for downloading. Second, due to problems such as line noise, they don't really support transmission speed of 56Kbps for either direction, but more typically transfer data at speeds in the mid-40s.

NOTE Due to FCC restrictions on transmittal power, 56Kbps modems are currently not allowed to transfer data any faster than 53Kbps. There's some discussion of the possibility of removing this restriction, but at this point, it's no more than discussion.

So far as 56Kbps modems are concerned, the bottom line is that they're an inexpensive way of having a reasonably fast connection to the Internet. The Battle of the Standards led to low prices (at least during 1998; it looks as though prices may be stabilizing now that the V.90 standard has been ratified). The cost of a 56Kbps connection to the Internet, where available, is no more expensive than that of connecting at 28.8Kbps. In terms of speed, however, it's not nearly as fast as some of the other options—both those available today and on the horizon.

Are 56Kbps modems suitable for LAN use? For those running a modem pool intended for general corporate use, a 56Kbps modem should work just fine. Those wishing to set up a proxy server to share bandwidth may want something a little faster, however, and that's where some of the following technologies come in.

Integrated Services Digital Network (ISDN)

What are the alternatives to modems? Large companies with deep pockets have been working with leased lines (high-speed dedicated circuits for their exclusive use) for a long time. These solutions work very well, but they have one major drawback: they're very expensive.

In the mid-90s, a new solution began appearing in selected locations across the United States. This new technology made possible a link that might not offer 1.5Mbps dedicated bandwidth but *did* offer speeds greater than the 14.4Kbps modems commonly available at the time. Plus, it was something resembling affordable, at least in some areas. This solution was the Integrated Services Digital Network (ISDN).

At its simplest, the baseband version of ISDN, known as Basic Rate ISDN (BRI) comes with three channels: two data (D) channels and one bearer (B) channel responsible for transmitting connection information. The two D channels may be used either independently for full-duplex (two-way) access at 64Kbps, or multiplexed to a single logical channel at 128Kbps. For an additional cost, you can buy more channels, thus reaching possible throughput of 256 or even 512Kbps. Some ISDN connection devices also support data compression to increase possible throughput.

Whither goes ISDN? When ISDN was first released, it was very attractive for a number of reasons. First, it was enormously faster than standard modem access, which, you may recall, was running around 28.8Kbps tops at that point and more commonly at 14.4Kbps. Second, it offered a way of linking remote offices that were close to each other but far enough away to make an ordinary LAN impossible. Where available, it wasn't as cheap as Internet access, but it was a lot cheaper than a leased line.

These days, ISDN isn't dead but its advantages are much slimmer than they used to be. First, there's cost. The telephone companies no longer sell unlimited connection time. (Previously, it was not always available, but sometimes offered if the two sites connected with ISDN were close to each other.) Bell Atlantic, for example, sells three different plans under which you can buy up to so many hours of connect time, and after that point additional hours cost you more. For those looking for an all-day connection between offices or to the Internet, this gets expensive. This is especially true when you consider that it encompasses *all* ISDN time, including telephone services if you're using the digital line for everything. In addition to the connect charges, an ISDN connection requires some pricey hardware: a terminal adapter (like a network card) that goes in the communications server and a bridge or router to connect to the digital network.

Second, other means of data transfer have become available that close the gap between what ISDN can produce and what ordinary online access can produce. Cable modems are here and getting more widespread. Also, ADSL looks promising and should be available more than just experimentally during 1999 (ADSL has its own section later in this chapter). Where these newer options aren't available, ISDN is still a viable possibility, however.

When Is a Modem Not a Modem? Cable Modems

Beginning in 1997, a new online connection option began emerging in selected areas across the United States: cable modem. This high-speed network type can outclass 56Kbps modems and even ISDN. Cable modems aren't exactly modems, or (depending on their type) are only half modem. Cable modem connections come in two flavors: one-way and two-way. Two-way modems aren't really modems at all, but a connection on a very large Ethernet network.

When you get a cable modem connection, the installer puts a network card in your computer and runs a cable tap from your computer to the main cable pipeline. For one-way connections, this network card and cable are joined by an ordinary modem and telephone line connection, with the connection being initiated by a dial-up connection. Information going "upstream" (from the PC to the network) travels at modem speed. Information traveling "downstream" (from the network to the PC) travels via the cable and therefore up to the speed of the ISP's connection to the Internet. For two-way connections, information traveling in both directions is transmitted via the cable. Figure 8.11 shows the two types of cable modem connections.

FIGURE 8.11:

One-way and two-way cable modems

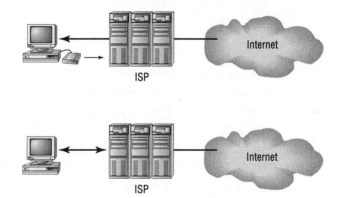

Although the one-way cable modems don't have the upstream data transfer speeds of the two-way modems, for most users this isn't important. How often do you upload information in proportion to the amount you download? I use e-mail for data transfer, but most of the files I send are 1MB or smaller—a size easily handled by a 36.6Kbps modem. Most of what I use an Internet connection for is downloading in the form of browsing the Web or getting e-mail. If you do upload a lot of information, then you'd need either a two-way cable modem connection or something else that's fast in both directions, such as ISDN.

NOTE If cable modem service is offered in your area, check with your cable company to see whether the connection is one-way or two-way. Generally, you'll have a choice of one or the other, not both.

How fast is the cable modem? As you're contending with all other cable modem subscribers for the same bandwidth, the answer to the question depends on both the pipe that the ISP has to the Internet and the number of subscribers currently using the connection. I typically see download speeds of about 60Kbps, with bursts of up to 130Kbps from time to time. These speeds are very workable with graphics-heavy pages downloading in seconds. However, as the cable modem is still in its infancy and is only beginning to be available in heavily populated areas, it's difficult to determine exactly how well it will perform under stress.

A year after the cable modem has become commercially available, it's still too soon to determine how well it will play to the general public, especially in the context of a LAN. Although the cable modem is better suited for proxy serving than a single modem, it won't necessarily have the bandwidth needed to support an entire LAN—certainly not if the members of that LAN are expecting blinding speed out of the connection. For corporate networks, ADSL or DSL Lite may be a more viable answer. Home networks, however, can probably be supported very well with cable modem access.

Asymmetric Digital Subscriber Line (ADSL)

I'm curious to see how this one shakes out.

Asymmetric Digital Subscriber Line (ADSL) is a technology designed to offer very high-speed data transfer (64-200Kbps upstream and up to 8Mbps downstream) on existing telephone wires. It's currently being offered in experimental stages at various locations in the United States; providers include PacBell, Ameritech, BellSouth, and others. DSL service allows you to have voice and data sharing the same line, so you no longer need two lines to serve voice and data.

What providers are offering isn't quite ADSL, however, but something called DSL Lite. Why the difference? The ADSL technology runs on telephone wires, it's true, but the easy installation forecast for the service is still presenting problems—specifically, the problem of splitting the line for voice and data at the high speeds. In an effort to catch up with cable modems, which have been quite popular in the areas where they're offered, the vendors developed a slimmed-down version of ADSL called DSL Lite. This new version still offered high-speed access (PacBell's offering runs in the 384Kbps-1.5Mbps range) but not the dizzying speeds possible with pure ADSL.

Cable modem or DSL? At this writing, the decision is an easy one throughout most of the United States as both technologies are so new that they may not be available in the same place. DSL's bandwidth is more appropriate to the levels required by a LAN, so it may be a better choice for those looking to share bandwidth among several users. The only catch is its cost; it's greater than that of cable modem access, which is already more expensive than ordinary dial-up access. This cost will likely limit the technology to power-users with deep pockets and corporate customers.

Application Servers

In the past year or so, there's been a lot of discussion about the best ways to reduce the cost of PC ownership/administration. As prices drop, it becomes clear that the expensive part isn't the PC, but maintaining it.

One of the expensive parts of PC ownership on a network is the problem of keeping up to date with applications. How can you make sure that everyone on the network is using the same applications, complete with any necessary patches or other changes? To simplify this problem, some people load all office applications on application servers, centrally locating the files so that everyone's using the same applications and versions.

Not sure why this would be a problem? Consider the trouble that can arise when people who are working together are using incompatible application types. The original version of Office 97, for example, could not save .doc files in a format compatible with Word 95 or Word 6.0. If you wanted compatibility with these programs, you lost formatting information when the files were opened in the older operating systems. If Word 95 is the network standard and someone comes in with their home copy of Word 97 and upgrades, then you've got a compatibility problem. You've also got a licensing problem, but that's a matter for Chapter 11, "LAN Applications and Licensing."

I recently heard of another problem from a network administrator with Visual Basic developers to support. When some of the developers upgraded to the most recent version of VB, they had access to library objects not present in previous versions and were therefore able to accomplish things with their software that the other developers could not. This was a good thing because it made for more powerful software, but it was a bad thing because it meant that the developers who might need to work on the applications developed with the new objects could not do so.

Part of the way to solve this is with a managerial policy: Thou Shalt Not Install Unauthorized Software on Your Computer. This is a good idea anyway, for licensing reasons, production reasons, and to reduce the likelihood of Trojan Horse viruses (viruses packaged within innocuous software) getting onto the network. But if everyone's got their applications loaded locally, it can be harder to control this. If applications are stored on and run from the server, then people should be less likely to mess with them and thus affect everyone on the network.

The cost of manually updating a network full of locally stored applications can also be a consideration. Setting up the computers in the first place can be made easier with some sort of disk imaging software, but updating can be more difficult unless you've got Systems Management Server or some other centralized administration tool. In that case, centralizing applications on a single server can make life easier.

You can centralize application use in a couple of different ways. First, you can simply install all applications on a central server and provide links to the executable file, running the application on the client. For many applications, this works, although some may not run unless installed locally, in which case you're back to where you started. Second, you can install the application for network access if it provides such an option. A third method runs the application in server memory, only downloading to the client the interface to the application.

NOTE   Whichever method you choose, you still need proper licensing for your applications. Turn to Chapter 11, "LAN Applications and Licensing," for more information on software licensing.

Storing Applications on the Server

To run applications from a central server, you need only install the application on the server's hard disk and share it with the network. Network clients can then run the application after mapping to the shared volume.

Alternatively, with Windows 2000 you could store the installation procedures for the application on the server and make them available to the client from there. There are two ways to do this. If you publish the application from a server, the application will be listed in the Windows client's Add/Remove Programs applet in the Control Panel. Another method is to make the application available as a shortcut on the client's desktop. When the client clicks on the shortcut, the application is automatically downloaded to the client, installed, and started up. Doing this requires applications that support this kind of remote installation, but Windows 2000 will include tools to package applications that aren't already designed to work in this environment. Any applications that bear the "Designed for Windows 2000" logo will have to support remote installation.

Running a Terminal Server

Another approach to the problem of how to centralize applications for the network is to install them on a server running a multiuser operating system, such as UNIX, Citrix's WinFrame, or Microsoft's Windows Terminal Server. Then let people run the applications on the server while displaying them on the desktop. Such a server is called a *terminal server* as its clients are acting as terminals. No matter how much horsepower is available on the client end, no real processing takes place on the client except for that required to display the application interface. This structure may also be referred to as *thin client computing*, as the resources are concentrated on the server, making fat servers and thin clients.

The subject of terminal servers and thin client computing is quite complicated and worth a book on its own. I'll have time for the bare basics here and in the next chapter on client types, but no more.

How Does Thin Client Computing Work?

Running a terminal server is a whole different ball game from the problems of running an application server with ordinary computer clients. On an application server, network clients use their own local resources to run the application; the only resources not used locally are the disk space required to store the application directories and (generally) the disk space used to store files. On a terminal server, almost all the resources used are those of the server—disk space, memory, processor time, and so forth.

How does this work? You can't do this on an ordinary server running a single-user operating system. Instead, you need a multiuser operating system. Each thin client connects to a session running on the server, each session being (almost) unaware of the others. In that session, the client can run any applications that have been made available.

NOTE   Some multiuser operating systems permit clients to run only single applications while others must give clients access to an entire virtual desktop.

What's actually happening is that the applications are running on the server and the clients are watching and able to manipulate the applications. To do this, images of the application front end are downloaded to the client of a particular session and the client's mouse clicks and keystrokes are uploaded to the server to be executed (see Figure 8.12).

FIGURE 8.12:

How thin client computing works

The multiuser operating system sorts out the client input according to which session it belongs to and then executes the client requests.

What Resources Does Thin Client Computing Require?

Remember, thin client computing requires a hefty server. You'll need fast CPUs and lots of memory. Consider it: the server must not only support itself, but also the needs of every client who's running a session. Sessions must contend for processor time and memory as well as hard disk space. Thus, terminal servers tend to be truly monstrous in terms of resources, sporting hundreds of megabytes of memory, multiple processors, and enormous hard disks. Conservatively, you need to have at least 4-8MB of RAM installed for each client that will be accessing the terminal server, in addition to whatever's needed for running the operating system. The terminal servers I've seen in a production environment tend to be two-way SMP machines at a minimum.

> **NOTE**   With Windows 2000, it may be possible to reduce the load on the server end by introducing client-side application caching.

A potential problem for the Windows NT terminal server types is a shortage of virtual memory. Windows NT 4 and earlier can support up to 4GB of virtual memory addresses. Say 30 clients are logged into a terminal server, each using 100MB of memory addresses (not unreasonable, given the size of some modern applications and files). Then memory addresses start getting hard to find when you take the operating system's needs into account. When interviewing one builder of a WinFrame solution, I asked him what happened if the server ran out of addresses. He hadn't seen this happen under controlled conditions, but in his experience, it led to a system crash. A crashed terminal server is not good as that kills every application in use without giving anyone a chance to save.

NOTE   Windows 2000 will be able to address virtual memory up to 64GB, but only on hardware that supports it.

Thus, the number of thin clients that can concurrently use a terminal server is limited not only by what the operating system can do but also by the virtual memory remaining. The computer can only issue as many virtual memory addresses as are available.

Summary

In this chapter, you've looked at some of the specialized server types you may need on your network and the hardware that they'll require. Almost without exception, a server will need the basic kind of horsepower described in Chapter 7, "Building the Better Server," but the special needs of each kind of server may require a bit of fine-tuning.

Each server type described here was taken in isolation—that is, it was assumed that each server was performing only one function: print servers were printing, file servers were storing files, and so forth. Generally speaking, you can't assume that this is going to be the case. Particularly in smaller networks, you may have to double up on server capabilities, and that means doubling up on required server resources.

I've had to talk a lot about basics in the past two chapters without getting into some of the fun technology out these days that really doesn't have much effect on the server end of things. In Chapter 9, "Client Workstations," I'll talk about the technologies that can make your clients shine.

EXERCISE 8

1. Data is most often shared from servers known as
   _____ servers.

2. Which of the following pictures illustrate how data are found
   on a tape drive? What is this difference called?

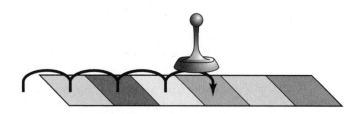

3. You want to back up a 30GB server. If you want to use as few
   tapes as possible, which of the following tape forms would be
   most useful to you?

   A. DLT

   B. DAT

   C. QIC

   D. None of the above

4. What component does a networked printer need more than a
   printer connected to a print server? Why?

5. _____ devices make it appear to network clients as
   though only one piece of hardware is present, when in fact,
   several physical devices may be supporting a single logical
   connection.

EXERCISE 8 CONTINUED

6. How fast do 56Kbps modems typically transfer data?

7. What's the difference between ADSL and DSL Lite?

   A. ADSL transmits data downstream more quickly than upstream, whereas DSL Lite transmits at the same speed in both directions.

   B. DSL Lite transmits data more slowly in both directions.

   C DSL Lite can only transmit in half-duplex mode, whereas ADSL can transmit in full-duplex mode.

   D. ADSL transmits data upstream more quickly than downstream, whereas DSL Lite transmits at the same speed in both directions.

8. In half-duplex mode, ISDN transmits data at up to _____.

9. Where is the map of the directory structure stored with a disk server? With a file server?

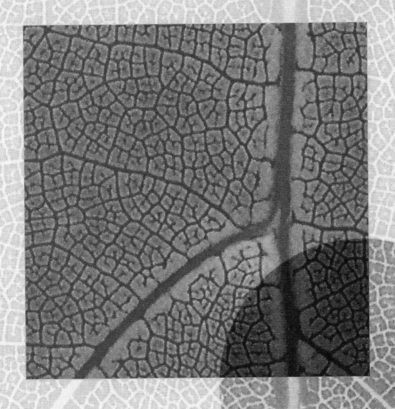

9

Client Workstations

I've spent two chapters talking about what the servers need, but what of the clients? Depending on what your LAN clients are doing, the client end can sometimes be the more interesting as that's where all the jazzy hardware goes. What good are high-level graphics on a server? They're certainly sometimes useful on a client, where a human sits and has to spend the day looking at the screen.

In this chapter, I'll take a look at two main classes of clients: ordinary PC workstations and thin client devices. Obviously, you don't have to include all the hardware described here in a particular client machine, nor is this a complete list of all the hardware that you *could* include. Instead, this chapter represents a reasonable sampling of the hardware that you might expect to need in a client machine and makes some recommendations about configuration.

Hardware for Network Clients

The point of networking is to lighten the load of the network clients by centralizing resources. If all the network clients can access the hardware located on the servers, then they need less themselves.

I've talked about the base components of a computer in Chapter 7, "Building the Better Server," so here I'll stick with making recommendations for client computers and discussing those technologies relevant to network clients that aren't really part of the server paradigm.

NOTE   The client hardware recommendations I make here are in the context of those times when you're buying new hardware, not for every client. That is, if you've got client machines that don't completely conform to these recommendations, don't despair. For most purposes, an older machine will function very well as a network client. You may not want to give the 486 you've still got to the head of the graphics department, but for someone doing word processing, that machine will be perfectly adequate.

The Central Processing Unit

CPU speed isn't as crucial in a client machine as in a server as only a single user's needs must be taken care of. Other than that, though, what's important in a server is important in a client. Given a choice between caching ability and MHz, pick caching ability. That way, you'll have a CPU that can process a lot of recently used data pretty fast instead of having to hunt down that data from memory to process very quickly. Once you start talking about the blazingly fast CPUs that have become available in the past couple of years, a difference of even 100MHz isn't going to be crucial.

Is it worthwhile to get a motherboard with a base speed of 100MHz rather than 66MHz? It depends on the application, but in most cases, the additional expense can't be justified in a client machine with its comparatively light load. For those machines belonging to power-users doing complex equations, there may be some reason to use the faster motherboards. But for someone who's doing word processing, there's little reason to get the faster motherboard.

What about CISC versus RISC on the client end? As with the server, the answer will be determined both by the kinds of processing you need to do and the operating system you want to do it on. In the PC world, it's not always easy to find a client operating system that will run on RISC chips; for example, the only Windows-based operating system that will is Windows NT Workstation. UNIX client operating systems will run on RISC CPUs, and MacOS will run on Apple RISC chips.

Whither Goest the CPU?

As of late 1998, current CPU speeds have topped out with the 450MHz Xeon chip. At present, the Xeon is intended for server machines. Just as 486DX66 was once the server platform of choice for some networks, however, I'd expect the Xeon to become a client CPU. Of course, then we'll need faster server CPUs so the servers don't feel inadequate. At this point, the roadmap for the next five years of x86 architecture looks like this:

Q199 Look for the Katmai chip, a next-generation MMX chip with an additional instruction set (called the Katmai New Instructions, or KNI) that includes enhanced support for 3D rendering and floating point processing. Katmai will run at 450–500MHz, using the 100MHz motherboard speeds. This CPU is expected to have a larger L1 cache than the current generation of MMX chips and a 512Kb L2 cache. The Tanner, a 500MHz Xeon CPU including KNI, will be released later in the quarter. Tanner will include an L2 cache of up to 2MB. In later iterations, it's expected to use the 133MHz motherboard.

Q299 The next generation of the Katmai chip supports a 133MHz bus and internal speeds of 533MHz.

Q399 Coppermine, a CPU using KNI, will be released. Coppermine will run on the 133Mhz motherboard and have internal speeds of 530–600MHz.

Q499 Cascades, a version of the Xeon chip, will be released to run at speeds of 600–667MHz. This chip will include an onboard L2 cache, providing faster access to the secondary cache.

Continued on next page

Q200   Merced, the first 64-bit *x*86 CPUs, will be released. This CPU will be more software-dependent than its 32-bit predecessors because some logic has been taken out of the CPU to speed up operations, and this logic will have to be included in the OS. Merced is expected to have a three-level cache, adding an L0 cache. The CPU, said to have speeds of 600MHz–1GHz, will be able to run six or eight threads of instructions at once, making it about three times as fast as Tanner. Merced is intended to run on a 200MHz motherboard. This product of Intel/Hewlett-Packard cooperation will feature built-in support for up to 4-way SMP systems, with support for 8-way, 16-way, or even 32-way computers to be provided by third parties.

Q400–Q101   Intel replaces P6 architecture used in Pentium II chips with a new one for the Willamette (client) and Foster (server) CPUs. The new architecture is designed to permit internal clock speeds of up to 1GHz for both models. Both CPUs will also include at least 1MB of on-board L2 cache.

Q401   McKinley, a workstation CPU, will replace Merced. Like Merced, McKinley will run at 1GHz. It's expected that by its release Intel should have more experience with the 64-bit architecture, so McKinley is anticipated to seriously rival—or even replace—its competitors from Hewlett-Packard and Digital.

Sometime in 03   Deerfield, a lower cost consumer version of McKinley, will be released, taking advantage of design improvements expected to be ready during 2002.

TIP   As chip speeds get faster, expect prices to keep dropping. If you buy one generation behind the currently fastest chip, you'll generally save some money. This won't impact client performance much—client needs aren't typically as great as server needs.

Physical Memory

Memory is very important to client performance as it's the place where all information waiting to be processed is stored. The more memory that's installed in the client machine, the more responsive the machine will appear. Given a choice between a slightly faster CPU and more RAM, I'd take more RAM.

As you may recall from Chapter 7, "Building the Better Server," there's one trouble with RAM: CPU speed has increased much more quickly than has RAM speed. Whereas the internal rate of a CPU is now measured in the hundreds of megahertz, the speed of the original RAM type—which really didn't change much for about 10 years—is measured in the tens. This means that the CPU has to spend a lot of time waiting for memory to find the data it's storing and bring it to the CPU for processing. In a multitasking operating system, of course, the CPU can be doing other things while the data is being called forth. However, the less time the CPU spends having to wait for other parts of the computer to catch up, the better.

How can you reduce these waits? Get faster memory. Today, two main memory types are commonly sold in PCs: EDO and SDRAM. Of the two, I'd pick SDRAM. EDO is faster than the standard FPM DRAM, but still only cycles at 40MHz. SDRAM, on the other hand, with current technology is capable of matching motherboard speeds of up to 100MHz. For a long-term investment, SDRAM is likely to be the better buy. The only time that EDO DRAM is preferable is if you're upgrading an older machine, in which case you may not have the option of supporting SDRAM.

Bus Type

As with servers, in modern PC-based client machines, you're faced with a choice between ISA and PCI slots. ISA cards are widely available, inexpensive, and slow, while PCI cards are available for many but not all plug-in needs, a little more expensive, and much faster than ISA cards.

NOTE   Those with laptops for network clients may be using PC-Card slots, but this isn't really a choice. With laptops, you're either using PC-Card devices or nothing—you can't plug an ISA card into a laptop.

PCI slots are good to have if you're buying new machines. For some adapter cards (notably video and network support), the faster bus speed will make a significant difference in performance. It will also provide greater flexibility in years to come, as ISA, one of these days, is going to be phased out. However, just because you have a computer with an ISA bus is no reason to scrap it. For many users, there won't be a noticeable difference in performance with ISA. Buy PCI support if getting new machines or if supporting power-users, but for those people doing basic office tasks, there's little point in replacing a machine you already have.

Hard Disks

I discussed the features of EIDE and SCSI in Chapter 7, "Building the Better Server," and I recommended SCSI for a server. When it comes to most client machines, however, I'd recommend EIDE.

First, client machines don't really need a lot of flexibility. Most client machines have a single hard disk for storing applications, and probably a CD-ROM. The ability to link many devices isn't important.

Second, the EIDE host adapter is only controlling a couple of devices and may not be doing much in the way of local access (assuming that files are stored on a file server). Therefore, the lag time resulting from the way that EIDE host adapters queue read/write requests isn't as important as it is with a server supporting a string of devices. Recall that a SCSI host adapter can multitask among read/write requests to all its devices in the chain. It starts a read for CD-ROM A, then starts a write for Disk B while CD-ROM A is accessing the proper track on the disk. Thus, doing a read from the slow CD-ROM doesn't slow down the write to the disk. EIDE doesn't have this capability, so CD-ROM reads will slow down disk access; however, this isn't likely to happen often enough to be a problem when only one user is accessing the disk. A server system needs to be able to cope with the conflicting needs of dozens of users at once, but a client system needs only to cope with the needs of the person using it. In fact, in a system with only one device on the host adapter, SCSI could actually slow down things because of the extra information passed along to handle the multitasking.

Third, even though storage space on the client end is getting more important as client software gets fatter, EIDE storage is able to keep up with client needs. You can buy 8GB EIDE drives now— a size undreamed of in a server a few years ago. Do you really need to be able to support more than 8GB on the client end? If your disk storage needs on the client end really are that large then perhaps you'll need to consider SCSI, but in most cases user data is stored on the file server, not on the client.

Fourth, and really the bottom line, SCSI drives are *much* more expensive than EIDE drives of a comparable size. For systems that won't see much or any performance increase with SCSI, getting the SCSI system is a waste.

Video Support

Essentially, I've just spent a couple of pages telling you not to bother spending too much money on most clients as they won't notice the difference—one function of the server is to make up for any deficiencies on the client end. There's one arena in which they *will* notice the difference: video support.

The display is the first thing that just about anybody notices about a computer they're seeing in person. A fast display won't make up for a slow machine, to be sure, but a small interlaced screen shown in 16 colors will make even the fastest machine seem slow and poky. Video doesn't matter much on a server, but the users of your client machines will be spending a lot of time looking at those monitors, so it's best to get something comfortable and attractive to look at. This doesn't necessarily mean getting all the latest bells and whistles as many office applications won't look any different with or without them, but get something easy on the eyes and responsive.

NOTE Games are the applications that benefit most from advanced video technology such as AGP and 3D acceleration, but rendering software will also benefit.

Video Boards

Like main memory, video memory serves as a buffer for data being manipulated and for instructions to be sent to a device—in this case, the monitor, for doing screen redraws. The more colors that are displayed on the monitor, the higher the resolution, and the more times per second the screen is redrawn (More redraws mean a steadier image.), the more storage space is needed to store all this data. The faster that data can be read from and written to this storage space, the more responsive the video.

What do you need to look for when choosing a video card? Three things, mostly:

- The amount of memory on the card
- The bus speed on the card
- The type of memory on the card

TIP   Don't worry about "video acceleration." All modern video cards support video acceleration whether or not it's explicitly mentioned in the card's specifications.

After the discussions about bus speed and memory needs, these first two factors are pretty self-explanatory. The third factor, type of memory used, may require a little more explanation of the kinds of memory that have been developed to optimize video performance. The type of memory used is important to video performance although the other two factors play a large part in performance as well and will affect the total cost of the card.

Regular (Fast Page Mode) DRAM As you may recall from the discussion of memory types in Chapter 7, "Building the Better Server," FPM DRAM is the oldest and slowest type of memory in use today, with access speeds typically running in the 60–70ns range. This type of memory can only handle one operation at a time. In short, it works and has the advantage of being inexpensive, but is most effective for low-end video supporting no more than 256 colors.

NOTE   All video memory is some form of DRAM. If the specifications for a particular video card say "DRAM," then this probably means that the card uses FPM (Fast Page Mode) DRAM.

A variant of FPM DRAM called Extended Data Output (EDO) RAM is used on some video cards. Like its counterpart used in main memory, EDO DRAM is a little faster than FPM DRAM because it can do the prep work for one read operation while completing another one. However, it's still not much faster than FPM DRAM.

For anything more than low-resolution 256 color, you'll probably want one of the other varieties of memory that's optimized for video output either by adding a second pipeline (VRAM), cranking up the speed (SGRAM and MDRAM), or both (WDRAM). All these types of memory are more expensive than FPM DRAM and EDO DRAM, but provide much better performance in some way. They are discussed in the following sections.

Video RAM (VRAM)   All RAM on a video card is VRAM, right? Not quite. VRAM is memory exclusively developed for video output. Its secret lies in a two-pipeline design. Whereas FPM DRAM can only handle one kind of operation at a time (meaning that reads and writes to memory must wait for each other), VRAM has two pipelines: one for reads and one for writes.

Synchronized Graphics RAM (SGRAM)   Unlike VRAM, SGRAM is single ported, but it manages to get performance more like that of VRAM than FPM or EDO DRAM because of its speed—it can only think about one thing at a time, but it can think about that one thing really quickly. SGAM is a common memory type as it provides excellent performance on medium-resolution systems. It won't perform as well with high-resolution graphics as, say, WDRAM (discussed next), but it's fast and cards with this memory type are easy to find.

Windows DRAM (WDRAM)   Those unhappy with Microsoft's position in the software world will be happy to know that the name of this type of video memory has nothing to do with the popular operating system, but instead refers to the type of output for which this memory type is optimized. Like VRAM, WDRAM is dual ported, but it's got some other speed advantages as well. First, WDRAM is higher in bandwidth than VRAM, allowing it to communicate with the CPU more quickly. Second, WDRAM has some built-in instructions commonly used in windowing subsystems, including those involved in text rendering and drawing large blocks of color. WDRAM is probably the fastest type of video memory available today. While it's capable of supporting complex color depth even at high resolutions, it's also the most expensive.

Multibank DRAM (MDRAM) Typically, video memory (or conventional memory, for that matter) is logically divided into blocks no smaller than 1MB. One megabyte can be accessed at a time, no matter how quickly or how many pipelines are open to that 1MB. This has a couple of effects. First, memory accesses aren't very flexible as you can only perform one read or write operation at a time from that entire 1MB block. Second, you must add memory in 1MB chunks even if you don't need that much more.

MDRAM splits memory into 32KB logical units to avoid these problems. This increases flexibility as read and write operations can be interleaved between these 32KB sections of memory. Why is this important? Largely because it removes the performance penalty for low-memory video cards. Consider this: if 1MB is the smallest logical unit of memory that can be addressed, then each queue for read and write operations applies to units no smaller than 1MB. If you want more queues to get faster output, you need to add more memory in units of 1MB. In other words, for most systems, a card with 2MB of video memory will always be faster than a card with 1MB of video memory. This is true even if a 2MB buffer isn't required for the desired video output, just because the card with 2MB has twice as many pipelines. With MDRAM, this ceases to be true. If you need the extra storage space, of course you'll still need the additional memory, but if all you need is the additional pipeline, that problem is taken care of.

The second advantage to MDRAM is that its memory design makes it theoretically possible to build cards with only the buffer sizes needed for the output that they'll be supporting. Typically, however, you'll still see those video cards using MDRAM sold with the same memory sizes as other cards: 2MB, 4MB, and so forth.

Which Monitor Should You Use?

The other aspect to the display issue is the monitor you use to create output. Generally speaking, the video card is quite powerful, and monitors try to keep up. It will do you no good to get a

PCI video card with 8MB of WDRAM if your monitor can't support its capabilities.

Like everything else in the hardware world, monitors have become both more elaborate and much cheaper than they used to be. New systems are typically sold with 17-inch monitors; more expensive systems support 21-inch monitors or even larger ones—sizes unheard of for normal applications only a few years ago. No matter how big monitors get, though, it seems as though everyone wants more room on their visual desktop.

TIP Some operating systems, such as Windows 98 and UNIX, support the use of more than one monitor at a time, so you can combine the viewing area of two small monitors into a single desktop. When Windows 2000 is released, it will include multiple monitor support as well.

When evaluating monitor characteristics, it's helpful to understand how the monitor works. There's a chip on the video card called the RDAC (RAM digital-to-analog converter); this chip is in charge of converting the digital information stored in video memory to analog information that the monitor can display. There are actually four parts to the RDAC: the converter, and one ray of each of the three colors needed to make any color on a monitor—red, green, and blue. The rays scan across the inside of the screen, shooting electrons at the phosphors there. As the phosphors are struck with the electrons, they glow. The colors and patterns in which they glow define the image on your screen.

That's the way that monitors work, but how do the specifics of an individual monitor's operation affect its output? The answer depends on a few factors. First, how often are the phosphors struck? Phosphors don't glow forever. The more often the rays scan and excite their electrons, the steadier the image will appear. It's as if the phosphors are allowed to fade enough for your eye to detect the difference, then the screen appears to flicker. This is especially a problem on larger screens as the rods in your eyes, located to the outside of the eye, are more motion sensitive than the cones in the middle of the eye. So you want a monitor that "repaints" the image regularly. The rate at which this happens is called the *refresh rate*. The higher the refresh rate, the better.

> **NOTE** Some older monitors tried to save money in their design by offering interlaced refreshing. *Interlacing* meant that every other row of phosphors would be replenished at a time. The phosphors might be replenished more often than would be possible otherwise, but the screen would also flicker. It's hard to find a modern monitor that supports interlaced refreshes, but if you do find one, avoid it. People will hate you if you make them look at an interlaced screen all day.

Second, what's the granularity of the image? The more dots there are on the screen, the sharper the image. In Monitor Speak, this is actually defined as the size of the dots—*dot pitch*—and is measured in millimeters. Modern monitors typically have a dot pitch between 15 and 30mm with most monitors falling somewhere in the mid-20s. The larger the monitor, the larger the dot pitch can be without looking strange, but smaller will always look sharper.

Third, what resolutions will the monitor support? Resolution is a function of the number of dots visible both vertically and horizontally. As the monitor screen isn't perfectly square, the resolution isn't either. So, for example, the lowest resolution possible on modern monitors is 640 dots across and 480 down: 640×480. The days of 640×480 being acceptable for most purposes are long gone; most of us are most comfortable at a minimum of 800×600, with 1024×768 useful on 17-inch monitors and larger. Some monitors support resolutions as high as 1600×1200. Modern monitors can support a variety of resolutions, so the resolution advertised is the highest resolution supported, not the only one supported. Generally speaking, finer resolutions look better on larger monitors.

TIP   Speaking of size, when choosing a monitor, look not only at the size of the monitor screen (measured diagonally, like a television set), but also at its viewing area. A 17-inch CRT (cathode ray tube) monitor never has a 17-inch viewing area, but somewhere more in the 16-inch range and possibly less on cheaper monitors.

What's most important in a monitor: refresh rate, dot pitch, resolution, or color depth? There's a trade-off between the color depth that can be displayed, the monitor resolution, and the refresh rate, with the refresh rate dropping as the images the rays have to paint get more complex. Certainly, monitors can support all four needs, but the better they support all of them, the more expensive the monitor is likely to be. Even the most expensive monitors see some kind of trade-off as their resources are stressed. If you want more colors, you may have to work at a lower resolution, and if you want a higher refresh rate, you may have to reduce the color map.

The good news is that these days it's pretty easy to find monitors that support 85Hz or so while displaying 16 million colors at 1024×768. Eighty-five megahertz is the minimum rate at which I'm comfortable, although some people can use monitors with refresh rates of 75Hz or even 60Hz without discomfort.

Flat-Screen Panels

Monitors keep getting bigger, and although they're better about footprint than they used to be, a bigger monitor still means both an increased power drain and a bigger box on the desk. Although too expensive for most of us these days, one answer to the problem of ever-bigger and more power-hungry monitors is the flat-screen panel. Despite being smaller than their cathode ray tube (CRT) compatriots that we're all used to, their viewing area is more efficient so that a 14-inch flat screen can give you as large a viewing area as a 17-inch CRT.

Continued on next page

Flat-screen panels have been in use for quite a while on laptop computers for two reasons. First, you can't lug a CRT while running for the next airport terminal. Second, flat-screen panels use much less power than CRTs. You can't run a CRT for very long even from a UPS battery, let alone from a laptop battery. Modern flat-screen panels using active matrix technology also support beautiful color depth and a rock-steady image that's very easy on the eyes.

These laptop screens have been getting bigger. Two years ago when I bought my laptop, its 12.1-inch screen was huge by laptop standards and now it's dwarfed by the 15-inch screens available today. There's an upper limit to the screen size practical on a laptop, though. Larger screens do use more power, even if they're more efficient than CRTs, and as the point of laptops is portability, the additional weight starts outweighing the advantages of more screen area.

These problems matter less in the desktop world, however. Power comes from the wall, not a battery, and no one expects to have to carry his or her desktop computer very far, so flat-screen panels can increase in size here. Some panels are even wall mountable, so you can have a desk *and* a monitor—a welcome change of pace for those of us who have to use L-shaped desks to get any work done.

What's stopping everyone from running out and buying flat-screen monitors? Price, mostly. At this point, you can expect to pay about twice as much for the same viewing area with a flat screen that you can get with a CRT. But as prices drop, expect to see people replacing outdated CRTs with flat-screen panels.

Client Computers That Aren't PCs

So far, this discussion has focused on client computers that follow the PC paradigm: they have monitors, onboard disk drives, keyboards, and the like. These client PCs are designed to do just about anything, if you give them the software to do it.

But what if the client machines don't *need* to be able to do just about anything? If a client computer is only going to be used for a specific task or subset of tasks, then it might make more sense to strip down the client to support only the applications that it's going to run. More task-oriented client computers can also have the advantage of being smaller and sometimes cheaper than their full-function counterparts. It can also be easier to train inexperienced users in the use of task-oriented computers. The person who freezes up when presented with a monitor, pizza-box computer case, and a keyboard may be just fine when presented with a touch-screen cash register.

The operating systems and applications available with these non-PC network clients depend on the model and what you need to be doing with the client computer. The operating system for such devices may be a proprietary one designed for a particular piece of hardware, or a more general one, such as Microsoft Windows CE, a cut-down version of the Windows NT API set that Microsoft developed for use in small computing devices.

> **NOTE** Incidentally, "proprietary" doesn't mean "bad." I prefer 3Com's Palm Pilot, which uses a proprietary OS, to Casio's Windows CE-based Cassiopeia. It's much easier to use.

On the application side, Microsoft has developed some lightweight versions of its more popular applications, such as Microsoft Word and Outlook. Other applications may be Web browsers offering access to Web-based applications. Still others may be running additional applications, such as inventory or cash register applications.

As of late 1998, these simplified network clients aren't common outside warehouses and restaurants—it's still more usual to see ordinary PC or Macintosh clients on a business network. The low-end clients are currently used to supplement the use of a PC rather than replace it. However, they're available now and it's possible that for the sake of simplicity more task-oriented business users, or those who need both mobility and network access, may begin using more specialized clients.

One example of a lightweight client machine is a personal data assistant (PDA). *PDAs* are small computing devices with lightweight operating systems (such as Windows CE) and lightweight applications. Typically, they're small enough to fit in a largish pocket with a small monochrome LCD screen.

What can you do with a PDA? Many people use PDAs for e-mail, taking notes, keeping an online calendar handy, or (if really bored) playing Solitaire; but they're not really practical for any kind of serious work. To produce the final product, you'll typically have to download the contents of the PDA into a PC. More specialized PDAs include support for accepting dictation, and beeper support is promised as well.

The input devices used with PDAs vary. Some have small keyboards (which some people can use quite competently, but I find a little small for serious typing). Others accept written input that you input onscreen using a stylus, following handwriting conventions that you have to learn. Navigation buttons take the place of the control keys on the keyboard.

Hardware for Thin Client Networking

I described thin client computing to some degree in Chapter 8, "Server Types and Additional Hardware," and I'll talk about it further in Chapter 12, "Thin Client Networking." As you may recall, the basic idea of thin client computing is that most processing takes place on a centralized server. The client is responsible only for drawing the images of the application on the screen and supplying keystrokes and mouse clicks to the server to interpret. Because this is the case, thin clients don't need nearly the horsepower as do ordinary computer clients. In thin client computing, the resources on the client end are devoted to making the client a highly efficient graphics engine.

Leaving aside such devices as personal data assistants and smart televisions, there are three main categories of computers that may act as thin clients:

- Any computer with client software installed that permits it to act as a thin client

- Network computers

- Windows terminals

Presumably, you know what a computer is. A *network computer* (NC) is a device that can either display applications running on a server or download them from the server to run locally; Java applets are the commonly used example for such programs.

Strictly speaking, Windows terminals don't run any programs locally; all processing takes place on the server and the terminal only displays the results. One Windows terminal device (without a monitor or keyboard attached) is shown in Figure 9.1. Everything the computing part needs to operate is in this box; the only external parts are the monitor and input devices.

NOTE   Network computers never did take off particularly well, but, just to make life confusing, many devices sold as Windows terminals have some features of NCs. That is, they can run Java applets using local resources and may even have small hard drives.

Note that what defines a thin client is not the hardware installed
in it (or not installed in it, as the case may be). A thin client may
be little more than a CPU, network connection, and some RAM
with a monitor and keyboard attached, or it may be a fully loaded
PC belonging to a power-user. The important part of being a thin
client lies with where the majority of processing takes place. If
the client machine is concerned largely or entirely with display
functions, it's a thin client no matter what its spec sheet looks
like. The one thing that all thin clients will have in common is
network support. By definition, a thin client must have a network
connection to the server running its applications.

Because thin client devices are geared toward graphic output, they don't need the horsepower that computers doing local processing require. A Windows terminal, for example, will typically include the following:

- CPU (100MHz or less in new models, slower in older ones)
- Enough RAM to support video output, say 8–16MB to begin with
- A video card and monitor
- A network card
- Input devices, such as a keyboard and mouse
- A serial and parallel port

With the exception of the mouse and keyboard, all these components are built into the Windows terminal or NC device. The thin client device may also include other hardware, such as speakers, PC-Card slots for modems or mini hard drives, and the like, but these are the basics.

Thin clients are *thin*. Even when running resource-intensive software, the thin client device's CPU can be slow, its memory limited, and its video card not necessarily the most powerful. (Because of the limitations on thin client video support, the display protocols can only work for up to 256 colors.) Devices, such as Windows terminals and network computers, are built for fast and efficient graphics display; but the actual output won't be anything spectacular. Even though thin client devices are network dependent, the network connection doesn't even have to be fast as so little information is being passed back and forth.

Computers acting as thin clients can also act as ordinary network clients at the same time and will need the resources of a network client to run applications locally. The good news is that they won't need *more* resources than an ordinary network client in their dual roles, as the requirements of thin client computing are so limited. Screen redraws are screen redraws whether they're locally generated or spread across the network.

Now you've had an introduction to thin client networking from a client's perspective. For more information, turn to Chapter 12, "Client Workstations."

Summary

As you can see, client computers don't have to have the horsepower of servers. Their demands are often simpler and their workloads lighter—even the busiest client computer has less to do than a server supplying a number of clients with resources.

When client needs are especially light, a traditional PC configuration may not be necessary at all. For some applications, a more lightweight computing device, such as a PDA or other task-oriented computer, may be appropriate. To really reduce the hardware needs on the client side, you could replace a client PC with a thin client device, such as a network computer or Windows terminal, which can display applications running on a terminal server. For most situations, however, the traditional PC is still most common.

In the past three chapters I've talked about the hardware requirements for servers and client computers. Turn to Chapter 10, "Network Operating Systems," to learn more about the operating systems running on this hardware and how they support the applications you'll use.

EXERCISE 9

1. What Windows-based client operating systems will run with a RISC chip?

2. True or false. Like WDRAM, SGRAM is dual ported.

3. Thin clients typically have lower memory and CPU requirements than fat clients; but by definition, a thin client device always has _____ support. Why?

4. Which disk controller type is preferable for most network client computers?

   A. SCSI

   B. EIDE

   C. IDE

   D. ESDI

5. The first 64-bit $x86$ CPU from Intel is code named

   _____ .

6. You have a client computer that's designed to download Java applications from a server and run them locally. This client is called a:

   A. Windows terminal

   B. Personal Data Assistant

   C. Task-oriented workstation

   D. Network Computer

7. Typically, a client's hardware requirements are lower than a server's except when it comes to _____ .

PART

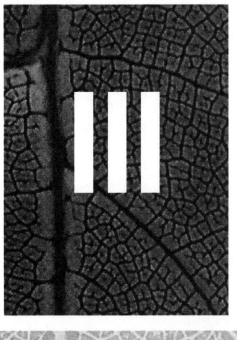

III

Breathing Life into Your
Network—Operating
Systems and LAN
Applications

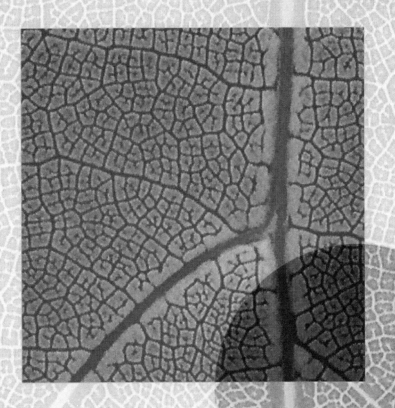

10

Network Operating Systems

So far, you've got a network of wires and the computers to attach to them. What you *don't* have is a network operating system (NOS) to provide network functionality, supplying network protocol support, file and print sharing, and other network-centric activities. In this chapter, I'll discuss some of the options available so you'll know what to expect from a network operating system and how they differ. This won't be an exhaustive examination of every network operating system on the market, but it's a start.

Most network operating systems have quite a bit in common in terms of the services they provide, which I've touched on in previous chapters. To be worthy of the name, an NOS must offer some network functionality in terms of sharing resources with other computers. Because of the competition in the market, once one NOS offers a feature, similar NOSes are likely to follow suit. The extent of this functionality varies—some NOSes are more powerful than others—and so does the way in which the functions work on an internal level. So, performance in a certain arena, such as video serving, may also vary depending on the way that the NOS is designed.

One major difference in NOSes lies in whether they're designed for client/server networking or peer networking. Client/server NOSes are designed to serve only network requests while peer NOSes are designed to serve both requests from the network and those generated by a local work. In English, this means that peer NOSes are designed to support someone working on the machine, making resources available to the network, and client/server NOSes are not. It's certainly possible in some cases to run user applications on a machine running a client/sever NOS, but the OS isn't designed for it. All other factors being equal, the applications won't perform as well as they would if run on an OS designed for that purpose. Similarly, network requests will be more speedily answered if a client/server NOS is used. The difference is not necessarily a matter of network design or dedicating server machines so that the computers aren't trying to do double duty in fulfilling two sets of requests. It's more a matter of factors inherent to NOS design and what it's intended for. The difference lies mainly in how network requests are prioritized for execution in comparison with those that are generated locally. Modern operating systems, in general, divide jobs requiring CPU time into threads and assign each thread a priority. A thread's priority governs how quickly it will get the CPU time it needs to complete whatever processing must be done—the higher the priority, the sooner it gets the CPU time. (This doesn't mean that threads with a low priority must always wait for the CPU to finish processing the higher-priority jobs, but it does mean that the lower-priority threads will have to wait longer.) This is important because the design of the operating system and the way it's configured determine how network-generated threads are prioritized in comparison to locally generated threads. A client/server NOS is designed to assign higher priority to threads initiated from the network while a peer NOS is designed to assign higher priority to local threads.

The difference between the scheduler of a server operating system and a client operating system leads to an interesting dilemma when it comes to terminal servers. Terminal servers run user applications, so it's to their advantage to schedule requests like a client workstation, not a server. For this reason, it will be possible to toggle the scheduler in Windows 2000, depending on whether the NOS is functioning as a terminal server or other server type. That's not the only difference between client/server and peer network operating systems. The former are optimized for network performance in other ways, too, such as providing:

- Greater security
- More efficient ways of organizing data for quick retrieval
- More advanced ways of storing files
- Better hardware sharing support

Also, generally speaking, they are more powerful than the network-capable peer operating systems that can provide resource sharing for small networks.

Peer Network Operating Systems

If you're running a small network and your needs are simple, a peer-to-peer network may be the appropriate choice. These operating systems don't offer everything the client/server ones do, but they have a couple of advantages:

- They're cheaper than client/server NOSes.

- They don't require a full-time network administrator to manage them.

You can reasonably expect a peer NOS to support file and printer sharing, and perhaps some remote administration tools, but there may not be much beyond that. Peer NOSes don't typically support any kind of advanced security or advanced remote network administration. However, if you can live with fairly low security and a clutter of shared resources, these operating systems can be quite adequate for a small and not very network-centric network.

NOTE   I've stuck with Windows operating systems here because they represent the most likely choices for a peer networking environment. Novell withdrew its peer network server product, and, as good as OS/2 was, Warp is dead. For the moment, peer networking is about Windows.

Ancient History

Windows has been network-capable for a long time, but until the early 1990s the operating system required a DOS networking add-on called MS-NET. (This add-on could be used to give MS-DOS networking capability as well, but I think I've delved deeply enough into legacy Microsoft operating systems as it is.) In late 1992, Microsoft released the first peer NOS, called Windows for Workgroups. It wasn't very different from Windows 3.*x* except in the File Manager, which offered support for mapping drive letters to shared directories and for sharing directories with the network. The Print Manager (the old Windows tool used for controlling print jobs and printer configuration) also had network support.

As NOSes go, Windows for Workgroups wasn't much by modern standards. It natively supported only NetBEUI, so it could only talk to other Microsoft networks, such as additional Windows for Workgroups machines or network-capable DOS. (TCP/IP support was only available as an add-on, so even Internet support was impossible out of the box.) However, it did allow file and printer sharing; it came with chat and office e-mail support; and the Clipboard was network-aware so you could cut and paste between local and network-accessible applications. It also had a graphical interface, which made what network administration was possible with the NOS much easier than it was from the command line, as contemporaneous NOSes demanded. Windows for Workgroups didn't sell terrifically well, but it was a good little network operating system for its time.

Windows 95

Windows for Workgroups wasn't bad, but it didn't offer enough functionality to make it worthwhile for most existing Windows users to upgrade to a network-ready version of the operating system they were using currently. You could already network with

Windows 3.*x*; you just needed an add-on from Microsoft or Novell. Getting a network version of Hearts just wasn't enough incentive for most people.

The first big hit in the Windows networking world came three years later, in the fall of 1995 when Microsoft released Windows 95. You might remember the hype that heralded the new operating system. Although the hype was a bit oppressive, the new NOS really was different from the previous versions in several ways.

First, it was a real operating system instead of a graphical environment for DOS. Instead of being purely 16-bit, Windows 95 had 32-bit components. Most of it ran in protected mode instead of using up conventional memory in real mode, so memory management became much less of a bear than it had been. The new 32-bit file system (VFAT) meant that you could use long filenames—so long as your applications were 32-bit as well and supported long filenames themselves.

> **NOTE** VFAT is the Virtual File Allocation table. Essentially, it's the FAT file system with support for long filenames added in.

Windows 95 included native support for TCP/IP and IPX/SPX-compatible protocols, so you could connect to NetWare networks or the Internet without having to track down and install new networking protocols. It came with 32-bit clients for both NetWare and Microsoft networks, too.

How did it fare as a NOS? Pretty well, for a peer-operating system. The interfaces for file and printer sharing are pretty simple to use. It's lacking the same thing that other peer NOSes lack: security and much hardware sharing beyond disk and CD drives. It also sold really well, so Windows 95 networks were possible. Windows 95 makes a better network client than a server, but for small networks that needed little in the way of security; it was and is quite adequate.

Windows 98

As of the fall of 1998, Windows 98 hasn't yet been out long enough to supplant Windows 95. Although it's not as radically different from Windows 95 as Windows 95 was from Windows for Workgroups, it has some additional features that make it more network capable than Windows 95.

First, it's got more interoperability services. Windows 95 was lacking in this department; although it included NetWare support, it only included *older* NetWare support. Newer versions of NetWare had to dumb themselves down to make their directory services available to the Microsoft-provided Windows clients. Additionally, NetWare IP was not supported, so the IPX/SPX-compatible protocol was the only transport protocol available for communication with NetWare networks. Windows 98 includes more NetWare clients and an optional client that allows Windows 98 client machines to connect to NetWare servers using the NetWare Directory Services (NDS). Windows 95, in contrast, had to use the bindery that was part of NetWare 3.*x* and earlier and hasn't been current for several years.

Although still designed primarily as a network client rather than a server, Windows 98 has more going for it on the server side, too. The addition of the Peer Web Server makes company Webs possible in offices with only a peer network. Furthermore, the Remote Access Dial-Up Server allows remote users to reach the network, or at least the Windows 98 remote access server. (The server supports only local access, not access to the entire network.) Support for FAT32, a file system that can handle hard disks up to two terabytes in size also helps. This is because support for hard disks larger than 2GB makes Windows 98 a more reasonable choice for large-scale file storage than Windows 95.

Windows 98's capabilities are limited and don't begin to compare with the wider-ranging capabilities of a client/server NOS, such as Windows NT; but they make Windows 98 a reasonable server platform for small and undemanding networks.

Windows 98—End of an Era

Windows 98 is the last of Microsoft's personal operating systems. All upgrades will be based on Windows NT technology, so only one product line will be continued. The new product line will be called Windows 2000, and it will include versions of Windows designed for computers from client desktops to servers that Microsoft is positioning to rival mainframes.

Is this a good thing? In terms of Windows as a peer NOS, it's probably not a *bad* thing. Windows 98 still has some undesirable DOS remnants, and the NT-based operating systems are DOS-free and more stable than Windows 98 or any other personal Windows operating system. The NT-based client version of Windows scheduled to be released in 1999 is designed to support many of the features that have been staples of personal Windows for some years now. The end of the personal line of Windows operating systems isn't going to limit OS functionality.

When considered as a client or a stand-alone OS, though, the news is less than good. Even personal operating systems are getting increasingly demanding, but NT-based operating systems make Windows 98 look meek and unassuming in its demand for hardware. NT technology is also picky about the hardware it supports, which will make life more complicated for those people who wanted to buy an operating system that they could more or less count on working, come what may. (Of course, given my experience with Windows 98, one NIC, and a CD-ROM drive I had, those days are arguably gone anyway; but *most* hardware still works with Windows 98.) Microsoft will likely hear from customers angry because their new computers, bought for Christmas 1999, don't work with their old scanners or other hardware.

Continued on next page

Another issue, worrisome to those viewing the new OS from the server side, is the question of what's going to happen to the core of Windows 2000 to make the operating system more palatable to personal users and network clients. NT is a security-conscious OS in a way that Windows 9.x never dreamed of. Finding a compromise between NT's security and W9.x's relative simplicity and openness is not going to be easy.

All that said, this isn't a problem you can avoid any more than you can avoid the dearth of new 16-bit Windows applications. You can be aware of it, however. From here on out, it's an NT-based world if you're a Microsoft customer.

Windows NT Workstation

Windows NT doesn't do Plug and Play. Its support for DOS applications is spotty—some applications work, some don't. It's a hardware hog but picky about what it eats. The list goes on. How could this NOS possibly be a better peer NOS than Windows 98? In three ways:

- Support for the NTFS file system
- Superior security
- Robustness

If you want glitz, go with Windows 98, but if you want a solid and dependable peer file and print server, go with NT Workstation 4. It has an interface similar to that of Windows 95; but underneath it's quite different, both in terms of its design and in its handling of shared resources.

New Technology File System (NTFS)

Like Windows NT Server, Windows NT Workstation supports the New Technology File System (NTFS). This is Microsoft's first file system designed to support long filenames, native compression, and large drives. FAT32 supports those options but does not support the security options that NTFS does—transaction logging that prevents volume corruption, file-level security, and a more coherent file organization.

Although only supported by NT-based Windows, NTFS is network accessible to any client, so all operating systems can benefit from the advantages of the file system. Until FAT32 came out with Windows 95 OSR2, NTFS was the only Microsoft file system to support volumes larger than 2GB. To this date, it's still the only Microsoft file system that supports file-level security and security logging.

Security Features

When it comes to peer networks, the logon security provided with Windows 9.*x* is less than perfect. If you attempt to log on with a known username and provide the wrong password, you can't get in. However, provide a new username and you're in. If you don't care about network support, you can press the Escape key at the "Welcome to Microsoft Networking" logon screen and still get in. You won't have access to the persistent network shares of anyone else who's used the Windows 98 computer. You will have to provide the share passwords to create any new shares. However, if all you care about is access to the machine itself, then getting in is a snap.

This is a problem from the perspective of a peer NOS for two reasons. First, the person using the machine can see the information stored on it. In a peer network, that's likely to be all the working data for the computer's usual operator, including confidential files. Second, the person using the machine can change network shares, editing their passwords, deleting new shares, or creating new ones. This situation is less than ideal.

NT Workstation avoids this problem by requiring explicit login. If you don't have an account on the machine, you can't use it, either locally or remotely. There is a guest account, but this account can be disabled or its password changed, or given such restrictive permissions that a person using it is not much of a threat to the integrity of the peer server.

NT can do this because it has a tool that Windows 98 and its predecessors lack: the User Manager. The User Manager is not as powerful as the User Manager for Domains that's part of NT Server. However, the User Manager can be used to create an account database not only to manage who's using the machine, but also what kind of access they're permitted.

In the NT world, access is a matter of rights and permissions. User and group accounts are assigned rights that define what they can do on a machine or on the network, and files and network shares are assigned permissions. On a peer network, you cannot access a resource shared from an NT Workstation computer unless you have an account on that computer, even if you're already logged onto the network.

NT Workstation comes with several predefined groups that have rights based on their function (see Table 10.1):

TABLE 10.1: NT Workstation Predefined Groups and Their Functions

Group	Description
Administrators	Can administer the local computer; this is the most powerful group.
Backup Operators	Can bypass file security to back up files so that even if they don't have access to a file they can run Backup to preserve it.
Guests	Guests in the workgroup or domain.

Continued on next page

TABLE 10.1 CONTINUED: NT Workstation Predefined Groups and Their Functions

Group	Description
Power Users	Can share directories and printers.
Users	Ordinary users, with no special rights.

Notice that ordinary users can't even share files under NT Workstation—you must be a member of the Power Users group to do that. All accounts are members of one group or another, but you're not locked into these options only. You can:

- Create groups of your own with their own sets of rights.

- Edit the rights associated with each group.

- Add and delete rights on a per-user basis.

- Make user accounts members of more than one group so that their rights are a combination of the rights assigned to the two groups.

NOTE In NT, user rights are cumulative. That is, the least restrictive set of rights applied to a user account will be the one used with one caveat: the right explicitly denying access always countermands any other rights with which it conflicts.

If you've formatted the data partitions with NTFS, you can add an extra layer of security to the system. Whereas FAT and FAT32 only support permissions on shared volumes and then only on a folder-level basis, NTFS supports file-level permissions both for network shares and for local use.

NOTE By default, everyone with access to the computer has full control over files, so it's a good idea to adjust file permissions when using NT Workstation as a peer NOS.

Increased Robustness

If you've worked with any Microsoft personal Windows operating system for very long, you've gotten good at rebooting after some application or other crashed and took the operating system down with it. It's certainly possible to crash NT, but NT crashes far less often than personal Windows. From an NOS perspective, this is important. You don't want a resource server crashing.

The Future of Windows NT Workstation

If you want to get picky about it, Windows NT Workstation *has* no future—in the fall of 1998, Microsoft renamed the product Windows 2000 Professional for the 5.0 version. (Yes, this was a deplorable marketing decision, to take a brand name currently associated with stability and dependability and trash it in favor of one associated with flash and little staying power.) The guess is that Microsoft was afraid of losing the brand recognition associated with Windows.

What are the new features? This isn't a complete book on Windows NT, but from a NOS perspective, Windows 2000 will offer improved security with Kerberos (more on that in Chapter 14, "Principles of Network Management") and some changes to NTFS that make the file system more flexible. Plug and Play support, long a staple of Windows, will be offered in Windows 2000, as will more system management tools, a new edition of the Microsoft browser, and power management. Most of these changes will apply most to the client/server version of the NOS, so I'll discuss specifics of those changes in the later section, "Windows NT Server."

Client/Server Network Operating Systems

Speaking in terms of people, not machines, the client is the important person in the network, not the server. As the name implies, the only reason for the server's existence is to provide something to the client. So—what do clients want?

- Quick and easy access to data and storage space
- Confidence of data integrity
- Confidence of data security

There are differences in the way that client/server NOSes are designed to address these issues, but there's also a lot of similarity as NOS manufacturers see what their competitors are doing and follow suit. In this section, I'll be discussing three main client/server operating systems: NetWare, Windows NT, and UNIX.

I'll talk first about general features of an operating system, then about some of the distinguishing design characteristics of each. This won't be an exhaustive guide to any of the three, but after reading this section you should be familiar with the features of all three NOSes and have an idea of how each is intended to work.

Features in Common

The more things change, the more they seem the same. NOSes get more and more alike as they develop, as their makers look at each other's products and think, "Gosh—that's a good idea. People seem to like that. I should add it to my NOS." From this kind of thinking stems the use of a GUI (graphical user interface) instead of a command-line interface, the need to support directory services, advanced security measures in terms of password protection and data encryption, backup services, and the like. Not all of the following are included in all operating systems, but they're either under development or available as part of an add-on pack, such as Microsoft's BackOffice.

TIP   Many features that are included in the NOS are also offered by third-party solution providers to provide features that the NOS does not. Backup solutions, RAID support, and directory services are all offered as third-party products.

Quick and Easy Access

When you ask someone who's job is dependent on using the network what they want out of the experience, that person's first response is often along the lines of, "Something responsive that doesn't crash." The following are features of NOSes designed to make that possible.

Unified Login So far as possible, the goal of network design is to make the problem of accessing shared resources as invisible to network clients as possible. This means that resources should be shared on a network (or portion of a network) basis, instead of on a per-server basis. What's the difference? As shown in Figure 10.1, if resources are shared on a network basis, then a network client must only log in once to access all shared resources on the network. If resources are shared on a per-server basis, then a network client must connect to all servers separately, starting with the network login server and moving on from there to follow resources as they're scattered about the network.

FIGURE 10.1:

Ideally, resources are shared as a group, not from individual computers.

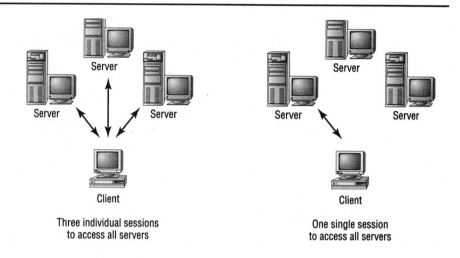

Three individual sessions
to access all servers

One single session
to access all servers

Sharing on a network basis doesn't always mean that logging into the network gives you instant access to all shared resources. For most network users, that would be more of a bother than a help as they tried to sort through all the shares that they didn't need. It does mean that you should only have to log in once to get to everything you need, however.

Directory Services Object organization and good search engines are key to ease of use. The three NOSes described in this section all support directory services either now (in the cases of NetWare and UNIX) or in an upcoming version. NT is a case of the latter; it does not presently support directory services but will in its next version, to be released sometime in 1999.

> **NOTE** Banyan's VINES supported the first network directory services, a design called StreetTalk.

Directory services are a means of organizing the entire network into a hierarchy of objects, some capable of containing other objects and some not. In a truly hierarchical directory service, the organization looks something like the drawing shown in Figure 10.2.

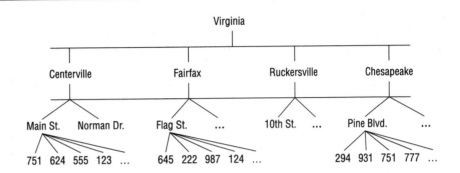

FIGURE 10.2:

Model of directory services

In the above illustration, I'm using street addresses in Virginia as an example of how objects can be implemented in a directory service. Virginia is the root. Below Virginia are city names; below city names are street names; below street names are house numbers.

Applying the naming scheme used by directory services, a house would have an identifier that looked like this:

```
751.Main Street.Centerville.Virgina
```

If a user came to the directory service and asked for access to that object, finding it would be a snap. First, the search tool (such as LDAP, the Light Data Access Protocol) would locate Virginia as the root that is last in the name.

Note that in a truly hierarchical directory service, different objects can have the same "first" name. The chances are excellent that there will be a house numbered 751 on Main Street in Chesapeake as well as in Centerville. However, this won't cause any confusion as the two house numbers referring to different locations will be in separate branches of the structure (see Figure 10.3).

FIGURE 10.3:

Objects can have the same "first" name so long as they're in different parts of the directory structure.

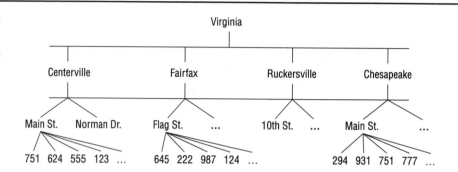

Of course, this is dependent on a hierarchical structure. If the directory service uses flat groups instead, then objects will be identified by their "first" names and won't be able to have common names.

Finding objects in a directory service is easy, but *organizing* them may not always be so easy because an object's location in the directory structure will determine who's got access to it. Planning the structure of network resources is always complicated as you've got to figure out where to put what to make sure it's available to the people who need it. But in the case of directory services, the complexity is compounded by size.

Advanced Hardware Support Quick and easy access doesn't just mean sharing hard disk space with the network but also requires the NOS to support lots of RAM and CPU power. Five years ago, a 486DX was a respectable server for some applications. As demands on servers increase, it's important for a server to be able to exploit the hardware that can help it meet those requirements. That implies support for multiprocessor computing and advanced CPU designs. Thus, all three NOSes mentioned in this chapter theoretically support up to 32 processors. That said, this is theory, not always practice. In its current iteration, NT Server, for example, only supports four processors out of the box. You have to get another version of the hardware accessibility layer (HAL), the part of the NOS that communicates with hardware to support more, and it really only works with up to eight.

One aspect of advanced hardware support will lie in the types of CPUs supported. Chapter 9, "Client Workstations," provided a time line of x86 CPU designs expected from the beginning of 1999 until 2003. One of the anticipated design advances lies in the introduction of the 64-bit chip, as opposed to the 32-bit CPUs now used. The 64-bit CPUs, beginning with the Merced chip and evolving to the McKinley, will be faster than their 32-bit counterparts in part because some logic has been removed from the chip. That logic has to come from somewhere, so it's in the operating system. Windows 2000, like other high-end operating systems, will include a version that supports the 64-bit architecture.

Web Server Support   The Web has become a vital part of many companies, both for internal use and for external use, so these NOSes can act as Web servers. NT and UNIX are both popular Web servers. Linux, a freeware version of UNIX, is also a popular Web server platform.

Terminal Services   Multiuser servers are old hat to UNIX but fairly new to the other two NOSes described in this chapter. As I'll discuss in detail in Chapter 12, "Thin Client Networking," multiuser operating systems let people run applications on a server from very lightweight computers on the network. The client machine is only responsible for displaying the application's output rather than doing any real processing. There are two main implications to this. First, client machines can be (don't have to be, but can be) lightweight and cheap. Second, they can be connected to the server via a slow link, as little data travels between client and server. It also allows network hardware resources to be used more effectively. This is because each network client only uses a CPU, for example—a small percentage of the time spent working. Multiuser systems can dole out CPU cycles as needed so that more work can be gotten out of the same kind of hardware.

UNIX was originally a multiuser NOS. Citrix Corporation developed the initial technology for multiuser NT and NetWare, and licensed it to other developers. Microsoft currently markets an add-on to NT 4 called Windows Terminal Server (WTS), but this add-on will be an optional part of the core operating system in the next version of NT.

Troubleshooting and Optimization Tools These tools aren't for the users; they're to help you make the network better serve user needs. Among them will be:

- Some kind of print management utility

- Some kind of file management utility to set up compression, file permissions, and the like

- Remote administration tools to configure client machines and automate software installation

- Network monitoring tools to keep track of network traffic and determine where bottlenecks are occurring

- Server performance monitoring tools to keep track of metrics such as CPU usage, memory usage, free disk space, packets sent to the network with a certain protocol, and the like

- Event logging, whether of errors, object access, user logons, starting services, and so forth

Using these tools, you should be able to manage resources more easily and troubleshoot problems.

TCP/IP Services

TCP/IP has become the default network protocol due to the spread of Internet access. However, with the use of TCP/IP, some network administration gets more complicated.

IP Address Leasing As discussed in Chapter 4, "Installing Cards and Cables," each node on a TCP/IP network needs an IP address to identify it on the network. TCP/IP networks tend to be large networks. The protocol and configuration is too complicated to make it worthwhile for most small networks not running an intranet to support it except for direct Internet communications. Therefore, the process of assigning individual IP addresses to each computer participating in the network could be pretty daunting if you had to do it all by hand. Thus, these NOSes support the Dynamic Host Configuration Protocol (DHCP), which maintains a pool of valid IP addresses and allocates them to computers on the network for a predetermined period of time. Only a few computers (the default gateway, for example, or the DHCP server) need a static address, so this greatly simplifies network administration.

Name Resolution Although computers on a TCP/IP network need IP addresses, most people are more comfortable calling a computer SERPENT than 24.48.12.161. Therefore, in addition to their IP addresses, each computer will have a NetBIOS name of up to 16 characters, a fully qualified domain name using the format `ftpserver.mycompany.com`, or, sometimes, both.

Humans can use these names, but the network cannot. Therefore, some kind of mapping from a human-readable name to network-readable name is needed. Initially, the most common way of mapping names to IP addresses was with a static list called a HOSTS file, if mapping fully qualified domain names to IP addresses, or an LMHOSTS file, if mapping NetBIOS names. This method worked but was time-consuming and wearying to maintain. This was because each computer needed its own HOSTS or LMHOSTS file and a change in name or IP address had to be reflected in all computers. Maintaining such a file in combination with a DHCP server, when a computer's IP address might well change every few days, didn't even bear thinking about.

The solution was to make a name resolution server and that's exactly what happened. NetBIOS names, used on NT 4 and earlier networks, are mapped to their IP addresses by a Windows Internet Naming Service (WINS) server. Fully qualified domain names, used on UNIX and NetWare networks, are maintained by a Domain Name Service (DNS) server.

Under NT 4, WINS was the easier to use as it could dynamically update itself and the DNS name mappings were static. But the next version of NT will support dynamic DNS for networks composed of W2K servers and clients. WINS will be supported for connectivity to older Microsoft networks and clients.

Confidence of Data Availability and Integrity

Getting to the server is important, but if the data isn't there or is inaccessible, then it doesn't matter how easily you can access the hard disk. Ensuring that users can get to the data they've saved, and that the data is preserved, is important.

Making Backups Backups are an essential part of any NOS. Backups include not only user data but also system configuration information (so that if you have to reinstall you don't have to hand-configure the computer all over again) and the structure of the directory services, if applicable.

One element that the out-of-the-box backup utility may not include, which you'll need, is the ability to back up open files. NT's Backup, for example, will skip any open files, including HOSTS files. It's possible to work around this by stopping the service that has the open files and then restarting after the backups are completed, but this isn't always a practical solution. Timed backups are also important so you're not required to be physically present to initiate a server backup. Additionally, multi-tape support is important for preserving large volumes.

A feature now part of NetWare and to be included in the next generation of Windows allows you to archive infrequently used data while still keeping it on the relatively inexpensive mass storage devices. When files haven't been accessed for a while, they're moved to the backup media. A link is maintained in the main directory so that when the client does a DIR, the file in question appears as though it were there. However, that link can be to a tape drive, optical drive, or some other media that's cheaper than hard disk space. There are two catches to such a system. First, retrieving data from a backup tape or optical disk takes longer than retrieving it from a hard disk. This means that network clients will definitely notice a difference in the system's responsiveness if they click a link to a file that isn't really on the hard disk even if it appears to be. Second, if the tape/optical disk/other backup media isn't where the link expects it to be, the operating system can appear to hang while it searches unsuccessfully for the link. This method is only recommended if you've got a very static archival system in place.

Data Replication One way to make sure that vital data is always available is to replicate it to another server on the network. If the first server fails, then the second one can be brought online either automatically or manually. It's not recommended that you do this with all data as replicating all user data over the network would use up a lot of bandwidth. But it can be done with data that doesn't change often and is necessary for the network to work properly at all, such as user profiles or logon scripts. Alternatively, selected data files needed at multiple sites can be replicated at night or at other times when the network isn't crowded.

RAID Support RAID, or the Redundant Array of Inexpensive Disks, is a blanket term for any of several methods of using multiple disks to ensure data integrity even in the case of disk failure. RAID can be supported in hardware with an external array of disks or in software by making hard drives in the server itself part of a RAID array. Software RAID support is most often offered out of the box, but hardware support is available as an add-on for all three NOSes.

There are five types of RAID support, but three are the most likely to be supported in software:

- 0 (disk striping without parity)
- 1 (disk mirroring)
- 5 (disk striping with parity)

RAID 1 and 5 are the two disaster-recovery options. Disk mirroring uses two separate physical disks, writing all data to both disks so that if one disk stops working, the second disk will still be available. Disk striping is more complicated, involving multiple physical disks (3-32, in disk striping with parity). Rather than being written to a single disk, data and parity information that can be used to re-create any missing data are written in blocks to each physical disk in the stripe set. If one disk in the array fails, then the parity information from the other disks is used to re-create the data on the dead disk. A replacement for the dead disk is not immediately required, but should be added as soon as is practical, as the array will need the disk to be fully protected.

The Role of Clustering   Clustering takes RAID a step further by ensuring data availability even in case of total server meltdown. A cluster is a collection of several servers made into Siamese twins with high-speed network or SCSI connections.

As I'll discuss in Chapter 16, "Disaster Recovery," clustering can be used not only for fault tolerance but also to improve server performance. Just as multiple disks can reduce the time it takes to read data from a volume because data can be read from more than one disk at a time, multiple servers tied together as a cluster can do the same thing.

Confidence of Data Privacy

Network clients want to be able to get to their data, but they don't want just *anyone* to be able to get to it. Client/server NOSes are designed to be secure and that security consists of:

- Password protection and the ability to set file permissions
- Authorization and authentication of system privileges
- Encryption techniques

There are two kinds of permissions on a network: what you're allowed to do and what objects you're allowed to access. For this discussion, I'll borrow the NT jargon and refer to them as "rights" and "permissions," respectively. In a client/server NOS, rights and permissions are established not with passwords but with a system of security settings that are mapped to network clients. A network server designed for this purpose maintains a database of all users allowed access to the network. Once user access to the network is authorized, the user's access to shared objects on the network (printers, directories, and so forth) is determined according to the permissions established for that object.

The method by which objects are organized in the network controls how that access is secured. For example, NT 4 allocates rights and permissions based on user or group ID, but NetWare can specify permissions based on SIDs or on placement in the organization.

Much Ado about C2

Some people get really excited about whether or not an NOS has C2 certification, meaning that it has been officially tested and certified to satisfy a set of requirements specified in the National Security Agency's Orange Book. NT 3.5 is C2 certified, as is NetWare 4.11, but NT Server 4 is not. Therefore, in the eyes of some, NT Server is officially less secure than NT 3.5 or NetWare 4.11.

Continued on next page

Not at all. Note that part about "officially tested." For any product to be tested takes time (years, actually) as does anything else in the federal government. NetWare 4.11 has been out longer than NT 4, so it's ahead in the queue (NT 4 is in the process of being tested). NetWare 5 is not C2 certified either, as it just came out in September 1998. This doesn't mean that it can't be.

What does C2 certification mean, anyway? This is from the official Web site at www.radium.ncsc.mil:

"A system that has been rated C2 provides a TCB [Trusted Computing Base] that enforces a DAC [Discretionary Access Controls] policy to protect information and allow users to share information under their control with other specified users, identification and authentication of users in order to control access to the system and enforce accountability, prevention of access to residual information from a previous user's actions, and provides for the auditing of security related events."

In English, this means that a C2-certified system allows users to control access to their files on a per-user basis, prevents object reuse, and can audit said access. That's all. Some government agencies require C2 certification before they can use a product, but it doesn't necessarily say anything about how locked down the system is beyond the parts specifically mentioned.

Microsoft's Windows NT

In its present form, NT was introduced in 1993, having originally been developed as an offshoot of Microsoft's LAN Manager with a distinct flavor of VMS. (Unsurprising, as several of the lead designers of NT had previously designed VMS operating systems for Digital before Microsoft hired them.) At one time, the OS/2 interface was to be used for the new NOS, but given the popularity of Windows Microsoft, a decision was made to replace the OS/2 GUI with Windows.

When NT was released, its security was stressed, but a lot of what made NT popular, especially at first, was that it looked just like Windows. It was an NOS that was easy to learn. You may not become expert with the NOS within a day or two, but you could have an NT-based network up and running in that time. That remains one of the reasons for its popularity and one of the reasons that the increased complexity of the next generation of NT is worrisome.

In the years that NT's been out, it's come a long way. From being a completely Microsoft-centric NOS, it's become compatible with NetWare. NT is also working on its UNIX interoperability with its Services for UNIX in final beta as of this writing. It's not as mature as either NetWare or UNIX, but for a six-year-old, it's coming along.

Master of the Domain—Basic NT Structure

From an administrative viewpoint, NT Server is based on the domain structure. A *domain* is a collection of up to 10,000 objects representing computers, users, user groups, file objects (directories and files), and printers, each with its own security identifier (SID) to identify it in the domain. It's a workgroup with a centralized security database. A network may be one domain or several, and a domain may consist of one part of a LAN or several of them; like workgroups, domains are an administrative division (see Figure 10.4).

FIGURE 10.4:

Domain structure is separate from network structure.

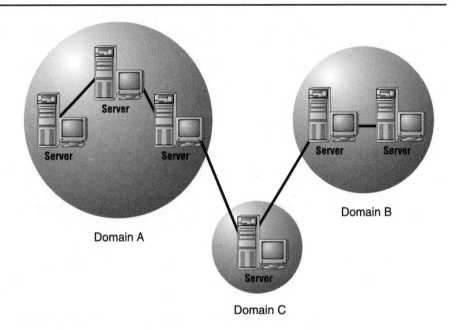

Domain A

Domain B

Domain C

Domains also have SIDs. Although you can't give two domains the same name, the reason for this is not identification to the NOS, but to the user. The NetBIOS naming scheme used with NT can't distinguish between two identically named domains for browsing purposes, but a domain's name is distinct from the SID. This means that if you stop using one domain and then create another one with the same name, you'll have to re-create the domain security structure from scratch—it won't be considered to be the old domain. Similarly, you can rename a domain without changing its SID.

The security structure of a domain is flat, meaning that objects are treated individually, not as members of a hierarchy. For example, there is no group of printers that contains all printers in the domain. Instead, there's Printer1, Printer2, and so forth, each of which is managed separately.

Security is based on group membership and all user accounts are members of one group or another. Each group has a predefined (but editable) set of rights associated with it. Permission to access an object is based on the permissions granted to groups or individuals and defined as a set of properties in the access control list (ACL). When a user attempts to access an object, such as a printer, the operating system examines the ACL for that printer and based on that information grants a certain degree of access. Every object has its own ACL.

Security is managed by special types of NT Servers called *domain controllers*. Domain controllers store the security database for the domain, authenticating user logons and object access. A domain controller must be present to authenticate access. NT Server 4 uses a two-tiered system of domain controllers. One primary domain controller (PDC) is in charge of domain security. Optionally, the security database is replicated to one or more backup domain controllers (BDCs) so they can help the PDC with its job of authenticating user access. Only a PDC is required for each domain, but it's a good idea to have at least one BDC in the domain both to help share the workload and to be promoted to the role of PDC in case the PDC fails. Extraneous BDCs, however, are not the best idea, as the traffic from replicating the security database to BDCs can take up a lot of bandwidth.

Trust Relationships   Although single-domain networks are simplest to administer, you may want to divide your network into more than one domain for one of several reasons. First, domains can hold only 10,000 objects, so very large networks with lots of objects may find this a restriction. Second, the security database must be replicated from the PDC to the BDCs. If the connection between the two domain controllers is over a slow or heavily traveled link, that can lead to traffic jams.

If you do logically divide your network into multiple domains, you'll reduce traffic in much the same way that using routers to physically divide the network can keep traffic to the segments in which it belongs. By the same token, however, just as routers in a network introduce latency, separate domains in a network cause administrative difficulties. What if you're a member of a group in Domain A but want to access a folder shared from Domain B? You're not out of luck, but you'll need to establish a *trust relationship* between the two domains.

A trust relationship is a mutual agreement between domains that one domain can use the resources of another, trusting them. This doesn't have to be a two-way relationship—in fact, by default, it's not—nor is it transitive. That is, if Domain A trusts Domain B, and Domain B trusts Domain C, then Domain A does not trust Domain C. You'd have to establish a separate trust relationship between Domains A and C.

The trust relationship structure is one reason that NT Server is best for smaller networks not encompassing too many domains. It's a real pain to set up, as to establish a two-way trust relationship between Domains A and C, you must follow these steps:

1. At Domain A's PDC, you must permit C to trust A.

2. At Domain C's PDC, you must add A to the list of trusted domains.

3. At Domain C's PDC, you must permit A to trust C.

4. At Domain A's PDC, you must add C to the list of trusted domains.

NOTE   You can't just trust another domain but first must have permission from that domain to trust it. Only after that permission has been explicitly granted can you trust the domain.

These steps must be completed at the two PDCs in the order listed here. Unless the two PDCs are physically next to each other, you either need to do a lot of running back and forth between computers, or have telephone access to the other server area. So you can talk to someone else through the process. Also, as these relationships aren't transitive, you have to do this for every domain with which you want to share resources. You can't just throw up your hands at the complications and decide to meld two domains, either. To move users from one domain to another you must manually add them, and to move the NT Servers you must reinstall and add them to the existing domain. Changing the domain name won't work, as domains are identified to the operating system not by their NetBIOS names but by their SIDs, and you can't edit SIDs from the user interface.

Making Resources Accessible Across Domains Assuming that your network is simple enough to make trust relationships practical, your work to make the resources of each domain available to the members of the other ones is not yet done. NT 4 and earlier versions identify two classes of user groups: local and global. Local groups are those that only exist within a domain, while global groups can span domains. Global groups can be nested within local groups, but not the other way around.

NOTE   There are only three global groups: Domain Administrators, Domain Users, and Domain Guests.

So far, so good. However, members of one domain cannot access the resources of another domain unless they're in a global group. At this point, you have three options:

- You can manually add each member of Domain A to Domain C's user account database. This is possible, but laborious, and increases the size of the security database with the duplicate entries.

- You can grant permissions to the global Domain Users group and make sure that everyone in Domain A is in it. This works but means that you have to reconfigure permissions on

Domain C to make sure that Domain A's Domain Users group has access as required.

- You can put all the people who get to access shared resources into Domain A's Domain Users group and then add that group to the local Users group on Domain C. This is the simplest option, as it immediately gives all the members of Domain A's global Domain Users group the same rights and permissions as Domain C's local group.

This implies that it's best to add users to global groups instead of (or in addition to) local groups where practical, if you think that you'll ever be setting up trust relationships between domains.

The Future of NT

Like NT Workstation, NT Server technically doesn't have a future as the product is being renamed to Windows 2000 Server, with NT Enterprise Edition renamed to Windows 2000 Advanced Server. Windows 2000 DataCenter, an additional product positioned to rival the mainframe market, is scheduled for release six months or so after the release of other versions of Windows 2000. All will still be built on the basic design of NT, however, so although the name is going away the product is not.

Improved Security   NT is marketed as a secure NOS, but some of its security standards have been less than secure because of the need for backwards compatibility. The next version of NT will include support for four security protocols:

NT LAN Manager protocol (NTLM)   For network clients that use pass-through authentication and for older versions of NT

Kerberos   A security protocol that's been used in UNIX networks for years and provides two-way authentication between client and server on a per-session basis

Transport Layer Security (TLS) protocol   A forthcoming version of the Secure Sockets Layer (SSL) protocol

Distributed Password Authentication (DPA)   Used in online services such as the Microsoft Network and CompuServe

WARNING Chapter 14, "Principles of Network Management," will look at these security measures in more detail, but for the moment understand that they don't necessarily apply to all networks. W2K will support NTLM (which is fairly vulnerable) for backwards compatibility with operating systems that don't support the more advanced protocols. In other words, if your network includes personal Windows machines or older versions of NT, you'll be using NTLM.

A More Flexible File System   Windows 2000 will support a new version of NTFS that supports some features that have been lacking:

- Disk quotas to monitor or restrict disk usage on a per-user basis

- Additional attributes to permit increased flexibility when searching for files

- A change log to record when files have been changed, not just their timestamps

WARNING The new version of NTFS is not backward compatible with the old one and the upgrade to the new file system is irreversible.

The new version of NTFS allows additional attributes to be assigned to files, thus making it possible to sort files or search for them by the new attributes. It also includes support for archiving infrequently used files on optical or tape drives, while leaving links to them in the main directory.

Directory Services One of the most hyped pieces of Windows 2000 Server is its support for directory services, called Active Directory. Active Directory is essentially a way of organizing users, groups, shared resources, and security settings for retrieval by the operating system when authenticating users. It's designed to make the domain structure manageable across large networks by allowing domains to be logically grouped into "trees" and "forests." Trees are collections of domains sharing a single name-space and forests are groups of trees.

Domains that are part of a tree are assumed to be in transitive trust relationships, simplifying cross-domain communications. If the implicit transitive relationship is not required in a particular situation, it can be replaced with an explicit one-way trust relationship. (If the trust relationship itself is undesirable, the domain shouldn't be in the tree in the first place.)

NOTE Cisco is developing a version of Active Directory for UNIX.

Novell's NetWare

NetWare 5 and NT have a lot in common in terms of what they're capable of doing. Either on their own or with the help of a third-party add-on, they're able to perform any of the functions that you should expect from a server operating system. How, then, are they different? One way lies in NetWare's directory structure (see Figure 10.5), which is radically different from the domain structure used in current versions of NT. As you'll see later in the section, "Structure of the Directory," they are also different from Active Directory.

FIGURE 10.5:

Resource organization
in NetWare 3.x and 4.x

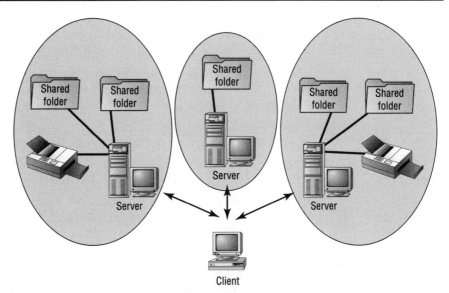

NetWare 3.x network

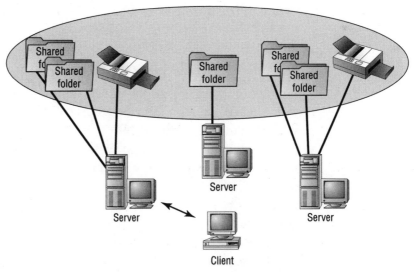

NetWare 4.x (and later) network

Sources of NDS

Like NT, modern versions of NetWare are not based on individual computers sharing their resources. Rather, they are based on a group effort to make all network resources transparently available no matter what computer they were stored on. As illustrated in Figure 10.5, this actually represents a break from the more server-centric design of NetWare 3.*x* in which network users had to log onto specific servers to access their resources. NetWare 4.*x* became more NT-like in its use of a unified logon system and that's still true in NetWare 5, the current version released in September 1998.

The reason for the change is pretty obvious. It's possible to organize a 100-person network for individual server logon, but it's time-consuming and complicated. Make that a 1000-user network spread over several locations and the job goes from difficult to practically impossible. In order to become scalable, NetWare had to change its view of the network as a collection of servers to a view of the network as a collection of resources.

Structure of the Directory

NetWare's unified logon is based not on a domain structure but on the NetWare Directory Services (NDS), introduced in 1993 with NetWare 4. Without NDS, each NetWare server maintains a personal flat-file database of system objects called the *bindery*. NDS, on the other hand, is a global database of all network resources, arranged in a multilevel hierarchy. This database is logically divided into partitions, and distributed and replicated among servers in the network. This accomplishes two purposes. First, even if one server goes down, the directory structure is maintained and the resources are still available. Second, a user should always be able to access a convenient server rather than perhaps trying to log onto a server across a slow WAN link or a very busy server.

This would perhaps be necessary in an NT 4 domain with only a single PDC and no BDCs to share the workload.

Two kinds of objects can exist in the NDS: container objects and leaf objects. *Container objects*, as they sound, can contain other objects, and include Organizations (Os) and Organizational Units (OUs). Os contain OUs; OUs can contain either other OUs or *leaf objects*, which are the individual resources rather than categories.

Servers, users, printers, and other leaf objects can be contained in any O or OU and are identified by a fully qualified domain name derived from their place in the hierarchy. NetWare uses a hierarchical system so its objects can have common "first" names so long as they're not in the same branch of the tree.

TIP   To keep names from being too complicated, Novell recommends making the directory tree no more than four layers deep.

Directory trees are often organized according to job function or geographic location, but the design is up to you. In fact, designing the directory tree is the hardest part of using NDS as that design will affect how resources are made available to the network clients. Generally speaking, when designing a tree, it's more important to pay attention to the resources that clients need than to their job titles or the buildings they work in.

How Is NDS Different from Active Directory?

Although both are called directory services, the two are not identical in a couple of different ways. The most important differences lie in the way that permissions are assigned and stored in the two services.

Organization of Object Permissions   NDS organizes object permissions not according to group or user ID, but according to O or

OU. If you move a user account from the ENGINEERING OU to the MARKETING OU, in this single step that user loses all permissions assigned to ENGINEERING and gains all the permissions assigned to MARKETING.

Active Directory, on the other hand, organizes object permissions according to user and group ID, similar to the domain system used in NT 4. Moving users from one OU to another doesn't affect their permissions at all. To change a user's set of permissions, you'd need to remove them from the ENGINEERING group and add them to the MARKETING group. If you only added them to the MARKETING group and didn't delete them from the ENGINEERING group, they'd keep both sets of permissions.

Which approach is better? It depends on how your mind works. If you find it easier to remember which set of permissions is associated with an OU, you'll like Novell's approach, but those used to thinking in terms of group memberships might be more comfortable with Microsoft's method.

Storage of Object Permissions The second difference lies in how those permissions are stored. NDS stores permissions as high up on the directory tree as possible and then extends those permissions to the objects lower in the tree. Active Directory, in contrast, stores each object's permissions with the object. This makes Active Directory objects (and, therefore, Active Directory databases) much bigger than those in the NDS, as they must store their own rights. However, having the permissions right there for evaluation by the operating system is a bit faster than having to go up the tree to see which permissions are defined at the top of the OU. Once again, it's a trade-off. Those who'd like to keep the database size reasonable will like the Novell approach, while those more interested in instant gratification will appreciate Microsoft's method.

Another difference lies not in how permissions are organized, but in how the tree itself is organized when spread out over several physical locations. In Active Directory, the smallest OU is the domain. In NDS, it's the partition, which may be smaller than a domain. Each company claims that its approach is superior— Microsoft because its domain structure means that network resources are more likely to be concentrated into a single location, and Novell because the partitions segment resource requests and keep traffic down.

The Many Flavors of UNIX

In the early days of networking, operating systems and hardware were commonly mutually dependent—to run a particular kind of computer, you needed an operating system designed for that computer. UNIX was originally developed by Bell Labs as a research tool in an effort to create an operating system with these characteristics:

- Platform independence
- Compatibility with other platforms and applications that adhered to its same rules
- Interoperability (in that it didn't require a single-vendor network)

AT&T couldn't sell the new NOS (UNIX was originally built for networking) because of antitrust laws, so the code was freely distributed to research and educational organizations. Over the years, these organizations tweaked the NOS into a number of mutually unintelligible operating systems all based on the UNIX core. There are actually about 20 different kinds of UNIX. The most popular are Hewlett-Packard's HP/UX, Sun Microsystems's SunOS/Solaris, IBM's AIX, and others.

Lightweight UNIX—Linux

In the last part of 1998, one version of UNIX in particular has been getting a lot of press: Linux. Since its beginnings in 1991 and open-source release in 1993, Linux has been developed by hundreds of programmers around the world. Its development has been enhanced by one simple means: the source code for Linux is free and people are welcome to develop it in any way that they like. The only catch is that any improvements or enhancements they make become part of the public domain. The actual changes to the operating system are determined by its creator, Linus Torvalds—not every change makes it into the "official" version.

As can be seen in the Halloween Documents referred to in the discussion of the OSI model in Chapter 1, "Basic Networking Concepts and Components," Microsoft is concerned about Linux as a threat to NT. They've got good reason. Linux has a dedicated group of developers behind it (many of whom would like nothing more than to prove Linux's superiority). The NOS runs atop *x*86 computers, the Digital Alphas, and Sun SPARC stations, so it's actually more flexible than NT, now limited to *x*86 and Alpha machines. For many, one of the best things about Linux is its relatively small hardware requirements—you can use it to run a Web server from a 486. Windows 2000's requirements are much, much greater. Linux is also getting support from some major hardware and software vendors.

At the moment, however, Linux doesn't seem positioned to take over the Windows world. It's definitely not going to take over the personal computing market any time soon—people not interested enough to download the operating system from RedHat's ftp site (accessible from **www.redhat.com**) or order it specially won't be running it. Right now, most Linux installations are personal or hobbyist installations instead of the business installations of NT. Other aspects limiting Linux as a server operating system divide processing time. Whereas NT and other major commercial operating systems divide CPU time on a per-thread basis, for kernel operations, Linux divides it on a per-process basis, making the division of CPU resources much less granular. Threads running in user mode, where applications execute, are also scheduled in a way that makes Linux applications less responsive than those designed for NT or Windows 9.*x*. It's actually more Windows 3.*x*-like, using

Continued on next page

cooperative multitasking to demand that applications release the CPU when they're done instead of the preemptive multitasking used by 32-bit versions of Windows that forces applications to give up the CPU at regular intervals. Finally, Linux can't effectively exploit multiprocessor hardware, as its code is designed to run on only one CPU at a time. Thus, it's unable to run many enterprise server applications.

For now, Linux is likely consigned to being a development platform and Web server. However, with some architecture changes and more user-accessible distribution, it could be a contender for at least parts of the NT market.

NOTE   So far, the efforts on the part of UNIX vendors have not yet produced a single unified version of the operating system, although the efforts continue.

What makes UNIX unique? First, there's the network file system (NFS), developed by Sun Microsystems in the late 1980s. NFS allows you to share files and resources from several machines transparently, as if from a single machine. NFS lets you do this even if the resources are not only on different machines, but are also using distinct platforms. Mainframes and NT Servers can appear to NFS as a single kind of resource. NFS exports these resources and then the network clients *mount*, or connect to, the resources as they need them, according to the permissions assigned to those resources. This is the basis of client/server networking technology.

The Network Information System (NIS) is another innovation of UNIX's that's become expected in an NOS. NIS is the piece that allows for unified logon to the network. Essentially, it's the directory services for the network, including such information as passwords, user groups, physical addresses, IP addresses, and so forth. If you need it to find a computer on the network, it's probably part of the NIS somewhere.

NT incorporates a lot of what makes UNIX a good operating system, so the two are quite a bit alike both structurally and in their capabilities as described earlier in this chapter under "Features in Common." Like NT, UNIX natively supports the obligatory file and print services, intranet services, object-level security, software RAID support, and so forth. What UNIX has that NT *doesn't* have, at this point, is good scalability. The Internet is mostly a UNIX network with some NT participation—as NT stands now, it wouldn't work if the situation were reversed. NT's domain system simply doesn't scale well, and if asked to juggle too many processes at once, NT can crash.

What does the future hold for UNIX? It's a mature operating system, so although it's likely that UNIX will adapt to some degree, it doesn't have the same job of catch-up as NT and NetWare. Most of NT's and NetWare's development lies in adding features that already exist in UNIX. The bigger question is whether a unified UNIX will ever be agreed on so that only a single platform will be offered, negating some of the current compatibility issues. At this point, it doesn't look likely. Too many vendors have too much to lose by going to a single standard. Furthermore, the political climate of UNIX doesn't really encourage the kind of unified thinking possible when a single company is producing a product, like Microsoft's NT Server or Novell's NetWare. Rather, it's more a culture of innovation, and Linus Torvalds isn't there to oversee all the changes. Thus, although UNIX isn't going away and still remains popular for large networks, it seems unlikely to stomp out either NT or NetWare.

Summary

According to a report published by the International Data Corporation in late 1998, UNIX still has the most market share, with 45.8 percent of all server operating systems sold in 1997. NT comes in second with 34.2 percent, and NetWare with 19 percent. UNIX's share of the market may be increasing—a surprise to those who thought NT was inexorably replacing UNIX.

NOTE   This report, incidentally, did not indicate how each of the NOSes was being used. UNIX in a test environment was counted the same as NT in a business environment.

But which NOS is best? This depends on what you're planning on doing with it. UNIX is a good, flexible, stable, and secure operating system for large-scale networks, but it should be—it's been a work in progress for 30 years, so you'd hope that some of the bugs had been worked out. Interoperability with the widely used Microsoft clients remains an issue, however, as does the fact that there is no single version of UNIX.

NT is still struggling to be taken seriously on a large scale. It's a good operating system for medium-sized networks where its simplicity and compatibility with the large Microsoft installed client base matter. However, it's still having trouble with the scalability problems brought about by its domain-based security system, so UNIX and, to a lesser degree, NetWare still rule the large network market. The addition of directory services to the NOS in its next iteration should help its scalability. But although they look hopeful as of this writing, Windows 2000 in its various forms is only in Beta 2; it's too soon to tell how well some of the good ideas will work when put to the test. Security also continues to be an issue, but this is a question addressed in the next version with the addition of support for Kerberos, the security system originally developed for UNIX. (It's interesting how much NT gets to look like UNIX as it's improved.)

NetWare? NetWare is losing market share to NT, but those who are using it have a well-established NOS with many of the features that NT is just beginning to add, such as directory services and real support for UNIX connectivity. NetWare has a large installed base as well, so it won't be leaving any time soon.

Whichever you choose, these are the major peer and client operating systems open to you. Chapter 11, "LAN Applications and Licensing," will examine the types of applications you can run atop these operating systems.

EXERCISE 10

1. You've added a new user to your peer network of Windows 95 and NT Workstation machines. The new user is attempting to access a folder shared from an NT machine, but can't do it—the system is demanding a password for an IPC share. She can access any resource shared from a Windows 95 machine. What's the problem?

2. All other things being equal, which directory services database is likely to be larger: one using Novell's NDS or one using Microsoft's Active Directory? Why?

3. What is the significance of NetWare 4.11 being C2 certified but not NetWare 5?

4. Why use UNIX over NT 4? Why NT 4 over UNIX?

5. True or false. Linux behaves more like NT than Windows 3.*x* when it comes to allocating CPU cycles among executing threads.

6. Linux competes with:

   A. NT

   B. Windows 9.*x*

   C. NetWare

   D. None of the above

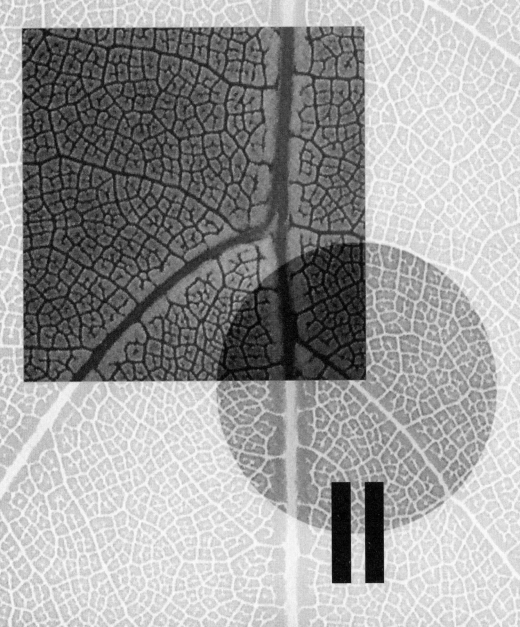

II

LAN Applications
and Licensing

The network operating system is only a support for the important tools of a LAN—the applications running on it. In this chapter, I'll talk about the kinds of applications your network clients may need and how the LAN affects them. After reading this, you should have a better idea of the kinds of capabilities that you can build into your LAN with application software, and how those applications must be licensed.

How Networking Affects the Applications You Use

Running applications in combination with a LAN isn't necessarily the same thing as running them on a stand-alone machine. Some applications are cheerfully unaware of the network, some require it, and others get some extra features if they're attached to the network.

LAN-unaware applications could care less whether a network is in place or not. The only additional functionality that they may see is more drives in which to store data, but the application can't tell the difference between a network-accessible drive and one available locally. An application, such as Microsoft Word 97, that can browse the Web is still LAN-unaware.

LAN-aware applications can function on a stand-alone machine but get extra functionality when connected to a network—functionality that enables them to cooperate with other computers on the network. For example, a database application on a stand-alone machine doesn't need record and file locking because only a single user can access a record at any given time. Once the database application is on the network, it needs record and file locking. The Windows operating system is a specific example of a LAN-aware application, as its interface and capabilities change when you add networking to a former stand-alone machine.

LAN-dependent applications do things that require a LAN to operate. Peer chat utilities, office e-mail, group scheduling, and the like are all dependent on the existence of a network.

What Makes a Good LAN Application?

Most of the time, a good stand-alone application is a good LAN application: it should be easy to use, provide the features its user needs, and be stable. Applications run in a thin-client-networking situation have more specific needs, but I'll discuss that in Chapter 12, "Thin Client Networking." Roaming users, however, require applications that can follow the user around.

Whether using thin clients or ordinary network clients, networks with roaming users have an additional requirement for their user applications: the ability to let users get their user preferences wherever they happen to log in. Some network types, such as Windows, support *user profiles* that store the user settings—colors, screen saver, contents of the Start menu, and so forth. When user profiles are enabled, these user settings are stored in a folder reserved for that network client so that when Sara logs onto the network, the desktop looks exactly the same no matter what computer she's using.

User profiles can contain application settings, too, so that Sara not only has her favorite screen saver, but also gets her custom dictionaries, file locations, and browser bookmarks. The only catch is that the application must be designed to store these user-specific preferences with other user-specific information, not with machine-specific information. Otherwise, Sara's dictionaries will be stored on one computer, not with her personal preferences that follow her wherever she logs on.

To continue with the Windows example, let's say that Sara logs into computer FROGGIE on Monday and uses Microsoft Word 97 as well as Netscape Communicator 4.5. Microsoft Word stores the user-specific settings for the word processor in the part of the Registry (the Windows system configuration database) that's devoted to the user currently logged in. Netscape Communicator, in contrast, stores user-specific settings in the part of the Registry devoted to the machine. Thus, on Thursday, Sara logs into computer EGRET and starts up Word and Netscape Communicator. She'll be able to access her personal dictionaries but not her bookmarks. Harry, on the other hand, has logged into computer FROGGIE and gets the default Microsoft Word dictionaries with Sara's bookmarks.

This isn't the worst problem in the world, but it's at best an inconvenience as Sara must either use the same computer all the time or resign herself to not being able to save bookmarks (definitely an inconvenience). At worst, it's a violation of Sara's privacy, and potentially even a security violation depending on what settings she'd used to customize Communicator. Thus, if you're supporting roaming users, you'll want to be sure to use applications that store user-specific information with the other user-specific settings.

Common Application Types

What kinds of applications are you likely to find on a network? Everything, really, but you can divide them into two main categories: applications that allow independent users to function and applications that allow users to function as part of a group. These two options are discussed in the following section.

Getting Work Done

Business applications are intended for single-person use. The project that the person is working on may be a group project, but while using the application itself, the user works alone. Business applications include just about anything you can do on the computer:

- Word processors
- Desktop publishing
- Accounting packages
- Spreadsheets
- Database clients
- Project management software
- Graphics packages

Although business applications are used by individuals, some kind of common file format is necessary so that users can share files if necessary. Typically, all network clients will use the same word processing package, not various and sundry packages. Even if it's possible to convert files from one format to another, it's simply easier to share files if everyone's using the same application.

Keeping in Touch

Communications software is often a bit more network-centric. It's used for such applications as e-mail, faxing, call management, and any other situation in which members of the network need to communicate with each other or the outside world.

Using E-mail E-mail has gone from being a curiosity, to a toy for geeks, to an indispensable part of office communications. E-mail isn't just about one more edition of the Darwin Awards making the rounds. Rather, it's a tool to provide timely and fairly private office communication. E-mail possesses the following benefits:

- It doesn't use up paper in memos.

- It doesn't require knowing someone's location at the exact moment that you realize you need to talk to them.

- It allows network users to attach files to bring them to the recipient's attention.

One thing you should remember about e-mail is that it's only fairly private, not completely. Even if you delete e-mail, it's not necessarily gone forever; e-mail is typically preserved in backups or it may be stored in a secondary location. As Microsoft and other companies have discovered in the course of the Department of Justice's investigation into Microsoft's business practices, e-mail can be subpoenaed. Many companies have started cracking down on the contents of e-mail and some have stopped using it to discuss very sensitive information.

Using Fax Services You've probably used faxing software before. In a stand-alone computer, it acts like a printer, rerouting print jobs from the parallel port to the modem connected to the serial port.

Just as a network printer doesn't work exactly like a locally connected printer, a network fax service doesn't work just like a stand-alone one. Instead, the network clients connect to a server running the fax software. Incoming faxes are routed to the clients (often with the help of the mail server, such as Microsoft Exchange) so that all incoming messages are available in a single inbox.

Using Call Management Software For those who want to combine e-mail, faxing, and even voice mail, there's call management software. All incoming message traffic is routed to a call management server. This server maintains a unified inbox of all message types for each client so that they can pick up all their messages from a single location.

Groupware—Playing Well with Others

Groupware is a blanket term for any application designed to help people function as a group. Particularly in widely distributed networks (implying that it's hard to get all the members of the workgroup together in one place), it can:

- Facilitate communications, making them faster or clearer, or even making them possible when this wouldn't otherwise be the case.

- Make it easier to coordinate schedules for meeting or project planning.

- Enable telecommuting or cut down on travel costs by improving group communication even when the group is separated.

You may think that these capabilities are what networking in general was designed to facilitate, and you'd be right, but there is a difference. Groupware is not designed for the membership of the network at large, but for the workgroup, no matter how large that workgroup happens to be. As such, it's different from the applications that address the needs of everyone, not just a closed circle. Groupware, if you will, is for the clique.

Typically, to fulfill all its functions, groupware supports e-mail, chat, group scheduling, personal calendars, to-do lists, document replication, Web or other document publishing, password protection for documents, and other functions needed to help all the members of a group work together. For this reason, groupware is also called *workgroup productivity software*, if you're getting paid by the word.

NOTE Still another term is *teamware*, which refers to any application that's designed to enable geographically dispersed coworkers to collaborate on a project, generally via the Internet. As modern groupware supports Internet connectivity, this distinction isn't very useful.

Whatever you call it, groupware has two sides: a client component and a server component. The server side is responsible for managing the groupware functionality: post office server, document publication, personal calendars, and so forth. The client side provides a user interface to all that functionality.

One groupware product today is Lotus Notes, now part of IBM. Why Notes? In part, because it's got a large installed base. Notes has been around since 1989, long before anyone else entered the market, and it got a good foothold in corporate America. Lack of competition wasn't the only reason, though: Notes' flexibility and portability to nearly all popular platforms at any given time has also had a lot to do with its success. Let's take a look at Notes as an example of what groupware can do, and how it's evolved from the local network to the Internet.

Notes-Worthy Groupware When it was first developed, Notes was a mainframe product called PLATO Notes. It was designed simply to stamp bug reports with the date and user ID, but its developers realized that they potentially had a good thing there and expanded its name and capabilities, making PLATO Group Notes capable of:

- Creating personal subject folders
- Creating access lists
- Sorting notes and responses by date
- Creating anonymous notes

- Marking up a document with user-specific comments

- Playing multiplayer games

All this looks like old hat now, but at the time, it was new. PLATO Notes puttered on until the mid-eighties when it became apparent that the personal computer market was endangering the mainframe market. With the support of Lotus Corporation, the developers created a PC-based Notes product, the first version of Lotus Notes. This version, officially bought by Lotus in 1986, supported e-mail, contact lists, and document databases. On the client side, it used either DOS 3.1 or OS/2, and on the server side was supported by DOS 3.1 or 4 and OS/2.

Since the 1989 release, Notes has expanded considerably. In its current iteration, the product supports document formatting, e-mail receipts, group scheduling, and sending documents via e-mail. It also supports many Internet hookups, including Web and newsgroup support, and even document publishing directly to the Web via a Lotus Domino server. The next version will use the Internet Explorer interface, so it may be hard to tell your Windows 98 operating system from your group scheduler. It also has more tools to help developers build applications for it. Notes was designed to be flexible and customizable, but its original designers were surprised to see how popular a development platform it turned out to be.

Groupware-Like Features As the network and the application become ever more intertwined, even products not normally placed in the groupware category have some features of groupware now. Microsoft Office 97 is a good example of this. Word, for instance, includes revision marking and has for several generations of the word processor. *Revision marking* is a groupware function, as it allows several people to review the same document and all mark it up independently so that each person's remarks stand out. (Every time I get back a chapter from the copy editor and technical editor for author review, I'm reminded of this Microsoft groupware capability.) Like the rest of the office suite, it also has Web access built in and can be used to create HTML documents for intranet publication if saved to a Web server. Perhaps not the most efficiently coded HTML documents you've ever seen, but HTML nonetheless.

E-mail also gets more groupware-like as the capabilities of some applications expand from simple mail and file sending to supporting to-do lists and integrated schedulers. Although "groupware" will likely remain a distinct category, you can probably expect its features in many applications to expand as networking becomes increasingly ubiquitous.

Software Licensing

One of the nice things about networking is that it can greatly simplify the problem of getting applications to network clients. No longer do you have to trot around from workstation to workstation installing and upgrading software; with many applications, you can install them on a central server. Even if the applications won't run properly from the server, you can use automated installers—such as the one that's part of Microsoft's Systems Management Server, or more advanced automated installations with Windows 2000—to install applications to user desktops.

There's one disadvantage to all this, or, more precisely, a caution: you need licenses for all the software users even if the software is only installed in one place. Buying a software package does not automatically give you the right to install the software wherever you like or let unlimited numbers of people use it. Otherwise, you're committing *software piracy*, a violation of intellectual property laws and a federal crime. You don't buy software, you buy the right to use it.

WARNING   This may be obvious, but I'll say it anyway: Any commercial software you download from so-called "warez" sites without paying license fees to its original developer is pirated software. Not only is warez software illegal, but it's also a good source of viruses.

What Is a License?

A *software license* is a user fee: you pay for the license and then you pay so much per head or per computer for the privilege to use it, with "usage" often defined as "present in RAM." It's also an agreement to abide by the manufacturer's rules for distribution. In its simplest form, a license is a proof of purchase that can take any of the following forms:

- The envelope containing the disks or CD on which the software was distributed, generally sealed with a sticker that says something along the lines of "By breaking this seal you are agreeing to the terms of the license agreement."

NOTE   My favorite example of the proviso, "When you break this seal you demonstrate that you're agreeing to the terms of the license agreement," comes from Citrix Corporation's MetaFrame (an add-on to Microsoft's Windows Terminal Server). The seal on the CD says that by breaking the seal you state that you have read and agree to the terms of the licensing agreement. The only catch is that the licensing agreement is *inside* the sealed CD case. Yes, we opened it anyway.

- The original disks or CD.
- The page in the manual that says, "Licensing information."
- A paid receipt for the software.

As you can install software multiple times, it's often simpler to buy one boxed application and a bunch of licenses than a boxed application for every person who needs to use the software. User applications typically come with a single license, while network operating systems often come with a small number, around five or 10. If you want more people to be able to use the software, you should buy more licenses.

Licensing's Watchdog—The Software Publisher's Association

The Software Publisher's Association (SPA) is a nonprofit organization based in Washington, DC. Twenty-five member companies created it in 1984 in an attempt to provide a voice to protect and represent the software industry; the SPA's anti-piracy campaign (only one part of what they do) began in 1989. As of late 1998, the SPA's membership included 1,200 commercial software companies, ranging from the largest like Microsoft, to small developers creating their first products.

Most of the SPA's anti-piracy actions begin with a tip on their hot line (800-388-7478), which gets about 30 calls a day. The person taking the call evaluates the tip according to its factual basis, the extent of the violation, and the apparent motives of the person calling. That is, is the person calling out of genuine concern about the licensing violation, or out of revenge, and if the latter, does the complaint sound legitimate? The evaluation of the report is based on the agent's instinct, information provided, and the SPA's own investigation.

Once the SPA decides that a tip is worth pursuing, it investigates the tip to attempt to verify the allegations. If it can't, then the investigation ends. If it can collect enough information to conduct an audit, then the SPA notifies the offender that it's identified a licensing violation and tells the offending company what action it intends to take.

Continued on next page

In most cases, the SPA will conduct an audit of the offending company, in which SPA auditors physically inventory the software on each machine against the proofs of purchase that the company provides. The best proof of purchase is often an invoice or paid purchase order. On average, an audit takes about six months, but the exact amount of time depends on the size of the company and their level of cooperation. During the audit, the company can still operate normally, working around the auditors. If the audit confirms the violation, then the company must pay a fine to the SPA based on a factor of the manufacturer's suggested retail price, and the illegal copies are destroyed or deleted. The organization is also required to repurchase any software necessary so that all users have access to authorized (or legal) software.

In some more serious cases, rather than performing an audit, the SPA files civil charges against the offending company. The SPA has permission from all its members to perform audits on their behalf, but members must grant explicit permission to file a lawsuit. If the lawsuit is successful, the offending company can pay up to $100,000 per civil violation, or $250,000 per criminal violation (assuming criminal charges are filed by the appropriate parties). Once again, all the illegal copies are destroyed.

In the most drastic situations, the SPA can ask a judge to issue a warrant to perform an unannounced raid on an alleged offender. In such a case, a federal marshal accompanies the auditors to protect them and to explain that they have the right to be there. This sounds dramatic, but mostly, it's an unannounced audit.

SPA actions are typically limited to their membership; they're not a federal agency or crusading organization. This means that if they get a tip reporting a license violation of a nonmember's software, they won't take action on the basis of that violation. However, if the violation is large enough to pursue, chances are good that the offender is violating a member's license agreement and the SPA may investigate anyway. If they collect enough information to perform an audit, the SPA will perform the audit on behalf of the nonmember as well as the member. This doesn't affect the outcome if the company is found to be in violation, as all fines are paid to the SPA, not to the software companies. The fines in turn are used to fund future investigations and educational campaigns designed to foster legal software use—and to pay the people who work for the SPA.

Not all software requires a license. The broad categories of licensing include:

Commercial software   This is the bread and butter of the commercial developers, such as Microsoft, Lotus, Adobe, and others. It must be purchased, may not be redistributed, and is ordinarily only released in final format instead of in source code before compiling.

Limited trial software   This is often done with "demo" versions of commercial products. They're generally crippled, time-bombed, or both, and are intended to spur purchase of the commercial version. Limited trial software may be freely distributed.

Shareware   Like commercial software, shareware is fully functional. Like freeware or limited trial software, it may be freely distributed. However, if you continue to use shareware past a stated trial period (10 days, 30 days, 60 days—it depends on the product), then its licensing requires that you pay for it. Most (not all) shareware is not time-bombed, but instead uses "nag screens" to harp at you about registering once the evaluation period is over.

NOTE   Some shareware is freeware-like in the form of the payment to be made; I've seen one shareware product whose author requested payment in the form of pizza delivered to his house in Australia. Apparently, he actually got several pizzas, one from a user in Germany.

Freeware   Freeware products are also fully functional (if somewhat limited in their functionality compared to shareware or commercial software) and free for redistribution, but do not require the user to pay for them. Some freeware is limited trial software, but some is distributed just for its own sake.

Non-commercial use   Nonprofit organizations and individuals may use the product free, but commercial entities must purchase it.

Royalty-free binaries   Royalty-free binaries consist of software that may be freely used and distributed in binary form only.

Open-source software   Both binary files and code may be freely distributed. Some open-source software (such as Linux) requires that any modifications made to it become part of the public domain.

To sum up, you need licenses for commercial software, noncommercial software unless you're part of a nonprofit organization, and shareware. Otherwise, you're free to use and distribute code according to the user agreement. In other words, you don't have a licensing problem on your hands if one of the software developers is tinkering with Linux or Mozilla code on her lunch hour.

Types of Licenses

Not all licenses give you the same powers and privileges. Licenses are most often granted according to the number of users or computers that will be running the software. However, depending on the licensing available with a particular product, you can license software on a per-user, per-workstation, network, site, or enterprise basis. These options are discussed in the following sections.

The Per-User License   Licenses allocated on a per-user basis give the owner of the license the right to load the software in as many places as he likes so long as only that person uses the software. For example, if you have one desktop and one laptop, it's okay to install your favorite word processor onto both the desktop machine and the laptop machine so long as they're for your use. It's not okay to install the word processor onto your desktop and your friend's desktop machine, or to let your friend use your laptop while you're running the same application on your desktop. Many client applications are licensed on a per-user basis, but read the fine print before you assume that this is the case with yours.

In a networked scenario, per-user licenses may be called "per-session," referring to the network session. If you've loaded licensed software (a NOS or user application) on a network server and a user can access it, then he or she has not used up a per-session license. If the user has accessed it, then the license has been used. For example, if you're running NT Server on your network server and have a 10-user license, Joe User does not use up a license by the simple fact of arriving for work in the morning. Once he logs into the network via that NT Server, however, he's used up one of those 10 licenses.

The Workstation (Per-Seat) License A *workstation license* authorizes anyone to use software so long as it's only loaded onto one computer at a time. It's like a user license except that the right is attached to the computer, not to the user. Therefore, at different times, both you and your friend could legally use the laptop with the word processor loaded. However, you could not load the word processor onto both the desktop machine and the laptop even if both computers were for your exclusive use.

In a networked situation, a per-workstation license may be called "per-seat." To return to my previous example, the fact that a client could access the network-accessible application uses up a license. This isn't as bad as it sounds. On one hand, this means that if you have 20 client computers in the office, all capable of accessing the software on the network, then you must buy a license for each computer. On the other hand, if your office runs in shifts and three users use each client computer every day, you don't have to pay for licenses for all those users.

Network, Site, and Enterprise Licenses As I said, most software is licensed on a per-user or per-computer basis, even if it's sold in blocks of 50 or a 100 users. However, sometimes you'll see licenses sold to a group, not to an individual. A *network license* grants all LAN members the right to use an application. A *site license* grants everyone in an office or building site the right to use the application, no matter how many LANs are involved. Finally, an *enterprise license* grants everyone in the organization, no matter how many or where they are, the right to use the software.

Creating and Implementing a Licensing Policy

Okay, you know what software you need to license and are familiar with the types of licenses available. How do you go about making sure that your software licensing is up to snuff?

There are two main issues when it comes to making sure that all the software being used in your organization is licensed. First, there's the problem of how to ensure that no unlicensed software (shareware and applications from home) is on the network. Second, there's the problem of how to make sure that no more than the licensed number of users are using any given package, and that you can prove it.

Solving the first problem may a matter of policy—of having users agree not to install any software themselves unless it's first approved by the network administrator or other responsible person. If you're not willing to trust, you can disable the floppy drives or CD-ROM drives on network client computers. You may even ditch the drives altogether and get the drive-less and disk-less terminal devices introduced in Chapter 9, "Client Workstations," and covered in more depth in Chapter 12, "Thin Client Networking." However, if network users have Internet access, you'll almost have to have some kind of policy in place. The Web is a fertile source of shareware, freeware, and (for the unscrupulous) warez that don't need floppy drives or CD-ROMs to be installed.

As described next, the second problem can be managed either with a manual tracking system or with software metering or monitoring.

Manual Tracking In small networks with locally loaded software, some kind of manual tracking may be possible. At one small consulting firm I used to work for, the user base was sufficiently computer literate to make all users responsible for their own software. All software was assigned a number and that number was assigned to an employee. Each employee had physical custody of the installation disks for the software installed on his or her computer. Additionally, each user prepared a personal inventory of the software on his or her computer and gave it to the business manager. This information was kept in physical form, but could also be entered into a user database quite easily.

TIP

If you decide to follow this model of software license tracking, assign software packages by number, rather than by name. Otherwise, when Jill leaves the company and is replaced by Timon, Timon will be assigned "Jill's Software Suite."

Manual tracking isn't for everyone. First, it requires some work and responsibility on the part of the network client base. If the client base doesn't live up to that responsibility, then your tracking system doesn't work. Second, physical custody isn't always a good idea. If users have physical custody of their software, it takes up a lot of room by each workstation—room that isn't always available. It also opens up the possibility of the network clients taking software home to install it there. This could be in violation of the license agreement and opens up the possibility of virus infections if the home computer is infected. Unless you simply have nowhere else to keep software, even if you are using a manual tracking system, consider locking up the software so it can only be taken out when necessary.

As imperfect a solution as it is (as peer networks won't support software license metering), in a small network with a computer literate user base, manual tracking can be a simpler way of keeping track of installed software.

Software Metering and Monitoring For larger client/server networks, the bookkeeping required may be too great to make manual tracking possible. In that case, there's no shortage of metering and monitoring software, available either from third-party suppliers or as a part of your NOS.

What's the difference between monitoring and metering? It's mostly a matter of control, not a fundamental difference in design—some metering programs can also monitor. *Metering* prevents violations by comparing the number of client accesses to the number of permitted connections. If the application in question is licensed for 50 users and the fifty-first person attempts to connect to it, then the user will receive an error message telling him or her that application isn't currently available. *Monitoring* only keeps track of the connections and logs them for future reference so you can find out exactly how many concurrent users of an application you have.

Summary

LAN applications are often the same applications that you'll find on a stand-alone machine: word processing, spreadsheets, desktop publishing, and so forth. Communications-based applications, such as e-mail, call management, and groupware, are more LAN-specific.

Whatever kinds of applications you're running, you'll need to make sure that they're licensed properly according to the rules established by their manufacturers. You don't buy software, you buy a license to use it. If you haven't purchased sufficient licenses for your organization, you can be held accountable and even criminally charged if the offense is made clear and the violation is sufficiently gross for the software manufacturer to press charges. To avoid this situation, you should keep tabs on software use in your network, either with a manual system, or an automatic software metering or monitoring program. Proper licensing is required whether applications are loaded on each client's machine, on an application server, or on a terminal server running a multi-user operating system for thin client use. Terminal servers and thin client networking are described in Chapter 12, "Thin Client Networking."

EXERCISE 11

1. Your office network has 20 network client PCs and a copy of WordPerfect stored on an application server. Assuming that WordPerfect is licensed on a per-user basis, how many WordPerfect licenses are used up at each of the following times?

   A. Before anyone logs into the network

   B. After 10 people have logged into the network

   C. When 15 people have logged into the network and five are using WordPerfect

   D. When 20 people have logged into the network, seven are currently using Word Perfect, one has it minimized on his screen while working on an Excel spreadsheet, and one stopped using it 10 minutes ago and closed the application

2. Your office network has 20 network client PCs and a copy of WordPerfect stored on an application server. Assuming that WordPerfect is licensed on a per-seat basis, how many WordPerfect licenses are required at each of the following times?

   A. Before anyone logs into the network

   B. After 10 people have logged into the network

   C. When 15 people have logged into the network and five are using WordPerfect

   D. When 14 people have logged into the network, seven are currently using Word Perfect, one has it minimized on her screen while working on an Excel spreadsheet, and one stopped using WordPerfect 10 minutes ago and closed the application

3. Why use per-seat licensing?

EXERCISE 11 CONTINUED

4. To support roaming users, where should LAN applications store user-specific information?

5. E-mail is an example of:

   A. Groupware

   B. Communications software

   C. A business application

   D. None of the above

6. How does groupware differ from communications software?

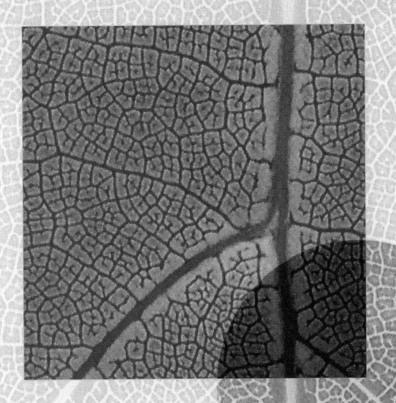

12

Thin Client Networking

*T*hin client networking refers to any network in which the lion's share of all application processing takes place on a server, instead of a client. The term refers to a network by definition, so it leaves out stand-alone small computing devices, such as personal data assistants (PDAs) and other specialized computers that use an operating system that is more streamlined than Windows. What makes thin client networking and computing "thin" is not the size of the operating system nor the apps run on the client, but where in the network the processing takes place.

> **NOTE** Multiuser NT is not the only multiuser server operating system available; UNIX, for one, supports terminal server functions. However, to keep things simple, this chapter will focus on NT-based thin client networking. Although the details for some other multiuser server products may be different, the essentials in terms of process and applicability will be the same.

To a degree, thin client networking represents a return to the mainframe paradigm—applications are located on a central server and accessed by client machines with little in the way of local processing power. The analogy isn't completely accurate, as modern applications can do things that mainframes didn't support, such as word processing. However, the degree of control that thin client networking offers is mainframe-like.

Why the move from centralized computing to personal computers and back again? Business applications drove the development of PCs; they simply couldn't work in a mainframe environment. Not all mainframes were scrapped, by any means, but the newer application designs were too hardware intensive to work well in a shared computing environment.

The return (to some extent, anyway) to thin client networking represents a recognition of two facts about PCs. First, they're a pain to administer. It's time-consuming to install and update locally stored applications. Also, PCs give network users a scary amount of control over their client environments to an extent that can mean a lot of reconfiguring when this control is abused. Second, many of the resources of client computers are wasted. As resource-hungry as modern applications are, they can't keep up with the high-powered CPUs and RAM available for client hardware. Particularly in environments wherein the network user is only actively doing something with the application from time to time, loading applications locally means that you're wasting resources supporting them.

Is thin client networking for everyone? Will it replace the PC-centric world or supplant the zero administration initiatives that are intended to reduce network administration costs? Almost certainly not. At least as of late 1998, thin client networking doesn't scale well enough to support many users and it's definitely not suited to all applications or all environments. But for task-oriented applications or light user load, it can be very useful.

Diagramming the Process

I've already alluded to thin client networking several times in this book, but I think it's time to get into some more detail.

There are three parts to a thin client networking session:

- The *terminal server*, running a multiuser operating system
- The *client*, which can be running any kind of operating system

- The *display protocol*, which is a data link layer protocol that establishes a virtual channel between client and server when the client logs into the terminal server and establishes a session with the server

A session starts when a client computer logs into the terminal server (see Figure 12.1).

FIGURE 12.1:

A client initiating a session on a terminal server

Client logs onto
terminal server.

Server starts new
session for client.

During this session, client input in the form of mouse clicks and keystrokes is uploaded to the server via the virtual channel. The commands to render bitmaps showing the interface are downloaded to the client via the same virtual channel (see Figure 12.2).

FIGURE 12.2:

Graphics instructions are executed on the client; all other processing is rendered on the server.

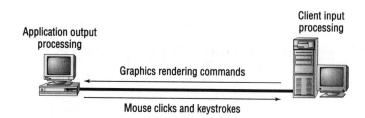

Application output
processing

Client input
processing

Graphics rendering commands

Mouse clicks and keystrokes

NOTE   In Windows Terminal Server, the multiuser version of NT 4, the image on the screen is updated about 20 times per second when the session is active. If the network client stops working, then the terminal server notes the inactivity and reduces the refresh rate to 10 times per second until client activity picks up again.

Image Processing

Once those commands are downloaded to the client, they're rendered using the client resources. The CPU and RAM installed in the client are almost wholly devoted to rendering these images. The processing demands placed on the client are reduced by two factors. First, the display is limited to 256 colors so the demands on the video card to produce complex color combinations won't be all that great. Second, at least some display protocols have a feature called *client side caching* that allows them to "remember" images that have already been downloaded during the session. With caching, only the changed parts of the screen are downloaded to the client during each refresh. For example, if the icon for Microsoft Word has already been downloaded to the client, there's no need for it to be downloaded again as the image of the desktop is updated. Data are stored in the cache for a limited amount of time and then eventually discarded using the Least Recently Used (LRU) algorithm. When the cache gets full, the data that have been there and unused the longest are discarded in favor of new data.

Session Handling

During the course of the session, the user can work on the terminal server as though he or she were physically at the terminal server, using its keyboard and mouse. As the client runs applications, loads data into memory, accesses shared resources on the network (see Figure 12.3), and generally uses the operating system, the applications use the CPU time and memory of the server. The only restrictions on the client are those defined by security settings and those inherent to the display protocol used. As I'll explain later in this chapter under "Preparing for Thin Client Networking," not all display protocols have identical capabilities.

FIGURE 12.3:

The client is not limited to accessing the terminal server, but it can use shared resources within the domain.

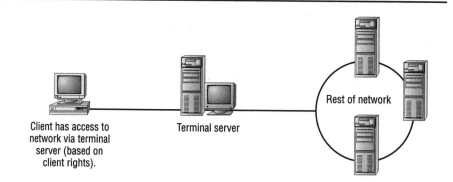

Client has access to network via terminal server (based on client rights).

Terminal server

Rest of network

To the terminal server, each session is treated both separately and as part of the whole of demands placed on server resources. That is, each session is separate from any other sessions already running or that begin while that session is in progress (see Figure 12.4). However, all sessions use the same resources—CPU time, memory, operating system functions—so the operating system must divide the use of these resources among all of them. The number of sessions supported depends on how many sessions the hardware can support and how many licenses are available. When a session ends, the virtual channel to the client machine is closed and the resources allocated to that session are released.

FIGURE 12.4:

Sessions are separate but tap into the same resource pool.

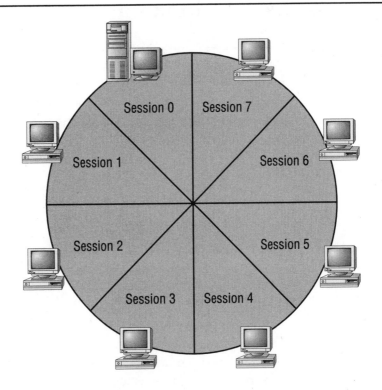

Note that in addition to each client session, there's also a session for the server's use. All locally run services and executables run within the context of this server session.

Preparing for Thin Client Networking

Getting ready for thin client networking takes a little more preparation than an ordinary client/server network. Your client needs are lower, but the server needs, unsurprisingly, are much greater and more complicated to arrange. The good news is that your network needs won't increase. In fact, if necessary, you can actually use a much slower connection than you'd ordinarily find comfortable with a traditional client/server network.

Server Requirements

On the server side, you'll need a multiuser operating system that supports the interface you want to present to network clients, enough hardware to support those clients, and a display protocol that will pass display data to the clients. These requirements are discussed in the following sections.

Hardware Requirements

First, there's the matter of supporting all the clients' hardware needs. To do that, you need to take into account the following:

- How much CPU power does the server need to support the compute cycles needed?

- How much RAM does the server need to support all client data and applications?

On average, you can figure on supporting about 12-15 clients per CPU in the machine, but the actual number will depend on how many compute cycles each client requires. This, in turn, is a function of both how often each client is using the computer and how compute-heavy are the applications each client is using. Thus, a server supporting clients for a bit of light word processing and periodic e-mail check-ins will be able to support many more clients than one used intensively throughout the work day for preparing Excel spreadsheets.

So far as memory's concerned, you'd better plan for using lots of it. Terminal servers typically have 256MB-1GB of RAM installed; the exact amount you'll need depends on the applications the terminal servers are running, how much data each client loads into memory at a time, and how many sessions are active at any given time.

TIP User training is one part of preparing for thin client networking. To get the most out of terminal server resources, encourage network clients to close applications and files that they're not currently using.

There is some good news: although each session in a multiuser operating system such as Windows Terminal Server is separate from all the other current sessions, objects used in more than one session can be shared. Therefore, the memory requirements for each application aren't quite as high as the memory requirements you'd see if you added up the virtual memory used among a like number of individual PCs. However, as is almost always true in a server, the more memory you have, the better the server will perform.

Software and Protocols

Once the hardware question is taken care of, there's still the matter of the software end of the support question:

- Will the server hardware be available to the clients connecting to the multiuser operating system?

- Will there be sufficient virtual memory addresses to support the client needs?

- Will the operating system support your clients' needs?

NOTE Not all multiuser operating systems (or protocols used to support the client connection to them) are created equal.

It's hard to provide hard-and-fast rules for these questions that apply to all situations, but here's some of the background data you need to answer them for yourself. All these questions depend on the multiuser operating system installed on the server and the display protocol you've got connecting server and client.

What Hardware Is Available? Will server hardware be available to client machines? This depends on the hardware, the operating system, and how the server is set up to handle requests. The issue is that not all operating systems can handle requests from multiple users for all hardware. It's not the same thing as routing requests from multiple network clients. With multiple network clients, all the requests are in the "network" queue. Recall that all client work is being done on the multiuser server, so users are technically working locally even though the data is being displayed and manipulated by a separate client machine. Thus, with multiple local clients, the information goes to a "local" queue. Some hardware, such as CD-ROMs, floppy drives, and serial and parallel ports were not originally designed to be shared among several people at once. This doesn't mean that they'll never work. However, it does mean that you may need to discuss your specific hardware needs with the suppliers of multiuser server operating systems to find out what you can reasonably demand from the operating system.

Virtual Memory Limitations What about virtual memory addresses? For those of us used to thinking in terms of single-user clients or servers, the problem of running out of virtual memory addresses isn't one we spend a lot of time on. Physical memory, certainly, but server operating systems support 4GB of virtual memory addresses, and it's hard to imagine running short on that much virtual memory on a single-user system. Even when you cut that down to 2GB for user-related data after 2GB is reserved for core functions of the operating system, it's still a lot of virtual memory addresses.

NOTE In NT 4 (with or without Windows Terminal Server installed), 2GB of virtual memory addresses may be used for user processes while 2GB are reserved for core functions of the operating system. With NT Enterprise Edition (or NT with Service Pack 3 loaded), this split can be made to be 1GB for the operating system and 3GB for user-related needs.

Make it a multiuser system, however, and the story changes. Say that you've got 100 users logged into a quad-processor system with a boatload of memory installed so that the physical resources aren't too strained. Each of those users requires 30MB of virtual memory for all the applications he or she is running—not an unreasonable amount, by any means. Factoring in the resources required by the operating system itself, you're getting perilously close to using up all 4GB of the virtual memory addresses that server operating systems can address. As one person I know found out, run out of virtual memory addresses and, at best, the terminal server will generate Stop errors. At worst, it will crash.

The issue is this: Recall that, to the server, each session is kept separate from each other, but all sessions compete for the same pool of CPU time and memory space. To the terminal server, there is only one stack of virtual memory, not one for each session. Thus, the hardware might be able to support all the sessions, but the logic of the operating system can't. For the moment, there's not much to be done about this except to distribute users among terminal servers and train users to close open files and applications that they're not using. With Windows 2000, the virtual memory address area will be larger than 4GB, so that will help the virtual memory crunch for WTS users.

Multiuser Server Operating System   Multiuser NT is a likely contender to answer the question, "What operating system will my terminal server run?" Two forms of multiuser NT are available:

- Citrix WinFrame

- Microsoft's Windows Terminal Server

WinFrame, developed first, is a set of extensions to NT 3.51 that allow it to function in a multiuser environment. Microsoft licensed the technology back from Citrix to develop Windows Terminal Server (WTS), which is essentially the same thing but with the NT 4 interface. WTS is currently an add-on product from Microsoft, but will be an optional service that can be toggled for Win2K Server and Win2K Enterprise Edition. Under the hood, WTS and Win2K running in single-user mode will be essentially the same operating system.

Application Scheduling in Multiuser Operating Systems

One difference that will exist between Windows 2000 Server and Windows 2000 Server in multiuser mode is related to thread scheduling. In Chapter 10, "Network Operating Systems," I mentioned one characteristic that distinguishes a server operating system from a client operating system. This is that the server operating system is optimized to give more priority to network-related functions than to personal applications. This is why you'll get better local performance out of a client operating system but better network performance out of a server operating system.

A terminal server presents a problem, though: it's a server running personal productivity applications like word processors and spreadsheets, and not just sharing the .EXEs with network clients but running the applications locally. This is a problem for NT 4, as it's not really one thing or the other once the multiuser extensions are added. Thus, Windows 2000 Server's task scheduler is designed slightly differently from that of NT Server. Windows 2000 Server will allow you to adjust the scheduler; either personal productivity applications will run more quickly, or network services will. Which you choose will depend on whether you're using the operating system's terminal server capabilities.

There are some behind-the-scenes design changes to NT that allow it to function as a multiuser operating system (namely, to allow it to organize memory usage and object access among several users, not just one). But the crucial points about how it operates are not directly related to the operating system. The operating system the client sees will be the one that the terminal server is running, interface and all. The key differences in operation are largely a function of the features of the display protocol that allows the client and server to communicate.

Display Protocols Recall that display protocols are the data link layer protocols that establish a virtual channel between the server and client, passing display information to the client for rendering and client input to the server for processing. NT-based multiuser operating systems support one of two display protocols: the Remote Display Protocol (RDP) and the Independent Computing Architecture (ICA).

NOTE   Familiar with the X protocol used with UNIX terminal services? RDP and ICA have much the same function as the X protocol.

RDP, which comes with Microsoft's Windows Terminal Server product, is based on the Microsoft T.120 protocol originally developed for NetMeeting, a video conferencing application. It supports only Windows clients (both 16-bit and 32-bit, including Windows CE); publishes the entire desktop to the client; and has limited communication between processes running on the client computer (if any) and processes running on the terminal server and displayed on the client.

ICA, the protocol at the base of Citrix's MetaFrame add-on to Windows Terminal Server, supports the following features, which RDP does not:

- Sound

- Access to multiple sessions

NOTE   RDP's design makes it technically capable of supporting multiple sessions, but the commercial product currently does not.

- Support for publishing individual applications instead of the entire desktop

- Support for non-Windows clients (DOS, Macintosh, UNIX) to run Windows applications

- Shared Clipboard between local applications and those running on the terminal server

- Support for both IPX/SPX and TCP/IP

- Support for *session shadowing* (allowing an administrator to take over a terminal server session for troubleshooting purposes)

- Support for local printing from applications on terminal servers

- Persistent client-side caching to reduce network traffic related to screen updates

Why use RDP at all, if it's more limited than ICA? One excellent reason: it comes with WTS, so you don't have to pay licensing fees for another display protocol. If your needs are simple (for example, Windows clients, no sound, no locally running applications, running a TCP/IP network), then RDP is perfectly acceptable.

RDP may be adding some functionality in any case. Although Windows 2000 is still in Beta 2 as of this writing (fall 1998), current plans are to add these features of RDP, which are currently restricted to ICA:

- Session shadowing

- Local printing from remote applications

- Shared Clipboard between local and remote applications

- Sound

In other words, when Windows 2000 comes out, if this functionality is still in RDP when the final product is released, RDP will have taken over some of the extra functionality presently restricted to ICA.

So far as speed goes, the conventional wisdom for a while has been that ICA is inherently faster than RDP. When the *Windows NT Magazine* labs performed a controlled test of the two protocols, however, this turned out to be not quite the case. Under some circumstances, RDP actually performs *better* than ICA. The difference lies in the number of windows that are displayed on the thin client. RDP is designed to send full-screen updates, so applications running in maximized mode and containing no child windows were painted more quickly with RDP than with ICA. Windowed applications, and applications with child windows, were redrawn more quickly with ICA than with RDP. These results were consistent regardless of the speed of the link between client and server. In short, if you're looking for speed, then choose RDP for running full-screen applications that don't spawn child windows, and ICA if redrawing windows will be necessary.

Client Requirements

The hardware requirements for a terminal server client vary depending on the client itself and what you're asking it to do. Memory and CPU requirements will depend on answers to the following questions:

- Will the client be running any applications locally?

- How complex will the display be? Will it include video or just still images?

The first question matters as the answer affects how resources will be used on the computer. As little stress as rendering images puts on a CPU or RAM, they put some on it—rendering images takes CPU time. If the CPU and RAM are having to support local data processing as well, then they're going to need to be more powerful than the CPU and RAM in a terminal device that's not running any applications locally.

Windows terminals, which do not usually run applications locally, have lower client-side requirements than microcomputers running their own applications. They don't store data locally, so they don't have hard disks. Generally, they don't have external devices such as CD-ROMs or printers attached, either. Most often, a Windows terminal will be a CPU and some memory, with ports allowing a monitor, keyboard, and network to be attached. Ethernet over UTP is the most likely network connection to be available out of the box, but coaxial Ethernet connections or Token Ring are often available either as an existing option or by request.

Network Requirements

The good news about thin client networking is that it won't place heavy demands on your network. Information passes from client to server pretty steadily, but there isn't much information to pass. Thus, you can actually run a thin client network over a relatively slow connection, such as a VPN running over the Internet or a dial-up connection, as described in Chapter 6, "A Tour of Wide Area Networks."

Display protocols won't transfer all data—they need a transport protocol. As noted in "Display Protocols," earlier in this chapter, both ICA and RDP support TCP/IP; ICA supports IPX/SPX; and neither support NetBEUI. For WAN or dial-up connections, both display protocols cooperate with a connection managed by PPP.

Choosing Thin Client Applications

Not all applications work equally well in a terminal server environment. The best applications:

- Are not demanding of compute cycles.

- Keep extraneous visuals to a minimum.

- Organize local and global data effectively.

- Refer to user names rather than to computer names.

Let's take a closer look at the reasons these features are important.

Low Appetite for Compute Cycles

As all sessions are sharing CPU time, CPU cycles are much more in demand than they are on a single-user system. Thus, the applications running on a terminal server should be fairly low in their use of compute cycles. Functions such as extensive number-crunching and other calculations should be relegated to client-side applications.

> **NOTE** As of this writing, all clients with active sessions must contend equally for compute cycles. However, Windows 2000 Server is supposed to support functionality that can limit a session's use of common resources so that one session's excessive use of system resources doesn't impact all other sessions.

Low on Unnecessary Visuals

Some visual updates are unavoidable: the screen changes that take place when you move from page to page with a Web browser, the updates needed when you open a new document or new application, and so forth. For unavoidable screen updates, just make sure your thin clients are capable of processing the data required to render the images.

Some visual updates, however, are not required and don't really serve any useful purpose. Animations are probably the worst of these, as they require both compute cycles and screen updates.

Applications should either not use animations at all or, if possible, those animations (such as the Office Assistant in Microsoft Office 97) should be turned off. Screen savers on client sessions are also a no-no for the same reason.

Keep Information Where It Belongs

A good application for a multiuser environment is well behaved about where it stores information. Some applications assume a proportion of one machine, one user, but this obviously doesn't work in a multiuser environment. This can wreak havoc in the wrong circumstances, as data that should only be available to a particular user becomes available to anyone using a particular machine. Custom user information should be stored in a user-specific location, such as a user's home directory, not in the system directory.

Identify Users by Name

Another aspect to the "one machine, one user" assumption is related to messaging between users. Applications such as Windows Chat have a machine-centric view of the world—a chat session is established between two machines, not two users. In other words, you can't use Chat between two people logged into the same terminal server because the application is actually running only on a single computer. The NET SEND command, in contrast, is user centric, looking for the names of logged-in users instead of machine names. If you must use a machine-centric messaging application, you'll need to run it on client machines, not on a terminal server.

Splitting Application Deployment—New Moon's Liftoff

One company has made it possible to publish applications to run on thin clients without even needing a multiuser operating system at all. In 1998, New Moon Software released a product called Liftoff, which divides the processing of "Liftoffized" applications between the server and the client without requiring any other extras. Instead of being a terminal server giving network clients access to virtual sessions on the server, the computer is an application server still running the single-user operating system but publishing the Liftoffized applications.

The execution of the published applications is split so that (as with a terminal server) the data processing happens on the server and the client only has to render graphics commands. However, the application appears to be running on the client side—it's not part of a terminal server session.

Why bother with terminal servers, then? The choice of which approach to take is largely dependent on the clients you're using or want to use. Liftoff only works with 32-bit Windows clients. There's no add-on to permit non-Windows clients to run Windows applications. Furthermore, the high resource requirements of the supported clients means that Liftoff is probably not the best way of using old hardware, as the clients have to be able to support NT Workstation or Windows 95/98. The lack of support for any OS other than 32-bit Windows also precludes the use of Windows terminals, even those running Windows CE. However, it's an approach that may work well for those who have high-end clients and don't want to get a terminal server but still want some elements of thin client networking.

Why Use Thin Client Networking?

Now you know what thin client networking is and what you need to support it. Now for the hard question: Why should you go to all that work?

A year or two ago, when the idea of Windows-based thin client networking was starting to take off, you'd hear a lot about how it was a better idea than a traditional LAN because it allowed network clients to be so lightweight and thus so inexpensive.

Nope.

First, the price of new PCs capable of running client applications has dropped dramatically. You can buy a fully loaded PC for about $1000 now, sometimes including a monitor. A lower-end system can cost as little as $500 without a monitor. As memory prices rebound slightly, expect prices to rise accordingly, but desktop PCs simply aren't that expensive.

Second, Windows terminals and other thin client devices aren't all that cheap. Typically, a Net PC runs somewhere in the $300-$500 range, not including a monitor. For that, you're getting a computer incapable of running anything without the help of an expensive multiuser operating system that runs on a fully-loaded computer, often a SMP machine to maintain all its users.

Third, it's not cheap to junk existing machines and buy new ones and a new server operating system. Advisable? Sometimes. Cheaper than buying new PCs? Possibly. But it's not cheaper than keeping existing PCs or performing spot upgrades to breathe new life into the machines you already had.

Clearly, the reason to go with thin client networking isn't a matter of reducing hardware costs. Rather than reducing the total cost of *ownership* (TCO), thin client networking reduces the total cost of *administration* (TCA). Thinking of it this way keeps you focused on where the money in the care and feeding of computers really goes. It's not the boxes that are expensive, it's taking care of them.

Reducing the Total Cost of Administration (TCA)

The costs of a PC are a lot more than just hardware. They also involve the following:

- Fixing problems caused by user error

- Installing or upgrading applications

- Repairing broken PCs

- Upgrading PC hardware

- Resolving problems due to applications conflicting with other applications

Thin client networking helps you maintain control over the client computers in your network by centralizing everything about them in a single place. Applications, user settings—everything the clients need to use the network is centrally located, down to the operating system. Combined with system policies that control what users can and can't do to their desktops, this can dramatically reduce the amount of support your help desk people have to do. If inexperienced users can't delete desktop shortcuts or turn their screens black, then they don't have to call Support to fix the problem after they've done it.

The increased control can be applied at the hardware level, too. Thin clients can be ordinary PCs (which is sometimes desirable), but they can also be stripped-down machines that offer little more than a keyboard, mouse, and monitor. These restrictions prevent users from installing unauthorized applications or games (or introducing boot viruses to the computer). Terminal devices have an additional advantage in that their smaller footprint means that they take up less space than a full-blown PC. This makes them good clients for crowded areas like kitchens or stockrooms.

Break the Upgrade Cycle

Another reason to use thin client networking is to give those old client PCs a new lease on life. Most commercial application software seems to do nothing but get fatter, which means that your computer must get fatter to accommodate it. It's not just the applications, either: the data itself gets fatter, as multimedia becomes more prevalent. The problem is cyclical. Parkinson's Law, which describes the nature of work to expand to fill available time, can be applied to data—that is, it expands to fill available resources. So, you get more resources (memory, disk space) to meet the requirements of your data and then the data expands again.

In short, the obsolescence cycle for a PC is about two years, so this can get to be an expensive hobby. Unfortunately, it's also a hard one to break, as opting out of the upgrade cycle is hard to do when everyone else is upgrading. The word processor that's two generations old might work perfectly well for in-house documents, but it won't necessarily be able to display the documents that your partner company sends you.

Computers aren't magically upgraded when they can't keep up with the latest application suite, however. If your PC can't keep up, then you have two options:

- Upgrade the PC

- Replace the PC

Upgrading is generally the cheaper of the two options in terms of hardware costs, but it's not necessarily cheaper in the long run. First, it costs time, a precious commodity for most of us, as you have to take the PC apart to add the new RAM or hard disk. Upgrading also eventually becomes difficult or impossible unless you replace the motherboard—tried to find 30-pin SIMMs for a 486 lately?

Buying new PCs every two years is the other option, but this option has hidden costs as well. Buying a new PC isn't just a matter of buying a new box and plugging it into the network, but requires making the new machine exactly like the old one. That means reinstalling applications, backing up locally stored data and user configuration settings and restoring them, and so forth.

> **NOTE** The issues involved in replacing an old PC with a new one are a convincing argument for central storage of all data and user configuration information, even if you're not doing thin client networking.

Now that I've thoroughly depressed you, there is a way to leave this cycle, or at least to simplify keeping up with it. As all applications are run on a single server in thin client networking, the client machines themselves don't actually have to be capable of running the applications—or even an operating system that supports them. The only machine that needs to be upgraded to keep up with application demands is the server. Thus, with thin client networking, you can dramatically extend the life of your client computers.

Sample Applications for Thin Client Networking

If you're still not sure what you could do with thin client networking, consider the following situations, derived from case studies of real-life thin client networks.

> **NOTE**   The full text of these scenarios, complete with hardware specifications and more details, is available at **www.winntmag.com** in the October 1998 and January 1999 issues.

Keeping Doctors on the Go

One Midwest clinic found itself in the position of needing to change the way it was storing data. For the previous 10 years or so, the clinic had been managing patient records and accounting with a combination of a mainframe and a few stand-alone PCs. The mainframe was getting old and unreliable, and the need for current patient information grew more crucial to manage the 10,000 patients the clinic saw each year.

The new solution had a couple of requirements. First, it had to offer reliable access to patient records so that hospital staff could do billing and other tasks that required patient information. Second, it had to give the staff physicians access to patient data without breaking the doctor-patient relationship. The doctors were accustomed to reading from a patient's file while at the patient's bed, and weren't keen about the idea of interrupting that communication by going to a client computer in another room. The end result was a combination of NT Workstation PCs for hospital staff and wireless Wyse thin client devices. The staff could use the PCs for fast and reliable access to patient data, while the doctors could carry the Wyse devices while making their rounds, making notes on the touch screen like a Clipboard.

Giving Students Computer Access

One of the biggest hassles about traveling is lugging along the laptop computer. Even the lightest laptops are heavy, bulky to store on an airplane, and (in most cases) less comfortable to use than the average desktop computer. However, if you don't take your laptop with you when you travel, you can't do anything computer related: work on files, check e-mail, browse the Web, or the like.

One executive training center decided to make things easier on its students by providing them with PC access for their two-day stay. Each hotel room in the center had its own computer that the guests could use to run any of a suite of applications: e-mail, word processors, Web browsers, and so forth. The guests were happy, but the network administrators were not. To keep each guest's data private, the network administrators had to wipe any files off each PC's hard drive after a guest had checked out. This was a major hassle when you consider that the center sees hundreds of guests a week and each only stays for a couple of days. Additionally, fixing broken and misconfigured computers took up a lot of administration time that could have been spent more usefully on designing network innovations.

To resolve this problem, the network designer decided to trade the PCs in each room in for thin client devices—network computers, in fact. The system policies for these users permitted them access to only a specific suite of applications, not any Control Panel settings. Two servers supplied login capabilities for the network; one provided file storage with user-specific home directories (with a script the training center staff developed) that could be automatically created at check-in and deleted at check-out. Four application servers provided access to network applications. With this configuration, users had limited control over the desktop (and thus limited ability to misconfigure the desktop), but they did have access to the applications they needed.

Centralizing Control of the Desktop

Not all thin client networks are homogenous—many, like the one in this example, represent a mixture of thin clients and fat clients as appropriate for users' needs. In this case, the network designers were lucky enough to be in a position to scrap their existing network—a collection of OS/2 servers, Windows 3.1 PCs, a mainframe, and some dumb terminals.

In the name of presenting a more consistent face to the network, and getting access to some applications that wouldn't run with either Windows 3.1 or dumb terminals, the company decided to replace the existing network. The company used a combination of Net PCs (devices that, like network computers, can run applications locally or remotely) and a terminal server. A few NT Workstation PCs were included for the power users who needed access to all applications and could be trusted not to misconfigure their computers. The rest of the user base was given the Net PCs and access to only selected applications. Some users objected to not being able to personalize their desktops (a common complaint when you use system policies to lock down part or all of the system configuration). However, most ended up being happy with the system's responsiveness and stability.

Summary

Thin clients for everyone? Not at all. I don't believe in "magic bullets" that will solve all problems. Thin clients are suitable in networks where it's desirable, possible, and cost effective to centralize the network's computing resources, and for use with applications that perform well in a distributed computing environment. The more task oriented and intermittent your network client use, the better suited your network is to thin client networking.

Thin client networking isn't desirable for network clients running compute-heavy applications. It requires a very stable server environment, one that may be more power hungry than every network can afford. It also requires a network staff capable of maintaining a centralized server. In short, thin client networking doesn't always fit the needs of the network, or fit the needs of every person on the network. This is one reason it's worth your while to check out the possibility of running a network that's a hybrid of thin and fat clients.

One excellent application for thin client networking is running a centrally stored Web browser. In Chapter 13, "Creating a Corporate Web," I'll talk about building an intranet server to provide that Web browser with a little content.

EXERCISE 12

1. Six clients are logged into a terminal server. How many sessions are running?

2. Name the two display protocols supported by Windows Terminal Server.

3. Which display protocol could you use in each of the following situations—RDP or ICA? (In some situations both may be possible.)

   A. The client is using Windows CE.

   B. The client needs support for sound.

   C. The client is running UNIX.

   D. The client is running Windows 95.

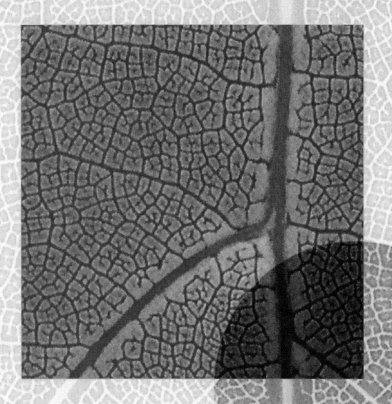

13

Creating a
Corporate Web

Near-universal access to the World Wide Web and other parts of the Internet have made the browser an essential office application. Why create an *intranet*-based Web, though, if no one's going to see it but the people in the office?

In this chapter, I'll discuss what you can do with a corporate Web and explain the basics of creating and publishing Web content, including the kinds of formatting options that are open to you and the tools you'll need to publish the data. You won't come away from this chapter an expert on Java programming, but after reading this, you'll know what's involved in creating a page or site and have some ideas to explore.

What Can You Do with a Corporate Web?

Although the first use for a Web you may think of is publishing information about your company, that's only a small part of what you can do. Get creative and you can do any or all of the following:

- Post must-see information and get confirmation of who's read it and who hasn't.

- Host virtual meetings between people not able to meet in person.

- Automate initial queries to the help desk or other office information.

- Give people easy access to a corporate database.

- Run a corporate FTP site.

- Publish in-house research to allow people to share information.

NOTE   Several (not all) of the corporate Web applications that I describe in this chapter stem from case studies I prepared for the "1999 NT Innovators" issue of *Windows NT Magazine*, which showcases ingenious uses of NT every January. If you'd like to read more about these inventive uses of corporate Webs, turn to `www.winntmag.com` and browse the archives for the January 1999 issue (available online as of April 1999).

Can't think of anything else to do with a corporate Web? Make it a testing ground for new ideas for the content of your Internet-accessible Web site. If you're not sure whether a concept is going to fly in the real world, why not publish it where only office people can see it, and ask for feedback? Better to find out in-house that an idea's a flop than on a network accessible to the entire world. You might even be able to save the idea from being a flop with the feedback you get.

Distribute Information Easily

Like e-mail, intranet Web content can be a big paper saver. Rather than creating memos informing people of a change in company policy or inviting them to the company holiday party, you can create a Web page with the information. This not only saves you the trouble of distributing the memos, but also allows you access to design elements not always possible in e-mail—without requiring people to have access to the application in which the original document was created. Posting the documents to the Web site also prevents people from getting cute and tampering with the original document.

Another advantage to publishing must-see documents on the Web is that you can confirm that people have read them—you're not limited to just posting the information and hoping it got to the people who needed to see it. Just create a section where people can click on a button saying, "Yes, I've read and understood this," to send a confirmation e-mail to the business manager or whomever else needs to know. You could do something similar to have people RSVP for the office party or get-together, creating a form in which people can indicate whether or not they'll be attending, how many guests they'll be bringing, and any other relevant information, such as preferred dates or dietary requirements. Anyone who's had to coordinate an office get-together will appreciate that kind of automation.

Bring People Together

Chapter 11, "LAN Applications and Licensing," mentioned chat sessions as a means of getting people together for meetings when physical meetings are difficult or impossible. A chat application is one way of doing this, but a Web-based chat is another, and one that can be used by anyone with a browser, not just the people with the chat application installed. Video conferencing can also be supported via a Web interface.

In fact, with Web-based scheduling applications, the Web can also be used in group scheduling for those times when virtual meetings won't do the trick. Lotus Organizer, for example, has a Web plug-in so that people can plan their schedules on their personal computers or PDAs and then upload the information to a Web-based calendar.

TIP   Don't want just anyone able to see or read your calendar? Password-protect it for viewing and editing.

A corporate Web provides still another means of getting people together—helping them find each other in the first place. Many big companies are a maze of cubicles or offices, and, in a large company, not everyone can know one another by sight. One solution to this problem is to prepare an online map of the corporate offices that shows the location of each person's office. Let users plug in a name, and the map highlights the location of that person's office *and* pulls up a picture of the person whose name you entered.

Reduce Support Costs

A Web-based user help desk facilitates the support process. First, many user requests are predictable—they want access to a particular folder, can't reach their e-mail, or can't find a file. You can create a form listing common problems, inviting users to pick their problem from a list. If their problem isn't listed, they can explain it in a text box on the Web page.

TIP   Using a Web-based help desk allows people to complain about lack of e-mail access without using the telephone or relying on the e-mail they can't use.

Second, writing down the problem or choosing from a set of options encourages users to think about what's wrong and describe it more fully than they might over the telephone or in person. From my tenure supporting user requests, I've noticed that you often have to go through the initial process of isolating the problem, getting from, "WordPerfect isn't working" to "WordPerfect is shutting down after a message comes up saying that the computer is low on resources." Isolating the problem can take several minutes or even longer if the user and the support person both get frustrated. It's simpler—and less frustrating for everyone—to allow the user to write down the problem or choose his or her problem from a list. This won't completely eliminate the need to isolate some problems, but it should help. Telephone follow-up is always an option if more information is needed.

Third, submitting problems by Web-based e-mail reduces both the time it takes to report the problem and the time required for the support person to listen to it. Additionally, e-mail is always available—the person reporting the problem doesn't have to wait for a free line to the support center to open up.

Simplify Database Access

An increasingly popular purpose for a corporate intranet Web is to provide a front end to a database for salespeople or managers. It's a great improvement over printing out standard reports every month. First, a canned report may not answer a specific set of questions that a salesperson or manager has. Second, we're back to the distribution problem again—how do you get those reports to everyone in a widely distributed company? By fax? By e-mail? Who's going to take the time to create the reports?

TIP

I've seen one corporation in which users could send the database server queries via e-mail—without having to know Structured Query Language (SQL) syntax. The users had to phrase the questions using standard language that would trigger a previously prepared query, but this language was very simple—much simpler than a complex query would have been. More advanced users familiar with SQL syntax could e-mail queries using SQL and thus get custom reports.

Additionally, when people need to edit the database or create reports, with a properly designed Web application they can do it without having to understand how to use a database front end, such as Access. The interface on the front end can be designed to translate the user-phrased queries into the SQL that databases use.

Distribute Files

It's entirely possible that you may want people to have access to certain files but not to the directories in which those files are stored. Perhaps the directories are across a slow WAN connection, or other files are stored in the directories that you don't necessarily want everyone to know exist. In such a case, you can set up an FTP site to function as a central repository for files coming in and going out. Users can upload and download files from a more-or-less public directory. The degree of security depends on how you configure it, whether access is dependent on a password, restricted to certain users, or open to anyone who logs in.

TIP   To keep data files consistent, replicate them from their original directories to the FTP site.

You needn't restrict your FTP site to text files. If you have fairly computer-savvy users on your network, you can store software upgrades in a central location. Users can run the Setup files from the FTP site, saving themselves the trouble of looking for their own disks or getting the support person to upgrade their applications.

Publish Research

One more use for the Web is to share research between departments of a large organization. For example, several agencies in the U.S. Department of the Army share a corporate intranet. On this intranet is a Web-based database called IntelLink that publishes the data collected by the analytical departments. Users of IntelLink, including policymakers, soldiers ("warfighters," to use the military jargon), management, and anyone else with access, can refer to a database of country reports, pictures, maps, and military hardware. Without this Web-based application, these people would have to call the analysts to prepare reports for

them. Obviously, the analysts still make custom reports and brief-
ings, but often-requested information doesn't require any more
work on the analysts' part.

Why Use the Web?

You can share information and run virtual conferences with a
corporate LAN that has file sharing, chat, and e-mail access
enabled—no Web required. Why bother building Web sites and
applications? Mostly because a Web creates a simple means of
providing a consistent appearance for published data and an easy
way of regulating access to that data.

Create a Consistent Look

Building a Web interface for applications or information allows
you to customize the interface to make it as simple or as complicated as you like. Ordinary LAN access, using the applications
described in Chapter 11, "LAN Applications and Licensing,"
requires people to have access to those applications—either
locally or on an application or terminal server—and know how to
use them. A Web-based application interface means that people
need only a browser, not one application for each type of resource
access. Whether the network's users are accessing a database or
sending e-mail, they can use their Web browser to load the interface you've created. Not only does this limit the number of applications that must be accessible to network users, but it also means
that the application front end can be as simple or as complex as
your user base requires. For example, if users only need to prepare database reports for certain dates, you could create an
interface with a place to plug in dates and a button that says
"Generate Report." It's not necessary to teach anyone how to
use a database client.

Using Web-based forms enhances consistency not only for the users but also for the people or applications receiving the information input by the users. For example, some e-mail applications support HTML and thus could display formatted party invitations or official memos. Even if your office uses such applications, however, e-mail is still an inferior form of communicating important information because it doesn't support forms. People can RSVP to your e-mailed invitation but there's no way to force them to provide all the information you need. In contrast, a Web-based invitation to a pot-luck dinner could include an RSVP section in which users could say that they were attending, indicate the number of people they were bringing, and choose a dish to bring from a list of options. The same invitation sent in e-mail demands a free-form response that might include all that information, some of it, or none of it. Similarly, canned reports that a user can choose from a list eliminate the possibility of user syntax errors. Get the syntax right on the back end and the user doesn't need to know it.

Securely Distribute Information

Not only does Web-based distribution of information provide consistency but also some additional layers of security. For example, recall that online documents are harder to tamper with than documents distributed in a user-editable form, and FTP sites allow documents to be made available without opening up the source directory. There's more:

- Pages can be protected to limit access to certain users or those who know a password.

- Canned queries can be the only interface to a database so that information not in the canned queries can't be part of a report.

- Chat rooms can be restricted to a set of users rather than being open to anyone.

In short, if you want to present a consistent yet customizable interface for data dissemination and retrieval, a corporate Web is an excellent choice of medium. It's dynamic, almost endlessly forgettable, and can't be tampered with easily.

Creating Web Content

Web content can be as simple as posting text and a few pictures or as complex as linking content from back-end applications or other pages. When creating content, think about who's going to be using the pages; from that, choose the tools you need to create the desired effect.

Planning Content and Design

As with preparing anything else complex, the first step in creating a Web site is not sitting down with Notepad or your favorite HTML editor and a copy of *HTML for Dummies*, but planning. Ask yourself the following:

- Who's going to be looking at this information?

- How should the content be organized?

- Will everyone have access to all content or will some parts be shut off to all but a few people?

- Where will the content be coming from?

Thinking about all of this ahead of time will help you when it comes to figuring out how to organize material. Until you know who's going to be seeing the information, you can't plan an interface or plan for security. Until you know how the content will be organized and where it's coming from, you can't write the code that will make that content available.

Design Tips

A lot of good web design is related to simplicity and legibility. No matter how many Web sites there are that do nothing but play the theme from *Deliverance*, the grand majority of sites—including the ones on your intranet Web site—will be there for the purpose of imparting information. If your readers can't read that information easily, they'll give up. If they give up, then you might as well have saved yourself the trouble of creating the site in the first place.

Keeping Data Organized Web pages are typically three-dimensional structures, built not only on their own contents but also with links to other pages. It's certainly possible to build an intranet Web site that's a collection of unrelated pages, but it'll be much easier to navigate the site if each page is part of a coherent whole.

TIP   Protected pages are one exception to this rule. If you don't want everyone to be able to view a particular page, one simple way of limiting access to it is not to link the page to other pages and not publish its URL. (If the page's content is really private, password-protect it as well; this method will help keep out the idle curious if that's all you're worried about.)

Drawing a map of your Web site's data sources, page links, and other pieces may help you keep organized when planning (see Figure 13.1). Once you've got the site's design mapped out, you're ready for some content and page design work.

FIGURE 13.1:

Draw a map of your Web site before worrying about content.

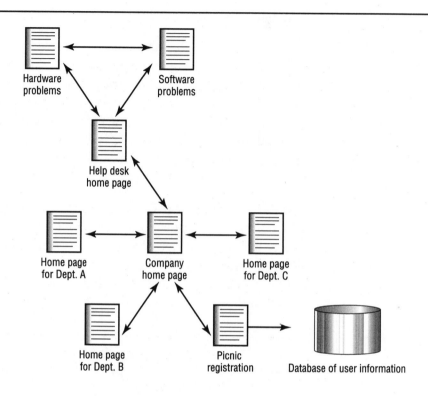

Hardware problems

Software problems

Help desk home page

Home page for Dept. A

Company home page

Home page for Dept. C

Home page for Dept. B

Picnic registration

Database of user information

TIP   Some HTML editors, such as Microsoft's FrontPage, let you create and graphically arrange pages, simplifying the process of organizing the Web site.

Don't Overload Reader Buffers   Flicker and backlighting make reading on-screen harder than reading hard copy; most people read from a monitor at about one-third the rate at which they can read print. Thus, one of the first rules of creating text is: Keep it simple. If at all possible, keep text on a single page so that people don't need to scroll down to read. If this isn't possible (for example, if you're coding a longish document for online dissemination), then use white space to break up the page a bit. Whatever you do, don't format the page so that people have to scroll horizontally to read it. Code the text to dynamically arrange itself in relation to the dimensions of the browser window.

Content organization is also important in getting the message across. The human brain can remember and absorb only about seven things at a time, so break up content accordingly. Eschew long lists of bullets and numbers for smaller sets, and if producing a long document for online publication, consider breaking the document into sections that can be loaded separately from a single table of contents.

Support the Text—Don't Squash It The first goal of an online document is readability. Once you've got that down, then you can worry about visual impact. To that end, keep backgrounds simple, supporting the text rather than distracting attention from it.

What about background bitmaps? They can work if they support the text instead of drawing attention away from it. Generally speaking, it's best to avoid backgrounds that:

- Have a repeating pattern the same size as the font you're using, as they'll make the letters hard to distinguish from the background.

- Are based on pictures or images that will distract the reader's attention from the text. If you want to illustrate the text, put pictures or photographs next to it, not under it.

- Are very bright or high contrast, hurting your reader's eyes.

- Are too close to the color of the text.

Speaking of color, you can't assume that subtle gradations of color will display the same way on every monitor. Keep the color scheme fairly bold or some elements may be lost in the translation.

Don't Overdo the Extras Animations aren't as much of a bandwidth problem on intranet Web sites as they are on the Internet, but they're still potentially distracting. Flashing signs, spinning globes, or the like can be a nice touch in small quantities, especially if they're used to focus the reader's attention. If overused, they draw attention away from the text. If *really* overused, they cause headaches and grouchy users.

What about sound? I'm not a huge fan of sound on Web pages in any case, but in the office environment, it's really undesirable unless everyone has their own office. Any kind of sound effects are distracting to people around you and not every computer has speakers that support sound well anyway.

Keep It Connected Make it easy to navigate the site. Back buttons on pages are a good idea, but an even better one is a site map that's accessible from anywhere in the site. If you're comfortable with frames, you can put a site map in a frame to one side of the currently displayed document. If frames are a bit beyond you, you can put links to important pages (such as the site's home page) on the top or bottom of each page in the site.

Intranet Content versus Internet Content

Now that you're thoroughly intimidated, the good news is that creating Web content for an intranet can potentially be much easier than creating it for the World Wide Web. First, you've got greater control over your user base in that you know what browser they're likely to be using and what features it supports. Not all browsers present the same information exactly alike or support the same capabilities. For example, Netscape Navigator does not natively support ActiveX controls (although you can download an add-on that will support them). For another, Microsoft supports a nonstandard Java type, so Microsoft's Internet Explorer is chancy at best when it comes to supporting pages running Java—sometimes they work, and sometimes they don't.

NOTE   Java is a programming language that Sun Microsystems designed to run on any computing platform without recoding. I'll talk more about Java and related languages in the section, "Functional Elements," later in this chapter.

Second, although you don't want to create pages that will bring your office LAN to a screeching halt, a corporate intranet doesn't have nearly the bandwidth problems of a World Wide Web page accessible only from a telephone line. A connection that runs at 100Mbps will download a Web page to a client's browser much more quickly than a 56Kbps modem. Even if the intranet spans WANs, traffic on the WAN may be lighter than traffic on the Internet during peak hours. It's certainly more easily manageable.

Third, security on the office LAN may be less of a problem than it is on the World Wide Web. There are security holes related to Web publishing that can lead to someone editing your Web page's content. (*The New York Times* public Web site found this out in the fall of 1998 when they got hacked and had to take down their page to keep the rest of the world from seeing what had happened to it.) However, a LAN has fewer potential culprits than the entire Internet. Thus, your chances of being hacked are reduced by a potential prankster's knowledge that he or she is more likely to be caught as the result of hacking a page.

TIP   These differences are worth keeping in mind when planning to migrate sites from the LAN Web to the World Wide Web. Pages that work really well on a LAN may not scale well to the Internet.

Text Markup Languages

People sometimes talk about "programming" a Web page, but formatting text to be readable by a browser isn't really programming. As the names of the formatting languages suggest, they're *markup languages*. That is, they're composed of characters or other symbols inserted in the body of a document that indicate how the file should look when printed or displayed, or to define its logical structure (such as paragraphs and bullets). Without such a markup language, the data to be displayed would be raw text with no character or paragraph formatting.

A markup language defines document appearance with codes called *tags* that take a form like this: <tag> </tag>. The first tag indicates the point where the formatting should begin and the second one (with the slash) indicates where the coding should end. If you forget the second tag, the coding for the first tag is applied to the end of the document.

NOTE

The markup language can be applied to raw text either by hand using a text editor (such as Notepad) or with a graphical tool that adds the code when you visually arrange the text as you want it to appear. Graphical tools are easier to work with when you're learning, but they're not always as precise as text editors.

HyperText Markup Language (HTML)

HTML is the granddaddy of Web page coding and the backbone of most Web pages. HTML allows you to publish text and figures, the contents of spreadsheets, or even create database reports to be read online. It's good for any kind of static information, both for organizing it and for formatting. HTML codes let you:

- Set text size and font.

- Apply bold, italic, or underlined formatting to text.

- Define links to other pages.

- Insert images.

- Create a title for the page.

- Create tables.

- Insert metadata for use by search engines.

NOTE   *Metadata* is hidden data that does not appear on the Web page but may be picked up by a search engine to direct people to that site.

There are three types of HTML tags: those that format text or individual characters, those that format paragraphs or other chunks of text, and those that are invisible but provide other functionality, such as metadata for searches.

HTML has one significant advantage over all other markup languages: near-universal support. Just about any browser (certainly any modern and graphics-capable browser) supports the current version of HTML, something not true of Dynamic HTML (DHTML), XML, or Java and ActiveX. If you need your Web sites to be accessible to a variety of browser types, HTML is the way to go.

Dynamic HTML (DHTML)

Dynamic HTML makes HTML a bit more flexible. Rather than presenting a static Web page to the world, you can use DHTML and make a page customizable by the person using it, without corrupting the original document source. For example, a page prepared with DHTML can include elements that a user can drag around on the page to rearrange its contents. When the page is refreshed, however, the changes are lost and the page is restored to its original appearance.

DHTML has support for the following features not included in HTML:

- Dynamic styles
- Precise positioning
- Data binding
- Dynamic content

Not sure what all this means? Fear not—it's explained below.

Applying Styles to Web Documents *Dynamic styles* are based on the principles of cascading style sheets (CSS), applying style sheets to a page instead of formatting the various sections by hand. If you use a modern word processor, then you're probably familiar with style sheets that automatically format text blocks a certain way depending on the style you assign to them. This formatting can include text color, font, positioning, visibility, and just about anything else to do with how text can be presented. CSS, and by extension DHTML, is the same kind of thing, only applied to Web pages instead word processors.

DHTML's dynamic styles have capabilities not included in word processors. For example, you could mark up text to make links automatically change color when you position your mouse over them, or show text when you move your cursor over a certain blank space. The only catch to these styles is that they require you to put most documents in style sheets, a time-consuming task for those new to style sheets or who are having to convert documents.

Placing Text Where You Want It Another feature of DHTML is its ability to define exactly where on a page an element will appear, using x (horizontal), y (vertical), and even z (3D) coordinates to define object placement. (Defining object placement in 3D allows you to make objects overlap.) Precise positioning makes wrapping text around images possible and repositions objects according to the size of the browse window.

NOTE   HTML without CSS does not support exact placement; the positioning of elements depends on the browser.

Embedding Data in a Page   To give users access to back-end information, such as that stored in a database, normal HTML pages must contact the server holding the original data and ask for permission to let users manipulate data. DHTML allows the data to be bound to a particular page, permitting users to work with the bound data without disturbing the source data or even touching the server storing the original data. Instead, the data source is part of the page and can be sorted and filtered like a database. Not only does this reduce load on the servers, but it also allows users to view and manipulate data without giving them access to the source.

Creating Dynamic Content   *Style sheets* allow the Web *publisher* to easily change the appearance of a page or set of pages. *Dynamic content* allows the Web *user* to change the appearance of a page by running a script in order to:

- Insert or hide elements of a page.
- Modify text.
- Change the page layout.
- Draw data from back-end sources and display it based on a user request.

Unlike HTML, which can only change page contents before the page is downloaded to the user's browser, DHTML can accept changes at any time. When used with scripts that allow users to define the elements they want to see, dynamic content can provide a high degree of interactivity.

TIP	In the section, "Bring People Together," earlier in this chapter, I described a Web-based map of a building that could display the location of a particular office and a picture of the person the user was trying to find. That map was created with DHTML, using the markup language's dynamic content feature.

EXtensible Markup Language (XML)

XML is a new Web coding language that doesn't replace HTML (certainly not at this point—there's little evidence of it in live Web pages) but supports it, making Web pages a little more flexible.

The idea is this: when you're formatting a page with HTML, you can change the appearance of text with the tags for boldface, italic, paragraph break here, and so forth. These tags don't really tell you anything about the text's content but only format its appearance. XML is not limited to tags that say what text is supposed to look like; instead, you can use it to tag the text with what it is (names, addresses, product names, and so forth).

Why is this helpful? First of all, this metadata can make it easier for search engines to find predefined elements. If you searched your corporate Web site (created with HTML) for "name," looking for all the names mentioned, the search would return all the instances of the *word* "name," not names. If the site were coded with XML, however, the search would return any text tagged as a name. Second, tagging parts of speech is useful if you want to apply a rule (such as color or language) only to parts of a Web document. Say that the online document is a short story in Spanish with translation in English. Rather than having to switch from Spanish to English support in the document, you could define all the parts of the story with a <story></story> tag and apply the Spanish rule to those parts only, with the translations remaining in English. Essentially, if your Web page design would be made easier by making certain parts of its text isolated elements, then you could benefit from using XML.

Application and Scripting Languages

Want your Web page to actually *do* something instead of just displaying text and images? You'll need to add support for some mini-programs. On the client side, this could take the form of ActiveX controls or Java applets. On the server side, the mini-programs might use a common gateway interface (CGI) front-end to a program stored on the server, or a script embedded in the page itself with Microsoft's Active Server Pages (ASP).

Client-Side Web Applications

Client-side Web applications and executables are downloaded from the Web server to the client, to be executed on the client using the client machine's resources. Client-side applications may include such features as chat programs or other applications likely to be used more than once while a page is still open.

The Java Language *Java* is a cross-platform language developed by Sun Microsystems. The concept behind Java is interoperability: Java *applets* (miniature applications) are able to run on any platform—DOS, Windows, UNIX, NT, or what have you. When a Java applet runs, it first creates an execution environment (called a *sandbox*) for itself, and then runs in the context of this sandbox. Theoretically, this sandbox has two effects. First, it lets an applet execute on any platform because the sandbox creates the operating environment the applet needs. Second, it keeps the applet from doing anything to the native operating environment, as it never actually touches it.

Java applets that you might already have encountered include Netscape Communicator's Netcaster as well as the trip planners used on some travel Web sites. Netcaster is the front end to Netscape *pull* technology (that is, pulling content from Web sites without requiring that you actually visit the sites). The trip planners take the preferences you enter and search a database of airline flights that correspond to your needs and then return the possible matches.

You might have heard various and sundry terms associated with Java. While this isn't intended to be a complete tutorial on Java, Table 13.1 explains some related terms.

TABLE 13.1: Java-Related Terminology

Term	Description	More Information
HotJava	The first browser to support Java. The browser itself is written in Java.	HotJava supports any combination of several different views (online applications), allowing you to customize the features available to those using the browser.
Java Beans	Components that can be used to assemble a larger Java application.	Simplifies Java programming by allowing developers to easily reuse code.
JavaScript	CA scripting language developed by Netscape. Not all browsers support JavaScript equally well; Netscape Navigator (unsurprisingly) is most reliable.	JavaScript can be used to support forms, timers, make calculations, and identify the browser being used, among other possibilities.

NOTE   Not all browsers support Java equally well. Internet Explorer's support for Java is spotty and Microsoft's version of Java (J++) enables some features not found in Sun's Java but which depend on Windows functions. A browser running on a non-Windows operating system may not get full functionality from J++ applets.

ActiveX Controls ActiveX is similar to Java in that it's a way of attaching mini-applications to Web pages, but it's not identical. Rather than being a platform-independent programming language, ActiveX is a set of controls that can make applications written in a variety of languages—C++, Delphi, J++, and Visual Basic, to name a few—accessible via the browser. ActiveX controls do *not* run in a sandbox; they run like any other application in the user operating environment.

Server-Side Web Applications

Server-side Web applications execute on the server, using a server operating environment and resources. Server-side applications are more likely to be one-time applications, such as search engines. The advantage to server-side applications is their universality: the browser doesn't have to support the client-side application language. The approaches to storing and loading these programs may differ. CGI servers access an application stored on the server, whereas Active Server Pages store the script to be executed in the HTML page itself.

Common Gateway Interface (CGI) *CGI* is a standardized way of passing information from a Web user's input to a back-end application or script and then passing back information to the client's browser. For example, when you fill out an online registration form and click the Submit button, the information that you supplied may be passed via a CGI to a database. Once the information has been processed, you get a "Thank you!" message back, via the CGI.

CGI's biggest advantage is its consistent interface. It doesn't matter what platform the server is running on; the data can be passed from the user to the application, regardless. The functionality you can get using CGI to access a back-end application isn't necessarily different from what you might get from using a scripting language; it just works differently. A script is attached to a specific Web page, but an application accessible through CGI is not linked to a specific page, rather to a specific gateway. Any Web page can associate itself with that gateway.

Active Server Pages (ASP) Some Web pages have scripts embedded in them that can be run when conditions require it—when a user clicks a search engine's Find button, for example, or fills out a form and clicks OK. You can create an ASP file by including in an HTML document a script written in VBScript or another supported scripting language, and then renaming the document with the ".asp" suffix. When the user loads that page and fulfills the conditions, the script will run.

NOTE   Active Server Pages are only supported by Microsoft's Internet Information Server (IIS), which requires NT.

Publishing Web Documents

Now you're aware of the tools you'll use to create Web pages for your site. Putting that site together is going to require one more tool: the Web server.

Where Do You Get Server Software?

If you're using Microsoft products, you may already have a Web server product installed; if not, one is readily available. NT Server 4 comes with version 2 of the Internet Information Server (IIS); Service Pack 3 and later for Windows NT will automatically upgrade IIS 2 to 3. But version 4, as well as the Peer Web Server for Windows 95 and NT Workstation, are available as part of the Microsoft Option Pack. The Windows 98 CD includes the Peer Web Server product.

Where on the Microsoft Web site? As Microsoft seems to rearrange its site about once a month, I can't guarantee that a specific URL will be accurate, but the Option Pack should be in the Free Downloads section of the site.

In addition, a 90-day evaluation version of Microsoft Site Server (an intranet product for NT Server) is currently available for download.

Those running NetWare networks can use one of Novell's intranet products:

IntraNetWare   Essentially NetWare with FTP and IP/IPX routing capabilities added.

IntraNetWare Host Publisher   Publishes information stored on IBM mainframes.

GroupWise Web Publisher   Supports Web publishing by any member of a GroupWise group (groupware).

Limited-user evaluation versions of Novell's intranet products are available for download from **www.novell.com**.

The current version of Lotus Domino also supports intranet Web publishing services.

Example—Installing IIS 4

NT Server 4 comes with IIS 2, which you can install by running the SETUP program found in the Internet Tools folder located in the Programs section of the Start menu. IIS 3 is part of Service Pack 3 and later. For the latest version of IIS, IIS 4, you'll need the

Option Pack, available on CD as part of the Microsoft TechNet monthly subscription (and handed out at Microsoft's 1998 TechEd conference). It's also available as a free download from the Microsoft Web site. One way or another, IIS 4 is readily available to just about anyone who needs it.

Preparing for IIS 4

Before installing the Option Pack, you'll need to install Internet Explorer 4.*x* (IE4) and Service Pack 3 (SP3) or later onto your NT Server machine if you haven't already done so. You don't have to use IE4 as your browser on the Web server if you don't want to, but IIS 4 calls on some IE4 files.

Where do you get these files? SP3 is available as part of the Option Pack; SP4 is available on the Microsoft site. Although it's included on the Option Pack CD, IE4 is not part of the Option Pack on the Web site; download it from the Internet Explorer part of the Microsoft Web site.

Downloading the Installation Files

If you don't already have the Option Pack installation files, you can get them from the Microsoft Web site at www.microsoft.com. I'm not including a specific URL because Microsoft rearranges its Web site about once a month, but you should be able to find these areas if you follow the links I've described. The Microsoft home page offers links to all areas of the site.

1. Go to the Free Downloads section of the Microsoft Web site and move to the Sever Software link. From the list of products, click IIS 4.

2. On this page, click the link for the Windows NT 4 Option Pack.

3. On this page, choose the options you want to download for installation:

    Internet Information Server 4

    Transaction Server 2

    Microsoft Message Queue Server 1

    Internet Connection Services for Microsoft RAS

    Windows NT Service Pack 3

    The options you need to install are IIS 4, IE4, and (if you haven't already installed it) SP3.

4. On the next page, you'll find the hardware and software requirements, and more information about the options—I recommend that you read it. At the bottom of this page is a link to registering for the download and downloading the Option Pack.

5. On the next page, fill out the form (the only required entry is the one asking what CPU platform you're using on the download computer) and choose the options to download.

6. On the next page, choose the kind of Option Pack you want to download (in this case, NT Server); on the following page, choose a language.

7. On the following page, choose a download location.

NOTE   Netiquette calls for using a download site close to you in the interest of minimizing Internet traffic.

---

8. On the final page, *read the instructions* (they're important) and then click each link to download its contents. You don't have to download the files in order, but they'll all need to be in the same directory, and you can't run the SETUP program until all the links are downloaded.

WARNING The time required to download all the files will vary according to two factors: the speed of your Internet connection and how heavy traffic is at the time you download the components. As you must manually download each of 52 parts of the 70-odd MB required (you can't just start the download and go to lunch), this is one time when a fast Net connection *really* pays off. A slow connection can cause this process to take all day.

Installing IIS 4

Okay, you've got the files, you've installed SP3 and IE4, and have restarted the computer. You're ready to install IIS 4 as follows:

1. From the folder to which you downloaded the files, run SETUP.EXE. (Don't run INSTALL.EXE—you'll get an error message demanding that you supply parameters for master .INF files and source folders.) You'll see the beginning screen to the Option Pack installation Wizard. Click Next to get past it and then accept the license agreement on the next page.

2. If you already had a version of IIS installed, once past the license agreement, you'll have the option of either simply upgrading the existing version or upgrading it and adding new components. To pick the first option, click Upgrade Only; to add new components, choose Upgrade Plus. Note that neither option gives you the choice of uninstalling previously installed components.

3. Choose Upgrade Plus and you'll see the dialog box shown in Figure 13.2, listing the components available. The components previously installed will be checked and their checkboxes grayed; you can't delete them. Make sure that "Internet Information Server (IIS)" is selected and click Next.

FIGURE 13.2:

Choose the components of the Option Pack that you want to install.

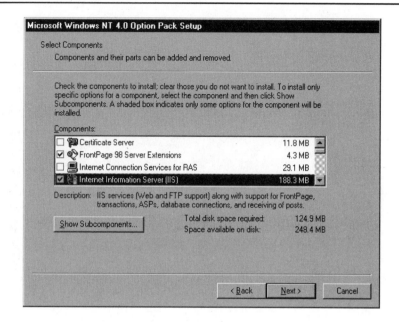

NOTE   Each component has subcomponents and IIS is no exception. Although you can't delete IIS, you can add new components that you may not have installed before, such as a news server (NNTP service) or SMTP service for doing e-mail. Be sure to review IIS's subcomponents and select the ones you want before moving on.

4. When prompted, provide the name of the locally available folder into which the files for each service should be copied. By default, the setup program will make them a subfolder of C:\Program Files.

5. If you want to be able to *remotely administer* (from another NT Server) IIS, then provide the name and password of the existing administrative account that will have that privilege (see Figure 13.3). If you'll do all the work locally (the default), you can leave these fields blank.

FIGURE 13.3:

Provide the name of a remote administrative account if you want to administer the Web server across the network.

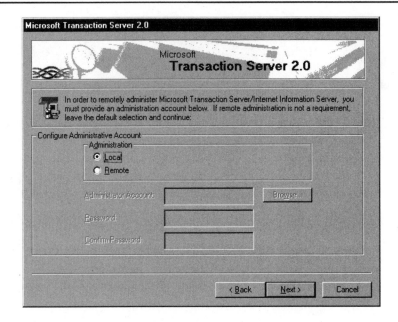

6. After you click Next, Setup will copy the needed files to the server's hard disk. This may take a while. When it's completed and Setup has updated the files, you'll need to restart the computer before you can use IIS.

Bare Basics of Setting Up an Intranet Web Site

This is not a complete tutorial on how to use IIS 4, but the basic steps to set up an intranet Web site with IIS 4 are pretty simple. Create a Web page using Notepad or some other HTML editor. Name the file DEFAULT.HTM and store it in the default directory of \InetPub\Wwwroot. If you've got a DNS server or other name resolution mechanism set up on your network, then users on the intranet will be able to type the name of the Web server to connect to the site. Otherwise, they'll have to type in the Web server's IP address. In short, you're storing files in an expected location and publishing them to the network. You can then configure security settings to permit or deny access to certain pages, customize the error pages used (such as the infamous 404 File Not Found that we all know and love), or do other operations.

Summary

By now, you should have a pretty good idea of how you could put a corporate Web to work. Publish reports, sign up people for the company picnic, speed up support calls, create maps of the office—if you can think of an information-related need, you can probably think of a Web application to support it.

To create those Web applications, you'll use a combination of markup languages (HTML, DHTML, or XML) and programming languages. Programming languages can run either on the client or on the server, depending on whether you'd rather use client-side resources or server-side resources, and whether your client browsers will support the client-side applications. Server-side applications can either embed scripts directly in the home page or include a common interface to a program stored on the Web server or on another machine. When creating these pages, don't forget to take your audience's needs into account—these pages are meant to make people's lives easier, not harder.

Once you've created the Web pages, you'll need a Web server to publish them on the corporate intranet. In this chapter, I discussed how to install Microsoft's Internet Information Server version 4 (IIS 4), but the idea behind all Web servers, like all server operating systems, is very much the same.

This chapter concludes the discussion of what you can do with a LAN. In the following section, I'll start getting more into the administration end of things. Let's begin with the principles of network management, the topic of Chapter 14, "Principles of Network Management."

EXERCISE 13

1. If you want to create a Web page that supports searching by subject category, which markup language would you use?

2. You want to create a Web page with functionality that can be interpreted by any client browsers. Which of the following tools will meet this need? Choose all that apply.

   A. ASP

   B. Java

   C. XML

   D. HTML

3. True or false. CGI embeds a script in a Web page, making the script available to any client.

4. What markup language could you use to create an online form?

   A. XML

   B. DHTML

   C. HTML

   D. All of the above

5. True or false. JavaScript is a scripting language developed by Sun Microsystems.

PART

IV

Holistic Network
Management—Resource
Organization, Security, and
Disaster Recovery

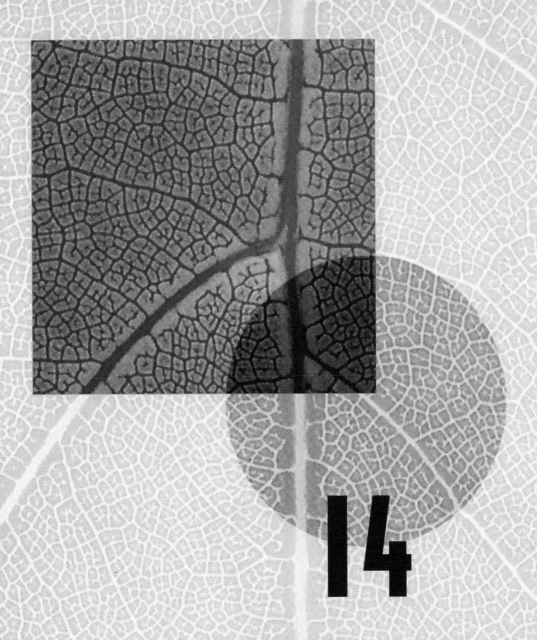

14

Principles of Network Management

In previous sections of this book, I reviewed the components of the network—cables, transport protocols, computers, operating systems, and applications. Putting together those pieces is in some ways the easy part. Once everything's up and running, a potentially thorny problem awaits: how to *keep* it up and running. It's just one of those annoying things about networks: people insist on using them and that can lead to problems.

Thus, this chapter will discuss some principles of network management, including:

- Knowledge of what you've got and where it is
- Tools you can use to monitor network traffic and hardware
- Concepts of zero administration
- Methods of changing the network without causing a mutiny
- Troubleshooting techniques

It's a lot of information, but the idea behind all these management concepts is the same: know what you've got and keep control over it. If you can do that, your job will be much easier.

Know Thy Network—Enterprise Documentation

The first step to effective network management is information, starting with an inventory and an outline of the network's layout and efficiency. In Chapter 4, "Installing Cards and Cables," I mentioned the importance of documenting PC settings to aid card configuration. The principle of documenting the network is the same thing on a larger level: how can you have any idea of how the parts of the network will perform together unless you know what those parts are? Document your network's organization, performance, and physical components, and when trouble strikes, you'll be in a better position to do something about it. You'll also be in a better position to avoid trouble.

Performing Audits

When the network is up and running and everything's quiet, that is not the time to relax. Instead, that's the time to do documentation. Get familiar with your network now, while it's working as it should. Documentation is a thankless task that doesn't always look like a useful expenditure of time, but it pays off when trouble strikes.

NOTE   Documentation is particularly necessary for disaster recovery, as I'll discuss in Chapter 16, "Disaster Recovery."

First, if you know what the network looks like when it's working, then it's easier to identify what's wrong when it's *not* working. "Not working" doesn't necessarily mean that something has changed that causes a failure; network or other failures can also indicate that part of the network wasn't stressed in a particular way until the occasion that brought the problem to light.

The second point is particularly applicable to large or widely distributed networks: knowing the physical layout of your network can be crucial to understanding problems, or to finding the errant piece of equipment.

You can perform two main types of LAN audits: physical and intangible. Inventory and facility audits are pretty physical in emphasis—use them to find out what you've got and where it is. Operational, efficiency, and security audits, are more intangible in nature: What kind of traffic levels does the LAN experience? Is the LAN run as efficiently as possible or should resources be redistributed to better supply user needs? What kind of security does the LAN require and are those requirements met? In the following sections I'll explain what you're looking for as you conduct each kind of LAN audit.

Physical Aspects of the Network

The easiest part of a network audit is the physical inventory: what you've got and where it is. This can be time-consuming, but it's mostly grunt work. Mostly, it's a matter of tabulating your hardware and software, and noting the patterns in which each is installed.

Conducting an Inventory In order to conduct an inventory audit, first find out what you've got.

For hardware, you should know:

- The type of machine, including general class (PC, router, bridge), manufacturer, and model number.

- The machine's serial number.

- Who's using the machine.

- How the machine is configured, including resource allocation, protocols used, and devices attached to PCs.

For software, you should know:

- The operating systems installed on all client and server machines, including version number and any installed patches or fixes.

- What applications are installed and, if possible, when they were installed.

NOTE Why does it matter when applications were installed? Sometimes, the answer can be the key to malfunctioning applications. Many Windows applications use pre-made libraries of data or instructions, called *dynamic link libraries*, or *DLLs*. Multiple applications can share a single DLL. Trouble can arise, however, when one application's DLL file overwrites another's with older information. Keeping track of when applications were installed can help you avoid or troubleshoot DLL conflicts.

- Who's got access to what applications.

- How many licenses you own for the software.

- How many licenses are used for the software.

The results of the hardware inventory can be invaluable for keeping track of hardware components, where they're used in the network, and how they're configured. The software inventory is important not only for tracking software versions, but it can also help you manage software licensing.

Conducting a Facility Audit Get a copy of your office's blueprints and take a walk around the building as part of your facility audit. On the blueprints, you'll need to note:

- Cable paths and the lengths of cable runs

- Where the network is terminated, if it's an Ethernet network

- The type of cable used at each part of the network (for example, a connected star network using Category 5 UTP to the desktop but fiber on the backbone)

- Network hardware (routers, bridges, switches, and servers)

- Color or numeric identifiers for cable runs

TIP If you haven't already labeled cable runs, do so during the facility audit.

Keep these blueprints safe and if anything changes be sure to update the record. The results of the facility audit are the basis of your network map (discussed later in this chapter under "Creating a Network Map").

A facility audit is also an excellent time to get familiar with your building, not just your network. Learn the locations of power and water shutoffs, air conditioning and heating equipment, and anything else that might potentially affect your network's operation.

Intangible Aspects of the Network

More subjective than the physical inventory and facility audit, but just as important, is the State of the Network in terms of performance and security. During this stage of the audit you'll evaluate your network in terms of its efficient use and distribution of network resources, identify how secure it is, and note its normal patterns so that you can identify any deviations from these patterns.

Recording Operational Efficiency An operational audit takes into account what's happening on the network without making any value judgments. During this audit, you'll need to note:

- How much traffic is generated on the network?

- What segments is that traffic concentrated on?

- How do traffic and server load vary over the course of the day?

- What aspects of the server are most stressed?

- How many application licenses are being used at any given time?

- Who's generating the traffic?

Even if the network is working well, the results of an operational audit can be valuable. Armed with this information, you can more easily identify changes that can cause trouble, or decide where new resources are needed should conditions change.

Evaluating Network Efficiency The operational audit is for finding out what's happening on the network. The efficiency audit, in contrast, is for taking that information and finding out whether it represents the most efficient way of doing business. This audit is derived from the results of the operation environment. Ask yourself:

- Is the load on the network evenly balanced or do some segments experience little traffic while others are overloaded?

- Can some traffic be rerouted to even up the load on the network?

- How busy are the servers? Can they meet user requirements at all times of day?

Compare the results of the operational audit with the efficiency audit to see how resources could be redistributed.

Evaluating Security Settings Finally, there's the security audit. In Chapter 15, "Network Security," I'll talk more about sources of security holes and how to test for them, but for now, here are the basics of what you're looking for:

- Can everyone get to the resources they need?

- Are resources protected from the people who shouldn't have access to them (both inside and outside the company, if your company has an extranet)?

- What methods are in place to keep people where they're supposed to be on the network (bindings configurations, passwords, user permissions, and so on)?

- What virus protection measures are in place?

- What data protection measures have you implemented?

Performing the security audit requires a combination of making an inventory of existing systems and getting user input. The security audit isn't just about locking people out, but about making sure that they can reach the resources they need. Find out what people need and whether it's practical or necessary to relax security to provide more access.

Storing Audit Information

Get all this information, and you need a place to keep it.

For most purposes, I don't recommend paper records (except of the blueprints). Paper reports are hard to update, easily lost or destroyed, possibly illegible if handwritten (if they're computer-generated, then why print out the records?), and not always easy to make accessible to the people who need them. The only time that hard copies of records are beneficial is during planning meetings, when you want to have reports available to management and the network support team.

The best way to store information, I find, is in a database. It's legible, easily updated, easily searched, and always there when you need it (so long as you back up regularly).

You can buy off-the-shelf audit databases. Creating one in-house isn't difficult, however, and is more likely to fit your needs exactly because you'll be doing the design work. To make it easier to enter the information, you can even create a form for the front end to the tables. If you've never created an application with which to enter data before, this is the process, in broad terms:

1. Identify the subject of each table (for example, inventory audit, facility audit, operational audit, and so on) and create the table.

2. Identify the categories within each table (type of device, serial number, packets sent per hour during a given interval, installation dates, and so on) and create the fields.

3. Design a front end for each table, creating places for user input.

> **TIP**   For fields likely to have predictable answers, you can create a drop-down list of items to choose from. This will save you from making spelling errors that can hamper searches.

Create all this and when you open the database you'll be able to choose one of a list of tables to open (see Figure 14.1).

FIGURE 14.1:

A database contains one or more tables, each devoted to its subject.

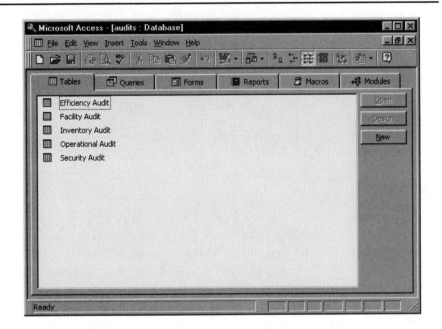

Open a table for which you've created a form and you'll see something like the form shown in Figure 14.2.

FIGURE 14.2:

An inventory audit
database created in
Access 97

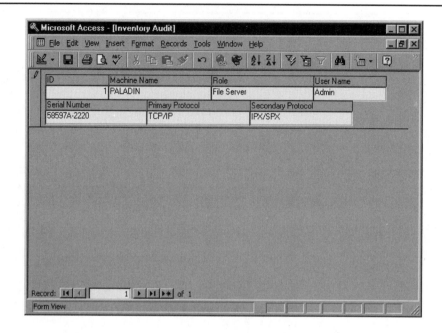

Creating a database might sound difficult, but it's really not; I'm far from an Access whiz, so if *I* can do it, just about anyone should be able to as well. The hardest part is identifying the information you need to enter. Once you've done that, the physical aspects of creating the tables and forms is mostly a matter of typing in the names of the fields and then drawing a front end that will be easy to use. It might take you a little time to get the database format just right. However, when you do, you'll have an application in which it's easy to store and update audit data, as well as a database from which you can create reports when the time comes.

Creating a Network Map

As a part of the audit, you can record not only in a database but also in map form, so it's easier to see how the parts of the network exist in relation to each other. Maps can be in hard copy or stored electronically, and will describe both the physical layout of the network and its logical organization.

The Physical Layout of the Network

You may actually have several physical maps of your network, depending on its size and complexity. The physical map is similar to the facility map, showing where components are in relation to each other. Thus, one map may show the extent of the network in your building, identifying each node on the network (see Figure 14.3). Another map may show the entire network, extending across the WAN (see Figure 14.4). The purposes for each level of detail are different; you'd refer to each to answer a different question.

FIGURE 14.3:

Physical network map for the building

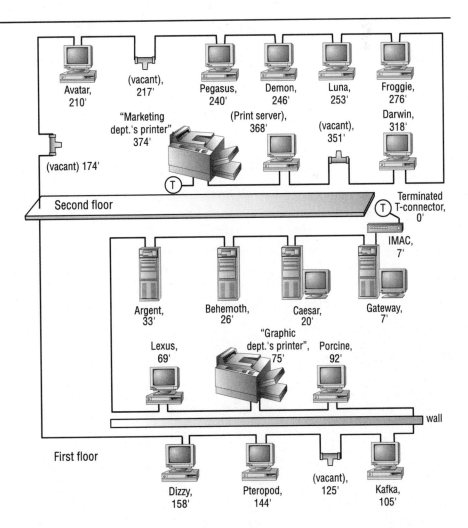

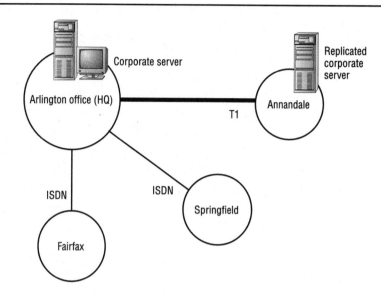

The Logical Layout of the Network

A physical network map shows how components are positioned in relation to other components. A *logical network map,* in contrast, shows how resources are organized (see Figure 14.5). Which clients have access to which servers? Which servers, or group of servers, hold what information? How is replication done across the network? The answers to these questions may correspond closely to the physical map or not at all.

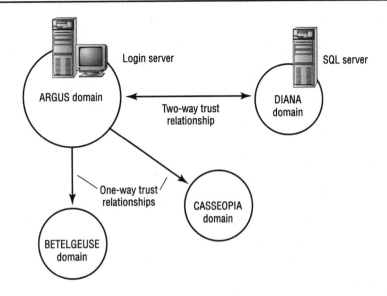

FIGURE 14.5:

A logical map showing organization of the network

Once again, you may need several maps to show varying levels of detail. On the one hand, you may need to know which clients log into which authentication server. On the other, you may need to know how the databases are replicated across the WAN, showing traffic flow.

A Survey of Network Management Tools

By this time, you're familiar with the information you need about your network. You can't pick up all the information you need by walking around the building, however. It may not be physically feasible to tour the network, and not all the information is physically manifested, anyway. Read on to learn more about tools you can use both to gather information about your network and make it do what you want it to do.

Server Monitoring Tools

One key to a successful network lies in server performance. If the servers can't keep up with demand, even if bandwidth is adequate, network performance will suffer. You can use a server-monitoring tool to keep track of server components and the demands on them, either watching current levels or logging results for later study.

If you're using NT, you've already got one server-monitoring tool: the Performance Monitor. For the purposes of example, I'll refer to this tool. Additional server-monitoring tools (including the other ones in NT) will be organized similarly to, if not exactly like, this one.

The Performance Monitor groups resources to be organized into objects and counters within those objects. *Objects* include general categories such as the processor, the server work queues, the physical disks, and the paging file, among many others. *Counters* within those categories include such specifics as the number of interrupts the processor must handle each second, the number of clients whose requests are serviced by a particular CPU, the time it takes to read from disk, or the percentage of the paging file in use at the time, respectively. Some counters are further subdivided into *instances*. For example, one of the counters for the Process object is a measure of the processor time devoted to each process running on the selected computer. Within this counter are instances—that is, you can monitor either the total percentage of all processor time used by all processes, or you can pick and choose processes to monitor.

To start monitoring the system with Performance Monitor, you'd choose the computer to be monitored, find the object you're interested in, then pick the counter or counters within that object. Click the Add button and you'll add a line for that counter to the chart. As shown in Figure 14.6, each counter's line will be a different color, so you can keep track of them.

FIGURE 14.6:

Use NT's Performance Monitor for charting demands on server resources.

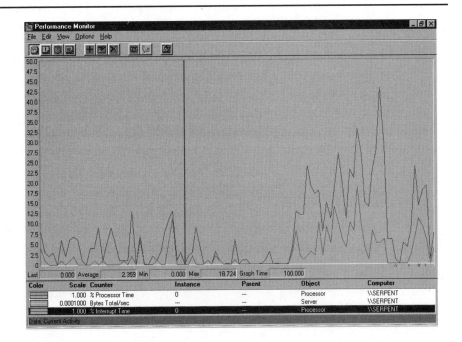

Monitor server performance remotely if possible. Otherwise, the monitor itself will use resources on the server. You'll also skew the results if some server CPU cycles and memory are devoted to supporting the monitor.

TIP

If you *must* run Performance Monitor on the server being monitored, then be sure to monitor the PERFMON instance of the Processor Time counter in the Process object. This will give you at least an idea of how much CPU time is devoted to the Performance Monitor.

Reading the output of the monitor isn't difficult. Knowing the implications of what you're reading can be a bit more difficult. To do that, you'll need to understand the way the parts of your servers interact and which hardware is responsible for supporting the various demands on the servers. At a minimum, you should be familiar with the description of the server in Chapter 8, "Server Types and Additional Hardware." To get as much out of a server monitor as you can, you'll need to know something about the server's architecture. It doesn't do you any good to watch an increasing value of the Threads counter if you don't know what a thread is, much less why their numbers might grow or what it means if they do. This chapter can't teach you everything there is to know about server monitoring, but Table 14.1 shows a few basics to watch out for. Based on your knowledge of server functions, you should be able to identify others that might interest you.

T A B L E 1 4 . 1 : Some Server Objects to Monitor and Their Importance

Object: Counter	Description	More Information
Logical Disk: % Free Disk Space	Ratio of unused disk space to used disk space on the selected logical volume.	Use this information to determine how much disk space you have left. On NT 4, you can't use this to restrict per-user disk use unless each user has an individual volume.
Logical Disk: Avg Disk Queue Length	Average number of read and write requests for a logical disk volume during a given interval.	Use this information to determine the demand on the disk at various times of day.
Memory: % Committed Bytes in Use	Ratio of memory committed to one process or another compared to the memory that could be committed.	Shows the percentage of virtual memory in use at a particular moment.
Memory: Page Faults/Sec	The rate at which data in use is being recalled from the paging file on disk instead of from physical memory.	Some page faults are to be expected, but a high rate of page fault indicates a shortage of physical memory for the demands placed on it.

Continued on next page

TABLE 14.1 CONTINUED: Some Server Objects to Monitor and Their Importance

Object: Counter	Description	More Information
Physical Disk: Avg Disk Queue Length	Average number of read and write requests for a physical disk during a given interval.	Use this information to determine the demand on the disk at various times of day. Based on this information, you may want to shift demand to a faster disk.
Physical Disk: Disk Transfers/sec	Rate at which data is read and written to a particular physical disk.	Illustrates how quickly the selected disk can respond to user requests.
Processor: %Processor Time	Ratio of how often the processor is doing something, instead of being idle.	Shows how busy the processor is. A busy processor isn't necessarily bad, but keep an eye out to make sure it's not becoming a bottleneck.
Server: Bytes Total/sec	Sum of the bytes sent and received each second.	Can break this sum down to reads and writes to show how fast the server is satisfying a particular kind of request, and how many requests of that kind there are.
Server: Errors Logon	The failed attempts to log onto the server.	A high rate can indicate an attempt to gain unauthorized access through guessing or password-guesser programs.
Server: File Directory Searches	The number of file searches performed during the selected interval.	This measure indicates how busy the server is.
Server Work Queues: Queue Length	The current number of waiting requests for CPU time. If more than one CPU is installed, this count is done on a per-CPU basis.	More than four waiting requests at any given time may indicate an overloaded CPU.

There's more, and there's plenty of information that you might need that's not in the Performance Monitor. But that's a taste of the kind of information you might pick up with the help of a server monitor.

To some extent, the categories that you're most interested in will depend on the role of the server you're monitoring. It will be more important to monitor disk space on a file server than on an application server, for example, and the number of CGI requests served only matters to a Web server. However, some resources are important to all servers—CPU cycles, memory-related objects such as both physical memory and the paging file, and the number of waiting requests are all examples of these.

You can monitor as many counters in as many object categories as you like. However, because of the wide array of data it's possible to gather with a server monitoring tool, you'll most likely concentrate your queries on the data that you're most interested in at a particular time. Especially during the information-gathering phase, focus your queries. How many requests per second is the server handling at a given time of day? How does this number change according to the time of day or month? Look for patterns and record them so that when there are deviations from those patterns you can identify the changes and track down their source.

Network Monitors

You'll use products based on network management protocols to gather information about the network and, sometimes, to pass commands to remote hosts. These tools aren't simply passive; if tolerances are exceeded, they can be used to notify someone in charge that there's a problem.

Network monitors have two parts: a client portion, located on the device to be monitored, and a server portion, located on the device doing the monitoring and recording the information gathered. How this client and server interact is defined in each monitoring protocol. Broadly speaking, however, all network monitoring software is designed for the same purpose—gathering information about the network. Doing so may require:

- Collecting transport protocol statistics
- Identifying nodes on the network
- Collecting data about hardware and software configuration
- Gathering performance and usage statistics for each computer
- Noting application usage statistics
- Recording event messages and error messages

The set of information collected depends on the elements that can be monitored and are supported by a particular network monitoring/managing product. Each host to be managed has a text file called a *management information base* (MIB, pronounced "mib") for each element to be monitored. The MIB contains information about the following:

- The objects being monitored
- The syntax of the objects being monitored
- The access provided to the monitor (read only or read/write)
- The status (mandatory or not) of the objects
- A description of the object

In short, a MIB lists the objects to be monitored on a system and defines their characteristics. The Windows NT Resource Kit includes a sample MIB (originally from an SNMP mailing list) called TOASTER.MIB to show you the syntax. One object from the MIB is shown below:

```
toasterDoneness OBJECT-TYPE
                SYNTAX  INTEGER (1..10)
                ACCESS  read-write
                STATUS  mandatory
```

```
DESCRIPTION
        "This variable controls how well done ensuing
        toast should be on a scale of 1 to 10. Toast
        made at 10 is generally considered unfit for
        human consumption; toast made at 1 is lightly
        warmed." ::= { toaster 4 }
```

Thus, the value associated with toasterDoneness would indicate how well done was that toast. The monitor could then assess whether that value fell within certain tolerances (say, between 3 and 7 for properly done toast) and issue a warning to a network administrator if those tolerances were exceeded. The value in brackets at the bottom of the sample ({toaster 4}) is the number of the object—toasterDoneness is the fourth object type defined in the toast MIB.

NOTE   This sample follows a standard called MIB-II. To be monitored or managed with recent implementations of SNMP, a device must use this format for its MIBs.

To use the most common collection method when you need information about a certain managed object, you can request that information from the network monitor. The monitor queries the host for that information, using the object's name. The host then looks up the name, finds the value associated with it, and reports back to the monitor.

Not all protocols used by network monitoring tools use the same MIBs, and not even all protocols of the same type support all the same MIBs. For a monitoring tool to be compliant with a standard protocol, it must only follow the data-gathering guidelines outlined in the protocol's standard. So long as a monitoring product uses at least one defined MIB, it's in accordance with the standard. In practical terms, this means that not all SNMP-based network monitors, for example, are created equal. You'll need to check to see exactly what information the product is collecting.

The Simple Network Management Protocol (SNMP)

The *Simple Network Management Protocol* (*SNMP*) is an example of a frequent occurrence in the networking world: a stopgap measure that becomes the standard option because the more advanced technology that was to replace it didn't measure up in some way by the time it became available. Originally, SNMP was designed to be a simple, lightweight method of monitoring TCP/IP-based internets. A more advanced networking protocol (the *Common Management Information Protocol*, or *CMIP*), based more fully on the OSI model, was supposed to replace SNMP, but this replacement never got off the ground. Two factors contributed to CMIP's failure to take over. First, CMIP was indeed much more powerful than SNMP and able to collect information that SNMP was incapable of gathering. But this increased power put an unacceptably heavy load on network and server resources. Second, by the time CMIP was as ready for prime time as it was ever going to be, SNMP had such a large installed base that the cost of replacing it was greater than the benefits that could be realized by implementing the more powerful management tool. Thus, by default, SNMP has become the most common protocol for network management tools.

Coulda Been a Contender II—CMIP

Chapter 6, "A Tour of Wide Area Networks," mentioned SMDS as a powerful technology that became supplanted by less powerful frame relay, originally intended to fill the gap while SMDS was being completed. This is a pretty common story—the same thing happened with CMIP.

Continued on next page

The Common Management Information Protocol (CMIP), based on the OSI model instead of the narrower TCP/IP protocol, was originally designed to be the more powerful replacement to SNMP. CMIP could support functions that SNMP could not; it would work on any platform (CMOT is the TCP/IP-only version); it would provide management capabilities that SNMP would not. Essentially, it worked opposite from SNMP. Rather than polling devices to discover their status or other information about them, CMIP waits for the devices to make reports to the CMIP manager.

Ironically enough, the root problem turned out to be CMIP's power. It demanded more in server resources than most networks could provide. As of the late 1990s, it's more or less history. There's hopeful information published about the protocol, cheerleading along the lines of, "If CMIP is ever commercially available, then it will have a huge customer base because of all the educational institutions that worked on developing it!" However, it seems unlikely that CMIP is going to replace SNMP any time soon. SNMP is too widespread and too well accepted at this point to be easily displaced, and if it's not quite as powerful as CMIP, it's not as power-hungry, either.

How SNMP Works SNMP uses MIBs like a census taker uses polls. At regular intervals, or when requested, the SNMP server portion queries a device about its status, referring to the device's MIB. When the agent gets the request, it returns the values requested. This information is passed between the client and server portions of the monitor with the User Datagram Protocol (UDP), a transport-layer part of the TCP/IP suite. UDP is a connectionless protocol—that is, it can pass messages without worrying about their receipt—so it doesn't contribute much to network traffic. Of course, SNMP or any other network monitoring tool will increase network traffic, but the impact of the monitoring is designed to be as low as possible. A network monitoring device that had to report heavy network traffic and its responsibility for a good share of the traffic would be, shall we say, less than useful.

NOTE   A standard exists for using SNMP over IPX/SPX-only networks, using IPX for the messaging protocol rather than UDP, but you're far more likely to see SNMP on TCP/IP networks. Not all implementations of SNMP support passing messages over IPX.

Recall that network monitoring protocols have two parts: a manager, located on the server, and an agent, located on the device being monitored. In SNMP, the relationship between manager and agent works as illustrated in Figure 14.7. In this simple example, the manager queries the agent (perhaps running on an FTP server) to find out how many connections it can support. Receiving this request, the agent retrieves the data from the FTP server and replies to the manager.

FIGURE 14.7:

SNMP communication between manager and agent

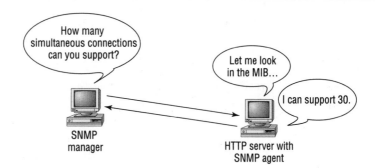

Not every device on a network will have an SNMP agent—only those devices that need monitoring and that you've configured to support SNMP will have an agent. SNMP-compliant devices such as routers or bridges already have an SNMP agent installed on them, but if you want to monitor a computer of some kind, then you'll have to install the agent yourself. In NT, this is done by running the SNMP service on the device to be monitored, as well as on the monitor.

By default, and by the terms of the standard, SNMP agents are configured to receive messages through port 161 and traps through port 162. If you need to install more than one SNMP agent on a particular computer, you can edit the port assignments. In NT, for example, this information is set in the SERVICES file (no extension, but you can open it with Notepad) found in System32\Drivers\Etc. Look for entries like these:

```
snmp           161/udp          snmp

snmp-trap      162/udp          snmp
```

The first column describes the service for which the port was assigned, the second the port number, the third the protocol used to pass the information, and the fourth the service alias.

WARNING This procedure is not idiot-proof. Only edit the SERVICES file or other port configuration if you're sure of what you're doing and know that you're not overwriting some other device's port settings.

An SNMP agent waits for a datagram from the SNMP manager requesting information. When the agent receives such a message, it performs one of the following operations:

get Retrieves a specific value for a managed object.

get next Retrieves the next value in the MIB.

set Changes the value of a managed object with read/write privileges.

When the SNMP manager receives the data from the agent, it may either display it or save in a database for future reference.

Get and set operations are performed only in response to a request from the SNMP manager. An SNMP agent will send unrequested messages only under two conditions: when the node is stopped or started, or when certain tolerances are exceeded and an alert is required. These alerts are called *traps* and are sent to the IP address, IPX address, or host name that you supplied when setting up the SNMP service on that machine.

SNMP Communities SNMP security is based on the concept of communities, logical organizations of SNMP machines organized under a common name, similar to a workgroup. Like a workgroup, members of a community are often physically proximate, but they don't have to be. Nor does the membership of the community have to bear any relationship to the membership of the workgroup or domain to which the computers belong. Essentially, the name of the community is a password and should be treated as such.

Only agents and monitors that are part of the same community can talk to each other. When a monitor sends a message to an agent requesting information, the community name is part of the message. When the agent receives the message, it checks to see whether it recognizes the supplied community name. If it does not, then it discards the message and, optionally, may register a trap noting the failed authentication. Only if the agent and monitor are in the same community will the message be processed at all.

By default, all NT servers running SNMP are originally part of the *public* community. For added security, you may want to remove this community name, or create another community. An SNMP machine—agent or monitor—may be a member of more than one community. If an SNMP monitor does not belong to any community, then this is the same as having a device that is not password-protected; any SNMP client may communicate with the monitor, regardless of the client's community membership.

Remote Monitoring (RMON)

Historically, hardware remote monitoring devices such as network monitors or network probes have been used for network management beyond what SNMP can provide. Typically (not always), these devices are stand-alone instruments devoted to the task of collecting network data, and one must be deployed at each segment of a routed network.

RMON, short for *remote monitoring*, is a way around the need for hardware to do complex network management functions. It's a protocol designed to collect information about the entire network from a single node instead of requiring the person doing the monitoring to physically go to the suspected trouble spot and analyze network data. From the central node, you can activate a remote monitor and have that monitor return information about its segment to the central console. The only limitation is the same one that applies to SNMP: to be monitored, a device must have an RMON agent resident on it.

Although they both use MIBs, RMON is not the same thing as SNMP. Both are network management tools, but RMON maintains a wider variety of MIB types, allowing the protocol to gather more information than is possible with SNMP. SNMP's main function lies in making sure that the various parts of the network are up and running. RMON is intended to do more—it's a network analyzer, used to measure data traffic on specific LAN segments to determine traffic patterns and the cause of any major bottlenecks. Under some circumstances, RMON can be used not only to read data, but also to write it, depending on whether it makes sense to impose values in a particular instance. As with SNMP, you don't have to watch the data collection in real time; it's possible for RMON tools to trigger alarms when conditions breach preset tolerances, or record data in logs to be reviewed later.

In its first incarnation, RMON gathered only data link layer information. But in its RMON2 version, standardized in January 1997, it now collects network layer information as well, all the way down to the port level if desired. It also supports some WAN-specific data and identifying conditions caused by physical layer problems, such as cable breaks. RMON doesn't note data link layer packet errors because the terms of the MIB can only identify errors by disassembling the frame and reading it. If there are errors at the data link level, there's little useful information to be derived. At the network layer and above, however, RMON can identify and report on protocol errors.

This data collected with RMON can come from any of the following categories:

Protocol directory   Lists the inventory of protocols the remote monitor is capable of tracking.

Protocol distribution   Records the percentage of packets created with each protocol on the segment.

Address mapping   Lists the mappings of data link layer address to network layer address and where those mappings were last observed.

Network layer host   Controls the amount of traffic sent between each pair of network addresses discovered by the probe.

Network layer matrix   Counts the amount of traffic sent between each pair of network addresses discovered by the probe.

Application layer host   Controls the amount of traffic sent between each pair of network addresses discovered by the probe, dividing the results according to protocol.

Application layer matrix   Counts the amount of traffic sent between each pair of network addresses discovered by the probe, dividing the results according to protocol.

> **NOTE** "Application layer" in the RMON standard doesn't necessarily refer to a protocol operating at layer 7 of the OSI model. Instead, it means any protocol operating above the network link layer, so it could include transport, session, presentation, or application layer protocols.

User history   Collects network data on a per-user basis.

Probe configuration   Controls the way the remote monitors can be programmed from the main console.

An RMON-compliant device doesn't have to support all those categories, but if it supports a category, it must support it completely. That is, an RMON-compliant device can't report on a subset of the network layer host information defined in the standard. Additionally, some groups are dependent on other groups. As you might expect, an RMON-compliant device can't implement the MIB related to the application layer matrix if it doesn't implement the network layer matrix. You can't count traffic between nodes according to protocol if you can't count traffic between nodes, regardless of transport protocol.

RMON is important not just because of the wide array of data it can collect, but also because it supports continuous collections, regardless of whether there's currently a live connection between the remote monitor and the main console. This constant stream of collected data keeps the system as up to date as possible.

For example, you can't be sure that a remote management device will always be in contact with the main monitoring console. Whether the break is because of network failures or scheduled downtime (something particularly likely if the monitor and main console are separated by a WAN), it's still cutting off contact between the main console and the device to be monitored. Using MIBs to collect data means that a remote system can be configured to compile its data even when it's not in contact with the main console.

NOTE   Understanding that the network may be monitored from more than one location, RMON supports reporting to more than one console.

RMON can be used to continually run diagnostics, collecting information not currently monitored for future reference. Even if the network goes down, the remote monitor is there to note the conditions that led to the problem—all the way up to the point at which the network no longer worked. When possible, the main console can review this information to identify the conditions that led to the network failure. RMON devices can also be programmed to note certain conditions. The devices are constantly collecting information; when the data recorded exceeds predetermined tolerances, the monitor can recognize the problem and notify the main console. All this data is a Good Thing because it makes the job of network management much easier. The more data you can call on, the easier it is to isolate the problem when the host that generates more errors or traffic than anyone else finally goes postal and takes down part of the network.

The only catch to RMON is compatibility. RMON1 is not entirely consistent, as individual vendors added capabilities to the protocol. These capabilities enhance the kinds of reporting that the protocol can do, but also make some RMON implementations incompatible with others. Before buying RMON devices, make sure that they're compatible with each other and can all be monitored by your monitor.

Other Network Monitoring Tools

What if you're not using SNMP or RMON on your network? You're not out of luck when it comes to network management; some other options await you. You can choose from literally dozens of management tools for various purposes, but the following are two pertaining to big issues: monitoring packet content and detecting and locating cable breaks.

Understanding Sniffers

A *sniffer* (on a TCP/IP network, also called a *packet sniffer*) is a computer or device that monitors data traveling over a network by intercepting all packets, not just those sent to it. This is called running in *promiscuous mode*.

> **NOTE** You can run a sniffer not in promiscuous mode, but in that case, you'll only be able to monitor the data sent to and from the machine the sniffer is running on.

Sniffers are popular cracking tools, as they can read the contents of private packets. They can also be used legitimately for analyzing traffic data, including types of broadcasts sent over the network, what computer is sending data and to whom, and so forth. This is the kind of information you'll need to conduct efficiency and operational audits. You don't have to read all information, but you can set up filters to pick up only the traffic that you want to see.

In short, sniffers are one method of monitoring traffic when your network doesn't support RMON. Microsoft's Network Monitor (included in NT) is one example of a commercial sniffer. Others are available commercially or on the Net at sites of varying degrees of legitimacy.

Time Domain Reflectometers

Time domain reflectometers (TDRs) use a sonar-like procedure to help you determine the location of network bottlenecks. The device broadcasts a signal called a *fast rise time pulse* over the network at regular intervals and waits for the echo. The amount of time it takes for the pulse to echo is noted and displayed as a function of cable length. Say, for example, that you know from your facility audit that a particular cable is 20 feet long. The results of the TDR test show a cable length of 15 feet, so there's a break at the 15-foot mark. TDRs were once used only for wire cables, but now are available for fiber networks as well (see Figure 14.8).

FIGURE 14.8:

A time domain reflectometer (TDR) sends out signals to test the network.

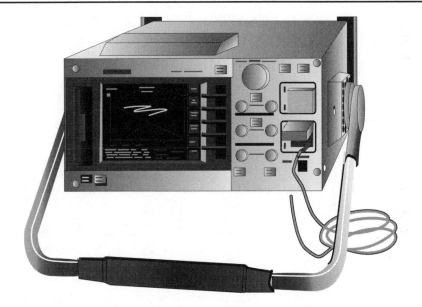

TDRs aren't cheap, to put it mildly; a wire TDR will run somewhere in the low thousands and a fiber one may cost as much as $20,000 or more. It might behoove you to think of other methods to isolate cable problems (see the following sidebar) unless you have a large network that can justify the price.

Ping—A Cheap Way of Isolating Network Discontinuity

If you're using TCP/IP on your network, you shouldn't start troubleshooting communication problems with a TDR; you've got a software cable break detector at your fingertips. One tool in the TCP/IP suite is a diagnostic called "Ping," which simply sends packets to the provided address and waits for a reply confirming that those packets got to their destination. If you can't connect to a certain address, try the following procedure to narrow the search for the problem child:

1. On the computer that can't connect to another one, type **ping 127.0.0.1** to send a message to yourself. If that works, the computer is connected to the network and the card is functioning.

2. Ping the default gateway for your segment. If that works, the problem is not on the segment.

3. Ping the DNS server. If that works, then the problem is not one of name resolution.

4. Ping a host on another segment. If that works, then you don't have a problem related to TCP/IP.

Once you've isolated the problem to a specific segment, *then* get out the TDR to find the break if you think one exists and you can't find it.

Ping can perform other diagnostic functions as well, showing the time it takes for packets to travel a certain distance, but the capabilities depend on the exact implementation of the TCP/IP suite you're running. Experiment with yours to find out what you can do with it. Even the simplest ping is easier—and cheaper—than getting out the hardware to detect cable breaks.

Zeroing In on Administration Costs

As discussed in Chapter 12, "Thin Client Networking," reducing the total cost of PC ownership is the hot concept of the moment. As also mentioned in Chapter 12, the biggest expense to PC ownership is not the cost of the boxes themselves, but the cost of administering them.

For a simple example of how these costs compare, consider the case of my friend, Joanne. Like many people their age, her parents have never had jobs that required them to use a computer. (Her father is a retired dentist; her mother is an artist and housewife.) Thus, Joanne bought her parents a fax machine last year for Christmas so they could send letters more easily, but she went all out this year. When she bought a new computer, she gave her parents her old one so they could use e-mail and ICQ (a Web-based chat and instant messaging program).

Since then, Joanne has spent several hours a month administering the darn computer over the telephone. It's definitely improved familial communication—or at least increased it—but it's also dramatically increased Joanne's long-distance bill and frustration level. It's frustrating for her parents, as well, to feel that every time they do something, they've broken the computer and have to ask their daughter for help. In short, computerizing communications has not had the intended effect. It was supposed to make life easier, but instead it's made life harder. (I'm lucky. My mom and dad just ask me about the finer points of using Netscape mail, which I don't use and can't help them with except in general terms.)

Realistically, my friend has two choices: she can continue to provide long-distance tech support, or she can install remote control software on her computer and her parents' and administer their machine long distance. The latter idea is one example of *zero administration*.

> **NOTE** Novell calls this "zero effort networking," but "administration" seems more descriptive, so I'll use the Microsoft terminology unless I'm specifically talking about Novell's approach. Both names are a little optimistic (*zero* administration? I think not) but at least represent the effort to reduce the time it takes to keep client machines up and running.

Zero administration is not a single concept but an array of tools and configurations meant to reduce administration costs. In a nutshell, the idea is to take control of the PC from the user and put it in the hands of the administrator, in order to:

- Reduce support requests caused by user error.

- Centralize the loading of applications, or making applications available from anywhere on the network.

- Permit administrators to remotely control client machines, loading software or rebooting as necessary.

Zero administration techniques are typically practiced from a server operating system such as NetWare or NT. The products available to do this depend on the operating system. Generally speaking, zero administration technologies will provide for centralized control of what users can and can't do to the operating system, including defining what programs users can run; installing applications from a central source; performing remote software and hardware inventory; and carrying out remote diagnostic operations.

There's one important caveat to zero administration: to make it work on the client end, you have to get it right on the server end. That's one reason it's not really *zero* administration; the dumber your clients, the smarter your servers have to be. Thus, when configuring the server side of zero administration, be careful about what you're doing and test extensively before implementing the final product.

Novell's Z.E.N.works

Novell's zero administration effort is called *zero effort networking* (ZEN) or, to use the product name, Z.E.N.works. Originally released in May 1998, this array of tools is designed to place the brunt of client administration on the server instead of the client. Client machines can be configured to automatically have new and updated applications downloaded to them. These applications are distributed across the network so that the apps don't have to be installed on a single server. Instead, when the client attempts to access an application, the one stored on the server closest to the client will be used. Additionally, all user preferences, procedures, and security rights are maintained in the directory services so that they're distributed throughout the network instead of just in a single location.

So far, it's a lot like Microsoft's ZAW (described next). What distinguishes the two administration tools at this point is an addition to Z.E.N.works made in November 1998. The 1.1 version of the tool includes support for remotely checking hardware and software for year 2000 compatibility.

Microsoft's ZAW

If you didn't listen closely to Microsoft's marketing literature, you may have thought that Zero Administration Windows (ZAW) was a new feature of the next generation of NT. Quite the opposite. ZAW has been part of NT since NT 4 was released. Presently, it takes the form of support for policies and profiles, Systems Management Server (SMS), and, as of the summer of 1997, the Zero Administration Kit (ZAK). Many people don't have any reason to use these features of the operating system, but they're there. The following isn't a how-to guide for Microsoft ZAW, but an idea of the tools that you can use to reduce the time and effort it takes to administer the network.

Policies and Profiles

Policies and profiles are two solutions to a similar problem: how do you maintain a consistent user interface? Many, many support problems arise from misconfigured machines, whether that configuration relates to the user display, hardware settings, installed applications, or some other configuration setting. Therefore, if you want to keep machines from becoming misconfigured, you prevent people from configuring them at all, or don't let their changes stick.

> **NOTE** Profiles may be maintained either on the client machine (assuming the client machine has a hard disk) or downloaded from a server when the user logs onto the network. Policies are always located on a server—they can't be used in a peer network. The server may be either an NT server or NetWare server, depending on the network type.

User Profiles Profiles maintain a set of user options, such as some application settings, colors, screen savers, and the like. On Windows 95 machines, for example, they're the set of information stored in the USER.DAT file that makes up the Registry—the central database of all system configuration information. The system information (stored in SYSTEM.DAT) is loaded when the computer boots—it's not user dependent. The user information can't be loaded until someone logs onto the machine. By default, every person who uses a Windows 95 computer uses the same profile. For example, say that Joe logs onto the computer, changes the color scheme from Windows Default to Storm, then logs off. When Tammy logs on, she won't see Windows Default, but Storm. Let Tammy change the color scheme back, though, and Joe's changes are lost.

That's the way it works by default: the change to the color scheme is stored in the common USER.DAT and when someone logs on, that USER.DAT is loaded. If you enable *user profiles*, however, then you prepare a custom version of USER.DAT for each person who logs onto the computer. When Joe changes the color scheme, the change is not stored in a common configuration file, but in his own file; changes he makes don't affect anyone else. Essentially, user profiles allow you to make changes that limit the collateral damage that one person can do to a computer used by several people.

> **NOTE** Changes to user profiles are made when the user logs off.

To really limit the damage that one person can do, you can use *mandatory user profiles*. A mandatory user profile (instituted by renaming USER.DAT to USER.MAN) returns the system to a common set of user-related settings; you can't make several mandatory profiles for a single machine. However, these settings are read only. If Joe changes the color scheme for the mandatory user profile and then logs off, the change he made is gone when Tammy logs on for her turn at the system. Similarly, Tammy can change her system for the current logon session, but those changes are lost when she logs off.

User profiles are a low-level ZAW tool. They apply only to the complete set of user settings; they don't include computer-related settings at all and they don't limit access to any of the configuration tools such as the Control Panel. However, they do reduce support costs incurred when one user messes up the settings for another. If you want more detailed control, you'll need to use system policies, discussed next.

System Policies System polices take control of the desktop one step further. Rather than granting or denying permission to change the entire set of user-related settings, they apply to specific parts of the user interface. Additionally, system policies can be used to control the way in which the computer itself may be configured. Policy settings are stored on a central server as .pol files so that they're downloaded to the client at logon time.

Configuring the level of user access to each and every picky detail of system configuration would be a serious pain, so system policies don't do that. Instead, you can explicitly enable or disable the features you care about and then leave the rest to be defined by the user profile; user profiles must be enabled to make system policies work. For example, you could set up system policies that forbid a user to share files with the rest of the network, set a default color scheme, but permit the user to share printers or not, at his or her discretion.

The Systems Management Server (SMS)

Policies and profiles take care of locking down the configuration settings to reduce the chance of user error. Systems Management Server (SMS) is a more proactive administration tool, responsible for the contents of each client machine. Using SMS, you can conduct remote software or hardware inventory, install applications or even an operating system, and reboot a client machine from the SMS console.

The Zero Administration Kit (ZAK)

The Zero Administration Kit (ZAK) is an NT add-on available from the Microsoft Web site. It's an extension to the idea of policies and profiles, meant to provide a standard type of access for client computers of two types: task stations and application stations. The ZAK is installed on the client end (the client must be running NT 4 Workstation or Windows 95/98) in one configuration or the other.

The difference between the two configurations is a matter of how many applications the user can access; configuring the system isn't an option for either. *TaskStation mode* is designed for task-oriented users, people who only require access to one application (such as a database client). When you boot a machine configured in this way, it boots directly into Internet Explorer or the previously specified application. The desktop is completely locked down; users can't run the Start button, Task Manager, Taskbar, Control Panel, or Explorer. *AppStation mode* is designed for workers who run three or four business applications but don't need or want to configure the system or install new applications. When you boot a client machine with this configuration, it goes directly into an administrator-constrained user interface that offers access to just the applications needed. The Task Manager, Control Panel, and Explorer are unavailable. Applications are run from the server, not on the client.

Forthcoming ZAW Features

Although some ZAW functionality is already present in NT 4 or the ZAK, other features are linked to the next generation of NT: Windows 2000 Server. The parts relevant to network administrators and not found in previous versions of the operating system include:

- Automatic system upgrade and application installation with IntelliMirror
- Microsoft Management Console's unified interface

Of course, Windows 2000 will include support for the currently available ZAW features. Policies and profiles are meant to be easier to work with to lock down parts of the system; the ZAK TaskStation and AppStation settings will be available in Win2K for anyone who didn't install the ZAK; and SMS 2 will still support remote management.

Automatic Upgrades and Installations Automatic upgrades and installations are based on IntelliMirror's push technology, in which data are downloaded to a client without the client having to ask for them, using a preset array of settings. This is how browser channels work. The purpose of automating these upgrades and installations is simple to grasp. The user doesn't have to know how the installation works; the administrator doesn't have to go to the client's machine to perform the installation.

When users log onto a Windows 2000 network, the central code server will note the version of the client's operating system and—with the preset permission of the user and/or administrator—download any upgrades to the client's desktop.

The Microsoft Management Console The Microsoft Management Console (MMC) isn't a tool in itself, but a front end for NT's basic suite of tools and for snap-ins from other vendors. It's meant to provide a central location for managing the network instead of the current system of doing one thing, shutting the relevant management application, and then doing something else; shutting that management application, then doing something else; and afterwards shutting yet another management application. Although I haven't been completely delighted with the appearance of the unified console, it saves time to have tools available from a central source.

Beyond Software

A final point about ZAW: it's not just about applications. One part of the ZAW design lies in making computers that are more easily managed. They forget the complicated hardware design and make computing devices interchangeable.

A big part of ZAW theory is tied to thin client computing in which the client PCs may be reduced not only to the role of terminals but also to the actuality of terminals. A Net PC is almost a "throwaway" computer. It has no hard disk and the case is sealed (I don't like that—it means they can't be upgraded easily). You're supposed to plug them in and forget about them or replace them with another client machine if they break.

Plug and Play (PnP) is another part of ZAW, as it reduces the amount of time it takes to set up hardware. A properly designed PnP device is recognized on system reboot—much simpler than fiddling with I/O addresses and IRQ settings. The DD2 monitors and video cards can even configure themselves for the optimal display settings so you don't have to worry about card configuration.

Troubleshooting Tips

Well documented or not, remotely administered or not, sooner or later, something is going to go wrong with some part of your LAN. Often, the hardest part of troubleshooting a LAN is not fixing the problem but figuring out the problem and determining what component is causing it. To that end, you need to:

- Be familiar with your network and data that is relevant to it.

- Be able to isolate problems in the network.

- Call on data from previously reported problems so you don't have to discover the same problem repeatedly.

Read on for more information about figuring out what's wrong and how to fix it.

The Web Is Mightier Than the TDR

The biggest tool in your troubleshooting arsenal is not expensive hardware but information. This chapter has devoted a lot of time to methods of gathering information about your network and the kinds of data you're likely to want. If you've been able to keep up with the suggestions I've made (unrealistic, but hopefully you've made a stab at it and have collected at least some of the data), then you should have records of expected network behavior, network layout, organization of resources, and the like.

Sources of Troubleshooting Information

Your network provides only one part of the data you need. The network's data tells you about your network's idiosyncrasies, traffic patterns, hardware, and so forth. Outside information is the second part. You need to know what your network's doing, but you also need to find out about known issues concerning the hardware or software you're trying to make work together.

Keeping Current The most current information is likely to be found in discussion lists devoted to some aspect of your operating system or hardware that you're interested in. The online guide with this book will offer some suggestions and places to look for other lists.

> **WARNING** Don't assume that everything you read in a chat room, online forum, or user mailing list is accurate. Some people who participate are experienced, but you can't assume that everyone who pipes up to answer your question knows what they're talking about.

Other sources of current information are bulletins released by the product manufacturer, either sent to you in e-mail or existing on the company Web site.

> **NOTE** Not quite as current, but much more manageable, are the monthly CD-based subscriptions, such as Microsoft's TechNet, which include a searchable database of white papers, bug fix information, and other technical data.

Some people also find newsgroups useful, but the signal-to-noise problem of newsgroups is as bad as ever. Half the traffic on technical newsgroups carries subject headers along the lines of, "Make Money Now!!!" The other half of the traffic typically isn't moderated and doesn't necessarily have anything to do with the main topic. You don't have to deal with newsgroup spam or irrel-evancies. Other online venues for information sharing among professionals exist. Check out the aforementioned mailing lists, discussion forums, or chat rooms attached to a Web site (see Figure 14.9).

FIGURE 14.9:

Avoid the spam of newsgroups in Web-based forums.

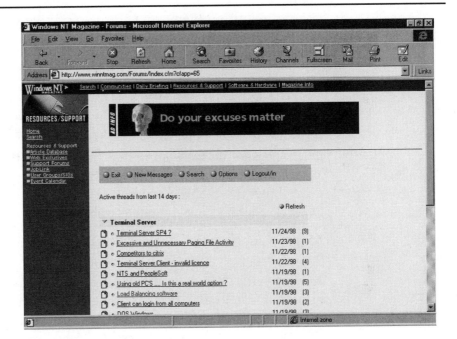

Collecting Background Information The most current informa-tion is not always the most complete. For a more in-depth look at the issues, read trade publications. Weeklies carry news or opin-ion pieces; technical detail is generally reserved for the monthly publications. Although the magazines won't be quite as current as the e-mail bulletins, they have the advantage of including back-ground information not included in mailing lists or other up-to-the-minute venues. Magazines can be an excellent source of tutorials, tips about specific problems, and new hardware sugges-tions. Read trade publications for the product reviews, too; a product review may comment on troubles that the reviewer had with the product and the methods used to resolve the problem.

Books are less likely to have up-to-the minute information than either lists or magazines because of the lead time involved in publishing a book. However, they can be excellent references for known problems and for background information that can help you figure out problems on your own or give you ideas of where to look for more information.

Keeping Up with the Flow

Anyone who's tried to keep up with the waterfall of technology-related information is probably a bit boggle-eyed by now, thinking, "She *can't* be suggesting that I keep up with everything!" You're right—I'm not. I can't do it myself. No one is expert in everything; the best most of us can hope for is to be a pretty good generalist who knows where to find the answer to a question.

You can manage the flow of information better with a couple of different tactics. First, pick the resources that help you most and keep up with them as best you can. Just because something is printed doesn't mean that it's any good or that it fulfills any particular need of yours. Microsoft, for example, issues hundreds of Knowledge Base articles addressing known problems in the course of a year. Most of us have no reason to read 90 percent of these articles, as they'll apply only to a particular model of network card or to an application we're not using. Search for the articles that include only the keywords you're interested in (see the following sidebar).

Online Search Tips

When sorting through online publications, a light touch with database searches is your best friend. Many major site and Web search engines support Boolean coding. These codes, derived from an algebraic system developed in the nineteenth century by English mathematician George Boole, make it easier to pinpoint the document most relevant to your problem by isolating the words you're looking for.

To search for documents that include all the words you're looking for, but not in any particular case or in any relation to each other, use AND statements. For example, **SCSI AND NT** will return all documents that include both words; "AND" is typically understood if not specified. That is, if you type **SCSI NT** in a search engine set up for Boolean statements, the engine will search for documents containing both words.

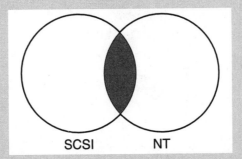

To search for documents that include any of the words you're interested in, use OR statements. For example, searching for **SCSI OR NT** will return all documents that include either word. I rarely use OR statements as they typically return too many hits for my purposes.

Continued on next page

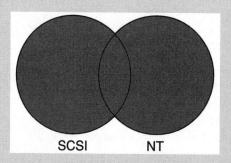

SCSI   NT

Say you want to find a document that does not contain a particular word. For example, if you wanted to find all documents that discussed SCSI but didn't discuss NT, then you'd use a NOT statement like this: **SCSI NOT NT**. NOT statements are useful to narrow searches that you know are likely to be broad.

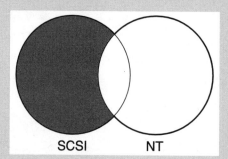

SCSI   NT

To find a document that contains one word or the other, but not both, use an XOR statement. For example, **SCSI XOR NT** will return all documents that contain either word but don't contain both words. XOR statements are like OR statements but will exclude any documents containing both words. Also like OR statements, they're usually a bit broad for my needs unless combined with other operands.

Continued on next page

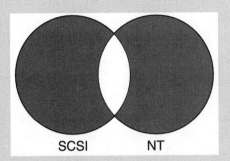

A Boolean search engine also supports two additional operands not technically part of Boolean algebra: NEAR and quotation marks. NEAR works like AND, except that it searches for instances of the words that are a certain distance from each other, usually within eight words. For example, **SCSI NEAR NT** would return all documents in which SCSI and NT were within eight words of each other, ignoring all documents in which both words appeared but were further apart.

Quotation marks are used to specify several words as a string to be looked for. In most search engines, searching for **Windows NT** returns all documents that include Windows AND NT—including instances of **"Windows NT"** but also including such phrases as, "Windows 3.x is a predecessor to NT." If you want the search to return only documents in which the words appear as a string, you'll need to use quotation marks around the string as in **"Windows NT"**.

The statements in these examples are pretty simple; I've only used two words and one operand in each statement. However, Boolean statements can include several words and multiple operands if necessary. For example, the statement **SCSI AND NT NOT network** would return all documents that contain the words SCSI and NT, but not "network."

Second, cooperate with others to share information. This is a good use of those mailing lists and online forums—if you don't know, someone else might. You can return the favor when someone asks what sounds to you like an easy question, but has been giving the questioner nightmares for two days.

Patches and Updates

What about updating not only your brain but your software? No software—driver, application, or operating system—is ever "done." Manufacturers frequently offer fixes or enhancements to their products in the form of new drivers, hotfixes that address a single problem, or service packs that address several problems and may include some additional features not part of the original product. Keeping up with these updates is one good reason to stay up to date on outside information pertaining to your hardware and software. Most updates are available from the manufacturer's Web or FTP site, or on a subscription CD like TechNet.

Keep up with these updates, but don't necessarily install them on production machines right away. First, don't install hotfixes unless you're experiencing the problem the hotfix is intended to correct.

Second, assuming that you do intend to install a hotfix or service pack, first make sure that the update isn't going to make the problem worse and that you can recover from the update if you have to. (Anyone who recalls the infamous Service Pack 2 to Windows NT 4 will understand why this is important. To make a long story short, more than a few people had to haul out the backups after installing SP2, as the upgrade broke their current installation.) Keep your ears open for a week or two after an update is released. Listen to what people are saying on the industry-related lists about the update, about any problems they're having, or what the manufacturer said when they called about a problem. If you can, test the updates yourself on a machine that can be broken without hurting anything. Essentially, do what you can to make sure that the update is going to help you out.

Even if it's not actually harmful, updates sometimes aren't complete, not entirely fixing the problem they were intended to address and leading to updates like the one from which I copied the following advice: "Microsoft highly recommends that all affected customers—including anyone who downloaded the original patch before November 18—download and install the updated patch to protect their computers."

Personally, I've better things to do than download and install patches twice. If you must have the functionality included in the software update, then install it immediately. Otherwise, wait at least a few days before installing. No matter what, always be sure that you've backed up all data and configuration information before you install any kind of updates. That way, if disaster strikes, you can at least go back to a system that worked.

Using Support Calls Effectively

The key to successful troubleshooting is background information to help you track problems and propose solutions. Without it, you've got nothing to help you, and you spend more time getting data about the problem than you'll probably need to fix the problem itself. In this section, I'll discuss the importance of documenting support calls and explain a couple of ways in which you can successfully do so.

One of the biggest favors you can do yourself is keeping a log of trouble calls, problems, and solutions. Part of the reason for doing this is self-protection; call tracking provides a record of your contribution to the organization. A better reason is to demonstrate the need for additional equipment or personnel, or demonstrating that a change breaks the network. If you can document the level of support calls has skyrocketed since a change was made to one part of the network, you may be able to prevent the change from being rolled out to the rest of the network until the change has been fixed.

A still better reason is to anticipate—or avoid—future problems by tracking trends. Trends can encompass either particular individuals ("Mr. X calls us whenever he can't figure out how to turn on the printer.") or particular situations. ("We can expect a call on files called 'Y' from everyone with WordPerfect.") This kind of background information can also be useful when you're training new support people or network administrators.

Thus, you'll need written or (my choice) electronic records of all support requests. Each trouble report should include the following information:

- Trouble report ID number
- Preliminary information:
  - Who reported the trouble?
  - When was the trouble reported?
  - How was it reported (e-mail, phone, walk-in)?
  - Is it related to previous trouble calls?
  - Where was the trouble reported?
  - What is the specific complaint?
  - Is this repeatable? Will your client/fellow employee be able to duplicate the problem before your eyes?
  - When did this first appear?
  - What (if anything) was done differently before the problem appeared and after the problem appeared?
  - Does it occur periodically? When?
- On-site information:
  - Comments on the PC environment: power, temperature, others
  - Your observation of trouble
  - Actions taken on-site
- If the PC was taken into your repair area or to a shop:
  - Date brought in?
  - What actions were taken?

- Result?

- Was the PC returned to the client/employee? Date?

- Summary information/keywords:

  - Was it a hardware, software, and/or user problem?

  - If it was software, what package(s)?

  - If it was hardware, what device(s)?

TIP   For common problems, create a FAQ that users can look at before they call the help desk. The FAQ can also be useful for support personnel, especially new ones.

Divide and Conquer

You've informed yourself of the state of the network. You're aware of the current technology. You've developed a database of known issues. What's left?

Well, there's still that broken network to fix.

Find the Problem—*Then* Fix It

The issue of dividing and conquering is twofold. First, there's the more obvious aspect of locating the problem. Is it in the network? Where? In which segment? Or, is it on the server side, perhaps in memory, in the CPU, in a hard disk? Second, there's the less obvious aspect of determining the problem. You're most likely to discover problems when someone reports them than in the course of normal checking, and when that report is made, your job is to get sufficient detail that you can isolate the real problem.

Not sure of the difference between the two divisions? For example, if Jesse calls the help desk and says that she can't get to her e-mail, you don't really know where the problem is.

Without further information, you don't know whether Jesse can't access the network, can't log onto the mail server, can't find her mail client, or (possibly—I've seen people be this vague) can't boot her computer. Once you have a more precise definition of the problem, you're in a better position to pinpoint the source of the trouble.

When you get a support call, get more information first, and go running around the office trying to track down the problem, second. It's a lot less work and significantly more rewarding.

One final word on the subject of garnering information: If you don't know what the problem is or how to fix it, then don't say you do and confidently offer a suggestion. First, doing this irritates the user unless you get really lucky with your guess, as they'll have to keep calling you back. One "I don't know—I'll call you back in an hour after I've done some research" is worth six "The problem is X—do Y. No? That didn't work? Try Z. That didn't work? Try A." If you actually call back, the former procedure builds confidence. The latter destroys it.

Second, if you make a preliminary statement about what the problem is, then the emphasis shifts from solving the problem to proving yourself right. It doesn't matter whether you're right the first time; the user will forgive a wrong guess if you fix the problem.

Tracking Down the Difficulty

Okay, you have a more detailed description of the problem. Now you can track it down. Ask yourself:

- Who's experiencing this problem? One person, one workgroup, one domain, one segment, or the entire network?

- What actions are associated with this problem? What's the user trying to do that's causing this problem? Does the problem occur only in a single circumstance or does it appear at various times? Is there any pattern?

- Does the problem only occur at particular times of day?

- Has this problem happened before? What was the cause and what was the resolution?

- What is different between yesterday (or whenever the problem wasn't a problem) and today (or whenever the problem arose)?

In short, you're looking for patterns and you're looking for prior experience.

Preparing for Change

Even the best-managed, most trouble-free network will be changed eventually. New hardware becomes available, new applications or new versions of existing applications are released, companies move; sooner or later, you're going to make changes, large or small, to the network. Your job is to make this change as simple as possible. To do that, you'll need to combine your technical skills with the delicacy of a diplomat—noting that a diplomat's job is not to get walked over, but to get his or her way while making the other person in the agreement feel good about it.

I've been part of some network planning sessions and from writing migration case studies I've observed many more. Successful migrations to new hardware or software almost invariably follow the same path:

1. Identifying requirements

2. Planning layout

3. Testing the new system and fixing any problems

4. Implementing the new system

5. Soliciting feedback

Let's take a more detailed look at these steps.

Performing a Needs Analysis

The first step in planning a change to the network shouldn't be identifying new toys to play with, but identifying an actual or potential need. Alternatively, you might identify a new technology or product that could be helpful once you introduced it. However, the most successful migrations I've seen seem to come from the mindset of, "How can we make our lives easier?" rather than, "This is a cool toy. How can we integrate it into the network?"

Preparing with Regular Meetings

In order to conduct needs analyses, many companies, especially larger companies, hold regular State of the Network meetings. During these meetings, they evaluate network performance, user satisfaction, and the like. If new technology is available, this is a good time to brief people about it. These meetings aren't attended only by the MIS staff, either—they're management meetings with representatives of user and network staff to offer input into what's wanted and what's possible. The exact number of people at the meetings depends on the company, of course. In one company, the meetings might include eight or 10 people (hopefully no more, or you won't get anything done); in others, they might have three attendees who all wear a lot of hats. Whomever's there, however, the following expertise should be represented:

- User management
- Building management
- Hardware support
- Software support
- Network support
- The user base

TIP The smaller the population of State of the Network meetings, the more likely you'll get something done. If some people are only needed occasionally, have them make guest appearances to make presentations relevant to their expertise.

Those support calls you've been tracking are one potential source of information about user needs. If you know that you're getting a lot of support calls about a particular word processor, but know from your reading that there's a new version available that's supposed to fix this problem, then you know that it might be time to go word processor shopping. On a larger scale, if you're getting a lot of complaints about the systems being unresponsive because you're trying to run Windows software in emulation, then it might be time to change the operating system to one that supports the applications you're already using.

Other potential sources include user satisfaction surveys and generally keeping your ear to the ground. That's one reason you need the user base represented. This person shouldn't always be assumed to speak for all users, but the people using the network to get work done are likely to have strong opinions about what features would make their lives easier, even if those opinions aren't always very precisely stated.

Soliciting User Input

If you're planning major changes, you'll need to talk to the people using the network so that you know what training and applications they need to get work done. The following is a user survey taken from a government agency migrating from UNIX-based workstations to NT.

1. Given that we'll be purchasing the MS Office Suite, check all applications listed below that you will need migrated onto

your new NT system. If possible, list the version you are currently running:

Applix Mail

Applix Spreadsheet

Applix Words

Corel Draw

Corel Presentation

FrameMaker

PhotoShop

WordPerfect

NOTE This is an example. The items in this list aren't important. The response you're trying to get here is, "If your computer vanished tomorrow, what applications would need to be restored for you to continue working?"

---

2. Will you need any software not listed in question #1?

3. Will you need any macros converted?

4. Do your customers require files saved in a particular format?

5. What database interfaces will you need migrated to the new operating system?

6. What training will you require? Please rate your level of expertise.

7. Do you have any additional comments or concerns about the transition?

When soliciting user input, remember a couple of points. First, the fact that someone asks for something doesn't mean that they have to get it. In this particular example, results from the survey showed that a couple of users in one division wanted 3D modeling software. They didn't have it at the time of the survey and their job descriptions didn't include any tasks that would require them to use 3D modeling software. But they wanted it because they knew how to use it. (The request was denied.)

The second point relates to the first: user input is advisory only, and both you (the person doing the asking) and the users need to understand that. Any time that you change part of the network, some advantages will be gained and some will be lost. If you attempt to maintain the fiction that the users are dictating the outlines of the network, then you're going to have resentful users when the network or applications don't work as they ordered it. Remember that network management and final design is a command decision. Although you're making changes to make life easier for the user population, you're responsible for the decisions made. Sometimes, that's going to include explaining trade-offs that have to be made for the sake of some other advantage.

Planning Infrastructure

Once you've identified the needs of the people using the network and have some ideas of what technology will fulfill those needs, it's time to start putting together the pieces of the infrastructure. Depending on the nature of the change you're making to the network, the questions will change, but overall they'll probably be something along these lines:

- What applications must be supported?
- Who needs access to these applications?
- What kind of control should users have over their machines?
- What kind of bandwidth will we need to support user applications?
- What kind of data protection do we need?
- What other networks will we need to communicate with?

- What existing hardware must be supported? What can be replaced? What needs to be added?

- Where are the network's needs going? Can we identify any needs not currently real, but which we'll have in the next year or two?

Based on the answers to these questions, you can choose hardware, software, and configurations that supply these needs. If you've been able to keep up with technology news (see, this is one application for those trade magazines you've been reading), then finding the tools that both fit your needs and work together may not be too difficult. For problems beyond your expertise, you may need to spend some time researching the latest offerings or calling in outside help.

TIP Don't forget about interoperability when planning your network's infrastructure. The lion's share of problems stem from, "This piece of the network won't talk to that piece." Save yourself some time by identifying pieces that will talk to each other or can be made to do so.

One part of planning the infrastructure may include training your client base in how to use the new pieces of the network. This isn't always necessary—if you've installed a new server operating system, the user interface may not change at all. However, if any users need training on new applications that they will have contact with, this is a good time to do it.

Testing Components

You've picked out the pieces of the network and know how you're going to put them together. Off to install them! The changes will be up and running by tomorrow morning!

Hadn't you better make sure the changes work before you replace a functioning network?

A successful installation is a tested installation. The nature of the testing may differ depending on the degree of change being made, the company's resources that can be dedicated to testing, and perhaps the experience of the client base, but testing is a usual part of the migration process. There's good reason. If you don't test the change, you know how it's theoretically *supposed* to work, but you don't know how it performs in the wild.

To test a change to the network, you can set it up in a lab if you have such facilities available. Lab tests are good for preliminary testing. During this stage, you can experiment with the best way to set up the changes, mess around with configurations, and generally tweak the system for best performance without worrying about how your tweaks will affect the people who are trying to get their jobs done. Data load can be simulated with automatic packet generators, so you can get some idea of how the network will perform under stress without having to pull in live users. Lab testing is also an excellent time to test for interoperability problems so you can resolve them before they inconvenience anyone other than the IS staff.

TIP   You can connect the lab to the main network if you put the lab on its own segment, behind a repeater, router, or bridge. That way, problems in the lab network won't affect the rest of the network, but you'll still be able to get to any network-accessible information you need.

Zoo animals don't act like animals living in the wild, and lab networks don't always act like "live" networks. The acid test of a change's stability is how it performs in a production environment; otherwise, you can't really tell how it's going to react to the stresses of the workday. You can handle this (without jumping straight from the lab to implementing the change across the entire network) in one of several ways.

If the change is a new element to the network (or the network itself is new), you can make a test site. At a test site, the change is fully implemented as it would be in its final version and used normally. The results of the test site can then be recorded and evaluated. If changes are necessary, you can make them and apply them to the test site again. Once the network's up and running on the test site, you can expand the implementations to other sites.

If test sites aren't possible, you may be able to isolate a change to an initial test segment or test workgroup, depending on whether the change is logical in nature, physical, or both. Once again, when the change is working as expected on a small scale, you can implement it across the network. Until that point, however, testing in isolated parts of the main network allows you to find and resolve problems while only affecting a limited population of the user base.

A third approach to testing can be incremental change, adding elements of the change in the network piece by piece. This kind of implementation can be something of a pain, but it isolates components, if not users. That is, if a component is causing problems, you can discover which one is the culprit more easily if new elements are introduced one at a time rather than as a group.

These testing methods aren't mutually exclusive—it's certainly possible to combine them or come up with new ways of testing the network. Regardless of the method used, however, the principles remain the same: isolate negative impact until you're sure the network is performing as expected. It's a lot easier to fix problems on a small scale and then implement the fix across the network than it is to fix the same problem across a large and complex network.

Implementing the Network

Finally, you're ready to execute the change. If possible, complete the task either away from the main client base or when they're not around and plan to give yourself time. Most changes take longer than we think they're going to, and if you're crunched for time, then you'll be more likely to cut corners that could cause you trouble later.

Even if you've tested the change in advance, expect to spend some time after the change ironing out bugs that didn't appear until the full-scale implementation. If you've tested carefully, however, you should have fewer problems with bugs than you might otherwise.

Summary

I said it before, and I'll say it again: putting together a network is often the easy part. The hard part comes when people want to use the thing and you either have to fix it or change it.

To make the job of fixing the network as trouble-free as possible, you can document it to death: know your network's pieces and layout as well as possible so that when something goes wrong it's easier to pinpoint the problem. Another complementary approach can be to lock down user desktops. Keep applications centralized and prevent users from configuring (and possibly misconfiguring) their machines. Also conduct inventories and installations from a central location so you don't have as much running around to do. In a nutshell, with adequate information about your network and a degree of control over it, you'll find the job of network management much easier than it will be if it turns into a free-for-all.

Management—keeping the network up and running—is a big part of keeping the workforce happy. In the next chapter, I'll talk about another aspect of keeping them happy: data security.

EXERCISE 14

You're attempting to find out the number of clients using the file server on weekday afternoons. Follow these questions relating to this inquiry.

1. What kind of audit will you conduct?

2. What tool described in this chapter could tell you *how many* client requests were waiting at any given time?

3. What tool could you use to determine *which* client machines were communicating with the server?

4. To identify a computer on a particular segment, you'd use the _____ network map.

5. Why is it a good idea to run a server monitoring tool remotely, if possible?

6. A management information base is a _____ file.

    A. text-based

    B. binary

    C. machine-readable

    D. None of the above

7. Which connectionless protocol is SNMP communication based on?

8. You're interested in monitoring the amount of IPX/SPX traffic created on one segment of the network. Which tool or protocol are you most likely to use? Choose all that apply.

    A. SNMP

    B. CMIP

    C. RMON

    D. TDR

EXERCISE 14 CONTINUED

9. True or false. SNMP requires TCP/IP.

10. Which zero administration technology currently supports checking for Y2K compliance over the network?

11. Which of the following ZAW features are not a part of NT 4 out of the box?

   A. System policies

   B. TaskStation configuration

   C. Y2K compliance checking

   D. User profiles

12. What documents will the following Boolean search statement return: "NetWare 5" NEAR Zero Administration?

13. Create a Boolean statement that will return documents referring either to NT or NetWare, but not to both.

14. List the three methods suggested in this chapter for testing a change before fully implementing it.

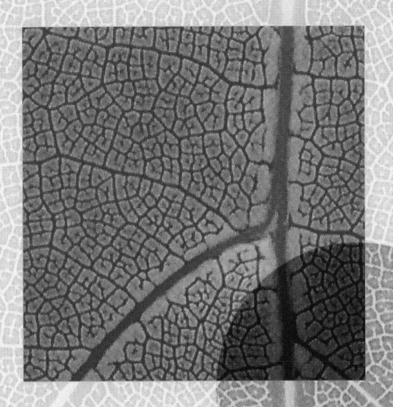

15

Network Security

What *is* network security? The answer isn't simple, as "security" encompasses several elements. It's not a monolithic concept, but instead comes in three parts, all fundamentally about protecting data.

First, there's the issue of securing the system against intrusion. How do you keep unauthorized people off the network, or keep authorized people from looking at data they're not supposed to get to? Second, there's the problem of protecting the data from loss. How can you be sure that data isn't destroyed or, more accurately, that you can get it back if it is destroyed?

NOTE   Securing data against loss will be discussed in Chapter 16, "Disaster Recovery."

Third, there's the problem of protecting the PCs of the network from viruses. Viruses range from harmless to destructive, but even the harmless ones are a nuisance.

In the course of this chapter, I'll talk about preparing for implementing a security system and the tools you can use to create one.

Preliminary Planning

The first step in securing the network lies in figuring out what you're securing it from and how much that security is going to cost. After you've done that, then you can worry about the finer points of user and group permissions or password policies.

Don't Chase Shadows

This might sound obvious, but it's worth saying: before lining up any security systems, you first have to think about the threats. Parts of the U.S. Department of Defense are devoted to *threat analysis*—the process of examining all the possible sources of danger and analyzing them to see how big the threat is and how likely it is to become active. Thus, the results of the threat analysis consist of two parts: Country X is deemed less of a potential threat to U.S. national security than Country Y, and Country Y is not deemed a serious short-term threat, although it might be one in the next decade or two.

Analyzing network security needs is a lot like that, as it also requires you to both identify threats and evaluate how likely it is that those threats are serious. For example, the person in charge of backups at your company represents a certain degree of threat—she could steal the backup tapes and sell them to someone doing corporate espionage. Is she *going* to do that? How bad would it be if she did so? The answer to those questions represents the degree of threat she represents. Once you make that evaluation, you know what measures are needed to keep her from stealing the backups.

You can identify threats and assess their seriousness in a couple of different ways. First, there's the intuitive approach that you can use if you've had some experience in securing a network. This works for small networks in which one person has sole discretion over what methods are used, but is unwieldy in larger networks or if you have to justify your reasoning to anyone.

A more exact method, and one more useful to people trying to assess a new or very complicated situation, is to systematically identify threats and rate each one individually. This works best if you can involve several people with different backgrounds in the brainstorming process so you're not working from a single point of view. Ask each person to write down the security threats they perceive, then compare the lists and remove any duplicates or truly off-the-wall ideas. What you're left with are some specific risks that you can assess and figure out how to countermand.

TIP   To perform a more informed threat analysis, it's a good idea to keep up with any security bulletins issued by the makers of your network's components. These bulletins will outline the problem and tell you about available fixes or workarounds.

Who Knows Best?

Should you depend on outside consultants specializing in security issues or internal people who know the situation? If you hire a consultant with a lot of experience working with companies or organizations like yours, you might be better off with the experience the consultant can bring to bear. The consultant shouldn't be solely responsible for designing the security system, but through his or her experience may be able to suggest solutions you hadn't thought of, or identify threats none of the internal people had noticed.

On the other hand, a security consultant doesn't know your personal organization as well as the people who are part of it. An outsider may be less willing to trust unquantifiable factors that may strike you as important to the threat assessment. He or she may also miss important elements that you see because of prolonged exposure. On the other hand, the outsider could be right in choosing to ignore some unquantifiable elements such as employee personality because they're not dependable.

The bottom line is that an experienced security consultant who draws both on your internal knowledge and his or her background can be an asset. An inexperienced consultant with a one-size-fits-all approach to problem solving isn't going to be any more useful in building a security system than he or she would be in doing anything else.

One final note about threats. The Internet is an excellent medium for information sharing. It's also an excellent rumor mill. Not every potential security threat you read about is a real one nor one that's led to a security breach. Similarly, not every patch offered to fix a security hole in your system is necessary for your system nor is it automatically valid. The principles of information gathering apply particularly well when it comes to security issues:

- Take the source of security threats into account when reacting to them.

- Unless it's a major security issue, don't rush to implement fixes. Wait a week to determine user reaction. Sometimes, fixes (such as the LAN Manager fix that was in NT's SP3 and later pulled) don't work as advertised.

- Don't implement fixes unless they're from a trusted Web or FTP site; you don't want to install a "fix" only to discover that it's a Trojan Horse, a virus concealed in a nominally helpful program.

Fundamentally, protect your network and yourself, but maintain a degree of skepticism while doing it.

Keep Protection in Line with Cost

Yes, Virginia, there *is* such a thing as a network that's too secure. Not too secure in the sense that the data protection it affords is more than what's needed. I don't think that many people are upset when it's discovered that the security measures in place prevented data loss or corruption. (Although someone who'd just gotten a bad performance evaluation that only existed in electronic form might not be too upset about the loss of *that* document.)

No, the problem isn't the degree of security but the cost incurred in the name of the security efforts. That cost takes a couple of forms. First, security measures are by definition a bit of a nuisance for both users and administrators because they're designed to make the data harder to get at. Users have to remember to change passwords and you have to set up encryption schemes, sort out user rights, configure firewalls…it's work and it takes time. The second factor is related to the first. Setting up security represents additional cost in terms of the dollar value of the systems themselves as well as the value of the manpower spent on implementing the systems.

The point isn't that security costs more than it's worth. Your data is the most important part of your computer and network; the only part that isn't replaceable. Parts of that data need to be kept private and all the data needs to be preserved. However, you need to do a little cost accounting to figure out the price of that security relative to the cost of the data it's protecting.

It's all very well to say that a security system shouldn't cost more than what it's protecting, but what are the factors needed to determine that cost? Thus, when you're evaluating a security system, compare how each of the factors in Table 15.1 will be affected by having a particular security system versus not having it.

TABLE 15.1: Creating a Cost/Benefit Analysis for Security Audit

Factor	Cost	Benefit
Productivity hours	How will it affect productivity to implement the security system?	How much will it cost in time and salaries to re-create or replace lost or compromised data?
Administrative hours	How much will it cost in terms of time and salaries to implement the system in the first place?	How much will it cost in time and salaries to get the system up and running again?
Business sales	How much will the security system impede people from doing business with us?	How much will business increase with the security system in place?

Continued on next page

TABLE 15.1 CONTINUED: Creating a Cost/Benefit Analysis for Security Audit

Factor	Cost	Benefit
Legal liabilities	What privacy-based liabilities are we open to if we implement this system?	What liabilities are we open to if we don't implement this system and data is lost or compromised?
Insurance costs	How will insurance costs be affected by the security system?	How will insurance costs be affected by the security system?

Each of these factors can be evaluated in terms of a dollar amount, which you can then balance on each side.

Once you know what the risks are and what you can afford to do about them, you can worry about the details described in the remainder of this chapter.

Get the User Base on Your Side

You can't secure the network if you're fighting the users.

A network security system is not just about technology but about management. Locking down the system will not solve security problems on its own. If the security system is too inconvenient, people will circumvent it. If you make it too difficult for most to circumvent, then they'll complain. Most people aren't expecting anything to go wrong, so the preparations against something going wrong are bound to be irksome.

So what can you do about this? The user base needs to be educated in the reasoning behind the security system. This doesn't mean that you need to consult all the users in its design. If you do that, then you'll have lower security because in the name of accessibility less security is better than more of it. Instead, tell the user base why they need to protect their passwords, log off at lunch, and so forth. Help them to understand why bringing in floppy disks from home is not an option and why incoming files must always be scanned for viruses. Fundamentally, teach people how the security that's in place benefits them. Otherwise, you're in for a difficult battle, one you'll probably lose just by being outnumbered.

The last thing you want to do is look like the bad guy who takes away access. To improve your image, how about locking down the network before people get to it? That way, you'll be able to unlock parts as people need access to them. Instead of looking like Scrooge, taking user access away, you'll look like Santa, making access possible. Just don't tell anyone that you're the person responsible for locking down the network in the first place.

Preventing Unauthorized Access

Hackers, schmackers.

Well, not quite.

NOTE   Technically speaking, a *hacker* is someone who "hacks around" with computers in the name of learning more about the system. You may have done that yourself. A *cracker* is someone breaking into secure systems for the purpose of stealing or corrupting data. Although the terms are used interchangeably in the mainstream press, they're not the same.

News stories about Pentagon break-ins or corruption of the *New York Times* Web site are about real exploits, and it's a good idea to secure your network from outside interference. However, you're far more likely to run into trouble from bored or idly malicious users poking around the network than you are from some guy in a basement with a modem. The real threat to network security is typically not brilliance on the part of an outsider but exploitation of a loophole in the system. Plug the loophole and you'll keep out 99 percent of the population.

With that in mind, it's time to think about the methods you can use to permit only authorized people on the network and to limit what they can do and see once they're logged in. In case you're feeling particularly paranoid, you can even monitor users to see what they're up to.

Authenticating User Identity

The first step to keeping unauthorized people off the network is to set up a *user account* for everyone who needs it. This user account denies the user access to network resources until he's provided a valid account name and password. On NT networks, for example, each user has a personal account with an internal security identifier (SID) that identifies them uniquely to the operating system. The only possible exception is usually a Guest account that can be used by anyone who's given its password, but in live networks, this Guest account typically has very limited access to the system.

This SID determines what each user can and can't do on the network. When a user attempts to open a file, for example, the security subsystem inspects the file and compares the user's identity with the list of users permitted to access that file, then noting what kind of access is permitted.

NOTE   The fine details of how permissions work depends on the server operating system.

Ending the Masquerade

One problem with user access lies not only in making users demonstrate their credentials before using network resources, but also in making sure an intruder hasn't compromised a valid account and assumed a user's identity—*masquerading* as the user, to use the jargon. In short, it's important to make sure that user accounts are protected and that no one can masquerade as an authorized user.

There are a couple of things you can do about this: hide user names and protect passwords.

Conceal User Names First of all, protect user names as well as passwords. User authentication is done by matching a user name with a particular password, not just by supplying the password. If an intruder doesn't know the user account name, they can't log on even if they have the password.

TIP Rename especially powerful accounts such as the NT administrator.

Rules for Password Protection Even more than you need to protect user names, protect passwords. A password should follow some basic rules.

NOTE You don't have to rely on good intentions to enforce these rules. Any NOS worth its salt supports minimum password length, reuse cycles, and the like. Some additional software will permit you to specify passwords that may not be used.

First, change passwords regularly. This means that a password can be no more than, say, 30 days old before it has to go to the Old Passwords' Home. It also means that you need to set rules about reusing passwords, insisting that people wait a certain period before recycling an old password. Otherwise, half the user base will plug in the same password over and over again to make it easier to log on. The older a password, the more likely that it's been compromised.

Passwords should be difficult to guess. Short and sweet is not what you're after here; define a minimum length for passwords (Microsoft recommends 11 or more characters) and don't let people use any of the following words:

- The user's name, spouse's, or children's names
- The user's birthday
- The names of the user's favorite sports teams
- Words related to their jobs
- A pet's name

TIP   Change any default passwords still in use immediately. Lists of default passwords for particular pieces of hardware (including the BIOS passwords you can assign to PCs) are widely available online.

To make passwords harder to guess, you can spell them oddly. Spell words backwards, make up nonsense words, or insert random characters into the password (for example, mort$ician). Or, if your NOS and authentication system support case-sensitive passwords, use random case settings (for example, FrOggiE). The most secure passwords are those created by a random password generator. Unfortunately, the user base won't like them because randomly generated passwords, such as JO%de)(Iwi82, are hard to remember and type accurately.

Just to complicate things, the final rule of password protection is that a password should not be written down. All these ploys will make it harder for people to type in their own passwords correctly, so they'll be inclined to keep passwords on a sticky pad on their monitor or under their keyboards. Discourage this.

These recommendations aren't all easy to implement, especially because some of them are contradictory. It's hard to think of a new 10-character word every 30 days. However, following these guidelines will make the passwords on your network harder to guess.

So, I'm Safe Now, Right? Following good password rules keeps casual prying out of the accounts but won't stand up to a really determined attempt to break into the system. You still need to keep people off the network.

Passwords that are difficult for humans to guess are still vulnerable to *dictionary attacks,* in which a piece of software supplies random combinations of characters to the login screen until there's a match.

Sniffers may also intercept passwords sent over the network. If the passwords are in cleartext, then the sniffer's operator will have the passwords without any further trouble. (Cleartext is unencrypted. More on what this means later in this chapter under "Using Encryption to Protect Data.") If the passwords are encrypted, they're still potentially vulnerable if intercepted, as password-cracking tools are far from uncommon (see the following sidebar).

L0phty Ideals

An organization called the L0pht (yes, that's a zero) has created a number of tools designed for stress-testing product security features. One in particular, called L0phtcrack, exploits a vulnerability in NT password encryption.

The problem is this: NT supports two challenge/response techniques: NTML2 and LM, LAN Manager's challenge/response system. If you're using the LM-compatible means of password authentication, you're very vulnerable to decryption. The problem lies in the way the hashed (encrypted) passwords are broken up and the password authenticated. LM authentication allows

Continued on next page

passwords to be attacked in seven-byte chunks. NTLM's authentication system, in contrast, is much harder to break. No passwords are invulnerable to a brute-force method, but it takes much longer to break down an NTLM challenge/response system than one based on LM—days, rather than seconds.

The one way to avoid the LM problem entirely is to have only NT machines on the network (just one Windows 95 client means that LM authentication must be supported) and have SP4 installed. For a complete technical description of the problem and proposed solutions, see `http://www.10pht.com/10phtcrack/rant.html` and `http://support.microsoft.com/support/kb/articles/q147/7/06.asp`.

And yes, this tool works. Feed the LM hash of a password into L0phtcrack and it will decode the password in as little as a few seconds, depending on the speed of the machine.

When Is a Password Not a Password? Biometric Devices and Smart Cards

Not all user authentication measures use typed passwords to authenticate user access. Installations requiring somewhat more stringent security measures may use smart cards, biometric devices, or some combination of the two to authenticate user identity. Such devices also can provide secure authentication for users not accustomed to passwords, or they may be used when passwords would be cumbersome but security is needed.

Getting Physical with Your Security System *Biometric devices* uniquely identify a user based on some physical characteristic, such as a fingerprint, handprint, retinal scan, voice print, or even some other identifier. The idea is to take the password system and make it better. The human brain can only think of so many 11-word passwords, but the pattern of blood vessels in a human's eye is unique and difficult to fake. This pattern, or any other pattern individual to you, can be picked up with a scanner and *digitized* (that is, converted to 1s and 0s—the same thing a modem does when translating analog data to digital for your computer). The digitized image is then stored in the equivalent of a password list file. When you present your fingertip/eye/hand/voice print to the scanner, the pattern in the original is scanned and digitized, then compared with the version already in the system. If the match is close enough, the system permits you to enter the area or the network.

Until recently, biometric devices were almost unheard of outside of a few high-security government installations. Voice print authentication suffered from the fact that people's voices sound different depending on the time of day and the speaker's mood, and retinal scanners were frustrated by bloodshot eyes in hay fever season. When the biometric authentication mechanisms didn't work, people would have to provide some other form of ID, or they were just waved along. An authentication system that gathers dust isn't very useful.

Improvements in voice recognition software and other technologies have significantly improved the creditability of biometric authentication tools. As they get more reliable, they're beginning to gain broader acceptance as a means of authenticating identity. But they're still not always popular mostly because they make people uncomfortable. If you can present them to your users as a way of making their lives easier ("We've got a new system that identifies you without needing a password!"), then you'll probably have better luck. Nontechnical users in particular seem to appreciate the convenience. Less invasive biometric devices such as fingerprint scanners seem to be easier to accept than more invasive ones such as retinal scanners.

Using Smart Cards At least in major metropolitan areas of the United States, more and more companies are requiring that their employees wear ID badges. The federal government has required this for ages; more recent developments include private firms and even public schools. Typically, these badges sport the pictures of their wearers and their names (or some identifier; very secure buildings may not use names). Often, the badges are color-coded, allowing a security guard to tell at a glance whether the wearer is allowed to be in a particular building or area.

In their simplest form, that's all there is to the badges: a picture and ID, like wearing your driver's license around your neck. *Smart cards*, in contrast, may include all that information but are characterized by some kind of electronic signature stored in a magnetic strip on the card. Your ATM card, which stores your account number on its magnetic strip, is one example of a smart card. Another example that does not require input from the user is a gate system that requires the badge holder to swipe her card through a digital scanner before the gate will open. Whether a pass code is required or the user just has to swipe the card, no match means no access.

NOTE   Smart cards can actually be biometric devices. Some companies make smart cards that use a digitized fingerprint as the digital signature.

We're pretty used to seeing smart cards in action as money cards or to authenticate access to a building. They're becoming available to authenticate access to a PC or network, too. Support for smart cards is becoming available in major operating systems and is already supported in some of them.

Organizing User Rights

One way or the other, the user has now been authenticated for access to the system. That doesn't necessarily mean that that user has full rights and access to files. On any reasonably secure network operating system, user access is defined by the group the user belongs to. The trick is to take advantage of that system by limiting user rights to the functions they need to perform. Chapter 10, "Network Operating Systems," describes some of the methods used by NT and NetWare to organize user rights and permissions; I'll touch on those methods again now.

NT Domains/Active Directory Whether using the domain structure or the Active Directory, NT/Windows 2000 uses essentially the same paradigm for organizing users. A *user* is a member of one or more groups that are associated with a Group ID (GID). Certain rights are associated with this group. Depending on the rights and permissions assigned, members of that group may read files, write files, create new files, use network-accessible devices, run administration utilities, and any other rights/permissions defined in the operating system (there are lots). Users may also be assigned rights and permissions on an individual basis, but they'll still be a member of at least one group.

> **NOTE** In the NT argot, the actions that users are allowed to do are defined by their *rights* and the objects they can access are defined by their *permissions*.

If a user is a member of more than one group with different rights assigned to each, the most permissive rule set applies. The only exception to this is if a group is specifically told *not* to do something; in that case, the user is denied the ability to do whatever that thing is even if it's permitted in another group he or she belongs to.

NetWare's Novell Directory Services (NDS) Rather than organizing rights according to users and groups, NetWare's NDS organizes them according to *organizational units* (OUs). An OU is typically some group of coworkers or part of a company, but it's user-defined so it can be pretty much any grouping that the designer of the organizational tree wishes.

In contrast to NT's domain-based system, NDS only permits a user to be a member of one OU at a time. Thus, to change the array of permissions associated with a particular user, you move that user to a new OU. The next time he logs on, he'll have the new permission set to work from.

Keeping Data Private

Authenticating users onto the network is only part of the process. Even once someone's logged in, you don't necessarily want that person to be able to peek in every network-accessible file. Therefore, you need to think about how files are organized and shared (or not shared), perhaps even password-protecting or encrypting important files.

Methods of File Organization

A basic feature of keeping people out of each other's files is proper file organization. It's much easier to protect files while still giving people the access they need if the files are logically grouped and those groups are protected. Here are a couple of suggestions that may help:

- Assign users home directories accessible only to them to store their work in progress.

TIP   Setting up user applications to automatically store files in the user's home directory also reduces the number of "lost" files—the ones the user accidentally saved to the default or program directory and now can't find.

- Put files into separate folders based on project or user group instead of pooling all company data files in one place.

- Don't share files or folders unless they need to be shared. Similarly, don't give people access to shared files or folders unless they specifically need that access.

You can still use user and group permissions to fine-tune access to shared directories, but this task will be made easier if the shares are subdivided a bit. The only catch is that the additional security will make it more inconvenient for users to access files that they are allowed to get to. Unfortunately, inconvenience is a common side effect to logical security. As noted at the beginning of this chapter, it's the nature of the beast.

Password-Protecting Files

The simplest method of protecting shared files on the network is to password-protect them, either with a password protection system built into the application or one that's part of the NOS's access control system. Password protection isn't very secure, particularly if more than one person needs to access the protected file, but it will keep the idle curious from reading private files.

NOTE I know I mention the idle curious pretty often, but that's the biggest security risk on your network—people who are bored and poking through files to see what's out there. Luckily, most people aren't interested enough to do any actual work to break into a protected file.

Not all NOSes support password protection—it's typically confined to the lower-end NOSes that don't support more advanced security. If your NOS doesn't support passwords and you want protection above and beyond that provided with user rights, you could encrypt the data (discussed next).

Using Encryption to Protect Data

A more secure method of protecting files is with *encryption*. Encryption is a blanket term for any method of garbling text using a certain algorithm called a *key* so that only the people who know the method can interpret the original message. This key may be really simple, such as substituting each letter for the one three letters later (see the following sidebar), or it may be very complex. The algorithms used in digital communications are complex, as computers have the calculating power to apply a complicated algorithm to plaintext.

NOTE   *Cleartext* or *plaintext* is any text that can be read and understood without special measures.

Is It Code or Encryption?

Although they're both used to make plaintext unreadable without help, encoding and encrypting aren't the same thing.

Encryption uses algorithms to obscure meaning. *Encoding* substitutes entire words or phrases to obscure the text's original meaning. For example, you might encrypt the plaintext "HELLO" to "JGNNQ," using the algorithm "take each letter and substitute it with the letter three places after it in the alphabet." If your message substituted "ZANY" every time the word "HELLO" appeared in the original, the message would be encoded.

So long as the key is kept secret, encoded messages may be more difficult to untangle than encrypted ones. Encrypted messages may be broken by brute-force methods or by application of a branch of mathematics called *crypto-analysis* in which patterns in the encryption are detected and analyzed. Encoded messages, in contrast, don't necessarily follow any kind of logic. Therefore, they're not as subject to systematic analysis—"HELLO" could just as easily be represented by "PIGGY" or "MY MOTHER WEARS ARMY BOOTS." As computers deal with numbers, not letters, they use encryption. Because computers are able to make calculations so quickly, they can use complex keys that are fairly resistant to cracking.

Types of Encryption   There are two main types of encryption: symmetric encryption and asymmetric (or public key) encryption.

Symmetric encryption uses the same algorithm to encrypt and decrypt plain text. Symmetric encryption works just fine for files to be used by only a single person because only that person needs to know the encryption algorithm. The problem arises when symmetric encryption is used for files shared by two or more people—

somehow, the person doing the encrypting must inform the person doing the decrypting about the key. Jane can encrypt data for Joe, but both Joe and Jane must know the key that locks and unlocks the data. If Jane works in Texas and Joe in Alaska, how does Joe determine the decryption key? Letters can be read, telephones can be tapped, trusted third parties can be suborned. It's not a secure system. One possibility lies in secure code books that list *ciphers* (encryption algorithms) that must be used in a certain way. For example, Cipher A is used on Wednesdays, so if you get an encrypted message prepared on a Wednesday, then you'd know you needed to use Key A to decrypt it. The trouble with code books, as both sides found out during the course of WWI, is that people steal them. Once a code book is stolen, it's useless. Not only is symmetric encryption not particularly secure, the lack of a preexisting key makes communication cumbersome between two people who don't have a standing relationship.

> **NOTE** Although the Data Encryption Standard (DES) created by the federal government uses symmetric encryption, DES is not usable for classified communications.

Public key encryption is the *de facto* standard for encrypting data intended for transmission. It uses two separate and user-specific keys for encryption and decryption—one public and one private. To encrypt data for someone, you must apply that person's public key to the plaintext. To decrypt the text, the recipient will apply their private key to it. Public keys are distributed, often as part of a person's e-mail signature. Private keys are kept, well, private.

> **NOTE** Some examples of public-key cryptosystems include Elgamal (named for its inventor, Taher Elgamal); RSA (named for its inventors, Ron Rivest, Adi Shamir, and Leonard Adleman); Diffie-Hellman (also named for its inventors); and DSA, the Digital Signature Algorithm (invented by David Kravitz, who apparently wasn't worried about being remembered for posterity).

An important element to this scheme is that the public and private keys are tuned to each other. To encrypt data for Doris, you must use her public key; to decrypt it, Doris must use her private key. There's no such thing as a general public key. Nor are the public and private keys related in any way; you can't guess or deduce one by knowing the other.

One example of a widely used public key system is Pretty Good Privacy (PGP), invented by Phil Zimmerman. Actually, PGP, widely used for Internet communications and possible to use for your own data, isn't purely a public key system. It has an additional symmetrical component called a *session key* that's unique to each encryption session. This session key is a number derived from the random movements of the mouse and the input from the keyboard.

The process of encryption with PGP works like this:

1. The plaintext to be encrypted is compressed.

2. PGP creates the session key.

3. The session key is used to encrypt the compressed plaintext.

4. The session key itself is encrypted using the public key.

When the recipient gets this package-within-a-package, he first decrypts the session key (using his private key) and then uses the session key to decrypt and decompress the plaintext. The next package he gets from the same sender will use the same public key and private key, but will have a new session key.

What Can Be Encrypted? Any data—passwords, text, or other information can and should be encrypted at least when passing it over a public network, and possibly at other times. Encryption is a very handy way of keeping locally stored personal files private on a machine that's used by more than one person. The more damage that could be done if the information were stolen, the more likely it is that you need to encrypt it.

Passwords, in particular, should never be sent over the network or stored as plaintext, but some may be nevertheless. (In the fall of 1998, Stanford University's internal network was compromised by someone with a sniffer, who over a period of about three weeks, picked up 4500 e-mail passwords being sent over the network as plaintext.) For anything remotely resembling network security, your network must encrypt passwords sent to the authentication server. Even the LM challenge/response system is better than nothing. Without encryption, an intruder doesn't even need L0phtcrack or the equivalent to decrypt passwords. Any NOS that doesn't use some method of encryption for passing passwords isn't secure at all.

NOTE   That said, you have little say in how or whether passwords are encrypted for user authentication. For example, with NT, you can pick one of two options in how passwords are encrypted: LM for Windows 9.*x* clients and NTLM2 for NT-based clients.

Remote Access Security Issues

Opening up the network to people dialing in from the outside exposes the network to new security risks. Local LAN access allows you to secure the building and keep out intruders. If you walk through the office, you can see everyone who's using a computer. This isn't possible with remote access—all you know about someone who's logged in remotely is what account they're using. That tells you nothing about who's using it. There's also the problem of that long, unprotected cable connecting the remote user to the network. Given that you can't prevent a public telephone line from being monitored at some point along the way, you need some method of preventing an intruder from picking up password information by tapping the channel.

Session Protection with CHAP and PAP

The most basic form of remote security lies in making sure that your remote users are who they say they are. As Point-to-Point Protocol (PPP) is the most commonly used line protocol for remote communications, this section will examine the two protection measures supplied with PPP: CHAP (the Challenge Handshake Authentication Protocol) and PAP (the Password Authentication Protocol). Both security protocols implement a secrets file to authenticate user identity, but each uses it a little differently.

> **NOTE**   PPP does not require authentication—it's just an option. Security is implemented after the logical link has been created but not opened.

How Does PAP Work? PAP is the least secure of the two protocols, but the one used by remote clients that don't support CHAP. When a client attempts to initiate a session with a remote access server, the client sends the account user name and password to the server. (This password may or may not be encrypted.) The server compares the user name and password to its secrets file. If there's a match, the client is in. If not, the connection is refused. The drawback to this method is that the password is actually sent over the PPP connection where it could be picked up. It's also vulnerable to repeated attacks.

How Does CHAP Work? The drawbacks of PAP led to the development of another security protocol: CHAP. CHAP's authentication process works somewhat differently. When the client attempts to initiate a session, the server sends the client the *challenge*—a randomly generated number—and the name of the server to respond to. The client is responsible for encrypting the challenge properly and sending back the right response. To do so, the client looks in its own plaintext secrets file for the response to that challenge. When it finds the right response, it combines the result with the original challenge, encrypts the entire string, and sends the encrypted string back to the server. The server then decrypts the package and compares the challenge and response to its own secrets database. If they match, the client session is authenticated and begins; otherwise, the session is closed or, in some implementations, rerouted to a session with extremely limited network access. The advantage over PAP is that at no time is the secret sent over the network so it can't be picked up and broken into.

Another advantage to CHAP is that the authentication process doesn't necessarily end with the original authentication. At intervals, the server may send another challenge to the client to make sure that an intruder didn't take over the session in the mean time. If at any point the client can't respond as required, the session ends.

Establishing a RADIUS of Fire

Not all remote clients can use CHAP or PAP; some will connect to the network with Telnet or a UNIX login. To provide a centralized authentication server for a variety of client types, the Remote Authentication Dial-In User Service (RADIUS) protocol was developed. RADIUS is used to transport authentication, authorization, and configuration information between a network access server that wants to authenticate dial-in sessions and a shared authentication server. This way, a single database of user accounts can be maintained for a variety of account types.

When a client uses RADIUS to dial up to a network, the initial connection is with the network access server. This server passes the authentication information from the client to the authentication server. The authentication server authorizes the connection (or indicates that the connection could not be authorized and refuses it). It also tells the network access server what kind of connection that particular client is expecting (Telnet, PPP, SLIP, or UNIX login).

Continued on next page

What about security between the network access servers and the authentication servers? Their interaction is CHAP-like, authenticated by a shared secrets database so that their passwords are never sent over the network connection. If the remote client's login method requires the remote user to supply the network access server with a password, that password is encrypted with the RSA public key cryptosystem when sent between the network access server and authentication server.

Restricting Users to Part of the Network

Once the remote user has been authenticated on the network, she's still not always able to roam freely amongst the network resources. Many network administrators restrict remote user access to the network; the permissions are more restricted than they would be if the user logged on locally.

How Far Does Remote Access Go? Not all remote access offers access to more than the server doing the authenticating. To isolate remote users from sensitive information, let them get to the remote access functions—e-mail, perhaps some read-only files—but keep them out of the main network. With some remote access servers— Windows 98's remote service, for one—this is the only option. Others, such as NT's remote access server product, permit you to specify whether a user may browse the network or only use server resources.

Configuring Bindings If you want to provide partial access to the network, you can do that by picking and choosing the protocols in play on each part of the network. As you may recall from Chapter 3, "Networking Protocols and Application Programming Interfaces," a protocol must be bound to a piece of network hardware or service to be accessible to that hardware or service; these configurations are called bindings. More simply, you can't send traffic on a part of the network for which you don't have an installed protocol.

In practical terms, dial-up users will be running TCP/IP. Therefore, if you want to afford remote users some access to the network, but not to all of it, unbind TCP/IP from servers you don't want the users to touch. No relying on security settings or authentication procedures—you simply can't get there from here because TCP/IP isn't supported on the segment. This works for ordinary LAN users, too.

Monitoring the System

As a final security measure, log access to the network. Any decent NOS supports some kind of security logging (such as NT's Event Viewer) to track who's doing what on the network. You can use this logging to monitor successful and attempted logins as well as successful and attempted access to files and folders shared from the server being monitored.

Only recent information will really help you much, and if you try to read too many log entries at once, you won't be able to concentrate well enough to get much out of them. Eliminate old entries, saving them to text files or spreadsheets if you want to have the old data to refer to, and review the logs once a week or so. By doing this, you can keep an eye out for repeated failed accesses that may indicate attempts to break into the network or secure files.

Save Those Log Files!

If you've set up your security logging to erase old entries after a certain period (say, a week) then *save the old logs before wiping*. You won't always detect an intruder in a week. When you do detect suspicious activity, you'll want to be able to see whether there's a pattern of user accounts used or objects accessed.

For example, say that you detect odd activity during the week of 5/17. Someone's hacked into the Microsoft Exchange 5.5 mail server. The intruder gave himself search capabilities and thus turned off everyone else's search capabilities, meaning that no one can read the global address book. Users start complaining to you that the mail server's broken, you check the security logs, and sure enough, the change in permissions shows up. So far, so good. You can fix the problem.

Wait a minute, though: How did the intruder get in? Is this the first stage of an attack or a continuation of a previous attack? You know that one of the UNIX servers on the network was hacked into on 4/30 and you disabled that account then. However, in your network, some users with low-level network administrator rights have two accounts with the same name and password—one for the NT domain and one for UNIX. (This, by the way, is a bad idea for reasons that are probably now obvious.) Is the account used to break into the Exchange server the one that matches the disabled UNIX account? You can't tell because you don't have the old logs. They were wiped when they were seven days old.

For log files to be useful, they need to be fairly small, so wiping old entries every week or so is probably wise. However, nothing says that you can't save old logs as a spreadsheet or even as a text file for later conversion.

Keeping Data Available

Not only does your network's data need to be hidden from those who have no business looking at it, that data also needs to be available in the first place. Preventing denial of service attacks and data loss due to accidentally or maliciously deleted data is part of your job.

Beating Denial of Service Attacks

A *denial of service* (DOS) is any condition under which some part or parts of the network becomes unavailable. Generally, this is done deliberately with a program that produces so much "junk data" that the junk crowds out the legitimate use. Examples might include:

- Generating spam to throw at a mail server, making it impossible for legitimate users to get to the mail server

- Consuming all CPU cycles on the server

- Causing the server to crash

- Repeatedly pinging a server, creating a lot of noise on the network as the server responds to pings

In short, if you can't use your network because of something someone else did to it, you've experienced a DOS attack.

Two of the better-known DOS attacks around are the Teardrop and Land attacks, which both exploit weaknesses in TCP/IP to interfere with networks connected to the Internet. Using either kind of attack, a remote user can crash a vulnerable server. For example, during a Land attack, an attacker might send repeated broadcast messages to a router connected to an Ethernet LAN. That router would then repeat the broadcast on the LAN, tying up traffic.

NOTE
Land attacks can come in any of several forms, but all have in common the use of IP address *spoofing* (that is, falsifying the source address).

Most DOS attacks come from outside the LAN, so the best way to prevent DOS attacks is to institute a *firewall* on your network. A firewall is a hardware or software router that stands between your internal network and another network—public or private. This router use *ingress filtering* to inspect incoming packets and drop any that shouldn't be accepted. As discussed in Chapter 14, "Principles of Network Management," some services use ports to listen for messages; for example, SNMP uses port 161. Depending on your network, you may want to block administrative ports from external access so that people can't administer the router except from the LAN.

NOTE
Actually, you should probably start by blocking all ports and then opening them only as necessary. That way, you'll know that the network is secure at first. You'll also look like the good guy, making resources available, instead of the bad guy, taking away resources.

To make sure that the firewall works properly, it should be updated with any patches issued by its manufacturer to close off vulnerabilities.

TIP
Keep track of the packets your firewall discards in case a pattern indicates a determined effort to break into your network.

Data Deletion

It might be hard to figure out what's wrong at first when you're hit with a DOS attack—the network slows down or stops, but you may not immediately realize why. Missing data, on the other hand, is a bit easier to detect. Therefore, to keep data available you need to make sure that backup copies of it exist and that destructive utilities aren't available to just anyone.

Back Up!

The first step to avoiding data loss is to keep copies of the data on hand in the first place. Chapter 16, "Disaster Recovery," will discuss backup strategies and other preventative measures in more detail.

Hide Destructive Utilities

Before Windows became ubiquitous, hiding destructive utilities used to be easier. If you didn't want someone to use FORMAT and wipe out his or her hard disk, for example, you'd rename FORMAT (or DELETE, or DELTREE) to something else. For an extra measure of protection, you'd use the –h attribute to hide tools so that they wouldn't appear in a DIR listing; for all practical purposes, you'd have to know the tools were there and what their names were before you could use them. This keeps disgruntled employees from typing DELTREE C: on their last day and wiping out the accounting files, or mistaken staff from wiping out the contents of a hard disk while attempting to format a floppy.

Ah, happy days. Now the tools of destruction are on every desktop and they're hard to remove. For users running dual-boot NT/Windows 95/98 systems, there's even a new peril in the form of the CONVERT command. CONVERT looks innocuous at first. It's a tool to convert FAT volumes to NTFS, thus using the disk space on large disks more efficiently and gaining some security features not available to FAT. The data on the drive is not affected by the conversion, so the tool looks harmless. The only trouble is that Windows 95/98 cannot read NTFS volumes and CONVERT is irreversible. The only way to make a converted volume visible to Windows 95/98 again is to reformat the drive with FAT and replace the data destroyed in the formatting.

TIP   Although NT 4 and earlier can't read the FAT32 volumes supported by Windows 95 OSR2 and Windows 98, it's not a disaster if a FAT drive on a dual-boot machine is converted to FAT32. A tool (called FAT32 for Windows NT, appropriately enough) that allows NT 4 to read FAT32 volumes is available from `www.sysinternals.com`. Install the tool and the volumes are accessible.

If your clients are using Windows and IE4, then the tools are *really* hard to remove because of the browser's integration with the File Manager interface. Anyone who's used IE4 and has more than basic computer skills has seen that you can view the contents of any logical drive by typing its drive letter. (Netscape doesn't support browsing the local drives with the browser.) Once you've done so, the interface changes to give you access to all the file management tools, including the aforementioned formatting and deletion tools.

What can you do about this? First, you can use system policies (described in Chapter 14, "Principles of Network Management") to limit the applications that network users can run. (By the way, this means disabling the Run command on the Start menu, disabling Explorer, and generally removing any interface that allows users to get to non-sanctioned applications.) Don't use IE4 or later unless it's okay to let users browse their logical drives. Limit the drives they have access to and keep those backups handy in case someone makes a mistake and formats the wrong drive.

Physical Security

There's more to network security than setting user permissions and authenticating identity. Some of the security issues relate to who's got physical access to the parts of the network, not just the logical components.

Securing the Servers

It's not yet exactly common to secure servers, but it's far from unknown. Big companies are likely to be especially security conscious about this matter, locking servers behind closed doors or removing physical shutdown.

Isolating Servers

The most extreme method of securing the servers is to put them behind a locked door—or a couple of locked doors, sometimes. To make it easier to change the locks in case of personnel changes, you can use a keypad to guard access to the server area.

Locking up the servers may sound a little extreme, but it's really not a bad idea if you have the resources to accomplish it. First, it keeps intruders away from the servers so that they can't perform network administration tasks, or even steal the hard disks. Second, it reduces the chances of accidental damage caused by someone just being around the server and damaging it in some way. You don't really want anyone around the servers except the IS staff anyway.

Removing Physical Shutdown

If locking up the servers isn't practical, then you can still secure them a bit by disabling the physical shutdown tools—the Reset button and The Big Red Switch. Without those, it's still possible to shut down a server if you really want to by severing the power cord, but it's more of a pain and much less subtle.

Almost certainly, you'll want to disable the shutdown tools on the login screen, if any exist. It should not be possible to shut down the server without logging on first. Granted, it's more inconvenient to reboot if necessary, but that prevents anyone from mistaking the production server for a test server and shutting it down while people have files open—something I saw happen a few years ago.

Combating Electronic Surveillance Attacks

Just in case you weren't already sufficiently nervous about having your network broken into, there's one more possibility to consider: electronic surveillance. This is a pretty remote possibility—most people aren't willing to try this hard to crack your system, and if you're dealing with the kind of data that attracts this level of attention, then you've probably already got prophylactic measures in place—but it's real.

Have you ever seen a movie in which a van full of people parks outside a house and intercepts electronic signals? There are several kinds of electronic surveillance, but one of them is called a *tempest attack.* Well-equipped system crackers can intercept the electronic emissions from your computers, and thus compromise your passwords and messages. It is possible to pick up signals from the radiation produced by a monitor and reconstruct the contents of the display. (Low radiation monitors help avoid this problem, but older monitors may not qualify.)

What can you do about this? The most effective way to avoid such an attack is with proper shielding to keep the electrical emissions in the room or building where they're generated. This can be done by shielding the room or shielding the equipment using

TEMPEST shielding technology. The people who use TEMPEST anti-surveillance technology most are government agencies and defense contractors. If you're really concerned about electronic surveillance, you can use a commercial version of this technology. It won't have all the bells and whistles of the official version, but it will offer some protection.

NOTE   TEMPEST is a classified code name, not an acronym.

For those of us who can't afford to use TEMPEST but are concerned about surveillance, there are still some simple countermeasures to take. No protection is perfect, but you can at least make it more difficult for anyone to intercept electromagnetic interference (EMI) from your computer or network.

Use quiet computers. Computers must be designed to meet certain FCC regulations about the number of emissions they can give off, but all computers make some emissions. The computers certified for home use (Class B) emit less EMI than the computers certified for business use (Class A); use Class B computers. Furthermore, don't operate the computer with the cover off and keep slot covers on any unused slots. This is better for your computer anyway, as the computer's fan will operate more efficiently in a closed environment.

If you're *really* concerned about emissions, you could keep your computer in a Faraday cage. This structure keeps EMI inside the cage so it can't escape to be picked up by surveillance equipment.

Shield your cables, or use cables that don't emit EMI at all. From the discussions of Chapter 1, "Basic Networking Concepts and Components," you know that the copper wires making up network cables are really just large antennae at heart. To keep them from exhibiting their true nature, they're shielded. The better the shielding, the lower the EMI radiation. For that reason, fiber optic cable is the best protection against electronic surveillance, as it doesn't emit EMI at all. Fiber isn't immune from tapping, but tapping it requires physical access to the cable.

NOTE   Ever picked up your wireless telephone to realize that you were accidentally eavesdropping on your neighbor's telephone conversation? If you're using a wireless network, you need to encrypt everything if you want any protection at all.

Network cables aren't the only potential sources of EMI, either. Protect power cords and telephone wires with EMI filters.

Finally, if you want to see how much EMI the components of your network are giving off, get a portable AM radio and walk around your office, holding the radio to the cables and PCs. Ideally, you shouldn't notice a serious increase in static when you hold the radio close to a component.

Don't worry about this overmuch. It's not likely that anyone is going to spy on you in this way; some of the measures suggested here (like that Faraday cage) are serious overkill for just about anyone who reads this book. Then again, a low-EMI network is a Good Thing anyway.

Avoiding Viral Infections

The last element of network security I'll talk about in this chapter concerns viruses. Technically, *viruses* are self-perpetuating executables introduced into your computer under stealth; more generally, you'll hear people call any malicious program, self-perpetuating or not, a virus. To keep things simple, I'll stick with the more general definition so I'm not forced to discuss attacks from worms, viruses, malicious but non-perpetuating executables, and Trojan Horses separately.

Just Because It's Not a Virus Doesn't Make It Benign

There's plenty of malicious code out there that is not self-replicating and therefore technically not a virus. It's still dangerous and undesirable, however. During 1998, one malicious executable (ME), called BackOrifice, got a fair amount of press time. When run on a Windows 95/98 computer, this program gave remote control access via the Internet to an intruder. Less well known than BackOrifice is a similar ME called NTBus that works on NT machines.

Not worried yet? Other possibilities include Java applets designed to crash your browser, ActiveX components that can be any executable, or innocuous sounding .EXEs that are in fact batch files that format your boot drive.

The lesson to be learned from all this is that it's a bad idea to run applications from an unknown source. Even if it's not a virus, it can still ruin your day.

Whatever definition you use, viruses really aren't something you want on your computer or network. Even if they're not blatantly destructive, they're annoying, interfere with your work, and consume resources you could be using for something else. A retired hacker/cracker friend of mine once told me that virus writers don't necessarily get respect even among the "black hat" (that is, criminal, or at least extralegal) elements of the hacker community. As my friend put it, if you're that good at coding and want to show off, make something useful (like WinZip) and put it in the public domain.

The sole benefit to society wrought from viruses is that they keep Norton, Dr. Solomon, and other makers of anti-virus software in business. Not enough of a justification, in my book.

Types of Viruses

Viruses aren't a homogenous group. Different viruses do different things and their methods of attack depend on their types. Most, however, have some elements in common:

- A replicating element (a worm)

- A payload

- A logic bomb that determines the conditions under which the payload will be executed

- A method of concealment (a Trojan Horse)

These elements allow a virus to spread, do their little routine (whatever it is), and conceal themselves so that you'll let them in to do their dirty work. Not all viruses have all components. A pure Trojan that pretends to be a screen saver and then wipes out your hard disk won't have much chance to replicate itself. Also, a worm that just keeps running, making more copies of itself so to eat up system resources isn't always concealed.

Another way to characterize viruses is by looking at their preferred operating environments. If a virus attaches itself to another program, then it's called a *parasitic*, or *program*, *virus*. If it's more comfortable hanging out in the boot sector of a data disk, it's a *boot sector virus*.

NOTE   Some viruses have characteristics of both program and boot sector viruses.

The one element that all viruses have in common is some kind of executable element. A virus is a program. It cannot be an ASCII file, so it can't be an e-mail message. It could certainly be sent as an attachment to an e-mail message, and if you were incautious enough to automatically run all attachments as soon as you got them, you'd be a sitting duck for a virus infection. However, the e-mail itself is not the virus; it's just an innocent bystander.

Program Viruses

Program viruses begin their work by infecting ordinary program files, perhaps those used in your operating system. When the infected program file is run, the virus is "armed" like a grenade. It doesn't necessarily go off once it's run, but it's ready when its logical conditions are met.

Document Infectors The most common type of viruses found "in the wild" (that is, outside of a virus lab) today are *macro viruses*. Macro viruses are Microsoft Office macros just like one you might create yourself, generally targeting Microsoft Word. Modern ones are written in Visual Basic for Applications (VBA) and supported by Office 97, but some are also written in Word-Basic and thus can infect files created with older versions of Word. The simple nature of the language makes it very easy for even unskilled programmers to write viruses—probably the reason why macro viruses have become so common.

The macro is attached to the document template. When you open the document, the macro infects any open templates (notably NORMAL.DOT, which is the alternate template for any document created in Word). The virus also does whatever its payload intends—forces you to save changes to a document in a new file instead of editing the existing one, attempting to delete system files, or just infecting every file that you open so that the virus spreads.

NOTE   Word macro viruses can't be passed to other word processors, even if those processors can display the infected documents. It's certainly possible to write macro viruses for any application that supports a macro language, but so far this hasn't yet happened, or at least no such viruses have appeared in the wild.

E-mail and the ubiquity of Word have permitted macro viruses to spread very quickly. Most people, these days, would hopefully exercise a little caution when it came to running a new program if they didn't know where it came from. (If you're not already careful about that, hopefully you will be after reading this section.) Documents are just documents, though, right? Someone sends you a file to look over, and you click on the link in your e-mail client to open it. You don't necessarily think about virus checking it first. Sadly, with macro viruses in the wild, PC users must do what Macintosh users have had to do for ages to ward off viruses: check everything. On a Macintosh, every data file is linked to an executable file, which meant that Macintosh viruses were rampant. Now that viruses are part of PC data files, PC owners have to be as careful as Mac users have had to be.

What can you do about macro viruses? One solution is to write-protect the global Word template (NORMAL.DOT), but that solution means that you can't change it either. If you're running Office 97, you can have Word prompt you when you try to open a document that has any macros in it, virus or no. You can then choose to enable or disable all macros in the document. (One effect that the spread of macro viruses has had is to diminish the usefulness of the macro tool, as people are apt not to use macros embedded in any document lest they be a virus.) Better (and the answer to avoiding most virus infections) to get a virus scanner and keep it updated. When someone e-mails you a document, virus-check it before opening it.

If your global template gets infected, you can delete NORMAL .DOT to kill the infection. When you restart Word, a new copy of the global template will be created.

A New Target—The System BIOS This is something new. I'm not going into detailed descriptions of most viruses, but this one is the first of its breed and potentially very destructive.

Until the summer of 1998, viruses were strictly a software problem. They might overwrite the master boot record (MBR) on your hard disk, or format it, but both of those problems could be resolved with backups. Annoying, and potentially destructive if you hadn't made preparations, but you could live with it.

That changed when the CIH virus was confirmed in June 1998. This program virus infects .EXE files, dividing the virus code among several .EXEs and hiding it in unused areas of the executables. The payload executes on the 26th of each month (or June 26, depending on the version you've got). It overwrites part of your system BIOS and the first 1MB of your boot disk, where the MBR is stored. This applies to any Windows 95/98 computer with a flash (updateable) BIOS. If your computer's BIOS is set to read-only as is the case on older PCs, then your computer can't be infected with this virus. Not sure whether your BIOS accepts flash updates? Check the computer's documentation or ask the manufacturer.

You can fix the MBR problem if you've backed up the MBR, but you can't boot until you've rewritten the BIOS. Some computers allow you to copy the BIOS, so if this is possible for your system and if you've done it, you might be able to recover. Otherwise, you'll have to buy a new BIOS and hope that the BIOS chip isn't soldered to the motherboard, or else you'll be buying a new motherboard to go with it.

Although it's difficult to tell just how widespread the CIH virus is, its existence in the wild is confirmed. As of late 1998, it's also already mutated to include at least two forms.

Boot Viruses

After macro viruses, the second most common type of virus in the wild today are *boot sector viruses*. These become active and infectious when the boot sector of the infected disk is read. From that time, they're loaded in memory and can infect other disks, such as floppies.

Boot sector viruses were easily spread when the most common method of passing information from PC to PC was to put the file on a floppy. Someone with a boot sector virus would give you the January sales spreadsheet on a floppy disk. You'd copy the spreadsheet from a floppy to the hard disk, but that wouldn't infect your machine. However, if you forgot that the floppy disk was in your A: drive and rebooted, you'd infect your computer when the BIOS read the floppy disk's boot sector. It didn't matter whether the floppy was bootable, just accessing the disk did the damage. Once it had infected your disk and every time you booted thereafter, the virus would be resident in memory and intent on infecting floppy disks.

These days, boot viruses still spread but are less common. The LAN makes file sharing much easier, so floppy disks and Sneakernet (walking between computers to copy files stored on floppy disk) aren't needed as much. Even more important, the omnipresence of the Internet and other e-mail access has made it easy to transfer files even between PCs on different networks.

The trick to avoid infection from boot sector viruses is not to boot from floppies. You can get yourself in the habit of always leaving the floppy drive door open, but there are also ways of keeping computers from booting from the floppy drive at all. Edit the system configuration settings so that the system searches for a bootable drive first at C:, *then* at A:. To avoid infecting floppies in the first place, write-protect them to keep the virus from writing to them.

WARNING Be careful when you're editing the boot order. If you accidentally set up the machine to boot from the CD-ROM drive, the machine will attempt to boot from a CD if one's in the drive. The error-handling for this isn't all it could be—on some machines, all you'll know is that there's a non-system disk error. Scary, when you think you're reading from the hard disk.

Alternatively, disable the floppy drive altogether; this is a common configuration on very locked-down machines. Thin client devices such as Windows terminals can't be infected with boot viruses at all because they have no hard or floppy drives.

Some boot viruses are *polymorphic,* meaning that they are memory-resident like the program viruses described in the next section.

Keep Infections at Bay

How scary are viruses? I've been working with computers in one form or another, in business offices and in consulting firms, since the early 1980s. Now that I've established my geezer credentials, I can tell you that in this time I have personally seen two viruses outside of a test setting—that is, that were unintentional infections. One was a macro virus and one was a boot virus. I've heard of a few other infections from people I was talking to, but not many. You need to be careful about viruses. You do *not* need to be panicked. If you take the precautions you should be taking in preparation for any other disaster (regular backups for one), then the worst that can happen to you with most viruses is a public relations nightmare when your client discovers that you've sent them an infected file.

Remember, a virus is a program. It cannot be an e-mail message. Someone sending you a virus as an e-mail attachment does not infect your computer. Someone giving you an infected floppy that you put in your drive does not infect your computer. Reading from the floppy doesn't infect the computer, so long as you don't run the program that has the virus in it. Run the virus, or boot from the infected boot sector though, and you're infected.

The best way to keep infections at bay is to get a reputable virus scanner or monitor. A *virus scanner* scans program files, looking for known *virus signatures* (hexadecimal strings). A *virus monitor* is a terminate and stay resident (TSR) program (like a virus itself) that watches for virus-like activity, such as writes to the boot sector. Keep the anti-viral tools up to date with the regularly posted updates from the manufacturers' Web sites or FTP sites, and you'll have the latest known virus signatures. A link to online reviews of anti-virus tools is on the Web site for this book.

TIP　Some will suggest you run two anti-virus monitors at once, on the principle that what one tool misses another might pick up. According to David Stang, virus expert and founder of the National Computer Security Association, you needn't bother. At best, you won't improve the situation. At worst, you'll cause the monitors to interfere with or crash each other.

How do you choose a virus tool? It's hard to get much out of some ratings systems. Some anti-virus tools say that they're better because they detect more viruses than their rivals, but going by the numbers in this way can be misleading. Some products count five variations of a single virus as five viruses, and some count that as one virus. Also, some viruses use the Mutating Engine's virus mutator to become polymorphic, meaning that one virus may be recognized but a close cousin may not.

More meaningful numbers might be seen from tests that pit several products against each other on the same set of viruses, with the product that detects the most being the most effective. Small differences won't be indicative of better performance (the scanner that detects 97 percent of the viruses in the test isn't necessarily superior to the scanner that detects 95 percent of the viruses in the test) but larger differences will be. On the whole, in addition to looking at these success and failure rates, I'd recommend that you choose a package based on the criteria described in Table 15.2.

TABLE 15.2: Anti-Virus Tool Criteria

Criteria	Description
Speed	How quickly does the scanner run? A slow scanner may make users impatient.
Memory usage	Does the scanner use conventional memory or upper memory? How much memory does it need to run?
False positives	A scanner that reports a lot of false positives (that is, viruses that aren't there) is worse than useless. Remember the boy who cried wolf?
Frequency of updates	New viruses appear all the time. How often is your tool updated to keep up with the changes? Do updates cost anything?
Cost	How much does the tool cost? How does licensing work?
Platform	Does the scanner work with your operating system? What do you have to do to thoroughly scan your PC?

Review these options and then choose an anti-virus scanner based on the answers you get. Preferably, you'll protect both the servers and the workstations, but if you have to choose one, choose the workstations. Servers are much less likely to become infected.

Summary

Network security is a big topic and this book only devoted a chapter to it. After reading these pages, however, you should have a taste for the kinds of situations you need to watch for and the measures you can take to protect your network from them. To review:

- Before putting any security plan into effect, figure out what viable threats exist. You can't prepare for everything, so prepare yourself for what's possible.

- Do cost accounting to figure out the cost of the protection relative to the value of the data being protected.

- Employ user authentication techniques to make sure that only valid users have access to network resources, and guard the security information for user accounts.

- If you want extra protection, encrypt data.

- Protect your network from attacks from the outside world that can disrupt service or destroy data.

If you can do all that *and* have a measure of luck, you can skip the final chapter, "Disaster Recovery." If you're like most of us, though, you'd better read on.

EXERCISE 15

1. What is the purpose of an SID on an NT network?

2. Microsoft recommends using passwords that are at least _____ characters long.

3. What is L0phtcrack and what is its function?

4. _____ divides users into groups to assign rights and object permissions; _____ divides users into organizational units to assign rights.

5. With NDS, how many OUs can one person belong to?

6. RSA is one example of a _____ cryptosystem.

7. True or false. PGP involves symmetric encryption.

8. DES is one example of a _____ cryptosystem.

9. What is CHAP and how does it work?

10. Which is more secure: CHAP or PAP? Why?

11. Under what circumstances would you need a server that supported RADIUS?

12. What are bindings and why are they significant?

13. An outside attack that ties up a server so no legitimate requests can be processed is one example of a _____ attack.

14. What does IE4 have to do with defining a set of permitted applications to run?

15. True or false. Viruses affect only software.

EXERCISE 15 CONTINUED

16. Which of the following does not protect you from a tempest attack? Choose all that apply.

   A. Using low-radiation monitors

   B. Using Class A PCs

   C Installing EMI filters for telephone and power cables

   D. Installing virus protection on the server

17. Which is the most common type of virus today?

   A. Boot sector

   B. Worm

   C. Macro

   D. BIOS

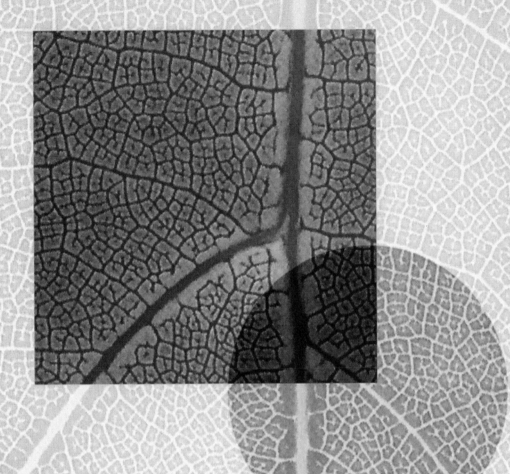

16

Disaster Recovery

This book started many years ago as a class on building, supporting, maintaining, and troubleshooting LANs. The people taking this class were all support people and network administrators, some coming up from the PC stand-alone world, some migrating to LANs from a mainframe environment, and some more experienced but looking to brush up on their skills. When we got to the part on disaster planning, whomever was teaching started a little exchange that went something like this:

"How many of you have disaster recovery plans in place?"

Most hands went up.

"How many of you have *written* disaster recovery plans in place?"

Many of the hands went down.

"How many of you have actually tested those plans and revised them where they didn't work?"

Most of the hands went down, most people looked sheepish, and it's a good bet that at least one of the people who still had his hand up was either lying or didn't hear the question.

There comes a time in everyone's life when a situation completely goes to pot. The server won't boot. The office burns down. The backups are destroyed. It's not fun to think about the file server going down in flames, but it's a heck of a lot better thinking about it ahead of time than explaining to your boss why you can't replace the network to its previous state. In this chapter, I'll talk about disaster recovery planning, including who's involved, what such a plan needs to encompass, and some possible solutions you can implement to avert or recover from disaster.

Exploring the Nature of Disaster

"Disaster" sounds terrifically melodramatic. If you think of disaster as limited to natural catastrophes or events on the order of the Oklahoma City or World Trade Center bombings, you might not think of disaster as being very close at hand.

A more realistic definition of disaster is any event or circumstance that could keep your company or organization from functioning for an undetermined length of time. That doesn't just encompass data loss, but anything that would interrupt operations; with that definition, disaster starts looking a lot closer.

You could divide the potential causes of disasters into three categories:

- Events
- Breakdowns
- Behavior

These categories aren't mutually exclusive, of course; an event could lead to a breakdown, or one breakdown could expose a behavior that exacerbates the disaster. For the purposes of recovering from a disaster, it doesn't always matter what caused it. For preparing for it, though, it does.

Event-Related Disasters

Having lived in one part or another of almost all the United States, I have a healthy appreciation of the power of nature to shut down a business. If you want an event-related disaster, a hurricane makes a good one. You have to shut down operations to evacuate; there's an excellent chance of water damage, or worse; you can't get needed supplies; and power shuts down. Then again, there are fires and earthquakes in California, tornadoes in the

Midwest, freak spring snowstorms that shut down power and roads for much of New England for days, and flooding and electrical storms just about everywhere.

A disaster-causing event doesn't have to be as big as an earthquake or Hurricane George, either. A fire that starts in one building of an office park is certainly a threat, as is a broken water main that floods part of your building. Even if the disaster doesn't touch your office directly, you can still feel its effects. A couple of years ago, there was major flooding in the Virginia city where I live. I live and work on top of one of the hills, so I didn't notice more than the heavy rain. Well, I noticed my telephone lines going out for two days because the river going through town had risen 30 feet and flooded out the telephone system. When you conduct your business remotely, downed telephone lines are a minor disaster in terms of making it difficult or impossible to conduct business normally or at all.

You get the idea. Events may not touch you directly, but they can cramp your style nonetheless.

Equipment Breakdowns

It is the nature of machinery—even solid-state machinery—to break down periodically. The more machinery you've got, the more likely it is that some of it will break at some point. Nor does the breakdown have to directly involve the machinery you need to function. For example, if the air conditioning goes out and it's hot outside, you may not be able to run the servers even if you can persuade the staff that they can function in 95-degree weather. Try to run a server for long in that environment and you'll bake it.

The good news is that breakdown disasters are often the easiest to plan for. More so than human-related disasters, at any rate.

Behavior Problems

Most of us who've lived in one part of the country for even a year or two can anticipate weather-related problems. Broken equipment problems can be resolved with redundancy in equipment.

Human-related problems can be another matter entirely. There are the obvious ones like major flu outbreaks, or strikes, but thankfully those aren't often the worry of the network administrator or other technical staff unless they're the ones who are sick or on strike. However, deliberate sabotage (that DELETE *.* gambit); ignoring safe computing advice and introducing viruses into the network; or someone bringing in unlicensed software, spreading it throughout the company and bringing the wrath of the SPA down on your head are also human-related problems, and ones likely to directly concern you.

Prepping for Disaster—Backups

Before you even think about a disaster recovery plan, you need to think about backups. Backups are so essential a part of a network administration plan that they should be an "of course" part of your network, not part of the disaster recovery plan.

In addition to the obvious role of permitting you to replace the network's data when someone puts a bullet through the file server's hard drive, backups are essential for a couple of less dramatic but still potentially bad situations:

- Replacing corrupted files
  - Data files
  - System files
  - Template files
- Needing copies of files last used several years ago

These are small problems in comparison to the difficulty of replacing the entire company data files, but they are not always inconsequential, either.

Understanding Backup Types

In the Windows world at least, there are four main types of backups (see Table 16.1). Each takes advantage of the file attribute archive bit to tune how the backup works.

TABLE 16.1: Backup Types

Backup Type	Copy Set	Resets Archive Bit?
Full	Copies all files selected for backup, regardless of whether their archive bit was set.	Yes
Incremental	Copies only files with the archive bit set.	Yes
Differential	Copies only files with the archive bit set.	No
Daily	Copies only files with the archive bit *and* timestamped for the day of backup.	No

NOTE These are common backup types; some backup utilities may offer further options. Version 7.*x* of Seagate's Backup Exec supports working set backups, for example, which back up all files accessed within a user-defined period.

It's not practical to copy every file every day, but you need a base set of all files on the system. Thus, an effective backup plan will incorporate more than one type of backup, most often a full backup at regular intervals (such as each week) and supplemented with a daily incremental or differential backup. Generally, daily backups are only useful if you're going on a trip and want to take copies of your most recently changed files with you, and not all backup software supports them anyway.

Backup types are important because part of outlining a backup plan lies in knowing what you want from your backups. What kind of flexibility do you want in your ability to restore data? For that matter, is flexibility or ease of use more important to you? How does the time it takes to back up figure in?

For example, the easiest backup to restore is a full backup because you're only restoring from a single source. Chuck in the same tape every day at 3 A.M. and you've always got a full backup. Of course, full backups typically take a long time and a lot of room—the more data that you're backing up, the longer it will take. It's more of a problem to run one full backup every night with the same tape because you can't archive backups. If it turns out that the version of a file that you really need is the one saved Wednesday, not the one you backed up on Friday after you'd revised it, then you're out of luck. How many full backups are you prepared to store? More often, you'll make full backups at intervals and supplement them with incremental or differential backups, described below:

Incremental backups   Create a record of the files that have changed since the last full or incremental backup was done. As such, they tend to be fairly small—certainly smaller than full backups and typically smaller than differential back-ups—and precise. They're useful when you want to find a single file to restore, but restoring an entire server's contents can be tedious as you have to restore each incremental backup separately.

Differential backups   Back up all the files changed since the last full or incremental backup was done. Thus, they're the easiest type of backup to restore—all you need to do is restore the full backup, then the latest differential. The only catch arises if you're trying to restore a particular version of a file, as tracking down the version you want can be tricky.

NOTE   The backup combination with the greatest degree of flexibility and ease of use I've seen is the full/differential one described in the section, "Creating a Schedule."

Creating and Implementing a Backup Plan

A few weeks ago, I was talking to an acquaintance of mine who's doing a consulting job. He's helping to install a network for a company in an industry that's historically been pretty paper based. In the process, he's incorporating new client machines, helping the company get up to speed with networking, figuring out some thorny communications problems and, of course, developing a backup plan for the company.

The biggest problem he was running into (well, after the problem of convincing them that they needed a backup system in the first place, which was more of a problem than he anticipated) was that it seemed as though no one wanted to do things the simple way. The people in the soon-to-be technical support department had been reading about all the new alternative media solutions available, liking the idea of writable CD-ROMs or some such. Tapes, according to the tech support people, were boring; everyone was using tapes. They wanted to use something different.

The time that you're designing a backup plan is not the time to get creative. To be informed, yes. To look at the various options available and see what kinds of backup systems will suit you best, yes. But not to discount a system out of hand just because a lot of people are using it already.

What's important to a backup plan is functionality, whether that's functionality in terms of backup media, scheduling, or any other aspect. Study the systems other people have put in place. If a system works for someone else whose needs are like yours, then there's a good chance it will work for you.

Outlining the Plan

The first stage of creating the backup plan lies with figuring out frequency and timing of backups. How often do you need to back up data to keep the organization running? When can you back up this data with the least inconvenience to people?

NOTE The answer to the second question depends, to a degree, on your backup software. Some backup utilities will let you back up open files, somewhat simplifying the timing problem.

How Often Do I Back Up? There's no set answer to the question of how often you need to back up—the answer depends on how much you can afford to lose. If you back up once a month, then you'd better hope you can re-create and/or live without a month's worth of data at a time. Most of us use some form of daily backups (perhaps supplemented with weekly full backups), but even that represents some data loss; I'd hate to lose what I create in a day. However, I'd hate even more to have to mess with running constant backups. My hardware seems stable enough to trust it for 24 hours at a time. As with security, the frequency of backups should represent the balance between the trouble it takes to do the backups, the value of the data you're protecting, and the likelihood that anything will happen to that data.

Timing Backups Constant backups aren't usually a practical solution. Running backups interfere with people working because they consume CPU cycles and may add to network traffic (if the files being copied aren't on the same system as the backup system). They also require software that can back up open files.

For these reasons, few companies use real-time backups. Instead, they choose the time of day that's least likely to inconvenience the majority of users and at which files are most likely to be closed. If you have a centralized backup system for a WAN that spans several time zones, it may be impossible to choose a time at which no one is working, but you can at least minimize the overlap.

TIP   Some operating systems, such as NT, run the file-sharing capability as a service that can be turned off and then turned on again. If users have left files open at the end of the day and your backup system doesn't support backing up open files, create a batch file that turns off the server service, runs the backup, then turns the server service back on.

Creating a Schedule   Table 16.2 shows a one-month sample backup schedule for a small office. An initial full backup (Full Backup Tape 1) must be done before you can adhere to this schedule.

T A B L E 1 6 . 2 : A Sample Backup Schedule (Rotating Biweekly)

Week	Day	Backup Type and Tape Used
Week 1	Monday	Differential Tape 1
	Tuesday	Differential Tape 2
	Wednesday	Differential Tape 3
	Thursday	Differential Tape 4
	Friday	Full Backup Tape 2
Week 2	Monday	Differential Tape 5

Continued on next page

TABLE 16.2 CONTINUED: A Sample Backup Schedule (Rotating Biweekly)

Week	Day	Backup Type and Tape Used
	Tuesday	Differential Tape 6
	Wednesday	Differential Tape 7
	Thursday	Differential Tape 8
	Friday	Full Backup Tape 3
Week 3	Monday	Differential Tape 1 (overwrite)
	Tuesday	Differential Tape 2 (overwrite)
	Wednesday	Differential Tape 3 (overwrite)
	Thursday	Differential Tape 4 (overwrite)
	Friday	Full Backup Tape 4
Week 4	Monday	Differential Tape 5 (overwrite)
	Tuesday	Differential Tape 6 (overwrite)
	Wednesday	Differential Tape 7 (overwrite)
	Thursday	Differential Tape 8 (overwrite)
	Friday	Full Backup Tape 5

On the Friday of Week 5, you'd overwrite Full Backup Tape 1 and restart the cycle. This backup schedule creates a two-week record of differential backups and a month record of full backups. An additional six-month archive might not be a bad idea either, for files that aren't often used and which are discovered to be missing or corrupted only months—or even years—after their original use.

More Recommended Backup Schemes

Table 16.2 maps out a simplified version of one of Microsoft's two most recommended backup models: Grandfather/Father/Son (GFS). In GFS, "Grandfather" is a monthly full backup; "Father" is a weekly full backup; and "Son" is an incremental or differential daily backup. GFS uses a total of 12 tapes or other media to store all backups for a three-month period: four for daily backups, five for backups each weekend, and three for the monthly backups.

Another backup scheme Microsoft recommends is called the Tower of Hanoi (ToH), after the math puzzle by the same name. Although more complicated than GFS, ToH keeps a longer record of backups than the other backup scheme—32 weeks instead of 12 weeks. In ToH, five tapes (labeled A–E here) are used in the following order: A B A C A B A D A B A C A B A E. In this method, tape A is reused every two weeks, tape B every four weeks, tape C every 8 weeks, tape D every 16 weeks, and tape E every 32 weeks. ToH only plans for full backups, so you'll probably want to supplement each weekly full backup with an incremental or differential daily backup.

To *really* keep things simple, get backup software that you can program to follow a certain backup scheme and prompt you for the correct tape. That way, you won't have to follow the plan quite so closely.

Choosing Backup Hardware

What are some good server-based backup devices? For practical purposes, a tape drive of some kind (Tapes are discussed in Chapter 8, "Server Types and Additional Hardware.") is probably your best bet: they're relatively inexpensive, have a high capacity, are reliable, and are widely supported.

Tapes aren't the only option, however. If there's a need for you to distribute the contents of your backups widely, then writable CD-ROMs might well be the perfect solution. Even though a CD-R holds less than 1GB and can be finicky for write options, you can be reasonably sure that just about all computers sold in the past three years will have a CD-ROM drive. The small capacity of Zip and Jaz cartridges makes the drives impractical for backing up servers. However, if your backup plan is client based instead of server based, the smaller removable drives may suit you well. The Jaz drive, especially, is large enough to back up user data, and if you use an external drive, it's easily swappable among SCSI-based client machines. If those backup options don't do anything for you, then you might consider backing up files to another disk, either on the server or on another networked computer entirely.

Ultimately, your choice of backup media will be influenced by its speed, capacity, and portability. These factors are discussed in the following sections.

Planning for Speed   If you're doing backups at night, fast backups might not be your first concern, but speed is likely to look a little more important when you're trying to *restore* data.

Speed is determined by two factors: the speed at which the media itself operates and the speed of the connection to the server. A switched fabric network connection will be fastest, but of the more likely options to be in use as of this writing, a SCSI connection will be fastest, with IDE second and a parallel port third. I've already recommended SCSI as the controller interface of choice for servers. (See Chapter 7, "Building the Better Server," if you don't remember the rationale behind this.) Parallel ports aren't a practical solution for server backup interfaces, although they might work if you're backing up individual client machines that don't support SCSI.

The access time of the media also matters. How quickly can you get data on and off the media? The data transfer rate for various media will impact the rate at which data can be read from and written to the media.

NOTE   The write and read speed are adversely affected by the degree of compression.

Capacity Planning How much data can one unit of the media hold? Will you be able to put all the backup data on a single unit, several units, or lots of units? The more data a backup storage unit can hold, the easier it will be to back up and restore data, as you'll have fewer media units to mess with. Backups will be simpler as you won't have to swap units; it's faster to restore data if you can do it from one or two units and it's much easier to store fewer units than more of them.

Planning for Portability So far, tapes are ahead of most other media. Although their access times run somewhere in the Zip drive range (see Table 16.3), they're high capacity and widely supported. The only thing that tapes don't necessarily have is portability. There are so many different types of tapes and backup formats that tapes aren't an easy way to distribute data, except within the confines of a single company. For those purposes, writable CDs and removable drives (described in Table 16.3) are likely to be superior. Chapter 8, "Server Types and Additional Hardware," examined some various tape formats; Table 16.3 examines some possible alternatives to tapes.

TABLE 16.3: Characteristics of Common Non-Tape Backup Media

Criteria	Hard Disks	CD-R/RW	Zip	Jaz
Connection Types Available	IDE, SCSI, network	Parallel, IDE, SCSI	SCSI, parallel, USB, IDE	SCSI
Access Time	>9ms	250–350ms, depending on model	29ms (parallel)	15.5–17.5ms
Capacity	Up to 13GB for a single drive	650MB	250MB	2GB
Unit	Hard disk	CD	Disk-sized cartridge	Disk-sized cartridge

Not all backup packages support all media types. In NT 4, NT Backup doesn't support any media but tapes, for example—you can't back up to a network or removable drive.

Choosing Backup Software

When choosing a backup utility, you need to keep in mind the product's flexibility and interoperability with the network components you've already got. Ask yourself the following about any backup applications you're considering:

- Compatibility:

  - Does it work with my operating system?

  - Is it compatible with any other backup systems that might already be in use?

  - What backup types does it support?

  - Does it work only on a per-server basis or can you use it to manage backups for multiple servers from a single console?

  - What types of media will the application support?

  - What tape format does it use?

- Flexibility:

  - Can it schedule unattended backups?

  - How much discretion does it give me in choosing files to be backed up (volume level, folder level, file level)?

  - Will it retry busy (open) files?

  - Will it back up open files?

  - Does it copy data structures or make a binary image of the disk being backed up?

- Reliability:

  - Does it have trustworthy error-correction available?

- Can you verify file integrity?

- Is it easy to use?

- Does it give you control over error correction?

- Does it keep dated revisions?

Most current network operating systems—even peer ones—have a native backup application you can use, so you don't necessarily have to shop for a separate one. NT's backup utility, for example, is a cut-down version of Seagate's BackupExec. For full functionality, including the ability to back up open files, you'd still need to purchase the Seagate version, but you can protect server data nicely with the NOS version of the utility.

Running the Plan

Once it's developed, running a backup plan is mostly a matter of administration, not technology. Plan for who's going to run the backup plan and where those backups will be stored, and practice restoring data.

Who's Minding the Store? The backup administrator needs to be someone trustworthy, both because the fate of the company's data rests in her hands and because she'll need to have access to the server that's less restricted than that of the average user. Make sure that this person understands procedures, and that she knows who to consult with if she runs into problems. Procedures may include any of the following:

- Backing up data

- Verifying writes

- Storing and labeling archive tapes

- Rotating and reusing tapes

For that matter, make sure that someone who can help is available. I remember one occasion when the backup administrator was having problems with the media, or the software—he wasn't sure which. The office expert on the backup utility traveled a lot and didn't have time to fix the problem when he was in the office, but the administrator figured that he'd catch the expert when the expert had time. You can probably write the ending; the file server crashed, the backups didn't work (the problem turned out to be poorly tensioned tapes, so the backups couldn't be restored), and it became a job for the data recovery people. Not pretty.

Finally, a responsible replacement backup administrator needs to be in place. If the main person is sick or on vacation, someone else needs to be ready immediately, not picked because he happened to be in the room when the usual person's absence is noticed. Otherwise, there's the danger that the job won't get done or won't be done properly.

TIP Posting the backup schedule, with a place to initial after a backup is completed and verified, can help on two fronts. First, it's a reminder that the backups need to be done. Second, having the schedule on the wall lets you see at a glance when the files were last backed up, what type of backup it was, and who signed off on the job.

Practice Restoring Data A key element to a successful backup plan lies in making sure that you can restore the data you're backing up. Problems could potentially arise due to operator error or hardware failure (remember those poorly tensioned tapes). It's nice to discover any such problems before the situation is critical. Thus, have the backup administrator verify the contents of all tapes and restore a file here and there (preferably one not changed since the backup was made.)

Archiving and Storing the Backups It won't do you much good if you back up your disk but find that the backups are useless. If your office is fire damaged, your backups won't help you if they sat on the shelf above your computer. Nor will they help you if you keep the box with the backups in it on a sunny window-sill—the disks will cook slowly in the sun and become useless. On another track, if you don't label the disks well or keep them organized, it will be difficult or impossible to find what you're looking for when you need to restore.

What, then, can you do to make your backups as effective as possible?

Label your backups clearly. Include the name of the machine, the drive, the date backed up, and the disk or tape number. A label or file card might look like this:

FULL BACKUP of PALADIN D: 07/15/98 #4/6

Keep your backups in a safe, cool, dry place. It's best to keep important backups off site so that if your office burns down, your backups don't burn with it. If you can't store them outside of your office building for some reason, at least keep them on a separate floor so that they can evade local disasters.

WARNING If you buy a fireproof safe in which to keep backup tapes, make sure you get a safe rated for data protection, not paper protection. Paper can stand fairly high temperatures before combusting. Tapes can melt in sunlight, let alone the middle of a fire. A data safe will be much more expensive (around $300 instead of $50) but the company data is worth at least that much.

Don't save backups you don't need; it will only confuse you later. If your company formats a computer's hard disk and starts over, get rid of the backups for that computer once you've established that nothing important was on the drive.

Test your backups periodically to make sure that they work. Heat, humidity, and electromagnetic fields can cause your data to deteriorate. Disks and people are generally comfortable in similar climates. If you wouldn't sit in your storage room for hours on end, your backups won't enjoy it either.

Don't keep backups for years and expect them to remain intact without help. The magnetic images on your disks tend to neutralize each other. A disk left on a shelf will slowly return to a *tabula rasa*. It would be as if you wrote in the sand on a beach; the writing would gradually fade unless you retraced it daily. You can give new life to your tapes by copying your backups to newly formatted media and then reformatting the old tape. Tapes are generally designed to last for two to three years.

Real-Time Data Protection Options

You may think of real-time backups as a practical impossibility—too expensive, too resource demanding, or the like. However, there are some methods you can use to maintain more-or-less constant updates of your data that will survive if a hard disk stops working. These methods have a couple of advantages. They not only provide data redundancy and improved up time, but also can improve network performance by introducing *load balancing*, distributing data access among multiple disks or servers. Ordinary backups, in contrast, only provide data redundancy.

Apply a Touch of RAID

RAID (Redundant Array of Inexpensive Disks) is a blanket term for the technology that allows you to combine the resources of multiple hard disks to improve overall disk reliability and/or performance. Hardware-based RAID is built on a RAID subsystem of SCSI disks, whereas software-based RAID uses software to build the array. RAID has the following characteristics:

- It can support the loss of one disk in the fault-tolerant array; the missing data can be supplied or re-created from the remaining disk(s).

- It is dependent on multiple physical disks working together. You can't combine logical volumes to create a RAID array, and if the physical disks aren't working together, they're Just a Bunch of Disks (JBOD).

- The physical disks in a RAID array do not have to be identical in size or type, but the logical divisions in the array must all be the same size. That is, each logical part of an array will be the same size as the other parts.

- You can use RAID to protect all or part of a physical disk.

TIP　　You can create software-based RAID arrays with EIDE disks, but you'll get better performance if you use SCSI. As I mentioned in Chapter 7, "Building the Better Server," SCSI supports multitasking for reads and writes on a single controller, whereas EIDE single-tasks.

RAID has become very common as disk prices have dropped and software-based RAID made the technology more available to the average person. The two types of fault-tolerant RAID most often supported are disk mirroring and disk striping with parity. These are discussed in the following sections.

Disk Mirroring　Disk mirroring protects all your data by writing it to two locations at once; every time you create or edit or delete a file, the changes are registered in both locations. It requires two physical drives explicitly associated in a mirror set. If anything happens to the data on one tape, you break the mirror set and a perfect and up-to-date replica of the data is available on the other disk. Mirror sets are inefficient in their use of disk space—the redundancy means that the data require twice as much disk space as they would ordinarily—but they are an excellent means of data protection. In SCSI systems, they can also reduce read times because the read operation can be multitasked among two disks.

NOTE   If each disk in the mirror set has its own disk controller (so that a disk controller failure doesn't render both drives inaccessible), then it's called *disk duplexing*. Otherwise, the mirror set works as described above.

Stripe Sets with Parity   Like disk mirroring, a stripe set with parity protects data by distributing the data among multiple disks. During write operations, data is written in stripes to each disk in the stripe set (stripe sets with parity must contain at least three physical disks). In addition to the original data, however, parity information for the data is also written to the disks and distributed among the physical disks like the original data, but stored separately from the particular data to which it applies. If one disk in the stripe set fails, then the parity information on the remaining disks can be used to reconstruct the missing data, so all data is still accessible. The proportion of parity information depends on the number of disks in the stripe set, as the parity is designed to make it possible to regenerate the data on a single disk. Therefore, a stripe set with three disks will use one-third of its capacity for parity information, while a set with 10 disks will use one-tenth for parity. The more disks in the stripe set, the greater the efficiency.

If more than one disk in the stripe set fails at a time, then the data are lost, but single disk failures are recoverable without any action required on your part. For example, say that you've created a four-disk array and used it as the foundation of a stripe set with parity. One of the disks dies. When you reboot the server and open the Disk Administrator, you'll see a message that a disk failed and that the missing data is being regenerated. People will be able to write to and read from the stripe set as though the missing disk were still there. Of course, you'll need to replace the dead disk as soon as possible. If a second disk fails, then the stripe set will be unrecoverable.

NOTE The parity information is crucial to the fault tolerance. One type of RAID—disk striping without parity—is not fault tolerant. Instead, it's designed to improve disk throughput by spreading read and write operation over multiple disks. As the disks are codependent and contain no fault-tolerant information, these disk arrays must be backed up regularly—one disk failure will make the entire array inoperable.

The Pros and Cons of RAID Types Should you use stripe sets with parity or disk mirroring? Disk mirroring has a lower initial cost, as the mirror set only requires a minimum of two disks instead of the minimum of three required for fault-tolerant stripe sets. Mirroring also has a speed advantage when it comes to write operations. In a SCSI-based mirror set, write options can be done more or less simultaneously because of SCSI's multitasking capabilities, so disk mirroring actually improves read and write speed. Stripe sets with parity, in contrast, take a performance hit for write options because they must keep recalculating the parity information as the data changes. Read operations aren't affected, but writes are slower than they would be if done to a single disk or in a mirror set. Finally, the calculations involved in supporting stripe sets place greater demands on server RAM and CPU time than does disk mirroring.

That said, stripe sets with parity are more common. Mirroring is very space inefficient, much more so than stripe sets, which become more efficient as more physical disks are added to the stripe set. The increased efficiency of space makes up for any performance hits, which aren't really large enough to be visible to the network client anyway. Cheap hardware means that the additional resources required to support stripe sets aren't really any deterrent to supporting the more efficient RAID method.

Data Replication

If you can't afford any down time at all, then you have a couple of options. One is clustering (described in the next section) and another is data replication. *Replication*—copying data and data structures from one server to another—is a popular way to both maintain data integrity and also distribute the data load among several servers. The data is originally written to one server (called the *export server* in NT networks) and then copied to another (called the *import server*). You can set up server connections to manually divide client access between servers or use load balancing to automatically divide the client load among the servers.

Generally speaking, people tend to replicate two kinds of data: that which they can't afford to lose and that which benefits from load balancing. Because of network bandwidth constraints, ordinary data aren't often protected with replication—copying each change to a large file server can take up bandwidth needed for other purposes, and it's possible to protect file data with RAID. However, replication can be a useful way to protect database or mission-critical information such as WINS mappings or the directory of logon scripts. Rather than trying to serve all client requests from a central location, replication makes it possible to let multiple servers help with the job, while at the same time making sure that redundant copies of the database exist.

Create Redundant Servers with Clustering

Clustering is a bit like RAID carried a step further. Rather than creating arrays of multiple disks to provide fault tolerance and improved performance, clustering creates arrays of servers to provide fault tolerance and improved performance.

Not all clustering solutions are identical, either in function or in the way they're connected and interrelate. So far as function goes, there are three main types of clustering:

- Active/active

- Active/standby

- Fault-tolerant

All cluster types provide some support for fault tolerance, but the degree to which they do it—and the speed with which one server will take over for another if the first server fails—depends on the cluster type.

In an active/active cluster, all servers in the cluster are functional and supporting users all the time. If any server fails, the remaining server (or servers) continues handling its workload and takes on the workload from the failed server. It takes from 15 to 90 seconds for the remainder of the cluster to take over for the failed server. In an active/standby cluster, one server supports user requests or does whatever it's designed to do while another waits for the first server to fail. This doesn't improve failover time; if the first server dies, it still takes from 15 to 90 seconds for the second one to take over the workload of the first. (Any connections or services running on the standby server are terminated when the standby takes over.)

Fault-tolerant clusters are designed to have less than 6 minutes of downtime a year and they are different from active/active and active/standby clusters. In a fault-tolerant cluster, each server in the cluster is identical to all the rest of them and operates in tandem, performing precisely the same operation as all other servers in the cluster. Thus, if one server fails, the rest of the cluster can take over more or less instantaneously. Fault-tolerant clustering uses resources less efficiently than active/active or active/standby clustering, but in case of server failure causes no downtime. The other cluster types, in contrast, may be down for as long as a minute and a half—even 15 seconds of downtime is long enough to spoil a write operation. Table 16.3 compares the three types.

TABLE 16.4: Comparing Cluster Types

	Active/Active	**Active/Standby**	**Fault-Tolerant**
Primary/Secondary Server Operations	Are different.	Are different.	Are identical for full redundancy.
Effect on Secondary Server if Primary Fails	Adds primary server's workload to its own.	Discards its workload for that of the primary server.	Are not affected, as both servers were doing the same thing before the failure.
Requires Identical Systems?	No.	No.	Yes.
Failover Time	15–90 seconds.	15–90 seconds.	<1 second.

The type of cluster describes whether the cluster is designed to offer fault tolerance or improved performance and the way in which workload is balanced between members of the cluster. Cluster *products* differ in terms of their data sharing techniques, the way in which the members of the cluster are connected, and how flexible they are as far as the hardware they support. Products also vary in the number of servers that may be in a single cluster—some clustering products only support two servers—a primary and a secondary—but the more expensive ones support more.

For data sharing, clusters may rely on replication, switching, or mirroring. In *replication*, the data written to the primary server's hard disk are replicated on that of the secondary server via the network connection between the servers. In *switching*, each member of the cluster has its own disk, but the disks are all connected to the same SCSI bus so that if the primary's disk fails, the secondary can take over. *Mirroring* works as described in the previous section, "Apply a Touch of RAID"—data is written simultaneously to the primary and secondary servers' disks.

The physical connection between the members of the cluster also varies with the product. Sometimes, the servers in the cluster will be connected with an ordinary network such as Ethernet.

Sometimes, they'll be connected with proprietary connectors. Other solutions, such as a switched fabric connection, are also possible—whether they're supported depends on the product.

Similarly, the degree of flexibility in terms of hardware type supported will vary. Some clustering products only support a single kind of hardware—bad news, to be sure. Better are those that will support any two servers. Best are those that support servers with different platforms (say, one x86-based and one Alpha-based). Fault-tolerant clusters can't use this kind of flexibility, however, as the servers in the cluster must be identical.

Creating a Disaster Recovery Plan

Backups are an important aspect of preparing for disaster recovery, but not the only part; they have a place in the entire disaster recovery plan.

A *disaster recovery plan* is a detailed document spelling out how to restore the business to working order after a catastrophic event. It's important that it be written down so that the instructions are available even if the person who created the plan isn't available. It needs to be as detailed as possible so that the person executing the recovery doesn't necessarily have to be a computer expert.

NOTE A complete disaster recovery plan involves nontechnical elements such as staffing, but I'll focus on the technical elements here.

A well designed plan will have the following characteristics:

- The support of upper management
- A clear purpose

- A clearly defined chain of command and delegation of authority

- No single point of failure

- Flexibility in case conditions change

These elements aren't part of an ideal plan, but are essential to any disaster recovery plan that's going to work as needed.

Support from upper management is important because you'll need their cooperation to develop and carry out the plan. A complete disaster recovery plan is too complicated and too involved with nontechnical concerns to be prepared fully in isolation from the rest of the company.

The clear purpose keeps the document on track. The plan shouldn't be a dissertation on network theory or nonessential tasks, but a tightly focused document explaining how to make the network operational again and detailing the steps required. Extraneous information may be saved for a "Meet Your Network" presentation for nontechnical staff members, or some such, but the plan itself should only include the essential instructions. Along the way to defining the plan's purpose, you'll need to answer the following questions:

- What is the scope of the plan? Is the purpose of the plan to restore the network to its complete state, or just to get it up and running for the moment, with more time to be taken later?

- What parts of the network need to be restored first? Some services are more essential than others and some services are dependent on others.

Defining responsibilities, both for preparing for disaster and for recovering from it, expedites the recovery process. If everyone knows what jobs they have to do, then there's no time wasted in determining who's responsible for what. Defining responsibility also makes sure that everything gets done—there's less chance of important elements slipping through the cracks.

NOTE One element of determining responsibility lies in defining response. When disaster strikes, everyone needs to know what's expected of them whether it means staying home and out of the way, reporting elsewhere, or working around the people reassembling the network. Customers may also need to be notified if some product will be delayed or coming from another location due to the circumstances.

Well-defined roles in preparation and recovery are important, but every reliable system has some redundancy. The success or failure of the plan shouldn't rest on one person's shoulders, or on one piece of hardware; no single element should be allowed to prevent recovery. This means that:

- A chain of command exists, showing who takes over if one person isn't available.

- Recent backups are stored offsite to reduce the chance of a catastrophe that destroys the original data taking the backups with it.

- Damaged hardware must be quickly replaceable if need be.

Finally, a good plan is flexible. The best plan is modular, not too reliant on the skills of any one person, or reliant on any other specific set of circumstances. Companies grow, staff come and go, and hardware and software changes. The plan needs to be adaptable without requiring a complete rewrite every time the network evolves.

Who's Involved?

A disaster recovery plan is not the work of a single person. Instead, it represents the combined input from and efforts of a team:

- The people using the network

- The people who support the network

- The people who control the resources available

The number of people required to supply all these perspectives depends on your company's structure. Regardless of whether one person is in charge of each listed element, or one person is in charge of multiple duties, you really can't create a useful plan without input from all these sources.

NOTE   Don't forget to get input from one other source—the boss. Someone has to sign checks and approve equipment redundancies.

People Using the Network

The people in the best position to know what services are essential aren't always the people running the network. As the network administrator, you should know service dependencies, but what about knowing which data sources or other servers are most crucial? For that, you'll need input from the people using the network, or their representatives.

People Fixing the Network

The network support people are the technical voice of the disaster planning team. It's up to them (to you, that is) to know what recovery systems are required, what's available, how much the components will cost, and where to find more information. The network administrator should be able to supply feasibility information to the user contingent, letting them know what's physically possible (for example, no, we can't replicate the file server to an offsite server with a 33.6 modem). Helping the people who control resources identify vendors and solutions is also part of the job of the support contingent.

The network administrator needs to know not only what's needed for disaster recovery, but also what's available now. For example, if the servers are SCSI based, then there's no point in buying backup IDE devices for them. An obvious point, but one sometimes missed. I recall one situation a few years ago in which a business manager bought some backup hard drives and controllers to have on hand in case the main ones failed. Unfortunately, the business manager didn't know what interface the existing controllers used. Thus, when the time came to replace one of the drive controllers with the backup, it turned out that the VL-Bus controller card that had been bought wouldn't work in the ISA/PCI server.

People Controlling Resources

The network administrator acts as one voice of reason, keeping tabs on what's technically feasible. The business manager acts as the voice of reason for cost and resource allocation. Sometimes the most effective disaster recovery plan isn't financially feasible. It's the job of the business manager to do the cost accounting required to make sure that the disaster recovery plan doesn't overprotect the network.

The business manager may also control the inventory of network hardware discussed in Chapter 14, "Principles of Network Management." Hardware inventory is important because it provides a reminder of how old hardware is, and also because it lets you know what parts need to be available (and perhaps, what can be cannibalized).

What's in a Plan?

The particulars of the plan will depend on the network design. Generally speaking, however, a disaster recovery plan will include the following:

- A statement of purpose describing the state to which the plan will restore the network

- Contact information for everyone involved in executing the recovery

- An organizational chart showing who's responsible for what elements of the recovery

- Instructions for recovery:

  - Instructions for getting the various network servers (file, application, DHCP, WINS, Web) back up and running again, including dependencies

> **NOTE** Dependencies are important! You need to make sure that in the process of recovery, the people restoring the network put the pieces back together in the proper order. Otherwise, the network may not function properly or at all.

  - Instructions for restoring data from backups

  - Instructions for regenerating data stored in a RAID array

Appendix C, "A Sample Disaster Recovery Plan," includes an excerpt from a disaster recovery plan that shows the level of detail you're shooting for. Creating a disaster recovery plan takes a lot of time and effort—one plan I know of ended up as a 145-page document—but when it comes time to get the network back up and running, perhaps without a full complement of the technical staff, it can be invaluable.

Some Final Thoughts on Designing Disaster Recovery Plans

Disaster recovery plans are essentially a really good piece of documentation. As such, they should be treated and tested as documentation. Make sure that the pieces work before forcing yourself to rely on them, and make sure you know what version of the product the documentation applies to.

First, test for accuracy. As each piece of the plan is written up, have someone else follow your instructions to make sure that you included everything and that your instructions are accurate. The ideal tester is someone who doesn't know how to do whatever the instructions describe—restoring backups, installing a DHCP server, or the like—because his inexperience will keep him from automatically filling in the blanks or correcting you where you're wrong, perhaps without even realizing that he's doing so. Second best is someone extremely picky, but you should never test the instructions yourself unless it's simply unavoidable. *Anyone* is better than you to fact-check your own instructions.

Second, test for feasibility. Can the plan work as you describe? Are all elements independent of special conditions? Do the pieces interoperate as envisioned? If the answer to any of these questions is "no," then redesign and test again.

Finally, keep a couple of dated hard copies of the plan in a safe place. If one copy is destroyed in the course of the disaster you're recovering from, you still have a copy of the plan. The dates are to let you know what version of the plan you've got, if more than one ever existed.

Calling in the Marines—Data Recovery Centers

Disaster recovery isn't always fully successful. Perhaps your backups don't work or are destroyed themselves. One more option remains before you have to tell everyone that everything they were working on for the past month is irretrievably gone: data recovery centers. Data recovery centers are staffed by experts at getting data off media (most often hard disks, but not always) that can't be accessed by normal means.

Not all data recovery centers are the same. Some data recovery centers (in fact, the first data recovery centers) are staffed with people who are really, really good at getting dead hard disks back up and running. Using their skill, they can resuscitate the dead drive, copy its contents to other media, and then return the data—on the new media—to you.

TIP   If you're interested in learning how to do this kind of data recovery, Mark Minasi's *The Complete PC Upgrade and Maintenance Guide* (Sybex, 1998) includes an explanation of how you can bring drives back from the dead, at least long enough to get the data back.

Other data recovery services can retrieve data not recoverable with ordinary methods. These operate at a binary level, reading the data from the dead media (sometimes even opening the hard disk, if the problem is serious enough) and then copying the data to your preferred media. Turnaround time is typically no more than a day or two, plus the shipping time.

The cost of data recovery depends on:

- The method of recovery used (The places that just fix hard disks tend to be cheaper, but they can't always recover the data.)

- Turnaround time requested

- The amount of data recovered

TIP   Consider storing irreplaceable data on a different physical drive from data you can easily replace. A data recovery service can't selectively restore data. That is, if the data files and the system files are stored on a single physical disk, you can't save yourself a little money by asking the center only to recover the data files, even if the data are on two different logical partitions.

Until recently, you had to send the hard disk to the data recovery center to have its data retrieved and this meant not having the data for at least a couple of days. Remote data recovery services can fix some software-related problems without requiring you to ship the drive anywhere or even take it out of the computer case. Using a direct dial-up connection, the data recovery center may be able to fix the problem across the telephone line. As of late 1998, the only data recovery center that offers this capability is OnTrack.

Summary

Disaster can take a variety of forms, some technical and some not. Whichever form it takes, your primary goal remains the same: getting the network back up and running. To do so, you'll need a combination of good backups and a good disaster recovery plan. Luck and skill are also helpful, but when neither is available, the backups and preplanning should help.

Most of the effort required for disaster recovery should take place *before* the disaster ever occurs. That's the time you should be making backups, testing those backups, and storing them carefully so that the data is easy to find and restore. Before the disaster is also the time that you may decide to implement a fault-tolerant system such as RAID, data replication, and/or server clustering.

In case these preparatory measures don't work, you'll need a well-planned disaster recovery plan. For best success, such a plan will be a detailed description of how to get the network back up and running as quickly and efficiently as possible, beginning with the most essential parts. If the plan isn't enough to let you fully restore your network's data, there are always the data recovery centers. It's a lot cheaper to preserve your data in the first place than to let a data recovery center get it back for you, but paying the money is better than the alternative of losing the data for good.

So, we've come to the end. If you've made it this far, then you have much of the ammunition you need to design a LAN, build it, and keep it up and running. Cabling is no longer a mystery to you; you know how to design the perfect server for your needs and pick the perfect clients; you have some ideas of applications to run on the network; and with a little luck and a lot of care and perseverance you'll keep the network organized and trouble free—or be able to fix it if it's not.

Not enough? You'll also find a glossary of terms used in this book. Turn to the appendices for more resources, including:

- A collection of URLs for useful Web sites (online)
- Some sample forms you can use to administer your network
- A selection from a real disaster recovery manual
- Answers to the exercises at the end of each chapter

Thanks for reading, and best of luck!

EXERCISE 16

It's Friday. Some Word documents have been infected by a macro virus that forces the user to save each iteration of a file in a new document. In other words, it's a very obvious virus. The people using the files say that they did not notice anything wrong with them when they were edited one day earlier in the week; they're not sure of the day but know it wasn't yesterday. It's assumed that the infection occurred when the files were reviewed either yesterday or today.

1. To recover from the infection and prevent further infections, what files need to be restored?

2. How can you restore the uninfected files without overwriting newer files on the same tape?

3. Given that you can narrow down the time of infection within a few days, what backup type would make the restoration job easiest? Why?

4. List the RAID types described in this chapter.

5. What type of RAID may be used on two servers in a cluster?

6. The failover time required for a fault-tolerant cluster is:

   A. <15 seconds

   B. 15–90 seconds

   C. <10 seconds

   D. None of the above

7. True or false: Using stripe sets with parity increases the time required to perform disk reads, relative to what it would have been on a single disk.

8. What data preservation method would you use to distribute databases across the network, updating the copies directly from the master?

EXERCISE **16** CONTINUED

9. Fault tolerant clusters have lower failover time than active/active clusters. Why?

10. When it comes to the way in which failover is managed, how is an active/active cluster different from an active/standby cluster? How does this affect failover time?

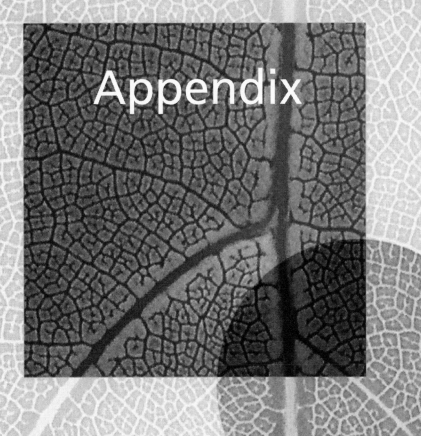

Appendix

A

Internet Resources

My favorite tool for the 1990s isn't the personal computer, it's the Web.

Computers are nothing but tools that let you get at information—the Web *is* information. In years past, I'd collect new drivers from bulletin board services, get documentation from fax-back services that demanded that you know the document number you wanted, receive tech support from telephone calls or newsgroups, and research background material from myriad magazine articles and newspapers. No more—the Web puts all the information you need in one place. I love it. You may not find all the answers you need there, but you can make an excellent start on how to find those answers elsewhere.

The following are links to some sites I've found helpful for one reason or another. Some are informational, some are good sources of utilities, and some are good places to get help. In case you want to do a little shopping, I've also included links to a couple of online shopping centers. This list is completely and utterly subjective, so if your favorite site isn't in this appendix, don't take it personally. No one's paid me to put their site here; these are just links I've found useful.

These links are also available on the Sybex Web site. You can access these links through the Web by visiting Sybex at `http://www.sybex.com`. To find the links and other information on this book, click Catalog, then type **2258** in the search field and press Enter.

A couple of things: First, the dynamic nature of the Web means that links are prone to move or disappear entirely. I've done my best to provide valid links, but I can't control it if someone else moves or deletes a page. (Microsoft's Web site is regularly rearranged.) If a link is no longer working, try searching for a keyword to that link on **Alta Vista** (my favorite search engine) at `http://www.altavista.com/cgi-bin/query?pg=aq&what=web`. If a link to a Microsoft page is broken, try using their site map to find the topical area you're looking for.

Second, there're so many manufacturers' sites that I haven't tried to list them all, concentrating instead on a couple of biggies. If I haven't listed a link to a manufacturer that you're interested in, try typing the name of the company you're looking for in the address bar of your browser (www.companyname.com). If that fails, search in Alta Vista for the product or company name.

Information

These links tell you how things are supposed to work and give you starting information. If you're looking for networking lore or background information, then check out the following:

Links to Requests for Comments Indices `http://www.rfc-editor.org/rfc.html` Requests for Comments (RFCs) are documents describing how Internet standards work. Final versions of the standards are called *standards*; versions still under revision (hence, the name "Request for Comment") are called *proposed standards* or *draft standards*. This site isn't a link to all the documents, but rather to search engines or pages of RFCs that allow you to find the document you're looking for.

My Favorite RFC Search Engine `http://info.internet.isi.edu/7c/in-notes/rfc/.cache` This engine allows you to search by keyword, returning all RFCs that include the selected keyword.

IEEE References `http://www.latech.edu/tech/IEEE/ieeeref.html` If you want the complete, gory details of any IEEE standard, such as Ethernet or Token Ring, then search this list, organized by committee number.

PC Webopaedia `http://webopedia.internet.com/` You need this site. The PC Webopaedia not only defines PC-related terms and gives you a list of related terms to look up, but it also provides links to sites that are related to the term you queried.

The Virus Bulletin `http://www.virusbtn.com/` For general information about viruses, turn here. From this page, you can reach reviews of anti-virus software, Joe Wells' most recent "in the wild" list of viruses, and reports of which viruses are most commonly reported. Excellent starting point for virus information.

ThinWorld Online `http://www.thinworld.com` Nice site for getting some basic information about thin client networking. Not a great deal of depth right here, but a good source of links.

Online Magazines

I know that this isn't a complete list of all online IT-related magazines, but these are some that I know and like, either for information or industry gossip:

Windows NT Magazine `http://www.winntmag.com/` The online version of Windows NT Magazine. Yes, I write for it, but I wouldn't plug the magazine—or write for it, for that matter—if it weren't good. The home page offers links to event information, article archives (All print articles are published online three months after the print date, and other pieces are published on the Web originally.), and other Duke Communications technical publications.

WUGNet `http://www.wugnet.com/` I first encountered WUGNet (the Windows Users Group Network) while using

CompuServe. At that time, they were a busy and useful forum for getting Windows-related questions answered. Since then, they've branched out to form this Web site, a source of reviews, news, and other useful Windows information. Paul Thurrot's daily Windows briefing is excellent.

CNet News `http://www.news.com/?st.cn.gp.tbtop.News` Not much hard technical news here, but good for industry news and links to related sites. CNet's site is also a good source of product reviews.

IDG Online `http://www.idg.com` This site provides links to headlines published in IDG publications, such as *PC World* and *InfoWorld*.

Manufacturers

When you're looking for product documentation, white papers and technical reports, or the latest product information or hot-fixes, the manufacturer's site is the place to start. I can't include every manufacturer of a networking-related product, but here's some official sites:

Microsoft's Web Site `http://www.microsoft.com/` Everything that Microsoft publishes is found here. Whether you're looking for user information or the latest developer news from the Microsoft Developer Network (MSDN), it's here. I spend a fair amount of time on this site.

Novell's Web Site `http://www.novell.com/` Like the Microsoft Web site, the Novell site is good for documentation and technical descriptions. I find its site map a bit easier to use than that of the Microsoft site, perhaps because the site structure is less complicated.

Linux Home Page `http://www.linux.org/` Want information about Linux, what you can do with it, or where to get it? Check out this site. This is an enthusiast's site, and its information reflects that, but it's no more slanted than the Microsoft or Novell sites. *And* the logo's better.

Java Technology Home Page `http://www.java.sun .com/` Interested in finding out more about Java? This is the official site developed and run by Sun Microsystems, the folks who invented this development language. You can get news, documentation, examples, and support here.

Citrix Systems `http://www.citrix.com/` If you're interested in thin client technology, you can read up on it at ThinWorld or on Microsoft's Windows Terminal section, but you shouldn't forget to check out the Citrix information about MetaFrame and the ICA display protocol. This site includes links to the relevant parts of Microsoft's Windows Terminal Server information, so you can start the research here.

Downloads and Online Utilities

Software is rarely complete out of the box; and even when it is, new enhancements and improvements are always appearing. Check out the following sites for upgrading your network or client operating system:

System Internals `http://www.sysinternals.com/` Mark Russinovich and Bryce Cogswell's site is an excellent source of heavy-duty tools and information for modern Windows operating systems. The page of utilities for NT is not to be missed. Some downloads are free, but even the ones that aren't are well worth the money.

Windows NT Server Upgrades `http://www.microsoft` `.com/NTServer/all/downloads.asp` This page contains links to all the Windows Service Packs (bug fixes and upgrades). It also contains links to tools, like the Zero Administration kit, and beta software to try out.

Pretty Good Privacy `http://www.pgpi.com/download/` If you'd like to download your own private and public keys, you can do it from this page. Documentation is also available.

Tucows `http://tucows.bealenet.com/` Good all-purpose site for picking up freeware and shareware for just about any computing platform. Software is rated and described, so it's easy to see what you're getting.

NoNags Freeware Shareware Center `http://www.nonags` `.com/` Want freeware? Check out this site. Most of it isn't very useful (it's free, after all), but sometimes you find a gem here.

Peer Support

Sometimes you don't need to read a static article, you need to find someone to talk to who can answer a specific question—someone who won't charge you $150 for the privilege of asking or make you listen to instrumental renditions of "Purple Haze." When you need this kind of support, you can try the online forums. The answer isn't always waiting there, and many peer support forums don't get enough traffic to be helpful, but it's worth a shot.

TIP I tend to avoid newsgroups these days because of the high signal-to-noise ratio. However, if you're interested in checking out product information, you can find Novell-specific information in the novell domain (as in `novell.zenworks.install`), and Microsoft-specific information in the microsoft domain (as in `microsoft.public.sms.admin`). Use your newsreader to browse for the name of the company you're interested in—a newsgroup devoted to it may exist.

Windows NT Magazine Online Technical Forums
`http://www.winntmag.com/Forums/Forum.cfm` Newsgroup-style Q&A without the spam, these forums cover a variety of special interests, ranging from Windows 2000 questions and Tricks and Traps, to Windows Terminal Server and SQL Server information.

Microsoft TechNet Peer Support `http://207.109.70.246/technet/peer/default.asp` This is another forum setting designed to get people peer support. Traffic for the NT and networking sections is respectable, but the forum isn't as readable as it could be. You have to know that it's there in order to find it (Well, that's taken care of, anyway.), and the posting format means that there's no word wrap for long lines. Hard to read. Wide array of subject matter, however, and chances are good that you'll get an answer, or at least a response.

Shopping

Try these online shopping sites:

CNet's Online Shopping Guide `http://www.shopper.com/?st.ne.nav.sh` Whether or not you actually buy from this guide, you can get a reality check for how much what you need will cost you. Plug in the type of product you're looking for, and the search engine will return a list of manufacturers who make that product and places to get it online, along with shipping and pricing information. I deliberately avoided including much pricing information in the book because the information from a site like this is much more current than a book could ever be.

JDR Microdevices `http://www.jdr.com/` I liked JDR Microdevices' print catalog, and I like this online version as well. They're an excellent source of just about anything you might want to flesh out your network: memory, peripherals, tools—you name it, it's here, and the prices are reasonable.

I hope this gives you a good start with getting the resources you need online. Have fun surfing the Net!

Appendix

B

Networking Forms

FIGURE B.1:

Workstation Information Sheet

WORKSTATION INFORMATION SHEET
PC Name:
Physical Network Address:
Logical Network Address:
Type of NIC (network interface card):
IRQ:
NIC RAM Addresses:
NIC ROM Addresses:
Base I/O Addresses:
Other Information:
Hard Drive Information (via CMOS):
Type of Video Card:
IRQ:
Video RAM Addresses:
Video ROM Addresses:
Other Info:
Other Hardware:
Serial #:

FIGURE B.2:

Server Information
Sheet

SERVER INFORMATION SHEET

Physical Network Node Address:		
Server Name:		
Network Operating System:		
Type of NIC (network interface card):		
	IRQ:	
	NIC RAM Addresses:	
	NIC ROM Addresses:	
	Base I/O Addresses:	
	Other Information:	
Hard Drive Information (via CMOS):		
Type of Video Card:		
	IRQ:	
	Video RAM Addresses:	
	Video ROM Addresses:	
Other Info:		
Other Hardware:		
Serial #:		

FIGURE B.3:

Special Hardware

SPECIAL HARDWARE	
Description:	Settings:

FIGURE B.4:

Network Information

NETWORK INFORMATION
Physical Topology:
Logical Topology:
Cable Specifications throughout:

Appendix

C

Sample from a
Disaster Recovery Plan

Not sure what level of detail you're shooting for when writing up the disaster recovery plan? The idea is to make it possible for just about anyone who can use a computer to restore the network to functionality. This isn't the time to be teaching the basics of using a mouse, but otherwise, yes, the document should be simple and spelled out to reduce the possibility of error. You can't be sure that the person restoring the network to working order will be the network administrator or similarly qualified person.

Keeping that in mind, this is a description of how to install the DHCP service and set up a range of addresses in a DHCP server, thus restoring IP address leasing to an NT network. This is *not* a complete description of how to set up DHCP (*Mastering Windows NT Server 4* [Sybex, 1999] provides that.) but an example of how to write a disaster recovery plan.

NOTE   Note that the instructions provide not only the tasks to be carried out, but also prompt the user for the tools he'll need. They also identify the computer on which the person reading the instructions is to install the service. (Strongly consider labeling servers with their names!)

Restore IP Address Leasing to the Network

To automatically assign IP addresses on the network, you'll need to install the Dynamic Host Configuration Protocol (DHCP) service on server PALADIN and set up the range of addresses (the *scope*) that may be leased to the network.

Installing the DHCP Service

1. Put the NT Server 4 installation CD in PALADIN's CD-ROM drive.

2. Start the Network applet in the Control Panel and click on the Services tab. Click Add.

NOTE   If Microsoft DHCP Server already appears in the list of installed services, then you don't need to install the service again. Skip to the following section on setting up the range of IP addresses.

3. Select Microsoft DHCP Server from the list (see below) and click OK. When prompted, supply the path to the NT Server CD. (Should be the G: drive.)

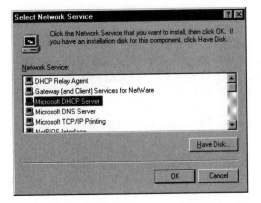

4. You'll see an informational dialog box telling you to change any IP addresses on the local network card(s) to static addresses. Click OK.

5. The setup program will copy to the server the files that are needed. Reboot when prompted.

Creating an Address Pool

1. Open the DHCP Manager, located in Programs➢Administrative Tools. You should see a dialog box that looks like this:

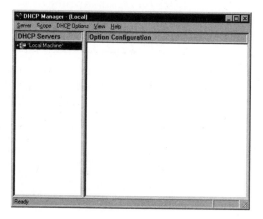

2. Choose Scope➢Create to open the Create Scope dialog box.

3. In the area for the Start address, type **199.34.57.60**. In the area for the End Address, type **199.34.57.126**. In the area for the Subnet Mask, type **255.255.255.0**.

4. Set the Lease Duration to 3 days, 0 hours, and 0 minutes.

5. Name the scope "Address Pool for Isinglass Productions." The final product should look like this:

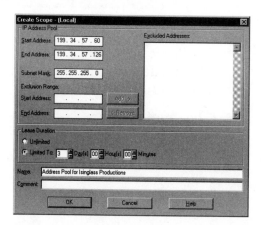

6. Click OK, and you'll see a dialog box telling you that the scope has been created, but not activated, and asking if you want to activate it. Click Yes to activate the range and make it immediately available. You do not need to reboot at this point.

Appendix

D

Answers

Exercise 1

Cable Type	Top Speed	Maximum Supported Length	Anti-Interference Measures Used	Connector Used
Coaxial cable	**10Mbps**	2500 feet	**Copper braid around transmitting wires**	BNC
Unshielded Twisted Pair (UTP)	100Mbps	300 feet	Twisted pairs	**RJ-45**
Shielded twisted pair	100Mbps	**300 feet**	Twisted pairs combined with metal shielding	**D-Shell**
Fiber Optic	U155Mbps or greater	**10Km**	Transmission without electrical signals	ST or SMA

Exercise 2

1. If the network fails due to a cable break, the star topology (shown with the network connections radiating to a central hub) would be easiest to troubleshoot. This is because each network connection has a dedicated connection to the central switching point. The bus and ring topologies both share a backbone throughout the network, so any break in the cable will affect the entire network.

2. The two are 10BaseT Ethernet, which uses the star physical topology and the bus logical topology, and Token Ring, which uses the star physical topology and the ring logical topology.

3. None. The two frame types are compatible without translation.

4. 802.4

5. Gigabit Ethernet

Exercise 3

1. IPX/SPX and TCP/IP could both be used to send the data. NetBEUI could not be used because it is not a routable protocol and this diagram includes a routed connection.

2. You can run either ODI- or NDIS-compliant drivers on the Windows 98 PC, but you will need to use ODI-compliant drivers for the DOS machine, as DOS runs in real mode and NDIS drivers run in protected mode.

3. TCP/IP

4. 32, 128

5. The redirector

6. Socket

7. A driver that includes both transport protocol and a device driver to allow the operating system to communicate with the network

Exercise 4

1. As the situation stands, you cannot install the card. Although two IRQs are free, neither of them is supported by the network card. To make it possible to install the card, you must change the IRQs used by another card so that that card uses one of the free IRQs and releases either 10 or 11.

2. B

3. Cables run under the floor should be placed in the middle of the room if possible. That way, they'll be easier to get at if necessary. Cables placed against the wall are more likely to be under a table or desk once the furniture's moved in.

4. False. These ranges must be separated, as data particular to a single device will be stored in the I/O address range.

Exercise 5

1. A

2. Store-and-forward, for checking packet integrity

3. Open shortest path first (OSPF)

Exercise 6

1. If the software you wanted to use didn't support frame relay, or if you were in an area with unreliable line quality and you wanted your WAN to support error checking, you would use the X.25 protocol.

2. B, C

3. The Layer 2 Transfer Protocol (LT2P)

4. It might be about the rate of a T1, but you really can't tell based on this information alone as CIR is based not only on line speed but also on network traffic.

Exercise 7

1. The L1 cache is a small portion of SRAM located within the CPU, used to hold recently accessed code and data. Storing this information in the L1 cache makes it faster to access than it would be if it had to be recalled from main memory every time it was needed.

2. The CPU is typically faster, as main memory runs at motherboard speed and the internal functions of the CPU can run at several times that.

3. 8; 33

4. B

5. See bold text below.

SCSI Type	Description
SCSI-2	Uses a 50-pin connector and an **8**-bit bus and supports data rates of 4Mbps.
Wide SCSI	Uses a **68**-pin connector and has a 16-bit bus.
Fast SCSI	Like ordinary SCSI, but doubles the clock rate to support data transfer rates of 10Mbps.
Fast and Wide SCSI	Combines the 16-bit bus of Wide SCSI and the doubled clock speed of **Fast SCSI** for data transfer rates of 20Mbps.
Ultra SCSI	Has an 8-bit bus but supports data transfer rates of 20Mbps.
Ultra Wide SCSI/SCSI-3	Has a 16-bit bus and supports data transfer speeds of **40**Mbps.
Ultra2 SCSI	Has an **8**-bit bus and supports data transfer rates of 40Mbps
Ultra2 SCSI Wide	Has a 16-bit bus and supports data transfer rates of **80**Mbps.

6. In an online UPS, all power travels through the battery to the power-protected device, so that the power is conditioned. When the wall power fails, there's no switching time needed to convert to battery support. In a switched UPS, the power runs from the wall to the device, siphoning off some power to charge the battery. When the power fails, there's a 4ms period during which the power-protected device is not being powered.

Exercise 8

1. File

2. Tape drives pull data using sequential access (shown in the bottom figure), meaning that to retrieve a piece of data, the drive must move sequentially to that data's place on the disk.

3. A. DLT, as its tapes can hold up to 35GB of data each.

4. Printer memory, as the printer must be able to hold entire print jobs in its memory alone without support from print server memory.

5. Pooling

6. At around 40Kbps

7. B

8. 64Kbps

9. Disk servers store the map of the directory structure on the client, whereas file servers store it on the server.

Exercise 9

1. Windows NT Workstation

2. False. SGRAM is single ported.

3. Network. If it doesn't have network support, then it can't connect to the network and access its applications running on the server.

4. B

5. Merced

6. D

7. Video support

Exercise 10

1. She doesn't have an account on the NT Workstation sharing the resource. Once she has an account, she'll be able to access the share without providing a password.

2. The Active Directory database, as each object's permissions are stored with the object rather than higher in the directory tree, which is the case with NDS.

3. NetWare 5 is a new NOS and (as of this writing) hasn't had time to complete the certification process. It doesn't mean that NetWare 5 is less secure than NetWare 4.11, but it does mean that certain government agencies will have to stick with NetWare 4.11 (or another C2-certified NOS) until the newer version has been certified.

4. UNIX is more stable and more scalable than NT, so it might be the better choice in a large network. NT is simple to set up and manage, so it might be the better choice for a medium-sized network with a network administrator who knows Windows.

5. False. Linux uses cooperative multitasking, which Windows 3.x used, not preemptive multitasking.

6. A

Exercise 11

1. **A.** 0 licenses

    B. 0 licenses

    C. 5 licenses

    D. 8 licenses

2. **A.** 20 licenses

    B. 20 licenses

    C. 20 licenses

    D. 20 licenses

3. Per-seat licensing is cheaper when you have more users than computers, as in shift work.

4. LAN applications should store this information in the part of the system configuration files devoted to user-specific information rather than in the machine-specific areas.

5. B

6. It differs primarily in terms of group membership. Groupware operates on the workgroup level, letting the people explicitly working on a project together communicate. Communications software doesn't limit communication to a certain group, but allows anyone to communicate with anyone else using the proper software.

Exercise 12

1. Seven. The seventh session is supporting services required to run the server. This session is different from the client sessions in that it doesn't download images to a client, but instead does all processing and image rendering on the local machine.

2. The Remote Display Protocol (RDP) and the Independent Computer Architecture (ICA) protocol

3. These are the possible choices for each situation:

   A. ICA or RDP

   B. ICA

   C. ICA

   D. ICA or RDP

Exercise 13

1. XML (the EXtensible Markup Language) or ASP with a Front-Page/IIS solution

2. A and D. ASP is dependent on the server equipment and HTML is universally supported. Java is not fully supported by IE and XML is only supported by IE.

3. False. This statement applies to ASP, not to CGI.

4. D. Form functionality is not part of the markup language.

5. False. Netscape developed JavaScript; Sun Microsystems developed Java.

Exercise 14

1. An operational audit

2. A server monitoring tool

3. A sniffer

4. Physical

5. Two reasons. First, running the monitor locally will consume server resources, diverting them from the job at hand. Second, running the monitor locally will skew the results of the monitoring by showing used resources not related to serving client requests.

6. A

7. User Datagram Protocol (UDP)

8. C

9. False. Some implementations of SNMP can send messages with IPX instead of UDP. However, not all implementations of SNMP support this.

10. Version 1.1 of Novell's Z.E.N.works

11. B, C

12. The search will return all documents containing the phrase "NetWare 5" within eight letters of the word "zero," including the word "Administration."

13. NT XOR NetWare

14. Creating a test site, installing the change on one part of the network, and installing several changes one at a time to make sure that each works

Exercise 15

1. The SID (security identifier) identifies a user account. If the user attempts to access an object, the operating system reviews that object to see whether that SID is permitted access.

2. 11

3. It's a tool that decrypts LM challenge/response passwords.

4. Microsoft's Active Directory or domain structure; Novell's NDS

5. One

6. Public key

7. True. The public key is used to perform the symmetric encryption used on the data.

8. Symmetric encryption

9. CHAP is the Challenge Handshake Authentication Protocol that's one of PPP's security systems. When a client requests a secure session, the server passes a random number to the client. The client is then responsible for finding in its secrets file the proper secret corresponding to this number and then passing the result back to the server.

10. CHAP, because it never passes a password over the network

11. If you had multiple network access servers for different kinds of remote connections and wanted to keep all remote access accounts in a single database

12. Bindings associate a network protocol with a service or adapter. If a protocol is not bound to a component of the network, the component can't use that protocol.

13. Denial of service (DOS)

14. Users can browse their local and logical drives with IE4, so they'd be able to run any executable files that were on those drives.

15. False. They can format hard disks or even corrupt the system BIOS.

16. B, D

17. C

Exercise 16

1. The document files and the infected templates must be restored.

2. Restore only the damaged files, leaving the rest intact.

3. It would be easiest to restore the backups from a differential backup because you know the last day that the files were edited. You also know that the final edits were done before the files were infected. An incremental backup would also supply the uninfected files, but you'd have to guess the right day or else the files wouldn't show up, or you wouldn't get the most recent version. So long as you restore the differential files from Wednesday, you should get all the edits—and no virus.

4. Disk mirroring or duplexing, stripe sets without parity, and stripe sets with parity

5. Disk mirroring

6. D (The answer is <1 second.)

7. False. It increases the time required for writes because the parity information must be recalculated, but not reads.

8. Replication

9. The failover time is lower on fault-tolerant clusters because both members of the cluster are doing the exact same thing.

10. When a server in an active/active cluster fails, the other server takes over the dead server's work in addition to its own. When a server in an active/standby cluster fails, the other server discards its own work and takes on that of the primary server. This doesn't affect failover time—it's the same for both cluster types.

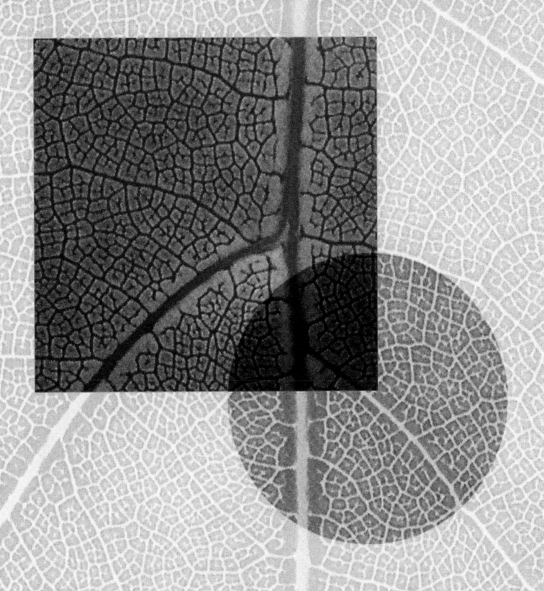

Glossary

Numbers

10Base2   Ethernet network arranged in the bus physical topology and running over Thinnet coaxial cable. So called because network segments can be up to 200 meters long. (Well, 187 meters, but who's counting?) See also *Ethernet, Bus Physical Topology, Coaxial Cable, Thinnet.*

10Base5   Ethernet network arranged in the bus physical topology and running over Thicknet coaxial cable. So called because network segments can be up to 500 meters long. See also *Ethernet, Bus Physical Topology, Coaxial Cable, Thicknet.*

10BaseT   Ethernet network arranged in the star physical topology and running over UTP. See also *Ethernet, Star Physical Topology, Unshielded Twisted Pair (UTP).*

802.3   Standards used in all types of Ethernet networks on all types of media. See also *Ethernet.*

802.4   Standards defining token-based networks that use a star physical topology and bus logical topology. Not very common, and not to be confused with Token Ring, which follows the 802.5 standard. See also *Bus Logical Topology, Star Physical Topology, Token Ring.*

802.5   Standard defining token-based networks that use a star physical topology and ring logical topology. See also *Star Physical Topology, Ring Logical Topology, Token Ring.*

A

Accounts   Containers for security identifiers, passwords, permissions, group associations, and preferences for each user of a system. The User Manager for Domains utility is used to administer accounts in Windows NT. See also *Security Identifiers (SIDs), Preferences, Permissions, Groups.*

Active Hub   A powered hub. See also *Hub.*

Active Monitor   See *Token Master.*

Adapter   Any hardware device that allows communications to occur through physically dissimilar systems. This term usually refers to peripheral cards permanently mounted inside computers that provide an interface from the computer's bus to another media such as a hard disk or a network. See also *Network Interface Card (NIC), Small Computer Systems Interface (SCSI).*

Address Resolution Protocol (ARP) Portion of the TCP/IP suite that maps IP addresses to hardware addresses. See also *Internet Protocol (IP), Hardware Address.*

Administrators Users who are part of the Windows NT Administrators group. This group has the ultimate set of security permissions. See also *Permissions, Groups.*

Advertising The act of a router's announcing itself and its connections to the rest of the network. Advertising is important to route discovery. See also *Router.*

Application Layer The layer of the OSI model that interfaces with user-mode programs, called *applications,* by providing high-level network services based upon lower-level network layers. Network file systems such as named pipes are an example of application layer software. See also *Named Pipes, Open Systems Interconnect (OSI) Model.*

Application Programming Interface (API) A standard set of functions that allow transparent access to operating system or networking functions. APIs allow programmers to use a standard interface for all related hardware types, rather than rewriting code for hardware variances.

Application Server A computer on which application software is installed and then shared with the rest of the network.

Asynchronous Data Stream Packets of information are passed one packet at a time rather than several packets in a synchronized burst. Resources can be physical, like your modem, or logical, like a fax service on your computer that utilizes the modem for the transmittal and reception of faxes.

B

Backup Browser A computer on a Microsoft network that maintains a list of computers and services available on the network. The master browser supplies this list. The backup browser distributes the Browsing service load to a workgroup or domain. See also *Master Browser.*

Backup Domain Controllers Servers that contain accurate replications of the security and user databases; servers can authenticate workstations if the primary domain controller does not respond or is overloaded. See also *Primary Domain Controller (PDC).*

Bandwidth   Describes the size of the channel (network or bus) available. Not necessarily an indication of connection speed, just of the size of the pipe between sender and receiver. Throughput is a more accurate measure of connection speed. See also *Throughput.*

Base I/O Address   The lowest I/O address in a range devoted to a particular piece of hardware. See also *I/O Address.*

Basic Input/Output System (BIOS)
A set of routines in firmware that provides the most basic software interface drivers for hardware attached to the computer. The BIOS contains the bootstrap routine. See also *Boot, Driver.*

Bayonet-Naur Connector (BNC)
Connectors used to connect lengths of coaxial cable to each other. For this reason, coaxial cable is also called BNC cable. See also *Coaxial Cable.*

Binary   Base-2 numbering system that uses combinations of only 1 and 0 to represent any number. Computers think in binary because it's the closest any number system can come to expressing a power on/power off situation. To make it easier for people to deal with binary numbers, they're often converted to decimal or hexadecimal. See also *Decimal, Hexadecimal.*

Bindery   A NetWare structure that contains user accounts and permissions. It is similar to the Security Accounts Manager in Windows NT. See also *Security Accounts Manager (SAM).*

BIOS   See *Basic Input/Output System.*

Boot   The process of loading a computer's operating system. Booting usually occurs in multiple phases, each successively more complex, until the entire operating system and all its services are running. Also called *bootstrap.* The computer's BIOS must contain the first level of booting. See also *Basic Input/Output System (BIOS).*

Bridge   A device that connects two networks using the same data link protocol; at the network layer, bridges are protocol independent. A bridge forwards packets destined for computers on the other side of the bridge. Some bridges, called *translation bridges*, can connect networks using two different data link protocols. See also *Router, Data Link Layer, Network Layer.*

Bridge Flooding   A normal condition in bridging wherein a bridge sends packets to all the segments connected to it, not just one. Flooding may be used for address discovery. In some cases, bridge flooding can lead to *bridge looping*, which is a problem, but flooding isn't automatically something to worry about. See also *Bridge, Bridge Looping*.

Bridge Looping   A possible side effect of bridge flooding in multi-bridge networks. A packet is propagated from the first bridge onto more than one segment because both segments eventually lead to the second bridge. This can lead to corruption of the second bridge's MAC tables, as it can't tell which path to take to get back to the segment on which the packet originated in the first place.

Browser   A computer on a Microsoft network that maintains a list of computers and services available on the network.

Browsing   The process of requesting the list of shared resources on a network from a browser.

Bursting Technology   Memory reading technology used to read not only the current four bits of data but an entire page (4KB on *x*86 systems) at once. Reduces wait states incurred by secondary searches within a single page of memory. See also *Wait State, Extended Data Output (EDO), Random Access Memory (RAM)*.

Bursty Transmissions   Transmissions that periodically send bursts of information, as opposed to a steady stream. E-mail is bursty; streaming video is not.

Bus   A collection of wires through which data is passed from one part of a computer to another, or from one computer on a network to another. The width of the bus and its speed determines the rate of data transmission along the bus.

Bus Logical Topology   Logical topology used in Ethernet networks, in which all nodes broadcast their transmissions over the entire network. All nodes can hear all transmissions, but only pay attention to the transmissions addressed to them personally or to all nodes collectively. See also *Ethernet, Logical Topology*.

Bus Mastering   A feature supported by some buses in which the device can manage the transfer of data from itself to main memory without requiring CPU time. PCI cards support bus mastering. See also *Bus, Peripheral Connection Interface (PCI)*.

Bus Physical Topology   Topology in which cable runs from network node to network node, making each computer the link of a chain. All computers on the network share a single cable, typically coaxial cable. This topology is found in 10Base2 and 10Base5 networks, and is commonly associated with Ethernet networks. Each end of the bus must be terminated for proper functioning. See also *Ethernet, Coaxial Cable, 10Base2, Logical Topology, Terminator, Thinnet, Thicknet*.

C

Caching   A speed optimization technique that keeps a copy of the most recently used data in a fast, high-cost, low-capacity storage device rather than in the device upon which the actual data resides. Caching assumes that recently used data are likely to be used again. Fetching data from the cache is faster than fetching data from the slower, larger storage device. Most caching algorithms also copy next-most-likely-to-be-used data and perform write caching to further increase speed gains. See also *Write-Back Caching, Write-Through Caching*.

Carrier Sensing Multiple Access with Collision Detection (CSMA/CD)   Ethernet method of making sure that only one network node transmits at a time. In short, each node listens to see whether the coast is clear before beginning transmission. If two nodes manage to transmit at the same time, then both nodes detect the collision and stop transmitting. See also *Ethernet, Collision, Truncated Binary Exponential Backoff*.

Cell Relay   WAN access technologies designed for handling steady streams of data. All packets transmitted over the WAN are 53-byte cells, regardless of the type of data they contain. When the cells arrive at their destination, they're processed in the order in which they left, so transmission is as smooth as possible. See also *Wide-Area Network (WAN), Frame Relay.*

Central Processing Unit (CPU)
"Brains" of the computer that manages all processing and executing of instructions. In PCs, the CPU is a single chip called a microprocessor, whereas in large computers such as mainframes it's located on a circuit board. Either way, a CPU has two parts: the arithmetic logic unit (ALU), which performs arithmetic and logical operations, and the control unit, which extracts instructions from memory and decodes and executes them, calling on the ALU as needed.

Certificate   Attachment to a data transfer that authenticates the sender's identity.

Circuit-Switched Network   WAN type that defines a static path from sender to recipient, to be used during the entire course of a transmission. Packets sent on a circuit-switched network don't have to carry routing information with them, as that data is inherent in the virtual circuit that's been established.

Client   A computer on a network (or the person using that computer) that subscribes to the services provided by a server. See also *Server.* Alternatively, the front end of a piece of software that provides the interface to a back end running on a server.

Client Element   Part of remote access or remote control software that runs on the computer that's initiating the connection to the remote computer. See also *Server Element, Remote Control, Remote Access, Thin Client Networking.*

Client/Server   A network architecture that dedicates certain computers called *servers* to act as service providers to computers called *clients*, which users operate to perform work. Servers can be dedicated to providing one or more network services such as file storage, shared printing, communications, e-mail service, and Web response. See also *Share, Peer.*

Client/Server Applications   Applications that split large applications into two components: computer-intensive processes that run on application servers and user interfaces that run on clients. Client/server applications communicate over the network through interprocess communication mechanisms. See also *Client, Server, Interprocess Communications (IPC).*

Client/Server Network   Network organized around a dedicated central server accessed by network clients. See also *Peer Network.*

Cluster   Logical grouping of sectors used in Microsoft file systems, and the smallest unit of storage possible. The number of sectors in a cluster depends on the file system and the size of the volume using that file system. Alternatively, a collection of several servers connected with a very high-speed network and designed to cooperate, either for fault tolerance or for increased performance.

Coaxial Cable   Made of a single copper wire (inner conductor) encased in insulation (dielectric) and then covered with a layer of copper or wire braid (shield) that protects the transmitting wire from interference. The combination is encased in a plastic jacket. Coaxial cable used in networking follows the RG58 standard. See also *Bayonet-Naur Connector (BNC).*

Code   The instructions used to build software. Also, a method of concealing meaning by substituting one word for another. See also *Encryption.*

Codec   Coder/decoder, the device at each end of a fiber optic cable that encodes the electronic pulses used by the computer into light pulses for transmission, and then decodes the pulses after transmission.

Collision   Event on an Ethernet network when two nodes transmit data at the same time. See also *Ethernet, Carrier Sensing Multiple Access with Collision Detection (CSMA/CD), Truncated Binary Exponential Backoff.*

Complex Instruction Set Chip (CISC)   Detailed instruction set built into a CPU's logic with microcode. CISC is used in CPUs using the *x*86 architecture. See also *Central Processing Unit, Reduced Instruction Set Chip (RISC).*

Components   Interchangeable elements of a complex software or hardware system. See also *Module.*

Compression   A space optimization scheme that reduces the size (length) of a data set by exploiting the fact that most useful data contain a great deal of redundancy. Compression reduces redundancy by creating symbols smaller than the data they represent and an index that defines the value of the symbols for each compressed set of data.

Computer Name   A 1- to 15-character NetBIOS name used to uniquely identify a computer on the network. See also *Network Basic Input/Output System (NetBIOS)*.

Connected Star   Variant of the star physical topology, in which hubs are daisy-chained together to connect several physical star connections. It's a combination of the star and bus physical topologies, and used in Ethernet networks. See also *Ethernet, Bus Physical Topology, Star Physical Topology*.

Connection-Oriented   Network communication that establishes a virtual connection between sender and recipient before data is sent. Used when data must be sent reliably. See also *Connectionless*.

Connectionless   Network communication based on datagrams that don't require acknowledgment of any kind. Connectionless transmissions start sending data without establishing any kind of virtual channel first. See also *Connection-Oriented*.

Container Object   Object in a directory service that can contain other objects. See also *Directory Services, Leaf Object*.

Control Panel   A Windows interface that provides access to applets controlling the function of specific operating system tasks. The Registry contains the Control Panel settings on a system and/or per-user basis. See also *Registry, Accounts*.

Cooperative Multitasking   A multitasking scheme in which each process must voluntarily return time to a central scheduling route. If any single process fails to return to the central scheduler, the computer will lock up. Windows 3.*x* and the Macintosh operating systems use this scheme, as does Linux. See also *Preemptive Multitasking, Windows 3.11 for Workgroups*.

Cost   The price of using a network device to reach a given destination, in terms of the hops required to reach it and other factors. The higher the router's cost, the less desirable it is to use it.

CPU Cache High-speed SRAM provided to the CPU for caching recent instructions. Current CPU design includes an L1 cache within the CPU itself and an L2 cache (generally) stored next to the CPU but not part of it. The L1 cache is quite small and very fast because it operates at the CPU's internal clock speed; the L2 cache is generally larger and somewhat slower because it operates at motherboard speeds. Future CPU designs include support for an internal L2 cache and a third cache. See also *Central Processing Unit (CPU), Caching, Static RAM (SRAM).*

CSMA/CD See *Carrier Sensing Multiple Access with Collision Detection (CSMA/CD).*

Cut-Through Switching A high-speed method of switching in which the switch only reads the MAC destination address of a frame before forwarding the frame to the port via which that MAC address is to be found. Cut-through switching is very fast, operating very nearly at line speed.

Cyclic Redundancy Checking (CRC) An error-checking method used in some packet-switched network access types such as X.25. Before a packet is transmitted, the sender runs an algorithm on the packet. This algorithm and the expected result are included in the packet along with the rest of the packet's contents. When the destination node gets the packet, it runs the algorithm. If the answer it gets doesn't match the one included in the packet, then the packet's recipient sends a message to this effect back to the original sender and asks the sender to resubmit the packet.

D

Data Link Connection See also *Logical Link Connection (LLC).*

Data Link Layer In the OSI model, the layer that provides the digital interconnection of network devices and the software that directly operates these devices, such as network interface adapters. See also *Physical Layer, Network Layer, Open Systems Interconnect (OSI) Model.*

Data Path   Width of the path leading into the CPU. The wider the data path, the more data can be loaded into the CPU at one time. See also *Central Processing Unit (CPU), Word Size.*

Database   A related set of data organized by type and purpose. The term can also include the application software that manipulates the data. For example, the Windows NT Registry is a database of system configuration information. See also *Registry.*

Datagram   A packet sent on a connectionless network. Datagrams are not acknowledged, so they use up little bandwidth. See also *Packet, Connectionless.*

Decimal   Base-10 numbering system used by most humans but not often used in computing. The main place you'll find decimal representations of numbers is in IP addresses. See also *Internet Protocol (IP).*

Desktop   A directory that the background of the Windows Explorer shell represents. By default, the Desktop contains objects that contain the local storage devices and available network shares. Also a key operating part of the Windows GUI. See also *Explorer, Shell.*

DHCP   See also *Dynamic Host Configuration Protocol (DHCP).*

Dial-Up Connections   Data link layer digital connections made via modems over telephone lines. The term *dial-up* refers to temporary digital connections, as opposed to leased telephone lines, which provide permanent connections. See also *Data Link Layer.*

Direct Memory Access (DMA)
Method of transferring data from a peripheral's on-board data to main memory with DMA chips on the peripheral device, without requiring assistance from the CPU. Requires dedicating a DMA channel to the peripheral device through which the data is moved. See also *Central Processing Unit (CPU), Programmable Input/Output (PIO).*

Directory Services   A means of organizing all resources and accounts on a network into a hierarchy of objects, some capable of containing other objects and some not. Novell's directory services are called the NetWare Directory Services (NDS), and Windows 2000's are called the Active Directory. See also *NetWare, Windows 2000.*

Disk Server   Networked computer that shares its disk space with clients on the network. The clients each maintain their own copy of the disk's volume structure, so each volume of the disk has to be shared separately to avoid confusion and corruption. Largely supplanted today by file servers. See also *File Server.*

Display Protocol   Data link layer protocol used in thin client networking to convey input from the client to the terminal server and output from the terminal server to the client. See also *Thin Client Networking, Terminal Server.*

DNS   See also *Domain Name Service.*

Domain   In Microsoft networks, a domain is an arrangement of client and server computers referenced by a specific name that share a single security permissions database. On the Internet, a domain is a named collection of hosts and subdomains, registered with a unique name by the InterNIC. See also *Workgroup, InterNIC.*

Domain Controllers   Servers that authenticate workstation network logon requests by comparing a user name and password against account information stored in the user accounts database. A user cannot access a domain without authentication from a domain controller. See also *Primary Domain Controller (PDC), Backup Domain Controllers, Domain.*

Domain Name   The textual identifier of a specific Internet host. Domain names are in the form *server.organization.type* (for example, www.microsoft.com) and are resolved to Internet addresses by domain name servers. In NT networks, may also refer to the name of a group of computers that share a common security database. See also *Domain Name Server.*

Domain Name Server   An Internet host dedicated to the function of translating fully qualified domain names into IP addresses. See also *Domain Name.*

Domain Name Service (DNS)   The TCP/IP network service that translates host names into numerical Internet network addresses. See also *Transmission Control Protocol/Internet Protocol (TCP/IP), Internet.*

Driver   A program that provides a software interface to a hardware device or part of the operating system, such as the file system. Drivers are written for the specific device they control, but they present a common software interface to the computer's operating system, allowing all devices (of a similar type) to be controlled as if they were the same. See also *Data Link Layer, Operating System.*

Dual-Boot   A computer configured to boot to more than one operating system. You choose the operating system you want to use at system startup, using a menu provided. For example, a dual-boot system might allow you to boot NT Workstation, Windows 98, and OS/2.

Dynamic Data Exchange (DDE)   A method of interprocess communication within the Microsoft Windows operating systems.

Dynamic Host Configuration Protocol (DHCP)   A method of automatically assigning IP addresses to client computers on a network.

Dynamic Link Libraries (DLLs)   Modular functions that can be used by many programs simultaneously. There are hundreds of functions stored within DLLs.

Dynamic RAM (DRAM)   Physical memory used for main memory. DRAM must have its contents refreshed every 4ms. See also *Random Access Memory (RAM), Static RAM (SRAM).*

E

Electrical Topology   See *Logical Topology.*

Electronic Mail (E-Mail)   A type of client/server application that provides a routed, stored-message service between any two user e-mail accounts. See also *Internet.*

Encryption   The process of obscuring information by modifying it according to a mathematical function known only to the intended recipient. Encryption secures information being transmitted over nonsecure or untrusted media. See also *Security.*

Enhanced Integrated Drive Electronics (EIDE)   Short for Enhanced IDE, EIDE is a newer version of the IDE mass storage device interface standard developed by Western Digital Corporation. EIDE supports data rates of 4–16.6MBps, about three to four times faster than the old IDE standard. In addition, it can support storage of 10GB or more, whereas IDE was limited to partitions no greater than 528MB in size. See also *Integrated Drive Electronics (IDE), Small Computer System Interface (SCSI)*.

Enterprise Network   A complex network consisting of multiple servers and multiple domains over a large geographic area. Enterprise networks are often assumed to include more than one network operating system and/or network protocol.

Environment Variables   Variables, such as the search path, that contain information available to programs and batch files about the current operating system environment.

Ethernet   The most popular data link layer standard for local area networking. Ethernet implements the carrier sense multiple access with collision detection (CSMA/CD) method of arbitrating multiple computer access to the same network. This standard supports the use of Ethernet over any type of media including wireless broadcast. Standard Ethernet operates at 10 megabits per second. Fast Ethernet operates at 100 megabits per second. See also *Data Link Layer*.

Exchange   Microsoft's messaging server application. Exchange implements Microsoft's mail application programming interface (MAPI) as well as other messaging protocols such as POP, SNMP, and faxing to provide a flexible message composition and reception service. See also *Electronic Mail (E-mail)*.

Explorer   The default shell for all 32-bit Windows operating systems. Explorer implements the more flexible desktop object paradigm rather than the Program Manager paradigm used in earlier versions of Windows. See also *Desktop*.

Extended Data Output (EDO)

Type of DRAM that can start the search for the next requested bit of data while passing the first to the CPU. Its access speeds of about 40ns are faster than FPM RAM (>60ns), but slower than SDRAM (10ns). See also *Random Access Memory (RAM), Fast Page Mode (FPM) RAM, Dynamic RAM (DRAM)*.

Extender

Device that amplifies an electronic or photonic signal so as to increase the distance that that signal can travel. Used in Ethernet networks to extend their reach without using a repeater. See also *Repeater*.

F

Fast Ethernet

Type of Ethernet that runs at 100Mbps over Category 5 UTP. See also *Ethernet, Unshielded Twisted Pair (UTP)*.

Fast Page Mode (FPM) RAM

Original DRAM type that reads one block of memory into the CPU at a time. Runs at 60-70ns. Common for about a decade, it's been largely supplanted with EDO and SDRAM. See also *Random Access Memory (RAM), Extended Data Out (EDO), Dynamic RAM (DRAM)*.

FAT   See *File Allocation Table.*

Fiber Distributed Data Interface (FDDI)

Fiber network using the physical and logical ring topologies. Typically, double-cabled for the sake of connection integrity

Fiber Optic Cable

Glass or plastic fiber surrounded with an insulating layer (cladding) and jacketed. Fiber optic cable is immune to electrical interference because it uses light to transmit data, not electricity.

Fibre Channel

Networking method in which peripheral devices and network nodes are all connected using the same high-speed network running at gigabit speeds. For example, a server could be connected to a hard disk located across the room from it, but the speed of connection would be as though the hard disk were internal to the server. The network may be point-to-point, connecting two devices, a physical ring connecting all devices, or a fabric in which devices are part of a logical mesh. Positioned to rival SCSI. See also *Small Computer Systems Interface (SCSI)*.

File Allocation Table (FAT) The file system used by MS-DOS and available to other operating systems such as Windows (all variations), OS/2, and the Macintosh. FAT has become something of a mass storage compatibility standard because of its simplicity and wide availability. FAT has few fault tolerance features and can become corrupted through normal use over time. See also *File System*.

File Attributes Bits that show the status of a file (for example, archived, hidden, read-only) are stored along with the name and location of a file in a directory entry. Different operating systems use different file attributes to implement such services as sharing, compression, and security.

File Management A general term for sharing, transferring, and securing information between networked computers.

File Server A computer that shares its files or directories with the rest of the network. The file structure is maintained on the file server and updated as network clients add or remove files from the shared directories.

File System A software component that manages the storage of files on a mass storage device by providing services that can create, read, write, and delete files. File systems impose an ordered database of files, called volumes, on the mass storage device. Volumes use hierarchies of directories to organize files. See also *Volume, Database*.

File Transfer Protocol (FTP) A simple Internet protocol that transfers complete files from an FTP server to a client running the FTP client. FTP provides a simple method of transferring files between computers, but cannot perform browsing functions. You must know the address of the FTP server to which you want to attach. See also *Internet, Uniform Resource Locator (URL)*.

Filtering The act of dropping a packet without forwarding it to another segment. Many devices can be configured to support filtering. Bridges filter packets they receive if the destination segment is the same as the sending segment—the computer for which the packet was intended already got the packet, so the bridge doesn't need to send it again. Routers and firewalls may filter packets based on IP address, protocol type, or other criteria, either to cut down on unnecessary traffic or for security reasons. See also *Bridge, Router, Forwarding*.

Flow Control   Mechanism for ensuring that a recipient never gets more packets than it can handle at once. Flow control can be managed either in hardware or in software.

Forwarding   The act of sending a packet to the port through which it can reach its final destination. Bridges forward packets destined for any segment other than the one from which they originated. See also *Filtering*.

Frame   Segment of data passed at the data link layer. See also *Framing, Data Link Layer*.

Frame Relay   WAN access method that transmits frames of variable length. Frame relay is distinguished by its technique of combining channel space for all those using the WAN, so that no bandwidth is wasted. This gives it higher effective throughput than would be possible if the channels were all maintained separately. Unlike X.25, frame relay does not support error checking, so it's best on reliable networks. See also *Cell Relay, X.25*.

Frame Type   Main parameter of IPX/SPX protocol. There are different frame types that can be run on your network. A frame can be considered a dialect—Ethernet has four possible frames or dialects, and Token Ring has two possible frame types.

Framing   The act of packaging data into segments called packets or frames. Framing takes place at the data link layer. See also *Frame, Frame Type, Packet, Data Link Layer*.

FTP   See *File Transfer Protocol*.

Full Duplex   Channel that can send data in two directions at once. See also *Half Duplex, Integrated Services Digital Systems Network (ISDN)*.

G

Gateway   A computer that serves as a router, a format translator, or a security filter for an entire network or subnet. Alternatively, a device that can connect two completely disparate computing devices, such as a mainframe and a PC.

GDI   See *Graphical Device Interface*.

General Protection Faults   A general protection (GP) fault occurs when a program violates the integrity of the system. This often happens when a program tries to access memory that is not part of its memory address space. This GP fault is a defense mechanism employed by the operating system and is designed to reduce the damage that an errant program can do.

Gigabit Ethernet   A version of Ethernet that supports speeds of up to 1 billion bits per second (Gbps). The NICs designed for these high speeds are currently very expensive and are designed for the high-end server market, rather than for network clients or ordinary servers. The first Gigabit Ethernet standard (802.3z) was ratified by the IEEE 802.3 Committee in 1998.

Graded Index Cable   A type of multimode fiber cable in which the light beams within the fiber follow a sine-wave path. See also *Fiber Optic Cable, Mode, Modal Dispersion.*

Graphical Device Interface (GDI) The programming interface and graphical services provided to Win32 for programs to interact with graphical devices such as the screen and printer. See also *Programming Interfaces, Win32.*

Graphical User Interface (GUI)   A computer shell program that represents mass storage devices, directories, and files as graphical objects on a screen. A cursor driven by a pointing device such as a mouse manipulates the objects. Typically, icons that can be opened into windows that show the data contained by the object represent the objects. See also *Shell, Explorer.*

Groups   Windows NT security entities to which users can be assigned membership for the purpose of applying the broad set of group permissions to the user. By managing permissions for groups and assigning users to groups, rather than assigning permissions to users, security administrators can keep coherent control of very large security environments. See also *Permissions, Accounts, Security, Local Group.*

Groupware   Blanket term for any application designed to help a defined group of people function together. Also called teamware, or workgroup productivity software.

GUI   See *Graphical User Interface.*

H

Half Duplex Channel that can only send data in one direction at a time. May have higher throughput than full duplex transmissions. See also *Full Duplex, Integrated Services Digital Systems Network (ISDN)*.

Hardware Address Unique physical address of a NIC, burned into the card at manufacture. In Ethernet cards, this address is 48 bits long.

Hardware Profiles A set of hardware devices that can be used or not used based on options chosen at system startup. Used to manage portable computers that have different configurations based on their location.

Hexadecimal Base-16 numbering system that uses sixteen numerals (0-9) and letters A-F to represent any number. Often used to shorten binary numbers for human consumption.

Home Directory A directory that stores a user's personal files and programs.

Hop An intermediate connection in a string of connections linking two pieces of networking hardware. Each time a packet is repackaged and propagated, a hop is registered. Routers, bridges, and repeaters all count hops. Extenders do not count hops, as they do not regenerate packets, but only amplify them to increase their strength. See also *Router, Bridge, Repeater, Extender*.

Host An Internet server. Hosts are constantly connected to the Internet. See also *Internet*.

HTML See *Hypertext Markup Language*.

HTTP See *Hypertext Transfer Protocol*.

Hub A common connection point for devices in a network, typically connecting segments of a LAN. A hub contains multiple ports into which each segment is plugged. When a packet arrives at one port, it is copied to the other ports so that all segments of the LAN can see all packets. See also *Active Hub, Passive Hub, Intelligent Hub*.

Hyperlink   A link in text or graphics files containing a pointer to another document or portion of the same document that, when clicked, moves you to another part of the document or another document, either one stored locally or on a Web. You can identify a hyperlink because it is usually underlined or a different color from the rest of the document. Hyperlinks are commonly used in online Help systems and Web pages. See also *World Wide Web (WWW)*.

Hypertext Markup Language (HTML)   A formatting language that uses codes to identify sections of a document as headers, lists, hypertext links, and so on. HTML is the data format used on the World Wide Web for the publication of Web pages. See also *Hypertext Transfer Protocol (HTTP), World Wide Web (WWW)*.

Hypertext Transfer Protocol (HTTP)   Hypertext transfer protocol is an Internet protocol that transfers HTML documents over the Internet and responds to context changes that happen when a user clicks on a hypertext link. See also *Hypertext Markup Language (HTML), World Wide Web (WWW)*.

I

I/O Address   Area in memory dedicated to a single hardware device. The device stores information here that it needs the CPU to process, and collects the results of data the CPU has calculated for the device. See also *Central Processing Unit (CPU)*.

IIS   See *Internet Information Server*.

Infrared Communications   Type of wireless communications that uses signals in the infrared (very high frequency) range to transmit data. Infrared connections are high-speed but prone to interference. See also *Wireless Networking*.

Industry Standard Architecture (ISA)   The design standard for 16-bit Intel-compatible motherboards and peripheral buses. Adapters and interface cards must conform to the bus standard(s) used by the motherboard to be used with a computer. The 32-/64-bit PCI bus standard is replacing the ISA standard.

Instruction Set   Array of instructions built into the logic of a chip such as a CPU. These instructions might be either hard-wired into the chip or written in microcode. See also *Central Processing Unit (CPU), Microcode*.

Integrated Drive Electronics (IDE)

IDE devices use a simple mass storage device interconnection bus that operates at 5Mbps and can handle no more than two attached devices. See also *Small Computer Systems Interface (SCSI), Enhanced Integrated Drive Electronics (EIDE)*.

Integrated Services Digital Network (ISDN)

A direct, digital, dial-up public switched telephone network (PSTN) data link layer connection that operates at 64K per channel over regular twisted-pair cable between a subscriber site and a PSTN central office. Up to 24 channels can be multiplexed over two twisted pairs. See also *Data Link Layer*.

Intelligent Hub

Powered hub that supports management protocols such as SNMP. See also *Hub, Active Hub, Simple Network Management Protocol (SNMP)*.

Internet

A voluntarily interconnected global network of computers based upon the TCP/IP protocol suite. TCP/IP was originally developed by the U.S. Department of Defense's Advanced Research Projects Agency to facilitate the interconnection of military networks and was provided free to universities. The obvious utility of worldwide digital network connectivity and the availability of free complex networking software developed at universities doing military research attracted other universities, research institutions, private organizations, businesses, and finally the individual home user. The Internet is now available to all current commercial computing platforms. See also *File Transfer Protocol (FTP), World Wide Web (WWW), Transmission Control Protocol/Internet Protocol (TCP/IP)*.

Internet Information Server (IIS)

A Windows NT Web server product that serves Internet higher-level protocols such as HTTP and FTP to clients using Web browsers. See also *Hypertext Transfer Protocol (HTTP), File Transfer Protocol (FTP), World Wide Web (WWW)*.

Internet Protocol (IP)   The network layer protocol upon which the Internet is based. IP provides a simple connectionless packet exchange. See also *Transmission Control Protocol/ Internet Protocol (TCP/IP), Internet.*

Internet Service Provider (ISP)   A company that provides dial-up connections to the Internet. See also *Internet.*

Internetwork Packet Exchange (IPX)   The network protocol developed by Novell for its NetWare product. IPX is a routable protocol similar to IP, but is much easier to manage and has lower communication overhead. The term IPX can also refer to the family of protocols that includes the Synchronous Packet Exchange (SPX) transport layer protocol, a connection-oriented protocol that guarantees delivery in order, similar to the service provided by TCP. See also *Internet Protocol (IP), NetWare.*

Internetworking   Connecting two or more networks so that they can communicate but remain separate entities. See also *Intranetworking.*

InterNIC   The agency responsible for assigning IP addresses. See also *Internet Protocol (IP), IP Address.*

Interprocess Communication (IPC) A generic term describing any manner of client/server communication protocol, specifically those operating in the session, presentation, and application layers. Interprocess communication mechanisms provide a method for the client and server to trade information. See also *Named Pipes, Remote Procedure Calls (RPCs), Network Basic Input/ Output System (NetBIOS), Network Dynamic Data Exchange (NetDDE).*

Interrupt Request (IRQ)   Often shortened to "interrupt," this is a hardware signal from a peripheral device to the CPU indicating that the device has data to be processed by the CPU. If the CPU is not running a more important service, it will interrupt its current activity and handle the interrupt request. PCs have 16 levels of interrupt request lines, numbered 0-15. Generally speaking, each device must have a unique interrupt request line. See also *Central Processing Unit (CPU).*

Intranet   A privately owned network based on the TCP/IP protocol suite. See also *Transmission Control Protocol/Internet Protocol (TCP/IP).*

Intranetworking   Connecting two or more networks so that they can communicate but remain separate entities. See also *Internetworking.*

IP Address   A four-byte (32-bit) number that uniquely identifies a computer on an IP internetwork. InterNIC assigns the first bytes of Internet IP addresses and administers them in hierarchies. Huge organizations like the government or top-level ISPs have class A addresses, large organizations and most ISPs have class B addresses, and small companies have class C addresses. In a class A address, InterNIC assigns the first byte, and the owning organization assigns the remaining three bytes. In a class B address, InterNIC or the higher-level ISP assigns the first two bytes, and the organization assigns the remaining two bytes. In a class C address, InterNIC or the higher-level ISP assigns the first three bytes, and the organization assigns the remaining byte. Organizations not attached to the Internet are free to assign IP addresses as they please for internal use. See also *Internet Protocol (IP), Internet, InterNIC.*

IPC   See *Interprocess Communication.*

IP Security (IPSec)   Network layer protocol used to create VPNs. Rather than tunneling, encrypts IP packets for transmission across a public network, authenticating sender with certificates. See also *Virtual Private Network (VPN), Certificate, Internet Protocol (IP), Encryption.*

IPX   See *Internetwork Packet Exchange.*

IRQ   See *Interrupt Request.*

ISA   See *Industry Standard Architecture (ISA).*

ISDN   See *Integrated Services Digital Network.*

ISP   See *Internet Service Provider.*

J

JBOD   Just a Bunch Of Disks—a collection of hard disks in the same server not made into a RAID array.

K

Kernel   The core process of a preemptive operating system, consisting of a multitasking scheduler and the basic services that provide security. Depending on the operating system, other services such as virtual memory drivers may be built into the kernel. The kernel is responsible for managing the scheduling of threads and processes. See also *Operating System, Driver.*

L

LAN Manager   The Microsoft brand of a network product jointly developed by IBM and Microsoft that provided an early client/server environment. LAN Manager/Server was eclipsed by NetWare, but it was the genesis of many important protocols and IPC mechanisms used today, such as NetBIOS, named pipes, and NetBEUI. Portions of this product exist today in OS/2 Warp Server.

LAN Server   The IBM brand of a network product jointly developed by IBM and Microsoft. See also *LAN Manager*.

Layer 2 Tunneling Protocol (L2TP)   Data link layer protocol used to create VPNs over any network that supports UDP datagrams. Designed to cooperate with IPSec, but will use PPP if IPSec isn't available. See also *Data Link Layer, Virtual Private Network (VPN), IP Security (IPSec), Point-to-Point Protocol (PPP), Datagram, Point-to-Point Tunneling Protocol (PPTP)*.

Leaf Object   Objects in a directory structure that cannot contain other objects. See also *Directory Services, Container Object*.

Leased Line   Dedicated private line for point-to-point WAN connections.

License   User fee for software. You don't purchase software, you purchase the right to use it for a certain number of people or computers. Licenses may be granted on a per-user, per-computer, or other basis.

Line Protocol   Data-link protocol used for dial-up connections to a server. This protocol establishes communication over the wire. See also *Data Link Layer, Point to Point Protocol (PPP), Serial Line Internet Protocol (SLIP), Remote Access, Remote Control*.

Local Area Network (LAN)   A network contained within the confines of a single building or office.

Local Group   A group that exists in an NT computer's local accounts database. Local groups can reside on NT Workstations or NT Servers and can contain users or global groups.

Local User Profiles   User profiles are part of 32-bit Windows. Local profiles are stored only on the local computer. If a user logs onto one computer, makes changes to the environment, and then logs onto another computer, the changes from the first computer are not reflected on the second computer.

Logging   The process of recording information about activities and errors in the operating system. Log files often have a .LOG extension and can be read either with a text editor or with a tool included for that purpose.

Logical Topology   The electrical layout of your network describing how data are passed around the network, how stations on the network are prevented from interrupting each other, and how low-level error checking works. Also called an electrical topology. See also *Bus Physical Topology, Ring Physical Topology, Physical Topology.*

Logical Link Connection (LLC) Part of the data link layer that handles the interface between all networking topologies and the network-layer communication protocols. Also called the data link connection. See also *Data Link Layer, Media Access Control (MAC).*

Logon Script   Batch files that automate the logon process by performing utility functions such as attaching to additional server resources or automatically running different programs based upon the user account that established the logon.

Long File Name (LFN)   A filename longer than the eight characters plus three-character extension allowed by MS-DOS. In 32-bit Windows, filenames can contain up to 255 characters.

M

MAC Address   See also *Physical Address.*

MAC Table   A table a bridge maintains to determine which port to forward a packet to. Bridges build their MAC tables by collecting the MAC source addresses of the packets they receive and noting which port the packets came from. See also *Bridge, Physical Address.*

Mandatory User Profile   A user profile that is created by an administrator and saved with a special extension (.MAN) so that the user cannot modify the profile in any way. Mandatory user profiles can be assigned to a single user or a group of users, and are generally used to present a consistent Desktop across the network. See also *User Profile.*

Master Boot Record (MBR) The MBR is a small program executed when a computer boots up. Typically, the MBR resides on the first sector of the hard disk. The program begins the boot process by looking up the partition table to determine which partition to use for booting. It then transfers program control to the boot sector of that partition, which continues the boot process. In DOS and Windows systems, you can create the MBR with the FDISK /MBR command.

Master Browser The computer on a network that maintains a list of computers and services available on the network and distributes the list to other browsers. The master browser may also promote potential browsers to be browsers. See also *Browser, Browsing, Backup Browser*.

Media Access Control (MAC) The part of the data link layer that supports the driver for the network card. This layer helps watch for errors in the transmission and conversion of signals. See also *Data Link Layer*.

Microcode Software language developed to program CPUs with their instruction set. More flexible than hard-wiring, and could be shorter (and thus less memory-intensive) than the hard-wired programs as the code could call on functions built into the chip. See also *Instruction Set, Central Processing Unit (CPU)*.

Microprocessor An integrated semiconductor circuit designed to automatically perform lists of logical and arithmetic operations. Modern microprocessors independently manage memory pools and support multiple instruction lists called *threads*. Microprocessors are also capable of responding to interrupt requests from peripherals and include onboard support for complex floating-point arithmetic. Microprocessors must have instructions when they are first powered on. These instructions are contained in nonvolatile firmware called a BIOS. See also *Basic Input/Output System (BIOS), Operating System, Central Processing Unit (CPU)*.

Modal Dispersion In fiber optic cable, spreading of the light impulse, thus slowing down the signal. See also *Fiber Optic Cable, Mode*.

Mode   A ray of light entering a fiber optic cable at a particular angle. Fiber optic cable may be single-mode (with one single ray of light) or multimode (with multiple rays of light). Single-mode fiber uses very intense beams of light, so this fiber type is typically used for transmitting data over long distances, often between buildings. Multimode fiber is more often used for interior work and is cheaper. See also *Fiber Optic Cable, Step Index Cable, Graded Index Cable.*

Modem Pooling   Sharing multiple identical physical modems under the same logical name, so that a request to use the modem with that name may be served by any of those modems.

Module   A software component of a modular operating system that provides a certain defined service. Modules can be installed or removed depending upon the service requirements of the software running on the computer. Modules allow operating systems and applications to be customized to fit the needs of the user.

Monolithic Device Driver   Device driver that combines the logic to control the communication between hardware and operating system with the network

protocol. Not often found today because of the lack of flexibility in this design.

Multibank DRAM (MDRAM)
Video memory split into several banks, so that reads and writes may be interleaved among several banks at once.

Multiprocessing   Using two or more processors simultaneously to perform a computing task. Depending on the operating system, processing may be done asymmetrically, wherein certain processors are assigned certain threads independent of the load they create, or symmetrically, wherein threads are dynamically assigned to processors according to an equitable scheduling scheme. The term usually describes a multiprocessing capacity built into the computer at a hardware level in that the computer itself supports more than one processor. However, *multiprocessing* can also be applied to network computing applications achieved through interprocess communication mechanisms. Client/server applications are, in fact, examples of multiprocessing. Windows 98 does not support multiprocessor computers. See also *Interprocess Communication (IPC).*

Multitasking   The capacity of an operating system to rapidly switch among threads of execution. Multitasking allows processor time to be divided among threads as if each thread ran on its own slower processor. Multitasking operating systems allow two or more applications to run at the same time and can provide a greater degree of service to applications than single-tasking operating systems such as MS-DOS. Microsoft operating systems support either cooperative multitasking (wherein applications are expected to relinquish control of the CPU when another application needs it) or preemptive multitasking (wherein application threads are allocated CPU time based on the threads' priority). See also *Multiprocessor, Multithreaded*.

Multithreaded   Multithreaded programs have more than one chain of execution, thus relying on the services of a multitasking or multiprocessing operating system to operate. Multiple chains of execution allow programs to simultaneously perform more than one task. In multitasking computers, multithreading is merely a convenience used to make programs run smoother and free the program from the burden of switching between tasks itself. On multiprocessing computers, multithreading allows the compute burden of the program to be spread across many processors. Programs that are not multithreaded cannot take advantage of multiple processors in a computer, although more than one single-threaded application may be able to run at once. See also *Multitasking, Multiprocessor*.

N

Named Pipes   An interprocess communication mechanism that is implemented as a file system service, allowing programs to be modified to run on it without using a proprietary application programming interface. Named Pipes were developed to support more robust client/server communications than those allowed by the simpler NetBIOS. See also *Interprocess Communication (IPC)*.

NCP   See *NetWare Core Protocol*.

NDIS   See *Network Driver Interface Specification*.

NDS   See *NetWare Directory Services*.

NetBEUI   See NetBIOS Extended User Interface.

NetBIOS   See *Network Basic Input/Output System*.

NetBIOS Extended User Interface (NetBEUI) A simple network layer transport developed to support NetBIOS applications. NetBEUI is not routable, and so is not appropriate for larger networks. NetBEUI is the fastest transport protocol available for Windows 98.

NetBIOS Gateway A service provided by the Windows NT Remote Access Service that allows NetBIOS requests to be forwarded independent of transport protocol. For example, NetBIOS requests from a remote computer connected via NetBEUI can be sent over the network via NWLink. See also *Network Basic Input/Output System (NetBIOS), NetBIOS over TCP/IP (NetBT), NetBIOS Extended User Interface (NetBEUI).*

NetBIOS over TCP/IP (NetBT) A network service that implements the NetBIOS IPC over the TCP/IP protocol stack. See also *Network Basic Input/Output System (NetBIOS), Interprocess Communication (IPC), Transmission Control Protocol/Internet Protocol (TCP/IP).*

NetBT See *NetBIOS over TCP/IP.*

NetDDE See *Network Dynamic Data Exchange.*

NetWare A popular network operating system developed by Novell in the early 1980s. NetWare is a cooperative, multitasking, highly optimized, dedicated-server network operating system that has client support for most major operating systems. Recent versions of NetWare include graphical client tools for management from client stations. At one time, NetWare accounted for more than 70% of the network operating system market, but Microsoft's Windows NT is rapidly gaining market share. See also *Windows NT.*

NetWare Core Protocol (NCP) NetWare servers communicate using a language called NCP. To communicate with a NetWare server, a client must be able to support NCP.

NetWare Directory Services (NDS) In NetWare, a distributed hierarchy of network services such as servers, shared volumes, and printers. NetWare implements NDS as a directory structure having elaborate security and administration mechanisms. Windows 98 supports connectivity to NDS volumes with the Service for NetWare Directory Services. See also *NetWare, Bindery.*

NetWatcher Interactive tool included with Windows 98 for creating, controlling, and monitoring remote shared resources.

Network Basic Input/Output System (NetBIOS)   A client/server interprocess communication service developed by IBM in the early 1980s. NetBIOS presents a relatively primitive mechanism for communication in client/server applications, but its widespread acceptance and availability across most operating systems makes it a logical choice for simple network applications. Many of the network IPC mechanisms in Windows NT are implemented over NetBIOS. See also *Interprocess Communication (IPC), Client/Server*.

Network Computer   Thin client device designed to run both applications on a terminal server and small (typically Java-based) applications locally. See also *Thin Client Networking, Terminal Server*.

Network Driver Interface Specification (NDIS)   A Microsoft specification to which network adapter drivers must conform to work with Microsoft network operating systems. NDIS provides a many-to-many binding between network adapter drivers and transport protocols, simplifying the driver development process by eliminating monolithic driver/protocol stacks. See also *Transport Protocol*.

Network Dynamic Data Exchange (NetDDE)   An interprocess communication mechanism developed by Microsoft to support the distribution of DDE applications over a network. See also *Interprocess Communication (IP), Dynamic Data Exchange (DDE)*.

Network Interface Card (NIC)   A physical layer adapter device that allows a computer to connect to and communicate over a network. See also *Ethernet, Token Ring, Adapter*.

Network Layer   The layer of the OSI model that creates a communication path between two computers via routed packets. Transport protocols implement both the network layer and the transport layer of the OSI stack. IP is a network layer service. See also *Internet Protocol (IP), Open Systems Interconnect Model (OSI)*.

Network Number   In IPX/SPX networks, the identifier for the physical segment to which a computer is attached. Also called the external network address. Together with the node number, this address identifies computers and their location on the network. See also *Node Number*.

Network Operating System (NOS)
A computer operating system specifically designed to optimize a computer's ability to respond to service requests. Servers run network operating systems. Windows NT Server and NetWare are client/server network operating systems, and Windows 98 is a peer NOS. See also *Windows NT, Server, NetWare, Client/ Server, Network Operating System (NOS), Peer Network, Operating System.*

Network Binding Interface   Interface between network card driver and protocol stack that makes monolithic device drivers obsolete. Similar in function to an API. See also *Driver, Protocol Stack, Monolithic Device Driver, Application Programming Interface (API).*

New Technology File System (NTFS)   A secure, transaction-oriented file system developed for Windows NT that incorporates the Windows NT security model for assigning permissions and shares. NTFS is optimized for hard drives larger than 500MB and requires too much overhead to be used on hard disk drives smaller than 50MB.

NIC   See *Network Interface Card.*

Node Number   Also called the internal network address, this number identifies a particular computer (or, more precisely, a NIC inside a computer; a computer would have more than one node number if it had more than one NIC) on an IPX/SPX network. Combined with the network number to fully identify a computer and its location. See also *Network Number.*

Non-Browser   A computer on a network that will not maintain a list of other computers and services on the network. See also *Browser, Browsing.*

NTFS   See *New Technology File System.*

O

Open Graphics Language (OpenGL)   A standard interface for the presentation of two- and three-dimensional visual data.

Open Shortest Path First (OSPF)
Route discovery protocol in which routers are logically arranged in a tree structure. Each router announces itself to the routers immediately adjoining it and collects data from those routers as well. From this information, routers develop paths to various destinations on the network, noting both a main path and backup paths (unlike RIP, which only maintains a single path). Routers using OSPF are divided into areas, to which flooding is confined. A backbone router forwards route tables from one area to another.

Open System   Networking system that can easily communicate with other networking systems because they all use the same communications model. See also *Open Systems Interconnect (OSI) Model.*

Open Systems Interconnect (OSI) Model   A model for network component interoperability developed by the International Standards Organization to promote cross-vendor compatibility of hardware and software network systems. The OSI model splits the process of networking into seven distinct services. Each layer uses the services of the layer below to provide its service to the layer above. See also *Physical Layer, Data Link Layer, Network Layer, Transport Layer, Session Layer, Presentation Layer, Application Layer.*

OpenGL   See *Open Graphics Language.*

Operating System   A collection of services that form a foundation upon which applications run. Operating systems may be simple I/O service providers with a command shell, such as MS-DOS, or they may be sophisticated, preemptive, multitasking applications platforms such as Windows NT. See also *Network Operating System (NOS), Preemptive Multitasking, Kernel.*

Optimization   Any effort to reduce the workload on a hardware component by eliminating, obviating, or reducing the amount of work required of the hardware component through any means. For instance, file caching is an optimization that reduces the workload of a hard disk drive.

OSI Model   See *Open Systems Interconnect Model (OSI).*

P

Packet   Portion of network data that contains addressing information, source and destination addresses for the packet, and sometimes error checking information. See also *Frame.*

Packet-Switched Network   WAN type that does not establish virtual channels between sender and receiver. Instead, each packet sent on the network carries its routing information with it so that it can dynamically choose its path. Not all packets in the same transmission may take the same path, if a lower-cost one appears in the middle of the transmission. See also *Frame Relay, X.25, Routing, Cost.*

Page File   See *Swap File.*

Partition   A logical section of a hard disk that can contain an independent file system volume. Partitions can be used to keep multiple operating systems and file systems on the same hard disk. See also *Volume*.

Passive Hub   An unpowered hub. See also *Hub*.

PC Card   See *Personal Computer Memory Card International Association*.

PCI   See *Peripheral Connection Interface*.

PCMCIA   See *Personal Computer Memory Card International Association*.

PDC   See *Primary Domain Controller*.

Peer   A networked computer that both shares resources with other computers and accesses the shared resources of other computers. A non-dedicated server. See also *Server, Client*.

Peer Network   In a peer network, all computers may share resources with the rest of the network, and there is no centralized organization of files or shared resources. A peer network is configured and used by end users with no particular need for an administrator to do anything on the server. Each node is administered by its user.

Peripheral Device   Any piece of hardware that attaches to the motherboard of your computer, whether directly or indirectly. Peripheral devices include both external devices such as printers and internal ones such as network cards.

Peripheral Connection Interface (PCI)   A high-speed 32-/64-bit bus developed by Intel and widely accepted as the successor to the 16-bit ISA interface. PCI devices support I/O throughput about 40 times faster than the ISA bus. PCI is a 64-bit bus, though it is usually implemented as a 32-bit bus. It can run at clock speeds of 33 or 66MHz. At 32 bits and 33MHz, it yields a throughput rate of 133MBps.

Permissions   Assignments of levels of access to a resource made to groups or users. Permissions are security constructs that regulate access to resources by user name or group affiliation. Administrators can assign permissions to allow any level of access, such as read only, read/write, or delete, by controlling the ability of users to initiate object services. Security is implemented by checking the user's security identifier against each object's access control list. See also *Security Identifiers (SIDs)*.

Personal Computer Memory Card International Association (PCMCIA)   A standard developed by the PCMCIA to describe small credit-card–sized devices that fit into slots in a laptop computer. Generally, you can swap PCMCIA devices in and out of your computer without rebooting.

There are three kinds of PCMCIA devices, all three the same length and width but of different thicknesses. Type I cards are up to 3.3 mm thick, and are typically used for adding additional ROM or RAM to a computer. Type II cards can be up to 5.5 mm thick, and are often used for modem and fax modem cards. Type III cards can be up to 10.5 mm thick, and are used for portable disk drives.

Each type of PCMCIA device has a corresponding slot type, which can hold either one of the cards of that type or one each of the cards or the lower types. For example, a Type III slot can hold either one Type III card or one Type II and one Type I.

Physical Address   A computer's address, as burned into its network card during the manufacturing process. This address identifies the computer (or, more precisely, the network card) at the data link layer. See also *Data Link Layer, Address Resolution Protocol (ARP)*.

Physical Layer   The cables, connectors, and connection ports of a network. See also *Open Systems Interconnect (OSI) Model*.

Physical Topology   The physical layout of the network. See also *Bus Physical Topology, Ring Physical Topology, Star Physical Topology, Logical Topology*.

Plenum   Coating for network cables that does not emit poisonous fumes when burning. Because of this, fire codes often demand the use of plenum cables between floors of a building. See also *Polyvinyl Chloride (PVC)*.

Plug and Play (PnP) Refers to the ability of an operating system to automatically configure expansion boards and other devices. You should be able to plug in a device and have it work on rebooting, without worrying about setting DIP switches or jumpers, or running configuration software. This technology allows you to install Plug-and-Play hardware into your system without having to reconfigure the hardware or the computer system.

Point and Print Used to install driver files for a networked printer by dragging the Point-and-Print printer icon from the networked PC to the Printers folder. Documents can be printed to networking printers by simply dragging and dropping onto the printer icon.

Point-to-Point Protocol (PPP) A data link layer line protocol that performs over point-to-point network connections such as serial or modem lines. PPP can negotiate any transport protocol used by both systems involved in the link and can automatically assign IP, DNS, and gateway addresses when used with TCP/IP. See also *Internet Protocol (IP), Domain Name Service (DNS), Gateway, Line Protocol.*

Point-to-Point Tunneling Protocol (PPTP) Data link protocol used to create secure connections between private networks through the public Internet or other IP networks, creating a virtual private network. Dependent on PPP. See also *Internet, Virtual Private Network, Point-to-Point Protocol (PPP).*

Polling Method of one device periodically checking with another to see whether the second device needs the first.

Polyvinyl Chloride (PVC) Inexpensive coating for cables that emits toxic fumes when it burns. Not always permitted in all installations, depending on the fire codes. See also *Plenum.*

PPP See also *Point-to-Point Protocol.*

PPTP See also *Point-to-Point Tunneling Protocol.*

Preemptive Multitasking   A type of multitasking implemented at the operating system level in which an interrupt routine in the kernel manages the scheduling of processor time among running threads. The threads themselves do not need to support multitasking in any way because the microprocessor will preempt the thread with an interrupt, save its state, update all thread priorities according to its scheduling algorithm, and pass control to the highest-priority thread awaiting execution. See also *Kernel, Thread, Operating System.*

Preferences   Characteristics of user accounts, such as password, profile location, home directory, and logon script.

Presentation Layer   The layer of the OSI model that converts and translates (if necessary) information between the session and application layers. See also *Open Systems Interconnect Model (OSI).*

Primary Domain Controller (PDC) The NT domain server that contains the master copy of the security, computer, and user accounts databases and that can authenticate workstations. The PDC can replicate its databases to one or more backup domain controllers. The PDC is usually also the master browser for the domain. See also *Backup Domain Controllers, Domain, Master Browser.*

Print Driver   A driver is software that controls a device, and each device type has its own set of commands included in the driver. Each printing device has its own command set. The print driver is the specific software that understands your print device. Each print device has an associated print driver.

Print Pooling   Logically combining several physical printers under the same name, so that a print job sent to that name may be printed on any of those physical printers.

Print Server   Print servers are the computers on which the printers have been defined. When you send a job to a network printer not connected directly to the network, you are actually sending it to the print server first.

Print Spooler (Print Queue)   The print spooler is a directory or folder on the print server that stores the print jobs until they can be printed. It's very important that your print server and print spooler have enough hard disk space to hold all of the print jobs that could be pending at any given time. See also *Print Server.*

Priority   A level of execution importance assigned to a thread. In combination with other factors, the priority level determines how often that thread will get computer time according to a scheduling algorithm. See also *Preemptive Multitasking, Thread.*

Process   A running program containing one or more threads. A process encapsulates the protected memory and environment for its threads.

Processor   A circuit designed to automatically perform lists of logical and arithmetic operations. Unlike microprocessors, processors may be designed from discrete components rather than being a monolithic integrated circuit. See also *Microprocessor.*

Program   A list of processor instructions designed to perform a certain function. A running program is called a *process*. A package of one or more programs and attendant data designed to meet a certain application is called *software* or an *application*.

Programmable Input/Output (PIO)
Method by which the CPU moves data from a peripheral device's memory to main memory. Replaced in some cases with a faster method called DMA. See also *Direct Memory Access (DMA), Peripheral Device.*

Programming Interfaces   Interprocess communications mechanisms that provide certain high-level services to running processes. Programming interfaces may provide network communication, graphical presentation, or any other type of software service. See also *Interprocess Communication (IPC).*

Protocol   In general terms, a convention for communications between two parts of a computer. Often used to refer to the network protocol, the convention for allowing two computers to communicate over a network.

Protocol Stack   Collection of networking protocols that work together to transmit data across the network. Protocol stacks operate at several layers of the OSI model. See also *Protocol, Open Systems Interconnect (OSI) Model.*

Proxy Server   Networked computer running software that allows it to act as a portal between one network and another, such as the Internet. May be used for security or load balancing, invisibly to the clients.

Punchdown Block   Unpowered connection area for network cables arranged in the star physical topology.

R

Radio Frequency Interference (RFI)

Interference generated by electronic transmissions. RFI is pretty much the same thing as EMI, except that EMI refers to interference caused by any large electrical output (such as a heavy motor) and RFI generally refers to interference generated by transmissions, as from cables or radios.

Random Access

An access method by which data can be pulled from any location as easily as from any other—it's not necessary to move sequentially through the volume. Hard disks are random access devices. See also *Sequential Access*.

Random Access Memory (RAM)

Physical memory that can be accessed randomly, not just sequentially. RAM is extremely important to computer performance, as it stores all data currently being used by the computer. See also *Static RAM (SRAM), Dynamic RAM (DRAM)*.

Redirector

A software service that redirects user file I/O requests over the network. Novell implements the Workstation service and Client Services for NetWare as redirectors, as does Microsoft with its Client for Microsoft Networks. Redirectors allow servers to be used as mass storage devices that appear local to the user.

Reduced Instruction Set Chip (RISC)

A microprocessor technology that implements fewer and more primitive instructions than typical microprocessors and can therefore be implemented quickly with the most modern semiconductor technology and speeds. Programs written for RISC microprocessors require more instructions (longer programs) to perform the same task as a normal microprocessor, but because their instructions are so simple, they are capable of a greater degree of optimization and therefore usually run faster. See also *Microprocessor, Central Processing Unit (CPU)*.

Registry

A database of settings required and maintained by Windows 98 and its components. The registry contains all the configuration information used by the computer. It is stored as a hierarchical structure and is made up of keys, hives, and value entries. You can use the Registry Editor (REGEDIT) to change these settings.

Remote Access

A service that allows network connections to be established over telephone lines with modems or digital adapters. The computer initiating the connection is called the guest; the answering computer is called the RAS host. See also *Remote Control*.

Remote boot   The remote boot service starts diskless workstations over the network.

Remote Control   Dialing into another computer and controlling it remotely. All applications run on the remote computer but are displayed on—and take input from—the one dialing in.

Remote Procedure Calls (RPCs)   A network interprocess communication mechanism that allows an application to be distributed among many computers on the same network. See also *Interprocess Communications (IPC)*.

Repeater   Device that regenerates an electronic or photonic signal so as to increase the distance that signal can travel. Used in Ethernet networks to broaden their reach. See also *Extender, Ethernet*.

Request for Comment (RFC)   Any of a set of written standards or proposed standards defining how the Internet works.

Resource   Any useful service, such as a shared network directory or a printer. See also *Share*.

Ring Physical Topology   Physical arrangement of the network in which the computers all share a cable and are arranged in a ring. Used in FDDI and fibre channel networks, otherwise rare. See also *Physical Topology, Fiber Distributed Data Interface (FDDI), Fibre Channel*.

RIP   See *Routing Information Protocol*.

RISC   See *Reduced Instruction Set Chip*.

Roaming User Profile   A user profile that is stored and configured to be downloaded from a server. Roaming user profiles allow users to access their profile from any location on the network. See also *User Profile*.

Root Bridge   Bridge with the lowest priority in a network; the one that all other bridges define themselves in relationship to. The root bridge is determined at network startup, while all bridges trade information about their priority and cost. See also *Bridge*.

Router   A device that moves packets between networks that use a common routable network layer protocol. Routers provide internetwork connectivity. See also *Network Layer*.

Routing Information Protocol (RIP)   A protocol within the TCP/IP protocol suite that allows routers to exchange routing information with adjoining routers, including the cost of a given route and the router's status. A variant of the RIP protocol also exists for the IPX/SPX protocol suite. See also *Transmission Control Protocol/Internet Protocol (TCP/IP)*.

Routing Table   List of addresses on the local segment that a router maintains. If the destination address of a packet a router receives is not in the router's routing table, the router will forward the packet.

RPCs   See *Remote Procedure Calls*.

S

Safe Mode   Safe mode bypasses loading the registry and bypasses the CONFIG.SYS and AUTOEXEC.BAT files. It does not load any network functionality or protected-mode drivers. It starts Windows 98 in standard VGA and loads HIMEM.SYS, IFSHLP.SYS, and the Path from MSDOS.SYS. Safe mode is useful for troubleshooting suspected problems with protected-mode drivers.

SAM   See *Security Accounts Manager*.

SAP   See *Service Advertisement Protocol*.

Scheduling   The process of determining which threads should be executed according to their priority and other factors. See also *Preemptive Multitasking*.

Screw-Mounted Adapter (SMA) Type of connector used on fiber optic cable, screwing into the end of the cable. Less common than spring-loaded twist (ST). See also *Fiber Optic Cable, Spring-Loaded Twist*.

SCSI   See *Small Computer Systems Interface*.

Search Engine   A Web site dedicated to responding to requests for specific information, searching massive locally stored databases of Web pages, and responding with the URLs of pages that fit the search phrase. See also *World Wide Web, Uniform Resource Locato (URL)*.

Sector   Smallest physical unit of organization on a hard disk. In Microsoft file systems, logically combined into clusters. See also *Cluster.*

Security   Measures taken to secure a system against accidental or intentional loss or corruption, usually in the form of accountability procedures and use restriction. See also *Security Identifiers (SIDs), Security Accounts Manager (SAM).*

Security Accounts Manager (SAM)
The module of the Windows NT executive that authenticates a user name and password against a database of accounts, generating an access token that includes the user's permissions. See also *Security, Security Identifier (SIDs).*

Security Identifiers (SIDs)
Unique codes that identify a specific user or group to the Windows NT security system. Security identifiers contain a complete set of permissions for that user or group.

Segment   Portion of a network divided from the rest of the network by a router. See also *Router.*

Sequential Access   Data must be accessed in the order in which it was written to the device. You can't skip around on a sequential access device such as a tape, but must proceed directly through it.

Serial Line Internet Protocol (SLIP)   An implementation of the IP protocol over serial lines. SLIP has been obviated by PPP. See also *Point-to-Point Protocol (PPP), Internet Protocol (IP).*

Server   A network-capable computer dedicated to servicing requests for resources from other computers on a network. See also *Client, Resource.*

Server Element   Part of remote access or remote control software that runs on the computer being connected to. See also *Client Element, Remote Control, Remote Access, Thin Client Networking.*

Server Message Blocks (SMBs)   A message format used by Microsoft network operating systems to share resources. SMB-based networks include LAN manager, Windows for Workgroups, Windows NT, Windows 98, and LAN Server.

Service   A process dedicated to implementing a specific function for another process. Most Windows NT components are services used by user-level applications.

Service Advertisement Protocol (SAP)   A NetWare packet that is broadcast from the server every 60 seconds that contains the server name and the shared resources it has. Windows 98 can also generate a SAP so that NetWare clients will see the Windows 98 box as a NetWare server.

Session Layer   The layer of the OSI model dedicated to maintaining a bidirectional communication connection between two computers. The session layer uses the services of the transport layer to provide this service. See also *OSI Model, Transport Layer*.

Shadow Packets   Extraneous packets created in an improperly terminated Ethernet network, by causing real packets to echo back at the end of the segment instead of being destroyed. Shadow packets can increase network traffic. See also *Ethernet, Terminator*.

Share   A resource (for example, a directory or printer) shared by a server or a peer on a network. See also *Resource, Server, Peer*.

Share-Level Security   The default level of security used in Windows 98. Share-level security is based on passwords assigned to shared resources.

Shielded Twisted Pair (STP)   Type of twisted pair in which the wires are protected from interference not only by their twists but by an additional layer of insulating foil. Most often used in Token Ring networks. See also *Twisted Pair, Token Ring*.

Shell   The user interface of an operating system; the shell launches applications and manages file systems.

Security ID (SID)   See *Security Identifiers*.

Simple Network Management Protocol (SNMP)   An Internet protocol that manages network hardware such as routers, switches, servers, and clients from a single client on the network. See also *Internet Protocol (IP)*.

Small Computer Systems Interface (SCSI)   A high-speed, parallel-bus interface that connects hard disk drives, CD-ROM drives, tape drives, and many other peripherals to a computer. SCSI is a parallel interface standard used by Macintosh computers, PCs, and many UNIX systems for attaching peripheral devices to computers. SCSI interfaces provide for faster data transmission rates (up to 80MBps) than do serial and parallel ports, or the IDE or EIDE disk controllers. You can attach several devices to a single SCSI port, so that SCSI is really an I/O bus rather than simply an interface.

SneakerNet   Copying data from a hard disk to a floppy, then walking to another computer to transferring the data there or print a file. Refers to the need to walk between computers to transfer data.

Socket   A temporary communication channel opened between a client application and server application. These applications may be running either on the same machine or on two separate machines connected with a network. See *Remote Procedure Calls (RPCs)*.

Solid Wire   A wiring configuration used in some copper cables. Solid-wire cable is made of a single wire.

Source Route Bridging   Bridging method used in Token Ring networks to identify the best path to a given destination and store a record of that path. It's more like routing than like STA bridging in that it does dynamic path discovery, rather than being updated when paths are found to be dysfunctional (like STA). See also *Bridge, Spanning Tree Algorithm (STA), Router*.

Source Routing   Routing method in which a router determines the best path to take to a packet's destination.

Spanning Tree Algorithm (STA)   Transparent bridging method used in Ethernet networks to determine the best path to any given segment, and then block off any other possible routes. If only one path is available, then a bridge can't loop.

Spooler   A service that buffers output to a low-speed device such as a printer so that the application sending data to the device is not tied up waiting for the data transfer to complete.

Spring-Loaded Twist (ST)   Type of fiber optic cable connector that clamps onto the cable's end. More common than the screw-mounted adapters. See also *Fiber Optic Cable, Screw-Mounted Adapter (SMA)*.

Star Physical Topology   Physical arrangement of the network in which each computer has its own cable connection to a central hub or punch down block. This hub provides a central switching point for all network nodes to communicate. See also *Physical Topology, Hub, Connected Star*.

Static RAM (SRAM)   Physical memory used in CPU caching that doesn't need to be refreshed. SRAM remembers everything it's told from the time data goes into memory until either the data is flushed or the computer is turned off. See also *Random Access Memory (RAM), Dynamic RAM (DRAM), Caching, Central Processing Unit (CPU)*.

Step Index Cable   Multimode fiber optic cable in which the modes take on a zigzag pattern. See also *Fiber Optic Cable, Mode, Modal Dispersion*.

Store-and-Forward Switching
Process by which the switch receives an entire frame and inspects it for errors before forwarding the frame to its destination MAC address. Only frames without errors get forwarded. This switching method is somewhat slower than cut-through switching, but has more error control. Both bridges and some switches support store-and-forward switching. See also *Switch, Bridge, Cut-Through Switching*.

Stranded Wire   A wiring configuration used in some copper cables. Stranded wire cable is made of several smaller wires combined. Stranded-wire cables are more flexible than solid-wire cables, but more vulnerable to signal loss.

Subnet   Segment of an IP network, identified by a particular subnet mask. See also *Internet Protocol (IP), Subnet Mask*.

Subnet Mask   A number used to determine to which subnet an IP address belongs. An IP address has two components—the network address and the host address—and although they're generally written in decimal format (dotted quad), the IP address is actually a binary number. The mask is also a binary number. All IP addresses that are part of the same subnet will have 1s in the same place in the network portion of the address.

Swap File Data are available for manipulation only when stored in RAM. But to allow modern computers to seem to store more data than there's room for in RAM, these modern computers use *virtual memory*. This is a construct in which data not being used at the moment are stored in a special area of the hard disk reserved for this purpose. If the data are needed, they can be restored from the hard disk and reloaded into memory. This area of the hard disk is called the swap file or page file. See also *Virtual Memory*.

Switch Intelligent hub that reads the (physical) destination address of a packet it receives and propagates that packet only on the port through which that address can be reached. See also *Hub, Cut-Through Switching, Store-and-Forward Switching, Physical Address*.

Synchronized Graphics RAM (SGRAM) High-speed single-ported video memory.

System Policy Created with the System Policy Editor, system policies are used to control the degree of discretion a user has over his or her environment and the actions that she or he can perform. System policies can be applied to a specific user or group, a computer, or all users. System policies work by overwriting current settings in the registry with the system policy settings. See also *Registry, System Policy Editor*.

System Policy Editor A utility found within the Administrative Tools group used to create system policies. This tool is not loaded automatically with Windows 98, but must be installed manually from the Add/Remove Programs applet. See also *System Policy*.

T

TAPI See *Telephony Application Program Interface*.

Taskbar The bar at the bottom of the screen that displays icons representing running programs as well as the Start menu button for accessing new applications. Used to switch between running programs or start new ones, the Taskbar also displays some system status information such as the time of day. Some applications also display information in the Taskbar, including a printer icon when a document is printing, or a letter icon when e-mail has arrived.

TCP See *Transmission Control Protocol*.

TCP/IP See *Transmission Control Protocol/Internet Protocol*.

TDI See *Transport Driver Interface*.

Telephony Application Program Interface (TAPI) TAPI is a standard way for programs to interact with the telephony functionality in Windows 98.

Templates ASCII files that correspond to subkeys and values in the registry. Template files (.ADM files) are used in creating system policies.

Terminal Emulation Method by which a PC pretends to be a dumb terminal so the PC can communicate with a mainframe.

Terminal Server Server running software that allows it to run applications locally while displaying application output on the desktop of a client machine. Input is generated by the client. See also *Thin Client Networking*.

Terminator Device used at the end of an Ethernet bus network to mark the end of the segment. Without proper termination, shadow packets will propagate on the network. See also *Ethernet, Shadow Packets*.

Thicknet Thick coaxial cable used as the backbone of 10Base5. Even though it can extend farther than Thinnet, it's not often used today because of its extreme stiffness.

Thin Client Networking Networking paradigm that combines a terminal server with client machines. Each client has its own private session on the terminal server, in which it can run applications. Input is generated on the client end and uploaded to the terminal server, and display commands are downloaded to the client. See also *Terminal Server, Display Protocol*.

Thinnet Thin coaxial cable used in 10Base2 networks. This cable type is more common today than Thicknet.

Thread A list of instructions running in a computer to perform a certain task. Each thread runs in the context of a process, which embodies the protected memory space and the environment of the threads. Multithreaded processes can perform more than one task at the same time. See also *Process, Preemptive Multitasking, Program*.

Throughput Effective network speed, calculated by combining available network bandwidth and network speed. See also *Bandwidth*.

Token Master   Node of a Token Ring network that manages tokens for the network. Also called the active monitor. See also *Token Ring, Token Packet.*

Token Packet   Administrative token used in Token Ring networks to determine which computer gets to transmit data. A computer can't transmit unless it has the token packet, or token. See also *Token Ring.*

Token Ring   Developed by IBM, Token Ring is the second most popular data link layer standard for local area networking. Token Ring implements the token-passing method of arbitrating multiple-computer access to the same network. Token Ring operates at either 4 or 16Mbps. See also *Data Link Layer.*

Transmission Control Protocol (TCP)   A transport layer protocol that implements guaranteed packet delivery using the Internet Protocol (IP). See *Internet Protocol (IP).*

Transmission Control Protocol/Internet Protocol (TCP/IP) A suite of network protocols upon which the global Internet is based, and in use now on many private networks. TCP/IP is a general term that can refer either to the TCP and IP protocols used together or to the complete set of Inter-net protocols. TCP/IP is the default protocol for Windows NT.

Transparent Bridging   A simple bridging technique in which the bridge accumulates information about which addresses are available via which ports. When the bridge gets a packet from a segment, it forwards the packet to the appropriate port.

Transport Driver Interface (TDI) A specification to which all Window NT transport protocols must be written to be used by higher-level services such as programming interfaces, file systems, and interprocess communication mechanisms. See also *Transport Protocol.*

Transport Layer   The OSI layer responsible for the guaranteed serial delivery of packets between two computers over an internetwork. TCP is the transport-layer protocol for the TCP/IP transport protocol.

Transport Protocol   A service that delivers discrete packets of information between any two computers in a network. Transport protocols may operate at the datalink, network, transport, or session layers of the OSI stack. Higher-level, connection-oriented services are built upon transport protocols.

Truncated Binary Exponential Backoff   Method by which Ethernet networks determine the order in which nodes should transmit after a collision has taken place. See also *Ethernet, Collision.*

Tunneling   Method of transferring packets using a given protocol over a network that doesn't support that protocol. The unsupported packets are wrapped in the supported one for the duration of the trip across the network, then unwrapped when they reach their destination.

Twisted Pair   Four-wire copper cable, with the wires within the cable twisted around each other, protect the wires from interference. Twisted pair comes in two main styles—shielded and unshielded—and currently five different categories, denoted by both wire type, the number of twists per foot, and the complexity of the twists. Category 5 (the highest standard) is most often used for new networks. See also *Radio Frequency Interference (RFI), Solid Wire, Shielded Twisted Pair (STP), Unshielded Twisted Pair (UTP).*

U

UNC   See *Universal Naming Convention.*

Uniform Resource Locator (URL)   An Internet standard naming convention for identifying resources available via various TCP/IP application protocols. For example, `http://www.microsoft.com` is the URL for Microsoft's World Wide Web server site, while `ftp://ftp.mwmicro.com/` is the file download site for MidWest Micro drivers. A URL allows easy hypertext references to a particular resource from within a document or mail message. See also *HTTP, World Wide Web (WWW), Hypertext Transfer Protocol (HTTP).*

Universal Naming Convention (UNC)   A multivendor, multiplatform convention for identifying shared resources on a network. See also *Mandatory User Profile.*

UNIX   A multitasking, kernel-based operating system developed at AT&T in the early 1970s and originally provided free to universities as a research operating system. Because of its availability and ability to scale down to microprocessor-based computers, UNIX became the standard operating system of the Internet and its attendant network protocols, and is the closest approximation to a universal operating system that exists. Most computers can run some variant of the UNIX operating system. See also *Multitasking, Internet.*

Unshielded Twisted Pair (UTP)

Type of twisted pair cable that's protected from interference only by twisting the wires in the cable around each other. Often used in 10BaseT networks. See also *Twisted Pair, 10BaseT.*

User Name   A user's account name in a logon-authenticated system. See also *Security.*

User Profile   Used to save each user's Desktop configuration, including colors, shortcuts, applications on the Desktop, and other user-customizable information. See also *Roaming User Profile, Mandatory User Profile.*

User-Level Security   The type of access control used for shared Windows 98 resources when that access is based on the rights associated with a particular user or group account. To enable user-level security, a Windows 98 machine must have contact with a Windows NT or NetWare server that's storing a user account database for the network.

UTP   See *Unshielded Twisted Pair.*

V

Virtual Machines   Windows 98 uses virtual machines to fool programs into thinking that they have exclusive access to all system hardware. These virtual machines run in Ring 3 and use a message passing technique to access memory and hardware.

Virtual Memory   A kernel service that stores memory pages not currently in use in an area on a mass storage device to free up the memory occupied for other uses. Virtual memory hides the memory swapping process from applications and higher-level services. See also *Swap File, Kernel.*

Virtual Private Network (VPN)   A private network running within a public network (such as the Internet). VPNs require the use of tunneling protocols such as PPTP. See also *Point-to-Point Tunneling Protocol (PPTP), Internet, Tunneling, IP Security (IPSec), Layer 2 Tunneling Protocol (L2TP).*

Volume   A collection of data indexed by directories containing files and referred to by a drive letter. Volumes are normally contained in a single partition, but volume sets and stripe sets extend a single volume across multiple partitions.

W

Wait State   CPU cycle during which the CPU isn't doing anything because it's waiting for data from another component. See also *Central Processing Unit (CPU)*.

Web Browser   An application that makes HTTP requests and formats the resultant HTML documents for the users. Most Web browsers understand all standard Internet protocols. See also *Hypertext Transfer Protocol (HTTP), Hypertext Markup Language (HTML), Internet*.

Web Page   Any HTML document on an HTTP server. See also *Hypertext Transfer Protocol (HTTP), Hypertext Markup Language (HTML), Internet*.

Web Site   A related collection of HTML documents at the same Internet address, usually oriented toward some specific information or purpose. See also *Hypertext Markup Language (HTML), Internet*.

Wide-Area Network (WAN)   A network that extends beyond the confines of a single building.

Win16   The set of application services provided by the 16-bit versions of Microsoft Windows: Windows 3.1 and Windows for Workgroups 3.11.

Win32   The set of application services provided by the 32-bit versions of Microsoft Windows: Windows 95, Windows 98, and Windows NT.

Windows 2000   Next generation of Windows NT. Windows 2000 is a suite of four operating systems ranging from network clients to a server operating system designed to rival mainframe operations. See also *Windows NT*.

Windows 3.11 for Workgroups   A 16-bit version of Windows, using the Windows 3.*x* interface, but providing basic peer networking services. As a 16-bit operating system, it can run only 16-bit applications.

Windows 98   A 32-bit version of Microsoft Windows that's designed for medium-range, *x*86-based personal computers. Windows 98 includes peer networking services, Internet support, and support for both 16-bit and 32-bit applications.

Windows DRAM (WDRAM) High-speed dual-ported video RAM optimized for use in windowing subsystems (hence its name).

Windows Internet Name Service (WINS) A Windows NT–based network service for Microsoft networks that maps IP addresses to NetBIOS names, allowing users to refer to computers by easy-to-remember NetBIOS names while still maintaining the IP addresses that TCP/IP requires.

Windows NT The 32-bit version of Microsoft Windows for powerful *x*86 or Alpha computers. This operating system includes peer networking services, server networking services, Internet client and server services, and a broad range of utilities.

Windows Terminal Dumb terminal used for thin client networking with a graphical operating system such as NT. Its processing power and memory are devoted to rendering the images from the applications run on the terminal server, rather than running any applications locally. See also *Thin Client Networking, Terminal Server, Network Computer.*

WINS See *Windows Internet Name Service.*

Wireless Networking Networking in which the physical medium isn't fiber or copper cable, but air. Wireless networking most often uses radio signals to transmit data, giving the network great flexibility and decent coverage but relatively low throughput. Infrared signals, which use a higher frequency signal, are more often used to provide wireless connections to external peripheral devices. See also *Radio Frequency Interference (RFI), Infrared Communications.*

Word Size Amount of data that a CPU can process at one time. See also *Central Processing Unit (CPU).*

Workgroup In Microsoft networks, a collection of related computers, such as a department, that don't require the uniform security and coordination of a domain. Workgroups are characterized by decentralized management as opposed to the centralized management that domains use. See also *Domain.*

Workstation A powerful personal computer, usually running a preemptive, multitasking operating system such as UNIX or Windows NT. Alternatively, any client computer.

World Wide Web (WWW)   A collection of Internet servers providing hypertext formatted documents for Internet clients running Web browsers. The World Wide Web provided the first easy-to-use graphical interface for the Internet and is largely responsible for the Internet's explosive growth since the middle 1990s.

Write-Back Caching   A caching optimization wherein data written to the slow store are cached until the cache is full or until a subsequent write operation overwrites the cached data. Write-back caching can significantly reduce the write operations to a slow store because many write operations are subsequently obviated by new information. Data in the write-back cache are also available for subsequent reads. If something happens to prevent the cache from writing data to the slow store, the cache data will be lost. See also *Caching, Write-Through Caching.*

Write-Through Caching   A caching optimization wherein data written to a slow store are kept in a cache for subsequent rereading. Unlike write-back caching, write-through caching immediately writes the data to the slow store and is therefore less optimal but more secure.

WWW   See *World Wide Web.*

X

X.25   Access method for packet-switching networks. Like frame relay in function, but supports error checking and is therefore both somewhat slower and more error-free on unreliable networks.

X86 Ring Architecture   The *x*86 architecture supports multiple levels of processor-provided protection for running programs. These levels are called rings. Transitioning between rings uses a lot of time and system resources. To increase speed and reduce errors, Windows 98 uses only two rings in the *x*86 architecture, Ring 0 and Ring 3.

INDEX

Note to the Reader: Throughout this index **boldfaced** page numbers indicate primary discussions of a topic. *Italicized* page numbers indicate illustrations.

D

E

F

Q

R

S